UNIVERSITY LIBRARY
W. S. U. = STEVENS POINT

W9-BIT-088

Readings for Social Studies in Elementary Education

SECOND EDITION

Edited by

JOHN JAROLIMEK
University of Washington

HUBER M. WALSH
University of Missouri, St. Louis

The Macmillan Company   **Collier-Macmillan Limited,** *London*

© Copyright, The Macmillan Company, 1969

All rights reserved. No part of this book may be reproduced or transmitted in any form or by any means, electronic or mechanical, including photocopying, recording or by any information storage and retrieval system, without permission in writing from the Publisher.

Second Printing, 1970

Earlier edition © copyright 1965 by The Macmillan Company.

Library of Congress catalog card number: 69–10645

THE MACMILLAN COMPANY
COLLIER-MACMILLAN CANADA, LTD., TORONTO, ONTARIO

Printed in the United States of America

LB
1584
.J29
1969
c. 3

PREFACE

Significant changes have occurred in the professional literature of elementary social studies since the first edition of *Readings for Social Studies in Elementary Education* was compiled. The overall volume of articles has increased substantially with authors addressing themselves to issues and developments surrounding the curriculum reform movement in social studies. This new collection of articles reflects the professional literature of the mid-sixties with little duplication of articles appearing in the earlier edition. In fact, of the sixty-seven articles in this volume, only six were included in the first edition. Therefore, the two books present the reader with some of the best periodical literature dealing with elementary social studies published in the past decade.

It is a common practice for instructors in social studies curriculum and methods courses to require students to sample some of the periodical literature relative to this field. In so doing, the student acquaints himself with current thinking and practices in social studies education. He also becomes familiar with the thinking and point of view of others besides his instructor and the author of the text used in the course. The practice of requiring such outside reading needs no defense as a sound instructional procedure.

Nevertheless, two problems invariably present themselves in meeting journal reading assignments: the selection of the articles to be read and their availability. If left unguided in his search for articles, the student is likely to select many that are irrelevant or inappropriate to his needs. Consequently, instructors often present students with a list of recommended articles. Although this solves the first problem, it complicates the second. Now the call for journals in which the selected articles appear becomes heavy and, as a result, periodicals are lost, articles are cut from journals, students must wait in line. The problem of availability is especially severe for students who live off-campus and for those who work. Inservice teachers who take late afternoon, evening, or Saturday classes find it difficult to spend enough time in the campus library to locate the articles and read them. *Readings for Social Studies in Elementary Education* is offered to make it possible for students to sample a wide range of recent literature in elementary social studies with a minimum amount of wasted motion in securing articles.

175574

The titles of the nine sections of this book suggest the changing emphases and new concerns of elementary social studies educators. The sections and articles within sections are arranged in a way that would logically correspond to the sequence followed in curriculum and methods courses. However, the articles do not have to be read in any particular sequence because each is complete in itself. As was the case in the first edition, the editors did not excerpt selected portions of articles but reproduced them in their entirety, just as they appeared originally in the journal in which they were published.

We wish to express our appreciation to the many authors and publishers who gave permission to reprint their selections. The authors are identified in the Contents and with their articles. The journals that gave permission to use their material in this book were as follows: *Childhood Education, CTA Journal, Education, The Educational Forum, Educational Leadership, Elementary English, The Elementary School Journal, Grade Teacher, Harvard Educational Review, The Instructor, Journal of Geography, Journal of Negro Education, NEA Journal, The PTA Journal, The Reading Teacher, School Library Journal, School Review, Social Education, Social Science Education Consortium Newsletter,* and *The Social Studies.*

J. J.
H. M. W.

CONTENTS

3.
Social Studies and Instructional Processes 107

Contents

The Social Studies Curriculum: Its Nature, Purposes, and Organization

THE SUBJECTS THAT COMPRISE the social studies have had a long history in American elementary education. Next to the basic literacy skills, no school subject is accorded the same degree of importance as social studies, if state legislative requirements are used as criteria. Nearly all states mandate the teaching of local, state, and national history, the Constitution, American institutions, and government. It is clear that the people of this nation have in the past and remain today committed to the idea that one of the basic purposes of elementary education is to educate pupils for social and civic competence in order that self-government will be enlightened and preserved.

To be effective social studies education must be attuned to the realities of present-day life. The United States today is a nation quite obviously facing different problems from those that confronted it in the days of Washington, Lincoln, Wilson, or even Franklin Roosevelt. For nearly 150 years this nation could correctly be described as rural and agricultural, although there were several large cities during that early period. But the basic style of life— whether one was a city dweller or lived in the country—was rural in outlook. Today the prevailing style of life—again, whether one lives in the city or in the country—is urban. This is reflected in food preferences, travel, entertainment, mode of dress, television programs, advertising, and, indeed, in practically all facets of modern life. A very high percentage of our people today are city dwellers, and even those who are not come under the influence of urban life.

Similarly, in international affairs the position of the United States has changed from what it was in earlier times. Today the United States is a powerful and influential nation in world affairs. The decisions it makes relative to international issues directly affect the lives of the people of many nations. With power and influence, of course, come increased responsibility, greater international visibility, and criticism. To a great extent, what the United States chooses to do or not to do in international affairs is governed by world opinion.

Thus, in contemplating the nature, purposes, and organization of elementary social studies, one cannot be unmindful of the sociological, technological, and cultural forces that are at work in the contemporary world, both domestically and internationally. Curriculum models that were adequate for the 1950's are not good enough for pupils in schools of the 1970's. The social forces at work even in local government are so complex that the citizen must be sophisticated in his political knowledge and skill if he is to participate in local civic affairs. Descriptive information about geography, history, and government is not sufficient to equip the citizen to exercise his civic and civil rights—and responsibilities.

The social studies curriculum has come under a considerable amount of study during the decade of 1950–1960. Some of the nation's most prestigious scholars from the social science disciplines, as well as social studies educators, have addressed themselves to problems surrounding the nature, purposes, and organization of the social studies curriculum. Out of their work are evolving some well-defined trends, many of which are discussed in the articles in the first section of this book. Profiting from the thinking of these authors, the reader may himself proceed to formulate his own conception of the nature, purpose, and organization of elementary social studies education.

Throughout the country there is presently discontent with social studies programs that are of the "tell-about" type—that is, largely descriptive and lacking in opportunities for analysis and application of knowledge. What most programs seek to do, at least in theory, is to select content and utilize teaching methods that enhance the pupil's thinking abilities. Concern for the thought processes and their development is a major thrust of most of the social studies projects in recent years. This emphasis and concern is also reflected in the 1967 yearbook of the National Council for the Social Studies entitled *Effective Thinking in the Social Studies*. In the opening paragraph of that volume, Kenneth D. Benne stresses the importance of intellectual skills as follows:

American society has long had a faith in education for democratic citizenship. In the midst of rapid and bewildering change, society expects education to be a major force in enabling citizens to take hold of this change, to turn it not toward dangerous confusion but toward inherent and even staggering possibilities for good. If education is to be such a force, it must develop in citizens their capacities for whole-hearted and penetrating thought.

Thus, the traditional goals of social studies education—the development of knowledge, skills, and attitudes—are focused on the one major goal, that of the development of thinking abilities of pupils. The reader will detect this emphasis in one way or another throughout the articles in this first section and in others throughout the volume. The achievement of this goal is the best hope for improved social studies programs in American elementary schools.

THE ROLE OF THE SOCIAL STUDIES *

National Council for the Social Studies

The social studies are concerned with human relationships. Their content is derived principally from the scholarly disciplines of economics, geography, history, political science, and sociology, and includes elements from other social sciences, among them anthropology, archaeology, and social psychology. The term *social studies* implies no particular form of curricular organization. It is applicable to curricula in which each course is derived for the most part from a single discipline as well as to curricula in which courses combine materials from several disciplines.

The ultimate goal of education in the social studies is the development of desirable socio-civic and personal behavior. No society will prosper unless its members behave in ways which further its development. Man's behavior tends to reflect the values, ideals, beliefs, and attitudes which he accepts. As used here, beliefs are convictions which tend to produce particular behavior in given circumstances. In authoritarian societies, the behavior desired by the rulers is brought about by fiat, threat of punishment, and manipulation of the emotions. In a free society, behavior must rest upon reasoned convictions as well as emotional acceptance. Knowledge and the ability to think should provide the basis on which American children and youth build the beliefs and behavior of free citizens.

Not all of the knowledge included in the social sciences can be used for instruction in the social studies. Indeed, the accumulation of knowledge in the social sciences is so vast that only a small fraction of it can be dealt with in a school program. Equally important, many of the concepts in the social sciences are too difficult to be grasped fully by children and youth. Since curriculum-makers must, therefore, decide what materials to include and what to omit, criteria for selection have to be adopted. The basic criterion put forward in this document is that those curricular materials should be included which will be most useful in developing desirable behavior patterns for a free society. Consequently, the knowledge included in the social studies will be related to important generalizations about human relationships, institutions, and problems, together with sufficient supporting facts to insure that these generalizations are understood. Instruction will also stress the methods

* Reprinted from *Social Education 26*:315–318*ff*, 1962, with permission of the National Council for the Social Studies.

used by social scientists in seeking truth. Some mastery of the methods of scholarly inquiry will enable citizens to make intelligent judgments on the important issues which confront them.

To use knowledge effectively, the student must develop a variety of skills and abilities. To obtain knowledge, one needs skill in locating and evaluating sources of information, in observing, in listening, and in reading. To make knowledge socially useful, one must be able to think reflectively about data and conclusions derived from them. One must also be able to express his views orally and in writing, and have the will and ability to take part in the work of organized groups.

A number of considerations grow out of the brief description of the social studies and what they are good for. Instruction in the social studies is part of the education which should be provided to everyone. The kinds of behavior, beliefs, knowledge, and abilities mentioned in this statement are needed by all members of a free society. To attain the goals suggested, a comprehensive program of instruction in the social studies is required throughout the elementary and secondary school. In addition to the required program, elective subjects in the social studies should be provided so that individuals may pursue and develop special interests. The effectiveness of the social studies program is impaired if it is assigned a host of extraneous responsibilities. Instruction related to home and family living, personal health, and driver education, for example, has been included in the school program by decision of the public. But it is generally accepted that this type of instruction can best be handled by teachers outside the field of the social studies.

The complex task of teaching the social studies involves a heavy responsibility. The effective teacher must have some understanding of all of the social sciences. A comprehensive program for the education of young citizens clearly cannot be limited to instruction in one social science. It is also clear that in a world of rapid and continual change it is impossible to prescribe a fixed and immutable content for the social studies. Even though most of the information currently taught will remain valid and useful, the total body of content will require frequent updating and sharpening as new problems arise and new ways of dealing with persistent problems are discovered.

In summary, this statement includes four major considerations: (1) The ultimate goal of education in the social studies is desirable socio-civic and personal behavior. (2) This behavior grows out of the values, ideals, beliefs, and attitudes which people hold. (3) In turn, these characteristics must be rooted in knowledge. (4) For the development and use of knowledge, people require appropriate abilities and skills. The perpetuation and improvement of our democratic way of life is dependent upon the development of individuals who achieve these goals.

The Behavioral Needs in a Free Society

Behavior is the reaction of an individual in any situation. Most behavior is learned in a variety of ways in the society in which the individual grows up. Some kinds of behavior are not acceptable in a democratic society at any time. It is also true that the process of historical change may demand new ways of acting.

In approaching the problem of behavior the school recognizes that in a democratic society responsibility for appropriate behavior must be assumed by individual members. A democratic society depends upon self-discipline and upon societal discipline approved by a majority. In any free society individuals must be willing and able to participate effectively in the solution of common problems. They must also be willing at times to arrive at decisions reflecting compromises among different points of view. Such compromises are acceptable when they help society to advance toward desirable goals, but the compromises must not result in the sacrifice of those inalienable rights, principles, and values without which democracy cannot survive. While it is true that other institutions share in the responsibility for the development of desirable behavior by members of society, it is also true that education has a great responsibility in shaping the behavior of individuals.

Among the behavioral patterns which may be identified as essential for the maintenance, strengthening, and improvement of a democratic society are the following:

1. Keeping well informed on issues which affect society, and of relating principles and knowledge derived from the social sciences to the study of contemporary problems.
2. Using democratic means in seeking agreement, reaching solutions, and taking group action on social problems.
3. Assuming individual responsibility for carrying out group decisions and accepting the consequences of group action.
4. Defending constitutional rights and freedoms for oneself and others.
5. Respecting and complying with the law, regardless of personal feelings, and using legal means to change laws deemed inimical or invalid.
6. Supporting persons and organizations working to improve society by desirable action.

7. Scrutinizing the actions of public officials.
8. Participating in elections at local, state, and national levels and preparing oneself for intelligent voting in these elections.
9. Opposing special privilege whenever it is incompatible with general welfare.
10. Being prepared and willing to render public service and to give full-time service in emergencies.
11. Engaging in continual re-examination of one's personal values as well as the value system of the nation.

The responsibility for the development of patterns of democratic behavior in pupils falls in large measure upon the social studies program. Behavior grows from the intellectual acceptance of new ideas, changes in attitudes, and the formation of a personal commitment to values which are basic to our society.

The Beliefs of a Free People

Values may be defined as the beliefs and ideas which a society esteems and seeks to achieve. They inspire its members to think and act in ways which are approved. To the extent that actual behavior is consistent with the values claimed, a society is meeting the standards it has set for itself.

A fundamental premise of American democracy is that men and women can be taught to think for themselves and to determine wise courses of action. In choosing a course of action they need to take into account the values which are basic to our society. These values are rooted in the democratic heritage and provide a stabilizing force of utmost importance.

In meeting new situations Americans not only must consider whether possible courses of action are consistent with democratic values but they may need to re-examine the values themselves. Although the basic values of American democracy are permanent, secondary values are subject to change. Furthermore, there is always need for adjustment whenever one value is in conflict with another, as, for example, liberty and authority.

Other agencies than the schools obviously have responsibility for the inculcation of basic values. Nevertheless, a primary objective of instruction must be the development of a better understanding of our value system. At all grade levels, instruction in the social studies should concern itself with the attainment of this objective. To the extent that Americans have a thorough understanding of the values underlying their way of life, and accept this code as their own, they will be able to do their part in achieving the great goals which they have set for themselves.

used by social scientists in seeking truth. Some mastery of the methods of scholarly inquiry will enable citizens to make intelligent judgments on the important issues which confront them.

To use knowledge effectively, the student must develop a variety of skills and abilities. To obtain knowledge, one needs skill in locating and evaluating sources of information, in observing, in listening, and in reading. To make knowledge socially useful, one must be able to think reflectively about data and conclusions derived from them. One must also be able to express his views orally and in writing, and have the will and ability to take part in the work of organized groups.

A number of considerations grow out of the brief description of the social studies and what they are good for. Instruction in the social studies is part of the education which should be provided to everyone. The kinds of behavior, beliefs, knowledge, and abilities mentioned in this statement are needed by all members of a free society. To attain the goals suggested, a comprehensive program of instruction in the social studies is required throughout the elementary and secondary school. In addition to the required program, elective subjects in the social studies should be provided so that individuals may pursue and develop special interests. The effectiveness of the social studies program is impaired if it is assigned a host of extraneous responsibilities. Instruction related to home and family living, personal health, and driver education, for example, has been included in the school program by decision of the public. But it is generally accepted that this type of instruction can best be handled by teachers outside the field of the social studies. The complex task of teaching the social studies involves a heavy responsibility. The effective teacher must have some understanding of all of the social sciences. A comprehensive program for the education of young citizens clearly cannot be limited to instruction in one social science. It is also clear that in a world of rapid and continual change it is impossible to prescribe a fixed and immutable content for the social studies. Even though most of the information currently taught will remain valid and useful, the total body of content will require frequent updating and sharpening, as new problems arise and new ways of dealing with persistent problems are discovered.

In summary, this statement includes four major considerations: (1) The ultimate goal of education in the social studies is desirable socio-civic and personal behavior. (2) This behavior grows out of the values, ideals, beliefs, and attitudes which people hold. (3) In turn, these characteristics must be rooted in knowledge. (4) For the development and use of knowledge, people require appropriate

THE ROLE OF THE SOCIAL STUDIES *

National Council for the Social Studies

The social studies are concerned with human relationships. Their content is derived principally from the scholarly disciplines of economics, geography, history, political science, and sociology, and includes elements from other social sciences, among them anthropology, archaeology, and social psychology. The term *social studies* implies no particular form of curricular organization. It is applicable to curricula in which each course is derived for the most part from a single discipline as well as to curricula in which courses combine materials from several disciplines.

The ultimate goal of education in the social studies is the development of desirable socio-civic and personal behavior. No society will prosper unless its members behave in ways which further its development. Man's behavior tends to reflect the values, ideals, beliefs, and attitudes which he accepts. As used here, beliefs are convictions which tend to produce particular behavior in given circumstances. In authoritarian societies, the behavior desired by the rulers is brought about by fiat, threat of punishment, and manipulation of the emotions. In a free society, behavior must rest upon reasoned convictions as well as emotional acceptance. Knowledge and the ability to think should provide the basis on which American children and youth build the beliefs and behavior of free citizens.

Not all of the knowledge included in the social sciences can be used for instruction in the social studies. Indeed, the accumulation of knowledge in the social sciences is so vast that only a small fraction of it can be dealt with in a school program. Equally important, many of the concepts in the social sciences are too difficult to be grasped fully by children and youth. Since curriculum-makers must, therefore, decide what materials to include and what to omit, criteria for selection have to be adopted. The basic criterion put forward in this document is that those curricular materials should be included which will be most useful in developing desirable behavior patterns for a free society. Consequently, the knowledge included in the social studies will be related to important generalizations about human relationships, institutions, and problems, together with sufficient supporting facts to insure that these generalizations are understood. Instruction will also stress the methods

* Reprinted from *Social Education 26*:315–318*ff*, 1962, with permission of the National Council for the Social Studies.

Among the values which instruction in the social studies should seek to engender in youth are:

1. Belief in the inherent worth of every individual—that each person should be judged on his merit.
2. Belief that all persons should possess equal rights and liberties which are, however, accompanied by responsibilities.
3. Belief that all persons should have maximum freedom and equality of opportunity to develop as they desire, consistent with their capacities and with the general welfare.
4. Belief that individual and group rights must be exercised in such a way that they do not interfere with the rights of others, endanger the general welfare, or threaten the national security.
5. Belief that citizens should place the common good before self-interest or group or class loyalty, when these are in conflict.
6. Belief that freedom of inquiry, expression, and discussion provide the best way for resolving issues; that the will of the majority should govern; that the rights and opinions of the minority should be respected and protected.
7. Belief that citizens should be willing to act on the basis of reasoned conclusions and judgments, even though personal sacrifice is involved.
8. Belief that government must be based on properly enacted law, not on the caprice of men holding office; that government has a responsibility for promoting the common welfare.
9. Belief that people are capable of governing themselves better than any self-appointed individual or group can govern them, that political power belongs to and comes from the people; and that the people have the right, by lawful means, to change their government.
10. Belief that the freest possible economic competition consistent with the general welfare is desirable; that government has the obligation to stabilize economic growth and reduce gross economic inequalities.
11. Belief that both competition and cooperation are essential to the democratic process and to our national well-being.
12. Belief that the separation of church and state is essential.
13. Belief that maximum individual freedom, under law, throughout the world is the best guarantee of world peace.
14. Belief that change in relations between nation states should be accomplished by peaceful means, and that collective security can best be achieved within an organization of nation states.
15. Belief that Americans should work to achieve a world in which justice and peace are assured to all mankind.
16. Belief that Americans should have reasoned devotion to the

heritage of the past, and a commitment to perpetuate the ideals of American life.

The foregoing beliefs and values have been subjectively derived. Quite possibly other lists would provide a different sequence and use different language. But the important point is that there would be a high degree of agreement on the basic beliefs included in such lists. A major purpose of instruction in the social studies is to help children and youth understand basic American values and develop loyalties to them. To attain this goal it is necessary to take values into account in the selection of content for social studies courses.

The Role of Knowledge

The attainment of goals in the social studies depends upon the acquisition and utilization of information, facts, data. Each of the social sciences, in effect, is a reservoir of knowledge to be used. But the kind and amount of knowledge which can be used from one or more disciplines is necessarily determined by curriculum requirements associated with a particular stage in the educational process. In any event, one cannot be concerned with the goals of social studies instruction without being drawn immediately into considerations of content. The National Council for the Social Studies, consequently, has made frequent examinations of content areas, notably in its yearbooks to which distinguished social scientists have contributed.

In the last few years the National Council for the Social Studies has recognized the necessity for making a more comprehensive study of the social studies curriculum. One report, issued in 1957, carries the title: *A Guide to Content in the Social Studies*. This report listed 14 themes which were proposed as guidelines for the selection of content. A second report, published in 1958, is called *Curriculum Planning in American Schools: The Social Studies*. The group which prepared this report showed special interest in the advances made by social science research in recent decades and was concerned that these findings be reflected in school programs in the social studies. Beyond noting some limited illustrations of these advances, the report underscored the need for cooperative effort among social scientists, educators, and teachers in the planning of the social studies curriculum. In such planning a fundamental problem would be the development of agreement on principles to be used in the selection and grade placement of content. Teachers have long recognized that the reservoirs of social science knowledge hold an embarrassment of riches. Indeed, the study of any one of the social sciences alone might well require all the time available in grades one through 12.

The Role of Abilities and Skills

If young people are to command the knowledge and develop the behavior and beliefs enumerated above, they must develop a variety of skills for locating, gathering, interpreting, and applying social studies information. Stated in another way, the purpose of teaching skills in social studies is to enable the individual to gain knowledge concerning his society, to think reflectively about problems and issues, and to apply this thinking in constructive action.

The need for the systematic teaching of social studies has become increasingly urgent for a number of reasons. With the development of modern media of mass communications and the expansion in the amount of scholarly material, there has been an enormous increase in the quantity and variety of social data that the citizens must deal with in locating and selecting information that is pertinent to a given issue. With the refinement and increasingly pervasive use of persuasion techniques in many areas of daily living, there is a correspondingly greater need for skill in appraising information and evidence and the sources from which they come. With the complicated forms of social organization which develop in an urbanized society, new skills of group participation are essential for effective action.

The development of some of these skills is the special responsibility of the social studies, such as those involved in understanding time and chronology. Others are shared with other parts of the school program, but have special application in social studies. The list of proposed objectives centering on abilities and skills includes both types, for students need both to deal with social studies materials.

The acquisition of abilities and skills is a form of learning. Consequently, some principles to guide instruction in them are essential to their development. These abilities and skills must be identified with sufficient concreteness so that the description helps in planning instruction and in evaluating various degrees of mastery. It seems clear that these abilities and skills cannot be developed in a vacuum but must be acquired by pupils as they study content derived from the social sciences. The nature of these abilities and skills is such that they will not be learned—nor should they be taught—incidentally, but rather through planned and systematic treatment. Effective instruction will recognize that the maturity of the students will largely determine at what grade level given abilities and skills can be developed most effectively. Teachers must also take into account that these abilities and skills should be developed in situations as nearly like those in which they will be used as possible, and that repeated practice will be needed if students are to become skillful in their use. Even so, there will be large differences in the facility with which students use skills at any grade level, as well as in the competence achieved by the end of the secondary school. The nature of these abilities and the individual differences exhibited by students indicate that complete mastery of most of them is never achieved. But the goal is to help each student achieve the highest level of performance each year that his own potential will permit.

The objectives listed in this statement involve abilities and skills needed for effective behavior; the abilities peculiar to the social science disciplines must be developed further as the college student pursues his specialized studies.

I. Skills centering on *ways and means of handling social studies materials*

A. Skills of locating and gathering information from a variety of sources, such as:

using books and libraries effectively, taking notes, using the mechanics of footnoting and compiling bibliographies

listening reflectively to oral presentations

interviewing appropriate resource persons and observing and describing contemporary occurrences in school and community

B. Skills of interpreting graphic materials, such as:

using and interpreting maps, globes, atlases

using and interpreting charts, graphs, cartoons, numerical data, and converting "raw data" into these graphic forms

C. Skills needed to develop a sense of time and chronology, such as:

developing a time vocabulary and understanding time systems

tracing sequences of events

perceiving time relationships, between periods or eras and between contemporaneous developments in various countries or parts of the world

  D. Skills of presenting social studies materials, such as:
    organizing material around an outline
    writing a defensible paper and presenting an effective
     speech
    participating in a discussion involving social problems

II. Skills of *reflective thinking as applied to social studies problems*

  A. Skills of *comprehension,* such as:
    identifying the central issues in a problem or argument
    arriving at warranted conclusions and drawing valid
     inferences
    providing specific illustrations of social studies gen-
     eralizations dealing with increasingly difficult and
     advanced materials

  B. Skills of *analysis and evaluation* of social studies materials, such as:
    applying given criteria, such as distinguishing between
     primary and secondary sources, in judging social
     studies materials
    recognizing underlying and unstated assumptions or
     premises, attitudes, outlooks, motives, points of
     view, or bias
    distinguishing facts from hypotheses, judgments, or
     opinions, and checking the consistency of hypotheses
     with given information and assumptions
    distinguishing a conclusion from the evidence which
     supports it
    separating relevant from irrelevant, essential from
     incidental information used to form a conclusion,
     judgment, or thesis
    recognizing the techniques used in persuasive materials
     such as advertising, propaganda
    assessing the adequacy of data used to support a given
     conclusion
    weighing values and judgments involved in alternative
     courses of action, and in choosing alternative courses
     of action

  C. Skills of *synthesis and application* of social studies materials, such as:
    formulating valid hypotheses and generalizations, and
     marshalling main points, arguments, central issues

comparing and contrasting points of view, theories, generalizations, and facts

distinguishing cause-and-effect relationships from other types of relationships, such as means and ends

combining elements, drawing inferences and conclusions, and comparing with previous conclusions and inferences

identifying possible courses of action

making tentative judgments as a basis for action, subject to revision as new information or evidence becomes available

supplying and relating knowledge from the social studies as background for understanding contemporary affairs

III. Skills of *effective group participation*

    A. Assuming different roles in the group, such as gadfly or summarizer, as these roles are needed for the group to progress

    B. Using parliamentary procedures effectively

    C. Helping resolve differences within the group

    D. Suggesting and using means of evaluating group progress

Certainly a major purpose of social studies instruction is to place emphasis on the development of those abilities which encourage the accurate and intelligent utilization of social science data and which make habitual the orderly processes of mind necessary to carrying on reflective thought and to taking action based on such thinking.

Looking Ahead

This preliminary statement of goals for the social studies is but a first step in a process that looks forward to making recommendations for the social studies curriculum in our schools. There remains for the future the major task of working out a logical sequence of grade placement that will present a systematic overview for the social studies curriculum. Here, there must be concern for a sequential development of the essential knowledge, skills, and attitudes that should be acquired by pupils going through the school program. Also consideration must be given to programs for pupils of widely varying abilities. Some experimentation with programs seeking to achieve all the objectives set forth will in all probability be called for in order to evaluate their effectiveness. Finally, it should be recognized that there is no single way in which the materials can be best organized in arriving at the goals, but that several alternative patterns might well be suggested.

WHY CHANGE MUST COME IN SOCIAL STUDIES *

Helen McCracken Carpenter

The teaching-learning process basically involves deciding the answers to the simple queries of "Why?", "What?", "How?", "With what?", "For whom?" and "How well?". The scholarly labor pains in the birth process of the new social studies have tended to accentuate the *what*—disciplines, structure, problems, concepts, generalizations; the *how*—inquiry, discovery, telling, large group, small group, simulation; the *with what*—teaching machines, programmed books, projectors, television sets, model kits; and the *for whom*—individual, group, disadvantaged, gifted. The most important query of all, the *why:* namely, the ends for which content, method, and materials are selected, has received less attention. Inextricably bound also with purpose is the factor of activation, the cornerstone of effective learning.

What are the goals, the directions, toward which the new social studies are, or should be, pointing?

Same But Different

Over the years, the intent of social studies goals in the schools has changed little. Few leaders in social studies education today would quarrel with the declaration, now a classic, of Charles A. Beard writing on civic instruction one-third century ago in his *Charter for the Social Sciences.*[1] Beard said, "Our fundamental purpose here is the creation of rich, many-sided personalities

Helen McCracken Carpenter is Professor of History at Trenton State College, New Jersey.

* An extension of an article from *The Instructor* 76:78–79, 1967, with permission of the Owen Publishing Company and Helen McCracken Carpenter.

equipped with practical knowledge and inspired by ideals so that they can make their way and fulfil their mission in a changing society which is a part of a world complex."

Here in capsule form are the primary characteristics of the effective individual in our nation which social studies instruction still seeks to develop—one with a sense of personal fulfilment and a world perspective who is knowledgeable, adaptable, humanly aware, and socially committed. Evidence of the continuing acceptance of these goals for democratic citizenship is found, for example, in the words of Donald Robinson, Director of the Civic Education Project of the National Council for the Social Studies, writing in *Civic Leader* a few months ago, "The bases for good citizenship in a democracy are unchanging . . . no citizen in any age can be complete if his citizenship training does not include these four factors: Gaining information or knowledge; learning how to use that knowledge analytically—to think; having appropriate feelings or affective reactions; and taking some kind of action as a citizen." [2]

The enduring nature of the attributes considered necessary for effective living in a democratic society is reassuring but it can also be misleading. The words may be strikingly similar but the implications can be markedly different from time to time. Failure to realize this distinction constitutes the danger and the challenge in the evolution of the new social studies. It is easy for local school committees, charged with recommending changes in the social studies program, to bypass, often unknowingly, analysis of the factors which give meaning to objectives and to settle quickly for patched-up old statements in order to move on to more tangible aspects.

New meanings in social studies goals accrue from the impact of change on three fundamental factors: the social realities of our times, the nature of the social disciplines, and current concepts of learning and the learner. Social studies instruction derives its direction from the interrelationships of these forces—society, disciplines, and learner—at the point where the lines of influence converge and interact.

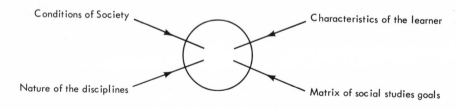

Conditions of Society   Characteristics of the learner

Nature of the disciplines   Matrix of social studies goals

Since each of these formative factors is changing and thereby producing fluidity in the import of social studies goals, periodic reinterpretation of the meaning of instructional objectives in the light of the needs and characteristics of the age becomes essential.

Re-definition Necessary Today

The faster the rate of change, the greater the need for re-definition of goals. Today finds social studies teachers at the vortex of a whirlwind with eddying currents pressing from all three formative forces.

The multiplicity and rapidity of change has never been greater in American life than it is today. John McPartland, speaking a short time ago of speed in the creation of scientific information, noted, "We are acquiring as much new information each two years as we acquired in the total of human history up to now; within five years that two-year span will have decreased to one year; within ten years it will have diminished to three months." Random illustrations of this momentum include manned space flight, active communication satellites, nationwide use of Sabin oral vaccine, coin-operated dry cleaning machines, electric toothbrushes—all commonplace in 1967 but not a part of American thought or things at the beginning of the 1960's. Prophecies for the not too distant future, such as computer hookups for homes to aid in housework, shopping, homework and recreation, suggest no lag in the reality of change as a continuing characteristic of our society.

The tempo of stirrings in the social sciences also is accelerating. Developments of the scientific revolution have aided the gathering and evaluating of data in all fields of the social sciences. We know more today than ever before, for example, about the political behavior of Americans, about their economic choices, about the interactions of various groups in our country and about the effects of resource use. In addition, the increasing concern of many social scientists over the contributions of the scholarly fields to social studies goals in the schools constitutes another ingredient of change.

New viewpoints on the process of learning and the capacities of the learner call for a re-examination of expectancies in social studies instruction. The recent recommendation of the Educational Policies Commission that public school opportunity be extended downward to age four and that learning experiences in the early grades be altered accordingly affirms both research findings and the experiences of many teachers concerning the learning capacities of today's children. From psychologists come also the suggestion that aspects of the scholarly disciplines can provide educational fare just as appropriate for younger children as for older learners, if it is served up properly.

The need to re-define goals is further attested in the adverse reactions of too many learners to social studies—not years ago but *now*. For example, "The school subject I dislike the most is history" writes Student Number 49631 as reported in the *NEA Journal* of October, 1966.[3] "I hated to study cities and long lists of things made in each," or "I thought it was unfair that the teachers never helped in making geography or history easy but all teachers helped with arithmetic or reading," quotes Mary S. Reynolds summarizing a recent sampling of elementary children in the *Journal of Geography* for December, 1966.[4] Poignant testimony to the irrelevancy of instructional goals to the needs, interests, and abilities of children exists also in the ten percent of our population age 18 or older who have completed less than six years of school. Most of these are illiterates; they are also voters, consumers, and parents.

Directions of Change

In discussions of aims today, there is frequent reference to "cognitive" and "affective." Advocates of the new social studies classify two well-known types of objectives—knowledge for one, and intellectual skills and abilities for the other—as cognitive. The old category of attitudes and appreciations, to which values usually are now added, belongs in the affective domain.

In the realm of the cognitive the balance for emphasis in social studies is tipped more toward the development of skills and abilities than the accumulation of knowledge. This weighting results from the prevalence of change, mentioned above, which is present in all facets of life and learning today. Knowledge becomes obsolete too fast to be feasible as the all-pervading aim of instruction to the extent it has been in decades past. Skills are conceived on a broad front with major focus on those which cluster around the core of problem-solving and decision-making in an effort to help the child accumulate experience which is transferable from situation to situation as life progresses. The implications of this focus for instructional procedures are far-reaching. Knowledge objectives are still conceived as *sine qua non*, but with different criteria for selection. Most important is functional relevance to life today which in turn implies selection from all the social sciences, not just from the fields of history and geography which have predominated as reservoirs for social studies content in the elementary grades.

In the affective realm, there is general agreement that social studies instruction should be much more concerned, than has been the case for a half century or more, with helping young Americans develop positive social-personal values. Few experts yet dare to tread confidently in this area with definite lists of "how-to-do-its." Nevertheless it is a most vital area which should command the thoughtful focus of each teacher and school system today.

If instruction is to further national purpose, the national and international interest, social studies goals must be defined in terms of today's needs. The concept of ends divorced from means is untenable, but focus on means without regard to ends is fraught with danger.

SOURCES OF QUOTATIONS

1. Charles A. Beard, *A Charter for the Social Sciences*. Scribner, 1932, pp. 96–97.
2. Donald W. Robinson, "Educating Citizens for the 21st Century." *Civic Leader*, May 16, 1966, p. 1.
3. Student 49631. See *NEA Journal*, October, 1966, p. 22.
4. Mary S. Reynolds, "Needed: A Social Studies Explosion." *Journal of Geography* 65:429–430, 1966.

ELEMENTARY SOCIAL STUDIES: CONTENT PLUS! *

Huber M. Walsh

In response to the widely recognized need for broader content emphasis in elementary social studies, teachers, curriculum workers and professors are effecting searching analyses and extensive revisions of existing programs. A result of this activity has been the emergence of a "new look" in elementary social studies in which programs are based (more distinctly than before) upon content drawn from the social sciences. In general this approach focuses upon major understandings or generalizations which are widely

Huber M. Walsh is Professor of Education at the University of Missouri, St. Louis.

* Reprinted from *Childhood Education* 43:124–126, 1966, with permission of the Association for Childhood Education International, 3615 Wisconsin Avenue, N.W., Washington, D.C. 20016, and Huber M. Walsh.

applicable key ideas taken from academic disciplines such as geography, history, sociology, anthropology, political science and economics.

Many persons welcome this approach for it promises to advance elementary social studies in several significant ways. *First*, this plan permits a more direct relationship between elementary social studies instruction and the parent social sciences—a relationship long in coming. *Second*, instruction built upon major understandings from the social sciences holds the promise of generally upgrading content coverage in the elementary school. *Third*, instruction in key ideas, according to authorities, can promote deeper comprehension, result in better transfer of knowledge and facilitate subsequent learning (2,4). Perhaps the greatest value of such instruction is that it prepares the learner for independent study (1).

Worthwhile though it is, this instructional plan may not be the panacea which many persons are seeking. Indeed, if made the sole basis for teaching, it could produce an undesirable imbalance in the social studies program. Present society demands that the schools of today equip future citizens with two essential ingredients for successful living: *knowledge* and *skill in working effectively with others*. Bringing youngsters into contact with big ideas from the disciplines will expose them to basic knowledge about man and his interrelationships. But, the acquisition of such information does not *ipso facto* insure the pupil will then apply appropriate aspects of this knowledge to improve *his own* human relationships. Teachers know that sometimes the child most able to verbalize eloquently about desirable behavior (*e.g.*, feelings of tolerance, patience with others) proves to be most inept in practicing what he preaches; obviously he has not learned beyond the level of sheer verbalism. If children are to extend knowledge beyond verbalism they must put it to work in deeds. This requires systematically planned learning experiences in which the pupil has the opportunity to *apply* what he has learned about desirable human behavior. These kinds of learning activities are the essence of what is commonly referred to as *social education*. Content alone, without provisions for social education, is not enough.

Content Plus

The child needs content *plus* social education. Content *alone* cannot constitute the whole social studies program any more than social education alone—both are essential and complementary; both must be in sensible proportion in a sound program designed for society's needs.

The present emphasis on subject matter does not automatically imperil acquisition and practice of important social learnings; but in some situations this stress on subject matter has been accompanied by a devaluation of social education. One reason is that educational respectability attaches more to the teaching of content than to the development and practice of social education. The danger is that social learnings in the elementary school will continue to receive diminished attention. If certain critics have their way, social education will be abandoned despite society's needs to the contrary (6). In some classrooms acquisition of information is regarded as an end in itself. Comprehension of key ideas and concepts is seen as the principal and exclusive instructional outcome. Little or no attention is given to providing social settings which give children opportunity to apply some of this knowledge in their day-to-day relationships under the guidance and direction of the classroom teacher. When this happens, teachers can miss determinate kinds of learning contacts in which the child's skill in human relations can be appraised, diagnosed and improved.

Overemphasis on content could now weaken the effectiveness of social studies programs in much the same way as overemphasis on social education did in the past. The former cry of critics was that the elementary child was being "socialized to death." Unless we avoid rushing to the opposite extreme, their future criticism may well be that the child is being "intellectualized to death." Why should we sacrifice either when we can have both? There is no reason to make it an "either/or" case. A sensible middle course can be maintained—*both* subject-matter and social learnings can be developed simultaneously without sacrificing either. They are compatible and complementary. Many social learnings taught and practiced in the elementary schools are predicated upon human relations skills closely allied to the funded knowledge in the social and behavioral sciences. Consider, for example, the major idea in political science: every known society has made rules on how its members should get along together and instituted coercive sanctions to help insure that rules are obeyed (3,5). This idea is germane to the classroom social context in which teacher and pupils together formulate guidelines and sanctions essential to their getting along together.

Specific social learnings in the classroom depend upon a variety of considerations. Examples for developing behaviors are: being a worthy group member (participating in discussion and resolution of questions and issues) ; practicing social amenities; communicating effectively (listening and speaking) ; respecting one's own rights and responsibilities and those of others.

These objectives can be served simultaneously through learning experiences in *both* subject-matter and social learnings. Illustrations of both follow.

Teacher-Led Group Discussions: Discussions with the entire class afford the teacher the opportunity to present new human relations ideas. For the pupil, such teacher-guided activities give practice in some of the social skills.

> John's group is of the opinion that the class has gathered sufficient information on the way of life in India, but Virginia's group believes further research is necessary. The teacher might ask: How shall we decide? What do we need to know in order to make a reasonable decision?

This activity can be a confluence of *both* content and social learnings. Social learnings deal with group processes in sound decision making, while content learnings involve subject matter which is the essence of the discussion. Exchange of ideas can be instrumental in developing skills associated with precise transmission and reception of ideas.

Study Sessions: Study sessions can be settings for social education while children investigate content—especially when the class is divided into study groups of four or five. These small groups give opportunity to practice sound *leadership* and *followership* skills.

> Paul, as group leader, determines with the others how the day's work shall be carried on. Each person may contribute ideas during the planning phase. Following that, each has an opportunity to practice directing his individual efforts toward reaching the mark. Through combined effort a team can work together to achieve the common goal.

Reporting: Groups of children can report to others the results of their studies. Usually reporting deals with content; but since it involves people working with people, it can function as settings for social learning. A group must decide what data and information will be presented and how this knowledge can be communicated clearly to the audience. During reporting time youngsters in the audience can practice what they have learned about courteous listening, respect and tolerance for the persons in the spotlight.

Each content experience need not unfailingly have a social dimension any more than every social learning must have content. As indicated above, there are worthwhile learning activities in which the two can be combined in a mutually beneficial way. Surely both are compatible in the same social studies program.

Most of today's pupils are destined to spend the rest of their lives dealing with others. Ideally, youngsters should begin learning and practicing good human relations during the formative elementary years. Teaching content and developing social learnings are not antithetical. Neither need be neglected if social studies programs are to be effective in preparing our future citizens. Wise educators responsible for improving social studies programs will be successful in finding the middle course which sacrifices neither content nor social education.

REFERENCES

1. Jerome S. Bruner, *The Process of Education.* Cambridge: Harvard University Press, 1960.
2. E. R. Keislar and J. D. McNeil, "Teaching Science and Mathematics by Auto-Instruction in the Primary Grades: An Experimental Strategy in Curriculum Development." Los Angeles: the authors, October, 1961 (mimeographed).
3. K. N. Llewellyn, "Law and Civilization," in *People, Power and Politics,* L. J. Gould and E. W. Steele, eds. New York: Random House, 1961, pp. 321–329.
4. Philip H. Phenix, "Key Concepts and the Crisis in Learning," *Teachers College Record, 58*: 137–143, 1956.
5. Robert Rienow, *Introduction to Government.* New York: Knopf, 1956.
6. Mortimer Smith, "Social Studies Challenged," *The Toledo Blade Sunday Magazine,* July 26, 1964, pp. 4–5 ff.

WHAT SOCIAL STUDIES CONTENT FOR THE PRIMARY GRADES? *

Ralph C. Preston

In recent years the "readiness" problem in social studies has focused upon the question: Are children ready to study, formally and systematically, remote places and remote times (as opposed to the "here and now") at an earlier age than children of a generation ago? Are children, in short, more precocious?

Those who answer affirmatively point to studies which report

Ralph C. Preston is Professor of Education at the University of Pennsylvania, Philadelphia.

* Reprinted from *Social Education 29*:147–148, 1965, with permission of the National Council for the Social Studies and Ralph C. Preston.

that as a probable consequence of the advent of television, of expanded family travel, and of increased availability of children's books, children today have wider experiences than children of a few years ago. Other studies have shown that children are sometimes taught what they already know. For example, Lowry tested and interviewed second-grade children concerning concepts they were about to be taught.[1] She concluded that they knew on the average of from 64 to 85 percent of the concepts. Such studies bring out the ever-present danger of under-challenging children. It is all too easy to belabor the obvious. Although teachers should begin with what children know, they should drive steadily on to the unknown.

The issue becomes confused, however, if we jump to the conclusion that present social studies topics are necessarily inappropriate and if we overlook the strong probability that it is usually shallow treatment of topics rather than the topics themselves which result in failure of children to be challenged.

An example of the confusion of the issue is seen in studies which seem to proceed on the two-fold assumption that (1) new topics are needed, and (2) the way to determine these new topics is by investigating children's interests. In one such study, children's interests were determined by analyzing tapes of discussions attended by 715 children of all elementary grades who were divided into small discussion groups.[2] The children talked about social studies topics up to one hour per day for one month. The discussions were not free in that a framework of promptings was devised. Thus, the children in grades 1 and 2 were given the daily reminder to "talk about people of long ago, people who live today, (people) that you like. Talk about people in this land, places in other lands, (places) you like."

The following conclusion was drawn with regard to grade 1: "The geographic interests of first-grade children seem to center about environments different from their own. . . . Generally, first-grade children, at the conclusion of their first year at school, are interested in dry lands (the desert), wet lands (the jungle), hot lands (lands of the elephant) and cold lands (the country of the reindeer)."

The reader cannot help but wonder how the data imply a set of

---

[1] Betty L. Lowry. "A Survey of the Knowledge of Social Studies Concepts Possessed by Second Grade Children Previous to the Time When These Concepts are Taught in the Social Studies Lessons." Doctoral Thesis, State University of Iowa, 1963.

[2] J. D. McAulay. "Some Interests Related to the Social Studies of Elementary School Children." December, 1960 (mimeographed).

interests that so neatly and explicitly correspond to conventional social studies topics. As a matter of fact, "cold lands" came up in just one situation, was discussed by two sub-groups, and 24 first-grade children (out of 85) participated in the discussion for a total of approximately three minutes (or an average of about eight seconds per child).

The study's evidence for this and other designations of interests seems tenuous. Can we infer from children's expressed interests (even if validly identified) anything about the topics they should or should not be studying? Surely not, unless we wish to return to the curriculum chaos of the 1930's. If a new set of topics is required, it seems sounder to proceed according to a logical model.

There is a real possibility that we are exaggerating the apparent sophistication of today's children. We may be mistaking their verbal glibness on Topic A as a sign of readiness for Topic B. These possibilities were investigated by Mugge with second-grade children whose mean intelligence and whose socio-economic status were above average.[3] She found that they lacked precision of knowledge with respect to matters about the community, the farm, and other topics normally studied in first and second grades. On the topic of the post office, for example, very few children could tell how much it costs to mail a letter or why a stamp is cancelled. By way of further example, they had difficulty in keeping cities, states, and countries in their proper hierarchical relationship. Those children who had traveled did not know significantly more than those who had not traveled. The disparity between Mugge's results and those of investigators who have found modern children well informed is probably attributable to the fact that Mugge, when asking children for a definition, was not satisfied with vague synonyms, minor usage, or trivial attributes; when children offered her these, she probed further and often found a sea of empty concepts beneath a facile surface.

Further reason for caution against precipitating children too early into studies of remote places and times is found in the literature of child development. What is known about children's thought structures at various age levels? Piaget, the Swiss psychologist whose importance is now being acknowledged by his American colleagues, found that seven-year-olds, in structuring ideas, were tied to concrete content, still bound to the here and now. Data consistent with Piaget's findings have been reported by various investigators. To be sure, Piaget is more concerned with cognitive

---

[3] Dorothy J. Mugge. "Precocity of Today's Young Children: Real or Wishful?" *Social Education* 27:436–439, 1963.

operations than with content, and the subjects of Piaget and of most other investigators whose conclusions are generally in accord with Piaget's were not reared in a television-saturated culture. Nevertheless, there are indications that the successive stages by which children structure their thought while growing up are independent to a surprising degree of the information and ideas to which they are exposed.[4]

How does Piaget's view relate to the view that, in Bruner's words, "there is no reason to believe that any subject cannot be taught to any child at virtually any age in some form"?[5] The views are complementary. As Bruner himself points out, "it is only when we are equipped with such knowledge [as produced by Piaget in the study of physical causality, of morality, of number, and the rest] that we will be in a position to know how the child will translate whatever we present to him into his own subjective terms."[6] There is no essential contradiction. A primary-grade teacher can assume, as would Bruner, that the geographical theme of man's adaptation to climate can be taught at any age. In applying the principle of readiness in accord with Piaget, the primary teacher may emphasize those applications which the child can observe and test at first hand. Without making formal study of the adaptation-to-climate principle as it applies to foreign lands and ancient times, the teacher can and should, nevertheless, make a number of comparisons and contrasts between the present scene and remote places and times.

The central problem of readiness is a question of fitting instruction—whatever its content may be—to the mental horizons and thought patterns of children at each successive stage of growth, whatever the pace of that growth. The point needs to be stressed that some elements of the "unknown" lie close at home. We should avoid being misled by children's glib talk about foreign places into concluding that they know all they need to know about that which is close at hand.

---

[4] Jean Piaget and Bärbel Inhelder, *The Child's Conception of Space*, London: Routledge & Kegan Paul, 1963. See also Piaget's many earlier works. Anselm Strauss and Karl Schnessler, "Socialization, Logical Reasoning, and Concept Development in the Child," *American Sociological Review 16*:514–523, 1951. Ralph C. Preston, *Children's Reactions to a Contemporary War Situation*, Child Development Monographs, No. 28, New York: Bureau of Publications, Teachers College, Columbia University, 1942. Harold V. Baker, *Children's Contributions to Elementary School General Discussion*, Child Development Monographs, No. 29, New York: Bureau of Publications, Teachers College, Columbia University, 1942.

[5] Jerome S. Bruner. *The Process of Education*. Cambridge, Mass.: Harvard University Press, 1961, p. 47.

[6] *Ibid.*, p. 53.

Rusnak has shown what is involved in teaching about the "here and now" in depth.[7] She experimented informally for three years with teaching children in the first grade about the home and community. Her report gives an apt illustration of how these important topics can be presented in a challenging way. Her pupils learned the profound aspect of home and community through analysis of historical sequence, cause-effect relationships, spatial relationships, environmental adaptation, and contrasts between simple and complex societies. They learned how to collect information, how to organize it, and how to report it. It may well be that the proper issue regarding readiness is not "here and now" versus "remote," but superficial study versus study which brings out underlying principles, relationships, and processes. Greater sophistication in the social studies on the part of today's children, if it exists, calls for teachers who know how to conduct studies in depth.

THE SCIENCE OF SOCIAL STUDIES *

Robert W. Hillerby

Social Science or Social Studies? goes a timeworn and continuing argument among curriculum planners, teachers, and anyone else interested in the educational program. What to include in the course of study and why? Whether the method of instruction be integration or correlation, coordination or separation matters not in the confusion resulting from the lack of agreement as to what constitutes a valid social studies or social science program. Social science and social studies teachers have long gone separate ways.

Let us briefly join the battle at the point of definitions. The social sciences are generally agreed to be any of the several related sciences that objectively study and analyze the significant aspects of human social behavior. The emphasis here may be placed on the separate disciplines of science as they are important to the social behavior of humans. Thus the content of the social sciences is de-

---

Robert W. Hillerby is Principal of the Hammel Street Elementary School, Los Angeles.

* Reprinted from *Education 86*:327–330, 1966, with permission of The Bobbs-Merrill Company, Inc., Indianapolis, and Robert W. Hillerby. Copyright © 1966.

[7] Mary Rusnak. "Introducing Social Studies in the First Grade." *Social Education 25*:291–292, 1961.

rived from the many interrelated and complex social experiences of man.

Social studies is usually defined as dealing with the interaction of people with their social and physical environment, stressing the importance of human relationships. So why the argument? It would appear that the social studies and the social sciences are concerned with the same entity, man.

If this be the case then it should be possible to draw upon the disciplines of the social sciences to develop a valid and useful curriculum in the social studies. And of course in many areas across the country this is just what has been accomplished.

The California State Curriculum Commission, for one, though by no means the only one, has within the past three years published and put into operation a new State Framework for Social Studies (2) in which the contributions of the related social sciences are brought into a meaningful context. One purpose of the California Framework was to indicate the interrelatedness of social studies and other areas of the curriculum, namely the social sciences. Essentially the social studies are considered portions of the social sciences, selected, simplified, and integrated for instructional purposes.

Curriculum Planning

The problem of curriculum planning in the social studies may seem quite simple from the foregoing, but such is hardly the case. A statement from a California State Curriculum Commission bulletin will illustrate. "All that mankind has acquired through a hundred thousand years and more of striving, experiencing and experimenting becomes the basic content from which the social studies curriculum must be selected." (3, p. 9)

The new California Framework is the product of the analysis of the basic generalizations that accrue within the social sciences. Unity is achieved by organizing a structure of related concepts and generalizations synthesized from all, or many, of the social sciences.

Actually the Framework outlines basic ideas or concepts from eight of the social sciences:

1. From *Geography* the sense of space and orientation toward the earth's surface
2. From *History* a sense of time and the record of what has happened to man
3. From *Political Science* the study of government and emphasis on civics and citizenship

4. From *Economics* an analysis of the production, distribution and consumption of wealth and income
5. From *Anthropology* the comparative study of man and the contribution of culture as a central theme
6. From *Psychology* the science of human behavior
7. From *Sociology* the scientific study of the social relationships which men develop in the interaction with one another
8. From *Philosophy* the appraisal of man, his conduct, values, and ethics.

From each of these sciences are drawn the prominent characteristics of society and the study of man which has always been the most valid and valuable segment of the social studies. Population growth, mobility, changes in family life, as well as man's historical identification at any time or place are provided from within the generalizations.

Implementing the Social Sciences

An example of how the social sciences can be implemented in the social studies curriculum, even in the lower grades, can be found in *The Course of Study for Elementary Schools* of the Los Angeles City Schools (4). The social studies course of study is a direct result of the California State Framework. At the third grade level the theme for social studies is "Los Angeles: A Growing and Changing Community; and the Contemporary Communities of the World." (4, p. 51) The following is a listing of the eight disciplines from the social sciences and appropriate unit titles from the third grade course of study.

Geography: Desert Communities, Mountain Communities
History: Spanish Explorers, Bringing Water to the City
Political Science: Municipal Government
Economics: A City of Business and Industry
Anthropology: Cultural, Educational, and Recreational Aspects
Psychology: People of Early Los Angeles
Sociology: Communications Between Communities
Philosophy: How People Live in an Urbanized Society

The vitality and utility of the social sciences, even for the eight-year-old, can readily be seen. However, the pertinence and amount of subject matter presented in any of the above titles would depend greatly on the kind of materials available and the techniques of the teacher.

At the secondary level the social sciences are more apt to be included in the curriculum as distinct entities and fields of endeavor in themselves. The Los Angeles City Schools require at least ten semester hours in the area of "Social Studies," five semesters in the junior high school, and five semesters in the senior high school (5).

The various units are far more discrete, and more advanced, as to subject matter than the themes of the elementary outline. Secondary courses include content from economics, international relations, psychology, sociology, current and world history, and geography, in addition to the expected courses in American institutions and United States history.

Some Disagreement

Everything noted so far seems easily accomplished and carefully considered, but not everyone agrees. An observation from K. William Kapp (1, p. vii) states that the social sciences are a "bewildering proliferation of subject matters, the preoccupation with trivia and the failure to make the maximum use of our knowledge for human welfare." In rebuttal the National Council for the Social Studies (1) points out that students receive a better education and experience in handling materials (from the disciplines of the social sciences) in a responsible way, and society receives people better educated to analyze the problems ahead.

Some disagreement seems inevitable, especially since content for the social studies does indeed come from more than one area. It has been stated that there are three major sources of content: the informal life of the community of which the child is a member, the formal social science disciplines which provide the warp and woof of the cultural pattern, and the pupil response to the first two.

In the California Framework it is recognized that the content of the social studies does not come exclusively from eight social sciences. Additional fields, especially in elementary school, are needed to provide the adequate degree of understanding. Young children need to learn on more than a mere verbal level, and so the instructional program includes natural and physical science, art, music, literature, even health and safety within the social studies program planned for elementary grades. Generalizations are then made from a broad base of experience.

Conclusion

Whatever the progress of the disagreement about social studies, one point should be clear and acknowledged by all sides. The generalizations derived from the social sciences provide a strong and vital foundation for the study of man and his environment, which most authorities agree is the essential and central aspect of general education. Thus firmly grounded, the social studies attempt to provide background and first-hand experience for successful living in American society.

It may be hackneyed to reaffirm that the children of today are the citizens of tomorrow; but still, the adult in year 2000 is going to school now. He must be equipped to analyze his own needs, to evaluate his own life and to use the processes at his command, whether they be social or scientific, which will enable him and his society to survive.

REFERENCES

1. American Council of Learned Societies and the National Council for the Social Studies, *The Social Studies and the Social Sciences*. New York: Harcourt, Brace & World, 1962.
2. California State Curriculum Commission, *Social Studies Framework for the Public Schools of California*. Sacramento: California State Department of Education, 1962.
3. California State Curriculum Commission, *The Social Studies Program for the Public Schools of California*. Bulletin of the California State Department of Education, Vol. XVII. Sacramento: California State Department of Education, August, 1948.
4. Los Angeles City Schools, *Course of Study for Elementary Schools*. Los Angeles, California, 1964.
5. Los Angeles City Schools, *Graduation Requirements and Curriculum*. Los Angeles, California, 1961.
6. Byron G. Massialas and Andreas M. Kazamias, *Crucial Issues in the Teaching of Social Studies*. Englewood Cliffs, N.J.: Prentice-Hall, 1964.

ASSESSING RECENT DEVELOPMENTS IN THE SOCIAL STUDIES *

Jack Allen

Of one thing, we can be sure. There is enough going on in the social studies (the magic word today is "ferment") to elicit complaints from some quarters, in the manner of the inimitable Jimmy Durante, that everybody wants to get into the act. Or, to use a more current idiom, if one wants to go where the action is, he needs only to peer around the nearest corner.

Consider the situation generally. First, at the local level. In the fall of 1965 the National Council for the Social Studies addressed an inquiry to almost 500 school systems. Virtually all indicated that they had some type of curriculum revision under way. Or, take many of the states. Here we find not only a sizable number of respectable state-wide curriculum projects, but a mushrooming within the past two or three years of social studies coordinator positions in the state departments. Finally, at the national level, we see some half a hundred projects, mainly in universities, supported by funds from the federal government and foundations.

And this by no means completes the list. One could cite a number of local social studies projects, many supported in part by outside funds, as yet largely unreported in the literature. Illustrative from my own experience would be the program at the Nova Schools in Broward County, Florida; a new elementary curriculum in Brentwood, Long Island; and innovative teaching with an inductive approach by the Christian Brothers in parochial high schools, mainly in the Middle West. Again, there is the broad movement in teacher education where one finds developing alliances, both formal and informal, between academic specialists and professional educators in colleges and universities, as well as the NDEA Title XI institutes and other federally-sponsored programs.

When we examine these many movements and fit them into the context of other developments currently influencing the program of the nation's schools, it seems reasonably apparent that the educational historian of, say, the 1990's, reflecting on the present decade, will report it as one of the most productive periods of change in

Jack Allen is Chairman of the Division of Social Sciences, George Peabody College for Teachers, Nashville.

* Reprinted from *Social Education 31*:99–103, 1967, with permission of the National Council for the Social Studies and Jack Allen.

the chronicles of American education. But how much of this change will represent genuine progress must still remain an open question. This brings us to the pesky question of significance.

Some insight into the present may be gained by recalling certain reasonably modern periods of change in the social studies. We might begin with a brief look at the 1890's.

Early in this educationally significant decade, important social studies developments began to emerge. They culminated, in a sense, in 1899, with the influential report of the famed Committee of Seven of the American Historical Association. A body of specific recommendations for curriculum content, the report had the effect of firmly establishing the dominant position of history in the social studies curriculum of the secondary school. Less noted, but an important feature of the report, was a wise statement on prevailing needs in the area of teacher education.

A second major curriculum thrust came in 1916 in the form of a report from the Committee on Social Studies, one of ten subject area subcommittees of the NEA's Commission on the Reorganization of Secondary Education. Challenging the exclusiveness of the Committee of Seven's secondary school history program, the 1916 committee directed its attention to the role of the social studies in the development of effective citizens. To implement this broad purpose, a course in civics was recommended for grade 9 and problems of democracy for grade 12, with the consequent replacement of history at these levels.

By combining the 1899 and 1916 recommendations, we find much that has remained influential in the secondary school social studies program throughout this century. Some have gone so far as to claim that nothing has substantially changed since these early pronouncements. This is a questionable judgment, however, in view of the many influential curriculum movements that have appeared in the intervening years.

Early developments and influences in elementary school social studies are more difficult to pinpoint. It perhaps suffices to note that elementary programs were recommended by the NEA as early as 1892 and 1895, by the American Historical Association's Committee of Seven in 1899, by another committee of the Association in 1908, and by Yearbooks of the National Society for the Study of Education in 1902 and 1903.

Much optimism about a bold new national effort in the social studies arose in the early 1930's with the establishment of the American Historical Association's Commission on Social Studies in the Schools. But, though the Commission succeeded in producing reports that ultimately ran to 16 volumes, many of lasting educational value, its curriculum pronouncements were confined to such generalities as "the development of rich and many-sided personalities" and the building of American society "in accordance with American ideals of popular democracy, personal liberty, and dignity."

Despite the inability of the Commission on the Social Studies to produce identifiable changes in the grade placement of subject matter, it doubtless had more subtle influences. In addition, the period of the Great Depression brought its weight to bear upon the social studies program by directing the bright light of inquiry on a host of social and economic problems. From it emerged such curriculum movements as intercultural education and such teaching strategies as the use of problem-solving techniques.

In the immediate aftermath of World War II came vigorous attention to the movement for international education, a movement that by the middle and latter 1950's was directing a considerable portion of its energy toward the study of the non-Western world. In the late 1940's the economic education movement emerged in much more explicit form and has continued vigorously without a break to the present. A citizenship education movement, heavily political in orientation, flowered in the early fifties, and, though it lost some of its force after a time, shows evidence of resurgence.

Now to our own decade. Here, in the America of the 1960's, we see a society of wealth and influence committed to the pursuit of excellence in its economic, social, and civic endeavors. Coincidentally, it is a society that may well be involved in the most revolutionary age in human history, a time when man's most fundamental values are being challenged and restructured. For us Americans, the unrelenting forces of history are being brought inexorably to bear on the most cherished of our institutions and ways—on the principles of individual freedom and the processes of constitutional government; on the functioning of a capitalist-oriented economy; on the nature of the family as a social system; even, as blaring headlines remind us almost daily, on the tenets of traditional religion. What is happening in the social studies today must be viewed within this context, for inevitably the various activities in the areas both of curriculum and learning are either explicitly or implicitly a response to such developments.

In our assessment of current developments in social studies, certain considerations should be kept in mind.

First, although some energetic school systems can justly claim to have been continuously in the process of curriculum revision, and a few movements, such as economic education, have been in progress for many years, most of the current major national efforts have come into being within the past three or four years. Thus, in a very real sense, we are only in the early phases of a movement. In any kind of historical perspective the clock has but recently been wound.

A second consideration relates to the nature of the projects themselves. Unlike the specific curriculum recommendations handed down in *a priori* fashion by national commissions in 1899 and 1916, the present movement is proceeding along a broken front, hoping in the process to fashion fresh points of view and build empirical bases for judgment. Thus we find work on individual units, as in the high school anthropology project; single courses, as in the high school geography project; limited studies of sequence, as with Northwestern's American history project; the preparation of specialized learning resources, as with Berkeley's Asia project; distinct student populations, as in Carnegie Tech's program for able students; particular teaching strategies, as with the Western Behavioral Sciences Institute's simulation studies. Interestingly enough, except for the work of some state and local school systems, very few studies are, like the Minnesota project, concerned with the total scope and sequence of the social studies curriculum.

No less important in its implications is a third consideration. Unlike the relative simplicity of the widely publicized recommendations for a new high school physics, or even a new elementary and secondary school mathematics curriculum, the social studies program is fashioned from a loose federation of social sciences, each discipline seeking what it regards as its proper role. To rationalize the conflicting claims of history, geography, political science, economics, anthropology, sociology, and social psychology into a balanced curriculum for children and youth has never been, nor will it ever be, easy. Some may well be led to the conclusion that it is virtually impossible.

Finally, even if some reasonable allocation of content could be made from among the various social sciences, there would still remain a whole complex of questions as to how it should be organized for instructional purposes. To illustrate this dilemma we need do no more than pose a pair of familiar issues: (1) Should the integrity of the disciplines be maintained, or should the approach be interdisciplinary? (2) Should specific subject areas be identified at separate grade levels, or should there be a sequential arrangement of non-graded units extending through the curriculum?

Within the context of the foregoing considerations, what are the current social studies curriculum developments seeking to achieve? Some commonality may be observed through an examination of their objectives. These might be categorized under three headings:

(1) the mode or process of inquiry, (2) knowledge of content, and (3) attitudes and values in the so-called affective domain. Here we find little that is distinctly new. Only in refinements and points of emphasis is there potential significance.

A mode of inquiry based on the process of induction appears to be a goal of paramount concern for a considerable number of projects. Illustrative of its philosophic justification was an observation by Alfred North Whitehead, many years prior to the current movement, that "our rate of progress is such that an individual human being, of ordinary length of life, will be called upon to face novel situations which find no parallel in his past. The fixed person, for the fixed duties, who, in older societies, was such a godsend, in the future, will be a public danger." Its psychological rationale has perhaps been suggested with greatest effect by Bruner in his *Process of Education* and other writings. In more explicit terms the goal has been amplified by Bloom and Krathwohl in their *Taxonomy of Educational Objectives: Handbook I, the Cognitive Domain.*

Content knowledge, likewise categorized in the cognitive domain by the Bloom-Krathwohl *Taxonomy,* is recognized as an objective of fundamental importance, but the tendency of the projects is to conceive it more as a means than as an end. In pragmatic terms this represents a contrast to traditional instruction both in schools and colleges where, in practice if not in theory, the tendency has been to regard acquisition of information as an end in itself. Current curricular efforts seem much less certain as to what knowledge is most important. What is more, they find their problems greatly complicated by the immense volume of data pouring from social science research, not to mention the inroads of other social science disciplines into the domain traditionally dominated by history and geography.

Less needs to be said at the moment about attitudes and values. A widely recognized body of goals, it is as yet a relatively unexplored dimension of current social studies activity.

As we examine curriculum developments in relation to objectives, certain emphases emerge and some deficiencies become apparent. From virtually every source, whether national project or local school system, attention is being directed in some manner to the basic concepts and structures of the various social sciences. The efforts range from the elements of a single discipline, functioning at a particular grade level, to a conceptual framework for a total k-12 program. In the process of development, a number of ideas and procedures are emerging that can be regarded as potentially significant for the future of the social studies.

For one thing, statements about concepts and structures are

being formulated for each of the social sciences in such a manner as to make them available for curriculum purposes. Particularly notable in this activity is the fact that social science scholars are being drawn directly into the work, a function that is tending to bring many academic specialists and curriculum workers into closer alliance and understanding. If the school person regards this as a means of bringing the university professor out of his ivory tower, the academic specialist thinks of it as a way of building more integrity into the program. A detached observer can only be inclined to regard it as a victory for both.

In the conceptualization process some other interesting things are occurring. Being challenged by other social sciences is the traditional dominance of history and geography in the upper elementary grades and junior high school, and history in the senior high school. As a concomitant, there is a growing emphasis upon a study of the contemporary world and current issues, for these things, after all, are the very stuff of political science, economics, sociology, social psychology—the broad realm of the behavioral sciences. Indeed, the behavioral movement is having its influence, both as regards scholarly research and curriculum development, in such areas as history, geography, and anthropology as well.

Finally, the conceptual framework is becoming increasingly global. More than such a comparatively simple process as making a world history course truly "world" oriented, it is the bringing of a global view into the social processes of the young kindergarten child, a questioning of the traditional perception of expanding environments in the early elementary years, and the permeation of other subject areas in a variety of ways, cutting across the whole spectrum of the school curriculum.

The search for a conceptual framework would seem to suggest a direct and immediate concern for curriculum scope and sequence. Often this is the case with the state programs and with many local efforts. School systems, after all, are confronted with the stark reality of dealing with a fresh collection of minds and bodies each fall. For good or ill, some kind of program has to be in operation. The national projects can afford to be more cavalier. They, as a consequence, have been inclined, as we noted earlier, to ride off in many different directions. The hope is that their efforts ultimately will react in some manner to the common good. In such a situation there may be some comfort for those who harbor fear of a superimposed national curriculum. If, in the past, there has existed some semblance of national consensus about the framework for a social studies curriculum—and I think there has—certainly one cannot detect a new one emerging from the various national endeavors currently under way.

Closely allied with the idea of concept and structure is a growing interest in what might be broadly labeled as skills development. Here we find new dimensions characterized by such terms as "discovery approach," "the method of induction," "simulation," "game theory," and the like. Integrated with newly developed course materials, they are leading to the development of interesting teaching strategies. In some learning situations, to paraphrase Carl Becker, they seek to make every man his own historian, or geographer, or sociologist, or archeologist, or economist. Often, the aim is to develop habits of self-direction on the part of the students. Again, the goal may be establishment of group initiative. Whatever the direction, there remains much to be learned in this crucial area of teaching strategy and skills development. Hard data on comparative performance in relationship to more traditional procedures is still in short supply.

Closely associated with the seemingly more sophisticated perceptions of skills development is an explosion in the area of learning resources. In many modern schools, the traditional single-purpose library is being replaced with exciting, attractive learning resources laboratories. And a few schools are moving closer to the limits of current educational technology through the development of information retrieval centers. To provide appropriate learning materials for these laboratories and centers is one of the responsibilities being undertaken by some of the national projects. A number, in response to an emphasis on inductive learning, are producing printed materials—document collections, case studies, selected reading to illustrate different interpretations of conflicting points of view, etc. One also finds such items as tape recordings, film-strips, transparencies, artifacts, and the like. Unquestionably, this multi-media approach to learning, old though it is in theory, is beginning to have a new kind of impact.

There is, of course, more to the enrichment of resources than the growing acceptance of new learning theory, important as this may be. For one thing, potentialities are being expanded by constant advances in technology. For another, our growing affluence is making it increasingly realistic to consider the use of these instructional tools. Not only is local support increasing, it is being enhanced by the benevolent arm of the federal government.

The expansion of conceptual frameworks to encompass all the social sciences, the enrichment of learning theory to provide, among other things, for more adequate development of skills, and the potentialities existent in a mounting volume of learning resources are placing heavy responsibilities on teachers in service and on teacher education institutions. Relatively little attention has been devoted to this problem by the national curriculum projects. Fortunately, however, one does find a growing recognition of the need at the local level, with school systems reacting in a variety of ways to in-service needs. Institutional pre-service programs are also being modified in an effort to adapt to new curriculum trends. Recently the federal government has moved into this area in ways that seem potentially promising. One example is the new Experienced Teacher Fellowship Program; another is the Prospective Teacher Fellowship Program.

But perhaps the strongest emotional shot in the arm for the social studies profession came in the summer of 1965 with the initiation of NDEA Title XI institutes in history and geography, a program now being expanded into other social science areas. It was my good fortune to serve as one of the evaluators for the first group of Title XI history institutes. To visit with institute participants and staff and, subsequently, to compare experiences with fellow evaluators, was something of an inspiration. Clearly, as with any beginning endeavor, there were glaring weaknesses in a number of institute programs; but one could not gainsay the professional attitudes of the great majority of teacher participants and the missionary zeal of institute directors and their staff. We evaluators were left with an abiding impression that the American social studies teacher was earnestly committed to the improvement of his professional competence in the light of new developments that were impinging upon him.

In the flush of renewed recognition, it is perhaps inevitable that the social studies movement in the United States should number in its camp a body of vocal new converts possessing all the zealousness that comes with the emotionalism of fresh conversion, as well as a staunch body of traditionalists who, by nature, tend to regard virtually anything different as threatening. From the former the claims are often excessive, from the latter the doubts unreasonable. Without endeavoring to find some rational resolution of these extremes, there are a number of deficiencies in the current efforts that seem clearly apparent.

There is, for instance, this fundamental question of teacher education. At the preservice level, both the academic community and professional educators have a lot of work before them. While one can develop considerable optimism about the sympathetic understandings emanating from both groups, the cooperation needs to move much further to be truly effective for purposes of effective preservice education.

Another facet of the preservice problem can be illustrated by the situation inherent in two such relatively unrelated goals as inductive learning and the development of global viewpoints. To assist students with the process of induction, teachers themselves need experiences with this teaching strategy. For prospective teachers, these should come from their own college classrooms. Similarly, if teachers are to be global in orientation, their college training should bring them into contact with content knowledge appropriate for this purpose.

The inservice teacher education problem is equally complicated—much more, it would seem, than the experience we have witnessed in recent years with the new mathematics. Here, as with the preservice problem, the situation will demand a high order of cooperation between the academic community and the profession.

The remaining unfinished business which I would like to mention relates more directly to current curriculum developments. As noted earlier, one of the strong motivating forces stimulating current curriculum change is the revolutionary character of our age. This is a circumstance that has special relevance to the affective domain. Yet, to date, we find very little work in this crucial values area. One of the national projects, that at Harvard, seems directly concerned with this objective. Also worthy of mention is the Good American Program, an elementary school project in Ossining, New York, conducted under the auspices of the Council for Citizenship Education.

Some of the soundest thinking in the values area is currently emanating from the Social Science Education Consortium in West LaFayette, Indiana, which is approaching the study of values by drawing a distinction between those that are personal, in the sense of tastes and basic needs, and those that are judgments or conclusions about the relative superiority of different procedures or entities based on the use of empirical data. One may hope, and reasonably expect, that a major thrust in the social studies in the immediate future will be work on the treatment of values in the curriculum.

Another relative deficiency of the current curriculum efforts relates to the social studies program in the elementary school, particularly at the earliest levels. There is, of course, some notable activity here that should be applauded. On any comparative basis, however, the elementary school is not receiving its just dues. Particularly in projects where university social scientists are intimately involved, the tendency has been to direct curriculum activity toward the secondary school. Perhaps, among other reasons, it is because the specialist feels more comfortable, as well as knowledgeable, at the more advanced levels, since they are closer to his own experiences in higher education. In this connection, it is interesting to note that of the 84 Title XI history institutes in the summer of 1965, 76 were devoted in some manner to the secondary school. In the geography institutes the elementary school fared somewhat better. Effective as these secondary school efforts may be, one is forced to observe that, if current curriculum efforts in the social studies are to make anything close to a maximum impact on the schools, much more attention will have to be directed to the education of young children.

Closely associated with the elementary school question is the need to establish better relationships between curriculum building and child development research. It is not enough for those responsible for current curriculum development to rely on experience and intuition in deciding how and what should be taught about the social sciences to children. To deal with this deficiency, it is just as important for child development psychologists to be brought into close alliance with curriculum workers as it is to involve social science specialists in this activity. By the same token, it is essential that available data on children's learning be inextricably interwoven into the preservice education of social studies teachers.

The final need I would mention is in the area of evaluation. We all recognize that curriculum is a terribly difficult thing to research. And yet we must surely develop better techniques and instruments for this purpose than we have had in the past. Many of the national projects speak confidently of evaluation as an essential dimension of their activity. But I am not yet persuaded that much really significant work in this area is emerging. There is no question about innovation. The woods are full of it. We must, however, distinguish between innovation and experimentation. Much of the innovative activity in social studies today is exciting, different, and interesting. It will have much more appeal for purposes of curriculum change when supported by experimental designs and results that are persuasive. Until this is accomplished, social studies curriculum development will move, as it has in the past, in response to prestigious voices, enactments of legislative councils, reactions to sources of money, and even sheer inertia. Should current curriculum activity degenerate into a movement influenced by those who can speak the loudest and most persuasively in the right places, then it would lose much of its significance, and negate the high level of expectation that we may have for it. The activity might bring substantial change, but there would be no assurance that it would also be progress.

Our faith today is that, at least haltingly, we are making some progress. Our sincere hope is that in the years to come we will find that it has been truly significant progress.

SOCIAL SCIENCE EDUCATION: A CURRICULUM FRONTIER *

Patricia Schmuck, John E. Lohman, Ronald Lippitt, and Robert S. Fox

Interest in the revision and improvement of social studies curricula by curriculum specialists, teachers and social scientists is clearly increasing. While mathematics and the physical and biological sciences have made great strides in bringing their curricula abreast of current knowledge, there has been no similar discipline-based movement in social studies. This is true, even though social science research and theory have progressed extensively in the past quarter century. Four limitations of current social studies education are briefly summarized here.

Some Limitations of Social Science Curricula

1. Social studies have been viewed primarily as a body of information to be mastered. Learning has focused on memorizing facts rather than the development of critical and analytical thinking.

2. There has been little distinction between value clarification or value inquiry and value indoctrination. It is important to teach children the distinction, on the one hand, between objective data

Patricia Schmuck is a doctoral student in Human Development at the University of Oregon; John E. Lohman is Research Associate and doctoral candidate in Social Psychology at the University of Michigan; Ronald Lippitt is Professor of Psychology and Sociology at the University of Michigan; Robert S. Fox is Professor of Education and Director of the University Laboratory School, University of Michigan, Ann Arbor.

* Reprinted from *Educational Leadership* 22:300–305, 1965, with permission of the Association for Supervision and Curriculum Development, Patricia Schmuck, John E. Lohman, Ronald Lippitt, and Robert S. Fox. Copyright © 1965, by the Association for Supervision and Curriculum Development.

collection, analysis and interpretation of phenomen⫽
other hand, the making of reflective value judgmen⫽
phenomena.

3. We have tended to make false assumptions ab⫽
potential of children and have expected too little from ⫽
the new math and physical science curricula have shown, children
can understand and use concepts that traditionally have been reserved for high school or even college students. We have also assumed an obligation to protect children from the "harsh realities"
of life. While we may view poverty, unemployment, discrimination,
crime and war as "harsh" realities, nevertheless, they are part of
children's lives—whether by exposure to mass media or through
the range of their own experiences.

4. The social studies curricula do not adequately represent the
disciplines that deal with man and his social world. Psychology,
social psychology, sociology, anthropology, and economics have been
ignored to a large degree, while history and geography and some
aspects of political science dominate.

Need for Social Science Education

It seems important to us to introduce a broadly gauged program
of social science education at all age levels. This should be done
because the social sciences represent bodies of knowledge that are
a significant part of the contemporary stockpile of science-based
information. Social scientists are playing an increasingly important
role in social policy, social legislation, and many other aspects of
social engineering. We have an obligation to expose children to this
body of knowledge and practice and to allow them to develop images
of social scientists and their work just as they develop images of
physical and biological scientists.

What is more important, children continuously do learn about
human behavior. They are required to interact within the context
of their family, their classroom, their peer group, their churches
and their clubs. They do make generalizations about human behavior and take value positions. We must, however, question the
accuracy as well as the adequacy of these unguided incidental
learnings.

The classroom can and should be a laboratory for guided learning
about human behavior. It is here that children can question their
assumptions and have an opportunity to delve into realms of
knowledge that have pertinence for their lives. A good social science
curriculum should provide an exciting experience with the use of
scientific methods to study human behavior and the social environ-

ment. Children need, and often are eager for, knowledge about motivation, learning, individual differences, human development, irrationality, and intergroup processes in order to help them function in their present day world, as well as to prepare them to solve some of the critical social problems of the world.

An Illustration of Social Science Education

Our Michigan Elementary Social Science Education Project [1] is developing a social science curriculum for upper elementary grades. This curriculum spans the fields of psychology, social psychology, micro-sociology and the small group aspects of social anthropology. Paralleling recent revisions in the physical sciences, this curriculum employs a laboratory approach to the scientific study of human behavior. Each unit uses the classroom as a laboratory where "specimens" of behavioral interaction are explored.

A number of inquiry projects, designed to enable the child to develop an understanding of social science content, to master the rudiments of social scientific methods, and to employ the scientific values of openness to inquiry, objectivity, curiosity, reliability, and validity are included in each unit. In addition to the discovery process of the laboratory, the units include rewrites of studies made by social scientists.

An introductory unit presents the domain of social science to the students and includes a series of activities focused on developing methodological skills such as observation, interviewing, and coding. The other six units are designed to encompass some aspect of behavior.

CRITERIA FOR CONTENT

Two criteria have been developed for determining the content of these six units:

1. The particular area of inquiry must have been the subject of a considerable amount of scientific investigation which has produced a coherent body of data and theory.

2. The area of inquiry must have relevance and meaning in the life of the child.

The six units selected are: Friendliness—Unfriendliness; People and Groups Different From Ourselves; Getting Work Done Alone

---

[1] The University of Michigan Social Science Education Project is affiliated with the Social Science Education Consortium of Midwest Universities and Colleges. This is a cooperative enterprise of 25 or 30 social scientists and educators engaged in social science curriculum projects. The Director of SSEC is Irving Morrissett, located at the Consortium central office, Purdue University, 404 Hayes Street, Lafayette, Indiana.

and in Groups; Social Influence; Decision Making; and Personal and Group Development.

The package of materials in each unit consists of a teaching guide, phonograph records of behavioral incidents, a children's workbook and a booklet of scientific studies and experiments rewritten for children. Each unit has been structured flexibly so that the teacher may adapt it to his pupils' past experience and readiness, methodological skills, conceptual knowledge and previous exposure to social science. The units are being developed for 4th, 5th, and 6th grade children. Instead of designing different topics for study at these different grade levels, we believe the child can study the same phenomena with increasing complexity and methodological sophistication. Each unit involves the following sequence of study phases:

Preparatory phases undertaken by the teacher prior to teaching in his classroom.

1. Teacher preparation—teacher reads prepared conceptual materials in teachers' guide; reviews skills needed for the unit; plans opportunities for direct study of behavior such as arranging for behavioral specimens in the classroom, or gaining permission to use another classroom for interviewing.

2. Classroom diagnosis—teacher uses a prepared questionnaire to diagnose the level of class information, attitudes and skills in order to adapt the materials to his classroom.

Inquiry phases undertaken by pupils to study the behavioral phenomena of a unit.

3. Question asking and inquiry design—pupils are involved in the process of asking curiosity questions about the phenomena under study and developing a study design to obtain data to answer some of these questions: what populations to study? what kinds of sampling? what kinds of methods for data collection are appropriate?

4. Data collection—pupils develop their own instruments or use those provided to collect data—questionnaires, interview schedules, observation procedures for direct study of the phenomena; finding out what scientists and other "experts" have discovered.

5. Data analysis—children learn how to organize and analyze (coding, frequency distributions, simple relationships) the data collected in order to answer inquiry questions.

6. Answering questions—pupils learn how to interpret the data they have collected and analysed and attempt to make tentative answers to their inquiry questions.

7. Value inquiry—a clear distinction is made between objective interpretations and predictions based upon data yielded by scientific study and the evaluation of these findings in terms of individual

personal and social values. These are seen as complementary aspects of the inquiry process. The child identifies the value preferences he maintains about social interaction and examines their bases.

8. Generalization—children develop implications of findings for other situations, for other people, at other times.

9. Evaluation—children evaluate the appropriateness of the methods they used to answer questions (involvement in issues of reliability, validity, size and representativeness of sample, etc.) and prepare new inquiry questions which the study has raised which might be answered for fuller understanding.

Phases three through nine may be repeated several times. In any one unit there may be 15–20 possible inquiry projects from which teachers and pupils will select those of greatest interest and relevance for study.

Summary and Evaluation Phases to bring together the learnings from the inquiry projects and to evaluate the unit.

10. Integration of findings—class integrates and summarizes the findings from its inquiry efforts; considers what the methods used in different studies contribute to understanding the phenomena under study.

11. Value inquiry—elaboration of phase 7 in context of the integrated findings from the total unit.

12. Generalization—children review learnings and make generalizations.

13. Replication, application (optional)—students apply the findings to their own lives and/or continue to replicate studies on their own.

14. Evaluations—both teacher and students evaluate the effectiveness of the unit; teacher evaluates the changes in information, attitudes and skills.

Each unit is focused upon the individual (psychological), the interpersonal (social psychological), and the group processes (sociological). Within each of these areas, conceptual understanding of the relationships among the internal elements (cognitions, attitudes and values, intentions and goals) is stressed. The behavioral phenomena under study are developed in the context of like-age and cross-age peer relations, and cross-generational and cross-cultural interaction.

Teacher Education

This new type of curriculum is a challenge to educators who must prepare future teachers and to curriculum planners who must prepare teachers already in the field to do an effective job of social science education. Ultimately, the strength of any curriculum does not reside with the curriculum planners. It resides with teachers in the classroom engaged in the task of teaching. A well-developed curriculum may be a necessary prerequisite for effective teaching, but it is not a sufficient condition. The success of any curriculum depends upon the knowledge and competence of the curriculum utilizer, the teacher. Consequently, curriculum planners cannot avoid or neglect the job of teacher involvement and education.

During the initial pilot testing of the social science materials, our project staff attempted to isolate the necessary components of teacher preparation for social science education. Collaborating teachers were engaged in a training program while teaching the curriculum materials in their classrooms. The task of the training sessions became threefold:

1. We found that teachers had varying degrees of knowledge and attitudes about social science. It was necessary to give basic scientific education about the content and methods to be taught.

2. Our materials introduced some new teaching techniques that required training and practice. We developed skill training exercises for teachers.

3. Teachers needed some "at the elbow" or reference help for problems that arose in the course of teaching. Consultants were made available.

In any wide distribution of curriculum materials, it is, of course, not feasible to depend on continuing personal consultation for teachers. In order to meet teacher-needs the project staff is developing a self-administering package of materials which may be used individually or by a group of teachers. We have identified six areas of activity that require understanding and skill for teaching these units. Each area is represented by conceptual and skill material which includes phonograph records, workbooks containing programed materials, teaching exercises and reference materials.

Curriculum Development and Applied Social Science

The needs for continued teacher education are probably more crucial in our present day than ever before. We have outlined one approach—training courses built into curriculum materials. Another approach might be through a new version of a university correspondence course in social science. A teacher could be involved in the university correspondence course for credit while teaching the materials in his class. Expansion of well designed in-service education programs sponsored by school systems is another approach.

To foster the development, diffusion and adaptation of the social science curriculum is in itself a scientific challenge. We must use our scientific resources to inquire into such questions as the following:

1. How can the concepts and methods of the disciplines best be related to the levels of development of children's concepts, interests, attitudes, and range of experience?

2. How can teachers be prepared to seek, rather than resist, the challenge of re-learning and continuing new learning of social science knowledge?

3. How can data on the learning experiences of the pupils be fed into the curriculum revision process?

4. What kind of orientation do parents need in order to understand, support and contribute to the development of social science education?

5. What teaching techniques will be most effective in achieving the goals of social science education?

We have identified variations on two current patterns of curriculum development and spread. In one pattern the social studies curriculum specialist (in a College of Education or a large school system) conducts a curriculum revision or development project, utilizing a cooperating school system or set of teachers for feasibility testing, and consulting knowledge specialists for validity checking.

Diffusion and adoption depend on the usual channels of commercial publication, professional journals, and local teacher committees. In a second pattern, the content specialists, the scientists, "call the shots" in the development project. Classroom teachers are recruited to try out the materials, while direct in-service education is conducted by the scientists, primarily in summer institutes.

Both patterns are weak when viewed in terms of a scientific theory of the process of change. Both patterns ignore the relevant research on change which has been conducted on the adaptation of new technical practices in industry and agriculture. Both patterns also ignore the ways in which the adoption of new teaching practices is a different process from the adoption of new technical practices.

EMERGING TRENDS

From an analysis of our experience to date, several generalizations are emerging for us:

1. Senior scientists and educators *must* be committed to joint learning from each other through joint production efforts.

2. Young scientists in training must be attracted to participate in some of the needed tasks of curriculum development, such as

knowledge retrieval, classroom observation, and development of evaluation tools.

3. Selected teachers must be an important part of curriculum development teams, and need to be representative of contrasting teaching situations, such as social class, ethnic differences and urban-rural settings.

4. School administrators and curriculum coordinators need to be consultants on issues of teacher training, curriculum adoption and parent relations.

5. Procedures should be developed which allow students to be active participants in curriculum design.

6. Because the changes in value, attitude, and skill required in social science education represent a deeper process of change than is typically required in new technical practices, there must be continued experimentation with the designing and redesigning of procedures and materials for teacher education.

7. The plans for diffusion of new curriculum models and materials must include as many substitutes for the "demonstration farm" in agriculture as possible, i.e., opportunities for direct observation and sharing of new practices among classroom teachers.

Because of the demand for revision and change, local school systems will be faced with a variety of curriculum adoption possibilities. Educators, boards of education, and parents must be helped to become sophisticated about the criteria of creative decision-making in this area of curriculum adoption.

Once the adoption decision is reached, teachers and administrators must decide how it fits within the context of the existing curriculum. There are several alternatives: finding time for the social science units as supplementary to the existing curriculum, or substituting in some of the current social studies periods, or introducing the new material as part of science education, along with physical and biological science. Certainly, such a decision will not be final for curriculum planners or school systems; it will be open to review and change.

It is to be hoped that the national associations of social studies educators and of curriculum specialists will find ways of collaborating with the scientific associations and teams of social scientists who have become convinced that the frontiers of new knowledge and scientific method must become part of the challenge and perspective of students at all age levels. Because the frontiers of knowledge are moving so rapidly, curriculum revision and teacher reeducation must be a continuing adventure in collaboration.

Social Studies and the Learning-Teaching Process

*E*FFECTIVE LEARNING AND TEACHING in elementary social studies depends to a significant degree on the application of sound psychological principles. If social studies programs are to concern themselves with the thought processes of pupils, it will be necessary for teachers to know how those thought processes develop and how they function. The research in education and psychology of the past fifty years has produced helpful guidelines for the development of psychologically sound teaching strategies. Nonetheless, a considerable amount of additional research is needed in many aspects of human learning. Our knowledge of this complex process is far from complete.

The intellectual operations involved in achieving the various types of social studies objectives are not identical, and therefore teaching and learning processes need to be varied. In forming and attaining concepts, for example, breadth of experience is important because the learner needs to encounter the concepts in wide and varied settings. When such broad exposure is lacking, the pupil is likely to develop a limited knowledge of the concept. Such instruction often contributes to the development of stereotypes. For example, when only one or two illustrations are given of a desert, the pupil comes to believe that those illustrations are representative of all deserts. Or, when limited examples are chosen of the ways of living in a country selected for study, pupils assume that the examples represent the way of life of everyone in that country. Pupils do not practice learning a concept in the way that they might practice a skill in order to develop proficiency in its use. Neither do they understand a concept very completely if they can only define it. There are certain principles regarding the formation and acquisition of concepts that can and should be applied in teaching them to pupils.

Similarly, there are basic principles of learning that need to be applied in teaching skills, values, and attitudes. For example, if a skill implies proficiency in doing something in repeated performances, the learner needs opportunities to practice and use the skill. In the case of values and attitudes the teaching ordinarily must be more subtle and less direct than is the case in teaching concepts or skills.

In practice learnings do not fall into neat categories or packages that can be labeled as understandings, attitudes and values, and skills. More often than not, learnings contain elements of each of these categories. Skills, especially intellectual skills that are so important in social studies instruction, have a substantive or cognitive base. How can a child, for example, learn thinking skills without having something of substance to think about? Values and attitudes also have a relationship to cognitive components. Indeed, ignorance is often the source of undesirable and ill-founded attitudes and values. In teaching, therefore, the teacher must plan for both the cognitive and neocognitive elements in almost all social studies instruction.

In addition to considering variables that have to do with the nature of the learning task, effective teaching and learning is a highly individual matter. Specific teachers have styles of teaching that are particularly effective for them, yet these same styles of teaching may be less productive for someone else. Individual pupils may have styles of learning that are especially well suited to them. It is well known that not all pupils learn in the same way. Some are endowed with well-developed verbal and linguistic skills and prefer learning styles that rely on such abilities. Other pupils are more visually oriented. Still others need kinesthetic experiences in order to learn readily. In addition to these idiosyncracies in learning styles, pupil variation is such that the sequence of learning is often different for individual children.

The articles that follow address themselves to these and similar problems. They offer a wide range of thought concerning the development of social studies learnings. Men have taught each other and their young for thousands of years. As a result, there has been built up a substantial amount of what might be called "conventional wisdom" about teaching and learning. Much of it is common sense and soundly based. Yet much of what we do in teaching is based on myths, feelings, and beliefs that have no foundation in modern psychology. It is indeed surprising how little is actually known about the teaching and learning process considering how long man has been engaged in it. The articles included in this section are rooted soundly in psychological theory and provide helpful guidelines for effective teaching and learning.

THE ACT OF DISCOVERY *

Jerome S. Bruner

Maimonides, in his *Guide for the Perplexed*,[1] speaks of four forms of perfection that men might seek. The first and lowest form is perfection in the acquisition of worldly goods. The great philosopher dismisses such perfection on the ground that the possessions one acquires bear no meaningful relation to the possessor: "A great king may one morning find that there is no difference between him and the lowest person." A second perfection is of the body, its conformation and skills. Its failing is that it does not reflect on what is uniquely human about man: "he could [in any case] not be as strong as a mule." Moral perfection is the third, "the highest degree of excellency in man's character." Of this perfection Maimonides says: "Imagine a person being alone, and having no connection whatever with any other person; all his good moral principles are at rest, they are not required and give man no perfection whatever. These principles are only necessary and useful when man comes in contact with others." "The fourth kind of perfection is the true perfection of man; the possession of the highest intellectual faculties. . . ." In justification of his assertion, this extraordinary Spanish-Judaic philosopher urges: "Examine the first three kinds of perfection; you will find that if you possess them, they are not your property, but the property of others. . . . But the last kind of perfection is exclusively yours; no one else owns any part of it."

It is a conjecture much like that of Maimonides that leads me to examine the act of discovery in man's intellectual life. For if man's intellectual excellence is the most his own among his perfections, it is also the case that the most uniquely personal of all that he knows is that which he has discovered for himself. What difference does it make, then, that we encourage discovery in the learning of the young? Does it, as Maimonides would say, create a special and unique relation between knowledge possessed and the possessor? And what may such a unique relation do for a man—or for a child, if you will, for our concern is with the education of the young?

Jerome S. Bruner is Professor of Psychology at Harvard University, Cambridge, Massachusetts.

* Reprinted from the *Harvard Educational Review* *31*:21–32, with permission of the President and Fellows of Harvard College and Jerome S. Bruner. Copyright © 1961.

[1] Maimonides, *Guide for the Perplexed*. New York: Dover, 1956.

The immediate occasion for my concern with discovery—and I do not restrict discovery to the act of finding out something that before was unknown to mankind, but rather include all forms of obtaining knowledge for oneself by the use of one's own mind—the immediate occasion is the work of the various new curriculum projects that have grown up in America during the last six or seven years. For whether one speaks to mathematicians or physicists or historians, one encounters repeatedly an expression of faith in the powerful effects that come from permitting the student to put things together for himself, to be his own discoverer.

First, let it be clear what the act of discovery entails. It is rarely, on the frontier of knowledge or elsewhere, that new facts are "discovered" in the sense of being encountered as Newton suggested in the form of islands of truth in an unchartered sea of ignorance. Or if they appear to be discovered in this way, it is almost always thanks to some happy hypotheses about where to navigate. Discovery, like surprise, favors the well prepared mind. In playing bridge, one is surprised by a hand with no honors in it at all and also by hands that are all in one suit. Yet all hands in bridge are equiprobable: one must know to be surprised. So too in discovery. The history of science is studded with examples of men "finding out" something and not knowing it. I shall operate on the assumption that discovery, whether by a schoolboy going it on his own or by a scientist cultivating the growing edge of his field, is in its essence a matter of rearranging or transforming evidence in such a way that one is enabled to go beyond the evidence so reassembled to additional new insights. It may well be that an additional fact or shred of evidence makes this larger transformation of evidence possible. But it is often not even dependent on new information.

It goes without saying that, left to himself, the child will go about discovering things for himself within limits. It also goes without saying that there are certain forms of child rearing, certain home atmospheres that lead some children to be their own discoverers more than other children. These are both topics of great interest, but I shall not be discussing them. Rather, I should like to confine myself to the consideration of discovery and "finding-out-for-oneself" within an educational setting—specifically the school. Our aim as teachers is to give our students as firm a grasp of a subject as we can, and to make him as autonomous and self-propelled a thinker as we can—one who will go along on his own after formal schooling has ended. I shall return in the end to the question of the kind of classroom and the style of teaching that encourages an attitude of wanting to discover. For purposes of orienting the discussion, however, I would like to make an overly simplified distinction between teaching that takes place in the *expository mode* and teaching that utilizes the *hypothetical mode*. In the former, the decisions concerning the mode and pace and style of exposition are principally determined by the teacher as expositor; the student is the listener. If I can put the matter in terms of structural linguistics, the speaker has a quite different set of decisions to make than the listener: the former has a wide choice of alternatives for structuring, he is anticipating paragraph content while the listener is still intent on the words, he is manipulating the content of the material by various transformations, while the listener is quite unaware of these internal manipulations. In the hypothetical mode, the teacher and the student are in a more cooperative position with respect to what in linguistics would be called "speaker's decisions." The student is not a bench-bound listener, but is taking a part in the formulation and at times may play the principal role in it. He will be aware of alternatives and may even have an "as if" attitude toward these and, as he receives information he may evaluate it as it comes. One cannot describe the process in either mode with great precision as to detail, but I think the foregoing may serve to illustrate what is meant.

Consider now what benefit might be derived from the experience of learning through discoveries that one makes for oneself. I should like to discuss these under four headings: (1) The increase in intellectual potency, (2) the shift from extrinsic to intrinsic rewards, (3) learning the heuristics of discovering, and (4) the aid to memory processing.

1. Intellectual Potency

If you will permit me, I would like to consider the difference between subjects in a highly constrained psychological experiment involving a two-choice apparatus. In order to win chips, they must depress a key either on the right or the left side of the machine. A pattern of payoff is designed such that, say, they will be paid off on the right side 70 per cent of the time, on the left 30 per cent, although this detail is not important. What is important is that the payoff sequence is arranged at random, and there is no pattern. I should like to contrast the behavior of subjects who think that there is some pattern to be found in the sequence—who think that regularities are discoverable—in contrast to subjects who think that things are happening quite by *chance*. The former group adopts what is called an "event-matching" strategy in which the number of responses given to each side is roughly equal to the proportion of times it pays off: in the present case R70:L30. The group that believes there is no pattern very soon reverts to a much more primitive strategy wherein *all* responses are allocated to the side that has the greater payoff. A little arithmetic will show you that the lazy all-and-none strategy pays off more if indeed the environment is random: namely, they win seventy per cent of the time. The event-matching subjects win about 70% on the 70% payoff side (or 49% of the time there) and 30% of the time on the side that pays off 30% of the time (another 9% for a total take-home wage of 58% in return for their labors of decision). But the world is not always or not even frequently random, and if one analyzes carefully what the event-matchers are doing, it turns out that they are trying out hypotheses one after the other, all of them containing a term such that they distribute bets on the two sides with a frequency to match the actual occurrence of events. If it should turn out that there is a pattern to be discovered, their payoff would become 100%. The other group would go on at the middling rate of 70%.

What has this to do with the subject at hand? For the person to search out and find regularities and relationships in his environment, he must be armed with an expectancy that there will be something to find and, once aroused by expectancy, he must devise ways of searching and finding. One of the chief enemies of such expectancy is the assumption that there is nothing one can find in the environment by way of regularity or relationship. In the experiment just cited, subjects often fall into a habitual attitude that there is either nothing to be found or that they can find a pattern by looking. There is an important sequel in behavior to the two attitudes, and to this I should like to turn now.

We have been conducting a series of experimental studies on a group of some seventy school children over the last four years. The studies have led up to distinguish an interesting dimension of cognitive activity that can be described as ranging from *episodic empiricism* at one end to *cumulative constructionism* at the other. The two attitudes in the choice experiments just cited are illustrative of the extremes of the dimension. I might mention some other illustrations. One of the experiments employs the game of Twenty Questions. A child—in this case he is between 10 and 12—is told that a car has gone off the road and hit a tree. He is to ask questions that can be answered "yes" or "no" to discover the cause of the accident. After completing the problem, the same task is given him again, though he is told that the accident had a different cause this time. In all, the procedure is repeated four times. Children enjoy playing the game. They also differ quite markedly in the approach or strategy they bring to the task. There are various elements in the strategies employed. In the first place, one may distinguish clearly between two types of questions asked: the one is designed for locating constraints in the problem, constraints that will eventually give shape to an hypothesis; the other is the hypothesis as question. It is the difference between, "Was there anything wrong with the driver?" and "Was the driver rushing to the doctor's office for an appointment and the car got out of control?" There are children who precede hypotheses with efforts to locate constraint and there are those who, to use our local slang, are "potshotters," who string out hypotheses non-cumulatively one after the other. A second element of strategy is its connectivity of information gathering: the extent to which questions asked utilize or ignore or violate information previously obtained. The questions asked by children tend to be organized in cycles, each cycle of questions usually being given over to the pursuit of some particular notion. Both within cycles and between cycles one can discern a marked difference on the connectivity of the child's performance. Needless to say, children who employ constraint location as a technique preliminary to the formulation of hypotheses tend to be far more connected in their harvesting of information. Persistence is another feature of strategy, a characteristic compounded of what appear to be two components: a sheer doggedness component, and a persistence that stems from the sequential organization that a child brings to the task. Doggedness is probably just animal spirits or the need for achievement—what has come to be called *n-ach*. Organized persistence is a maneuver for protecting our fragile cognitive apparatus from overload. The child who has flooded himself with disorganized information from unconnected hypotheses will become discouraged and confused sooner than the child who has shown a certain cunning in his strategy of getting information —a cunning whose principal component is the recognition that the value of information is not simply in getting it but in being able to carry it. The persistence of the organized child stems from his knowledge of how to organize questions in cycles, how to summarize things to himself, and the like.

Episodic empiricism is illustrated by information gathering that is unbound by prior constraints, that lacks connectivity, and that is deficient in organizational persistence. The opposite extreme is illustrated by an approach that is characterized by constraint sensitivity, by connective maneuvers, and by organized persistence.

Brute persistence seems to be one of those gifts from the gods that make people more exaggeratedly what they are.[2]

Before returning to the issue of discovery and its role in the development of thinking, let me say a word more about the ways in which information may get transformed when the problem solver has actively processed it. There is first of all a pragmatic question: what does it take to get information processed into a form best designed to fit some future use? Take an experiment by Zajonc[3] as a case in point. He gives groups of subjects information of a controlled kind, some groups being told that their task is to transmit the information to others, others that it is merely to be kept in mind. In general, he finds more differentiation and organization of the information received with the intention of being transmitted than there is for information received passively. An active set leads to a transformation related to a task to be performed. The risk, to be sure, is in possible overspecialization of information processing that may lead to such a high degree of specific organization that information is lost for general use.

I would urge now in the spirit of an hypothesis that emphasis upon discovery in learning has precisely the effect upon the learner of leading him to be a constructionist, to organize what he is encountering in a manner not only designed to discover regularity and relatedness, but also to avoid the kind of information drift that fails to keep account of the uses to which information might have to be put. It is, if you will, a necessary condition for learning the variety of techniques of problem solving, of transforming information for better use, indeed for learning how to go about the very task of learning. Practice in discovering for oneself teaches one to acquire information in a way that makes that information more readily viable in problem solving. So goes the hypothesis. It is still in need of testing. But it is an hypothesis of such important human implications that we cannot afford not to test it—and testing will have to be in the schools.

2. Intrinsic and Extrinsic Motives

Much of the problem in leading a child to effective cognitive activity is to free him from the immediate control of environmental

---

[2] I should also remark in passing that the two extremes also characterize concept attainment strategies as reported in *A Study of Thinking* by J. S. Bruner *et al.*, New York: Wiley, 1956. Successive scanning illustrates well what is meant here by episodic empiricism; conservative focussing is an example of cumulative constructionism.

[3] R. B. Zajonc. Personal communication, 1957.

rewards and punishments. That is to say, learning that starts in response to the rewards of parental or teacher approval or the avoidance of failure can too readily develop a pattern in which the child is seeking cues as to how to conform to what is expected of him. We know from studies of children who tend to be early over-achievers in school that they are likely to be seekers after the "right way to do it" and that their capacity for transforming their learning into viable thought structures tends to be lower than children merely achieving at levels predicted by intelligence tests. Our tests on such children show them to be lower in analytic ability than those who are not conspicuous in overachievement.[4] As we shall see later, they develop rote abilities and depend upon being able to "give back" what is expected rather than to make it into something that relates to the rest of their cognitive life. As Maimonides would say, their learning is not their own.

The hypothesis that I would propose here is that to the degree that one is able to approach learning as a task of discovering something rather than "learning about" it, to that degree will there be a tendency for the child to carry out his learning activities with the autonomy of self-reward or, more properly by reward that is discovery itself.

To those of you familiar with the battles of the last half-century in the field of motivation, the above hypothesis will be recognized as controversial. For the classic view of motivation in learning has been, until very recently, couched in terms of a theory of drives and reinforcement: that learning occurred by virtue of the fact that a response produced by a stimulus was followed by the reduction in a primary drive state. The doctrine is greatly extended by the idea of secondary reinforcement: any state associated even remotely with the reduction of a primary drive could also have the effect of producing learning. There has recently appeared a most searching and important criticism of this position, written by Professor Robert White,[5] reviewing the evidence of recently published animal studies, of work in the field of psychoanalysis, and of research on the development of cognitive processes in children. Professor White comes to the conclusion, quite rightly I think, that the drive-reduction model of learning runs counter to too many important phenomena of learning and development to be either regarded as general in its applicability or even correct in its general

---

[4] J. S. Bruner and A. J. Caron, "Cognition, Anxiety, and Achievement in the Preadolescent." *Journal of Educational Psychology* (in press).

[5] R. W. White, "Motivation Reconsidered: The Concept of Competence." *Psychological Review 66*:297–333, 1959.

approach. Let me summarize some of his principal conclusions and explore their applicability to the hypothesis stated above.

> I now propose that we gather the various kinds of behavior just mentioned, all of which have to do with effective interaction with the environment, under the general heading of competence. According to Webster, competence means fitness or ability, and the suggested synonyms include capability, capacity, efficiency, proficiency, and skill. It is therefore a suitable word to describe such things as grasping and exploring, crawling and walking, attention and perception, language and thinking, manipulating and changing the surroundings, all of which promote an effective—a competent—interaction with the environment. It is true of course, that maturation plays a part in all these developments, but this part is heavily overshadowed by learning in all the more complex accomplishments like speech or skilled manipulation. I shall argue that it is necessary to make competence a motivational concept; there is *competence motivation* as well as competence in its more familiar sense of achieved capacity. The behavior that leads to the building up of effective grasping, handling, and letting go of objects, to take one example, is not random behavior that is produced by an overflow of energy. It is directed, selective, and persistent, and it continues not because it serves primary drives, which indeed it cannot serve until it is almost perfected, but because it satisfies an intrinsic need to deal with the environment.[6]

I am suggesting that there are forms of activity that serve to enlist and develop the competence motive, that serve to make it the driving force behind behavior. I should like to add to White's general premise that the *exercise* of competence motives has the effect of strengthening the degree to which they gain control over behavior and thereby reduce the effects of extrinsic rewards or drive gratification.

The brilliant Russian psychologist Vigotsky [7] characterizes the growth of thought processes as starting with a dialogue of speech and gesture between child and parent; autonomous thinking begins at the stage when the child is first able to internalize these conversations and "run them off" himself. This is a typical sequence in the development of competence. So too in instruction. The narrative of teaching is of the order of the conversation. The next move in the development of competence is the internalization of the narrative and its "rules of generation" so that the child is now capable of running off the narrative on his own. The hypothetical mode in teaching by encouraging the child to participate in "speaker's de-

---

[6] *Ibid.*, pp. 317–318.
[7] L. S. Vigotsky, *Thinking and Speech.* Moscow, 1934.

cisions" speeds this process along. Once internalization has occurred, the child is in a vastly improved position from several obvious points of view—notably that he is able to go beyond the information he has been given to generate additional ideas that can either be checked immediately from experience or can, at last, be used as a basis for formulating reasonable hypotheses. But over and beyond that, the child is now in a position to experience success and failure not as reward and punishment, but as information. For when the task is his own rather than a matter of matching environmental demands, he becomes his own paymaster in a certain measure. Seeking to gain control over his environment, he can now treat success as indicating that he is on the right track, failure as indicating he is on the wrong one.

In the end, this development has the effect of freeing learning from immediate stimulus control. When learning in the short run leads only to pellets of this or that rather than to mastery in the long run, then behavior can be readily "shaped" by extrinsic rewards. When behavior becomes more long-range and competence-oriented, it comes under the control of more complex cognitive structures, plans and the like, and operates more from the inside out. It is interesting that even Pavlov, whose early account of the learning process was based entirely on a notion of stimulus control of behavior through the conditioning mechanism in which, through contiguity a new conditioned stimulus was substituted for an old unconditioned stimulus by the mechanism of stimulus substitution, that even Pavlov recognized his account as insufficient to deal with higher forms of learning. To supplement the account, he introduced the idea of the "second signalling system," with central importance placed on symbolic systems such as language in mediating and giving shape to mental life. Or as Luria [8] has put it, "the first signal system [is] concerned with directly perceived stimuli, the second with systems of verbal elaboration." Luria, commenting on the importance of the transition from first to second signal system, says: "It would be mistaken to suppose that verbal intercourse with adults merely changes the contents of the child's conscious activity without changing its form. . . . The word has a basic function not only because it indicates a corresponding object in the external world, but also because it abstracts, isolates the necessary signal, generalizes perceived signals and relates them to certain categories; it is this systematization of direct experience that

---

[8] A. L. Luria, "The Directive Function of Speech in Development and Dissolution." *Word 15*:341–464, 1959.

makes the role of the word in the formation of mental processes so exceptionally important." [9, 10]

It is interesting that the final rejection of the universality of the doctrine of reinforcement in direct conditioning came from some of Pavlov's own students. Ivanov-Smolensky [11] and Krasnogorsky [12] published papers showing the manner in which symbolized linguistic messages could take over the place of the unconditioned stimulus and of the unconditioned response (gratification of hunger) in children. In all instances, they speak of these as *replacements* of lower, first-system mental or neural processes by higher order or second-system controls. A strange irony, then, that Russian psychology that gave us the notion of the conditioned response and the assumption that higher order activities are built up out of colligation or structurings of such primitive units, rejected this notion while much of American learning psychology has stayed until quite recently within the early Pavlovian fold (see, for example, a recent article by Spence [13] in the *Harvard Educational Review* or Skinner's treatment of language [14] and the attacks that have been made upon it by linguists such as Chomsky [15] who have become concerned with the relation of language and cognitive activity). What is the more interesting is that Russian pedagogical theory has become deeply influenced by this new trend and is now placing much stress upon the importance of building up a more active symbolical approach to problem solving among children.

To sum up the matter of the control of learning, then, I am proposing that the degree to which competence or mastery motives come to control behavior, to that degree the role of reinforcement or "extrinsic pleasure" wanes in shaping behavior. The child comes to manipulate his environment more actively and achieves his gratification from coping with problems. Symbolic modes of representing and transforming the environment arise and the importance of stimulus-response-reward sequences declines. To use the meta-

---

[9] *Ibid.*, p. 12.

[10] For an elaboration of the view expressed by Luria, the reader is referred to the forthcoming translation of L. S. Vigotsky's 1934 book being published by John Wiley and Sons and the Technology Press.

[11] A. G. Ivanov-Smolensky, "Concerning the Study of the Joint Activity of the First and Second Signal Systems," *Journal of Higher Nervous Activity* 1:1, 1951.

[12] N. D. Krasnogorsky, *Studies of Higher Nervous Activity in Animals and in Man*, Vol. I. Moscow, 1954.

[13] K. W. Spence, "The Relation of Learning Theory to the Technique of Education." *Harvard Educational Review* 24:84–95, 1959.

[14] B. F. Skinner, *Verbal Behavior.* New York: Appleton-Century-Crofts, 1957.

[15] N. Chomsky, *Syntactic Structure.* The Hague, Netherlands: Mouton, 1957.

phor that David Riesman developed in a quite different context, mental life moves from a state of outer-directedness in which the fortuity of stimuli and reinforcement are crucial to a state of inner-directedness in which the growth and maintenance of mastery become central and dominant.

3. Learning the Heuristics of Discovery

Lincoln Steffens,[16] reflecting in his *Autobiography* on his undergraduate education at Berkeley, comments that his schooling was overly specialized on learning about the known and that too little attention was given to the task of finding out about what was not known. But how does one train a student in the techniques of discovery? Again I would like to offer some hypotheses. There are many ways of coming to the arts of inquiry. One of them is by careful study of its formalization in logic, statistics, mathematics, and the like. If a person is going to pursue inquiry as a way of life, particularly in the sciences, certainly such study is essential. Yet, whoever has taught kindergarten and the early primary grades or has had graduate students working with him on their theses—I choose the two extremes for they are both periods of intense inquiry—knows that an understanding of the formal aspect of inquiry is not sufficient. There appear to be, rather, a series of activities and attitudes, some directly related to a particular subject and some of them fairly generalized, that go with inquiry and research. These have to do with the *process* of trying to find out something and while they provide no guarantee that the *product* will be any *great* discovery, their absence is likely to lead to awkwardness or aridity or confusion. How difficult it is to describe these matters— the heuristics of inquiry. There is one set of attitudes or ways of doing that has to do with sensing the relevance of variables—how to avoid getting stuck with edge effects and getting instead to the big sources of variance. Partly this gift comes from intuitive familiarity with a range of phenomena, sheer "knowing the stuff." But it also comes out of a sense of what things among an ensemble of things "smell right" in the sense of being of the right order of magnitude or scope or severity.

The English philosopher Weldon describes problem solving in an interesting and picturesque way. He distinguishes between difficulties, puzzles, and problems. We solve a problem or make a dis-

---

[16] L. Steffens, *Autobiography of Lincoln Steffens*. New York: Harcourt, Brace, 1931.

covery when we impose a puzzle form on to a difficulty that converts it into a problem that can be solved in such a way that it gets us where we want to be. That is to say, we recast the difficulty into a form that we know how to work with, then work it. Much of what we speak of as discovery consists of knowing how to impose what kind of form on various kinds of difficulties. A small part but a crucial part of discovery of the highest order is to invent and develop models or "puzzle forms" that can be imposed on difficulties with good effect. It is in this area that the truly powerful mind shines. But it is interesting to what degree perfectly ordinary people can, given the benefit of instruction, construct quite interesting and what a century ago would have been considered greatly original models.

Now to the hypothesis. It is my hunch that it is only through the exercise of problem solving and the effort of discovery that one learns the working heuristic of discovery, and the more one has practice, the more likely is one to generalize what one has learned into a style of problem solving or inquiry that serves for any kind of task one may encounter—or almost any kind of task. I think the matter is self-evident, but what is unclear is what kinds of training and teaching produce the best effects. How do we teach a child to, say, cut his losses but at the same time be persistent in trying out an idea; to risk forming an early hunch without at the same time formulating one *so* early and with so little evidence as to be stuck with it waiting for appropriate evidence to materialize; to pose good testable guesses that are neither too brittle nor too sinuously incorrigible; etc., etc. Practice in inquiry, in trying to figure out things for oneself is indeed what is needed, but in what form? Of only one thing I am convinced. I have never seen anybody improve in the art and technique of inquiry by any means other than engaging in inquiry.

4. Conservation of Memory

I should like to take what some psychologists might consider a rather drastic view of the memory process. It is a view that in large measure derives from the work of my colleague, Professor George Miller.[17] Its first premise is that the principal problem of human memory is not storage, but retrieval. In spite of the biological unlikeliness of it, we seem to be able to store a huge quantity of information—perhaps not a full tape recording, though at times

---

[17] G. A. Miller, "The Magical Number Seven, Plus or Minus Two." *Psychological Review 63*:81–97, 1956.

it seems we even do that, but a great sufficiency of impressions. We may infer this from the fact that recognition (i.e., recall with the aid of maximum prompts) is so extraordinarily good in human beings—particularly in comparison with spontaneous recall where, so to speak, we must get out stored information without external aids or prompts. The key to retrieval is organization or, in even simpler terms, knowing where to find information and how to get there.

Let me illustrate the point with a simple experiment. We present pairs of words to twelve-year-old children. One group is simply told to remember the pairs, that they will be asked to repeat them later. Another is told to remember them by producing a word or idea that will tie the pair together in a way that will make sense to them. A third group is given the mediators used by the second group when presented with the pairs to aid them in tying the pairs into working units. The word pairs include such juxtapositions as "chair-forest," "sidewalk-square," and the like. One can distinguish three styles of mediators and children can be scaled in terms of their relative preference for each: *generic mediation* in which a pair is tied together by a superordinate idea: "chair and forest are both made of wood"; *thematic mediation* in which the two terms are imbedded in a theme or little story: "the lost child sat on a chair in the middle of the forest"; and *part-whole mediation* where "chairs are made from trees in the forest" is typical. Now, the chief result, as you would all predict, is that children who provide their own mediators do best—indeed, one time through a set of thirty pairs, they recover up to 95% of the second words when presented with the first ones of the pairs, whereas the uninstructed children reach a maximum of less than 50% recovered. Interestingly enough, children do best in recovering materials tied together by the form of mediator they most often use.

One can cite a myriad of findings to indicate that any organization of information that reduces the aggregate complexity of material by imbedding it into a cognitive structure a person has constructed will make that material more accessible for retrieval. In short, we may say that the process of memory, looked at from the retrieval side, is also a process of problem solving: how can material be "placed" in memory so that it can be got on demand?

We can take as a point of departure the example of the children who developed their own technique for relating the members of each word pair. You will recall that they did better than the children who were given by exposition the mediators they had developed. Let me suggest that in general, material that is organized in terms of a person's own interests and cognitive structures is material that has the best chance of being accessible in memory. That is to say, it is more likely to be placed along routes that are connected to one's own ways of intellectual travel.

In sum, the very attitudes and activities that characterize "figuring out" or "discovering" things for oneself also seem to have the effect of making material more readily accessible in memory.

SOCIAL CONCEPTS FOR
EARLY CHILDHOOD EDUCATION *

V. Phillips Weaver

One characteristic of the searching consideration now being given social studies programs, kindergarten through senior high school, is a concern for "beefing up" the content in the primary grades. True, some voices are raised in dissent; nevertheless, a preponderance of opinion, in tones ranging from cautious suggestion to loud outcry, seems to make a strong case for a judicious overhaul of the social studies curriculum for young children. It may be difficult to prove that children today are more precocious than were their parents, yet to say that children's experiences and interests are broader, and that the social scene has changed considerably, is to state the obvious.

In the late 1950's, several persons, such as John D. McAulay, Professor of Education at the Pennsylvania State University, were working toward a new curriculum for the primary grades. This new approach would take youngsters more quickly from the study of their immediate environment and the simplest of ideas to an examination of the world itself and its limitless challenges. O. L. Davis, Jr.,[1] pointed out that today's children are being hidebound by the theories of the 1930's which deferred the teaching of complex principles to the very young.

V. Phillips Weaver is Assistant Professor of Education at the University of Maryland, College Park.

* Reprinted from *Educational Leadership 22*:296–299 ff., 1965, with permission of the Association for Supervision and Curriculum Development and V. Phillips Weaver. Copyright © 1965, by the Association for Supervision and Curriculum Development.

[1] O. L. Davis, Jr., "Children Can Learn Complex Concepts." *Educational Leadership 17*:170–175, 1959.

Thus, Jerome Bruner in 1960 added fuel to a fire which had already been kindled. Educators became excited about his theory that complex social science principles can be introduced to young children when the framework is the experience background of those children. Bruner's "spiral" approach to teaching complex ideas, whereby concepts are introduced at an early age and retaught in succeeding years in an increasingly sophisticated fashion, made sense to many persons in education.

Trends in Social Studies

As a result of the work of the early trailblazers and Professor Bruner, trends regarding social studies opportunities for young children are beginning to emerge. There are now new directions for the primary grades in geography, in economics education, in political science and in history.

GEOGRAPHY

There is a marked trend to introduce the study of geography earlier in the primary grades than has heretofore been customary. The justifications are multiple: (a) the post-World War II emphasis on international understanding; (b) increased travel; (c) population mobility; (d) the "shrinking" globe; (e) new theories concerning the ability of young children to conceptualize.

It is increasingly common for kindergartners to use the globe to locate places of interest. They are able to understand the basic principles governing day and night, differentiate between land and water, begin to build concepts of the earth's size and shape, and begin to understand the sun's relationship, and importance to, the earth. Five-year-olds can also work with cardinal directions on the globe and on simple maps.

First graders use the environment as an outdoor laboratory to discover in miniature geographical features which they often reproduce on a sand-table. These youngsters, in addition to making observations about weather and climate, use the "lab" to draw conclusions concerning the relationship between land scope and water flow, concerning drainage, soils and other conservation topics. The ultimate goal is that the children begin to draw conclusions about the effect of environment on man's activities.

Second graders can read and interpret maps, particularly if there is a sequential progression from the use of aerial photographs, to pictorial and semi-pictorial maps, to teacher-made maps, to commercial maps. As the children learn to make their own maps they begin to use a legend. Rose Sabaroff recommends having the children, when possible, observe physical features from a high place in the community.[2] She also suggests that taking the children on a walk of exactly one mile will begin to give them an appreciation of distance. Sabaroff points out the benefits to children of early exploration of the environment when careful and scientific observations are the standard. McAulay's studies indicate that the second graders can move quickly from this type of map work to understandings concerning distant lands, using maps as one tool.

Some newer curriculum guides suggest that units concerning the home, the family and the community should incorporate material related to other cultures. When the plans for such topics capitalize on the interest of youngsters in customs, holidays, games, schools and homes, empathy for other peoples can indeed have its beginning!

ECONOMICS

Another dimension of content revision is the current emphasis on economic education. In an age when national and international economics are prime concerns, and are constantly paid heed by the various news media, this trend is not surprising. Citizens are presented with such data as the cost of living index, the Gross National Product, the unemployment rate, the gold outflow, the federal deficit and the national debt. What does all this mean?

Traditionally, the study of basic economic principles has been delayed until high school, but the work of Lawrence Senesh, Professor of Economic Education at Purdue University, has shown that young children can comprehend fundamental principles of economics when these principles are related to the children's own experiences. Senesh suggests that if such basic principles are introduced in first grade and rediscovered in succeeding grades in more complex forms, high school students will be ready for sophisticated economic generalizations.[3]

Professor Senesh uses cartoons to begin the development in first graders of appreciation for such principles as the conflict between unlimited wants and limited resources; the division of labor; the relationship between education and standard of living; the dependency of people's spending on taste, income and the price of goods; the relationship between price on one hand and supply and demand on the other. Senesh challenges the very young to tackle

---

[2] Rose Sabaroff, "Firsthand Experiences in Geography for Second Graders." *Journal of Geography* 57:300–306, 1958.

[3] Lawrence Senesh, "The Economic World of the Child." *Instructor* 73:7–8, 1963.

such perennial problems as the surplus of output on the nation's farms.

A typical Senesh cartoon illustrates for children how man's invention of money has encouraged specialization of work and how such specialization raises the standard of living. Children also see the importance of savings to an economy. They discover, too, that it is vital that people have faith in their nation's currency. The teacher's guides accompanying the cartoons sometimes suggest role-playing by the children as a good method for clinching understandings.

Pioneer programs in economics for the primary grades, such as the one in Detroit, indicate the growing success of an exciting dimension of the curriculum.

POLITICAL SCIENCE

The work of Professors David Easton and Robert Hess of the University of Chicago has placed renewed emphasis on the role of the early school years in citizenship education. A five year national study of 12,000 children conducted by Easton and Hess has resulted in some conclusions which should have a powerful impact on curriculum. This research indicates that the formative years in political orientation (knowledge, opinions and values concerning the political world) are those between ages three and thirteen. It is concluded that such orientation begins through the family before the child enters school, and that it is largely accomplished by the time the child reaches senior high school age.

According to Easton and Hess,[4] prominent in very young children is the concept of authority. For example, the child of five to eight has a very positive image of, and attachment to, the President. He attaches the same image he has of the office to the person of the incumbent—great power, kindness and goodness. Through his identification with his family, the child rather early becomes attached to a political party. He knows the controversy that surrounds the selection of authority. Easton and Hess also conclude that what youngsters learn about politics is related to religion and internal needs as well as to the family. What is learned at an early age is difficult to displace.

In light of this research, it is alarming that the curriculum for the primary grades rarely includes a study of government and politics. What is included is often incidental, and therefore lacking

---

[4] Robert Hess and David Easton, "The Role of the Elementary School in Political Socialization." *The School Review* 70:257–265, 1962.

in planned sequence. Trends resulting from the findings of Easton and Hess are not as yet apparent. Nevertheless, the research provides a strong indication that selected basic political science concepts should be introduced as early as kindergarten, with subsequent experience designated to insure that the elementary school does not divorce itself from responsibility for the child's political orientation.

When we examine the voting record of Americans (barely 60 percent of those eligible voted in the 1964 presidental election), it is obvious that something happens to the positive political learnings of the young child by the time he reaches adulthood. The challenge to those concerned with curriculum for the primary grades is clear. We should provide opportunities which: (a) teach youngsters the importance of commitment to the democratic process and of participation in government; (b) build fundamental concepts concerning the rule of law, and the role of government in formulating and enforcing statutes; (c) arouse early awareness of the realities of politics.

HISTORY

The deferment theories of the 1930's which still largely prevail today, call for exposing primary grade children to little, if any, history. Perfunctory attention is paid to the birthdays of Washington and Lincoln and to celebrations honoring Columbus and the Pilgrims, but historical studies in depth for grades K-3 are not widespread to date.

However, we are beginning to witness a change. While it is generally agreed that children in the early grades cannot grasp history in its chronological sense, there is a growing acceptance of the notion that the young child can begin to develop an understanding of the "structure" of history. Children of six can carefully explore the community for signs of recent changes, then begin to look for older landmarks and lore. The essential concept involved is *change*—change as good and bad, change as inevitable and continual. Hopefully, children are led to see that the study of history involves the interpretation of change.

As children of eight or nine begin to examine in depth a time and place in history, the emphasis must be on those aspects with which youngsters can identify: the customs, the food and shelter, the schools and recreation, the transportation. Little attempt is made to place colonial Jamestown or a 19th century western mining community in its proper chronological sequence. At this point, dates are unimportant, but an understanding of the ways in which people once lived is possible and worthwhile for youngsters. Emphasis is also placed on the method of the historian: how he evaluates evidence such as old newspapers, letters, diaries and other types of artifacts in order to interpret history.

Such emphases make a young child's first experiences with formal history both pleasurable and meaningful. The peoples, the places and the events of times past come alive. Children form positive attitudes toward history as a discipline and toward the historian as a scholar whose work can be as exciting as that of an atomic scientist.

In summary, the social studies curriculum for the primary grades has entered a period of great change. Directions and trends already seem to be emerging.

Characteristic of newer courses of study are: (a) more stimulating and exciting content, using as a basis concepts and generalizations recommended by social scientists; (b) greater scope in the program, with the inclusion of material from geography, economics, political science and history as well as the more traditional sociology and anthropology; (c) application of Jerome Bruner's "spiral" approach to teaching basic concepts and principles. Also there is a growing consensus that important learnings cannot be left to chance, or to "incidental" teaching. Opportunities must be planned to insure that in the primary grades children begin to build the foundation for the basic understandings so necessary for effective citizenship.

THE LEARNING OF CONCEPTS *

Robert M. Gagne

For those interested in the design of effective instructional conditions in the school situation, the learning of concepts is a matter of central concern. School learning is preponderantly conceptual in nature. Nevertheless, there is great variation in the ways in which the term "concept" is used by educational writers and, accordingly, a variety of descriptions of the essential conditions for learning concepts by students. What *is* a concept, anyhow, in a generic sense?

Robert M. Gagne is a Professor at the University of California, Berkeley.
Paper given as part of a symposium on "Concept-Learning and the Curriculum" at the annual meeting of the American Educational Research Association, Chicago, Illinois, February 12, 1965.

* Reprinted from *School Review* 73:187–196, 1965, with permission of The University of Chicago Press and Robert M. Gagne. Copyright © 1965.

How is it related to a "fact" or a "principle" or a "generalization"? How is it related to methods of learning, such as repetition, or to discovery?

Being a psychologist, I naturally think that one should attempt to seek an answer to such basic definitional questions in that body of partially organized knowledge that has originated from controlled experimental research on behavior. For surely it is true that human learning of concepts can be studied in the framework of controlled laboratory experimentation. Whatever may be the variation in concepts of science, mathematics, language, art, or other content subjects, when people speak of concept-learning they must be referring to a kind of change in human performance that is independent of such content. And if it is independent, then it would seem possible to arrange a set of conditions under which the learning of a concept can be studied systematically.

When one examines the experimental literature on "concept formation," "concept-learning," and related matters, it appears that here too the word "concept" is not being used with great consistency. Under the heading of concepts, one can find experimental studies dealing with such things as the learning of nonsense words, the acquiring of a new category word by children, the inferring of common functions of a set of objects, the combining of object qualities to achieve new categories, and even the solving of mathematical puzzles. All of these kinds of experiments undoubtedly represent studies of learning. What is not entirely evident, however, is whether they reflect the learning of the same kinds of capabilities. It is truly difficult to describe what it is that these experimental studies have in common, or whether they are in fact devoted to the study of a common problem.

What does "learning a concept" mean? The approach I should like to take here is one that depends largely on observations of what happens in school learning. I do this, not to suggest that one can study the problem systematically in this way, but rather that perhaps one can begin to *define* the problem in such a manner. Perhaps if there can be agreement on what a concept is, and on how it is typically acquired in practice, then it will be possible to design experimental studies to find out the effects on its learning of various conditions of the learning situation.

An Initial Distinction

Some anticipation of my conclusions needs to be stated at the outset in order to spare you the details of a historical account. As a result of examining the kinds of situations that are said to represent concept-learning, I have arrived at the following propositions:

1. There are at least two different, important kinds of phenomena commonly referred to as concept-learning. One refers to the acquiring of a common response, often a name, to a class of objects varying in appearance. This may best be called *concept-learning.* The second refers to the combining of concepts into entities variously referred to as "ideas," "facts," "principles," or "rules." I prefer to call this *principle-learning.*

An example of these two different kinds of capabilities can perhaps be illustrated by *number*. First of all, there are such things as number concepts. When a young child is able to correctly assign the name "three" to collections of any three objects, and at the same time not assign it to collections of two or four objects, it may be said that the child has learned the concept "three." But as mathematics educators will be quick to point out, this is only the most elementary meaning of what they have in mind when they speak of the child "knowing the concept three." Obviously, they want the child to know that three is a set that may be formed by joining the sets two and one, by taking one member away from the set four, by subtracting zero from the set three, by dividing six into two equal parts, by taking the square root of nine, and so on. Perhaps all of these together could form what might be called the "meaning of three." But each of these is a separate *idea* or *principle.* Each of them is achieved by *combining* the concept three (in the simple sense previously described) with some other concept, perhaps equally simple. There is, then, the concept three, the correct choosing of objects to which the name three can be legitimately assigned. And in addition there is a set of principles of three, which are actually combinations of simpler concepts.

2. The basic reason for the distinction between *concept* and *principle* is that they represent two different kinds of learned capabilities. In the first case, the criterion performance is simply being able to answer such a question as "Which of these collections of objects is three?" In the second case, the criterion performance is being able to *use* the concept three in combination, as in the question "What number added to two will give three?" These are quite different performances. Obviously, a child who is able to do the first may not have learned to do the second. If the second question is asked in a way which excludes the possibility of verbal parroting (as it needs to be), then it seems very likely that a child who does it correctly *will* be able to answer the simpler question correctly.

3. If it is true that knowing a concept and knowing a principle are two different capabilities, then it is also quite possible that

the conditions for learning them are also different. I shall have more to say about this presently.

Learning Concepts

How is a concept learned? What are the conditions that need to obtain in the instructional situation in order for a new concept to be acquired? It should not be too difficult to identify these conditions. For one thing, we know that animals can acquire concepts. The Harlows' monkeys acquired the concept "odd" when they had learned to choose the odd one of any three objects presented, two of which were nearly identical. If two identical cubes and a sphere were presented, they would choose the sphere; if two boxes and a stick were presented, they would choose the stick.[1] It is instructive to note that what the monkeys learned was the capability of choosing an "odd" one, regardless of the physical appearances of the objects presented. They learned to respond to a *class* of situations which the experimenter could classify as "odd."

How did the animals learn the concept "odd"? Actually, it required a lot of practice with a variety of specific situations each containing "an odd one" which was correct and each differing from the preceding one in the actual objects it contained. Human beings, too, can learn concepts this same way. In fact, sometimes psychologists force them to learn concepts this way in order to analyze the phenomenon. But one should not be led to suppose that humans *have* to learn concepts this way. In one way or another, it is almost bound to be true that the process of concept-learning gets shortened by human beings. Language is one thing that operates to bring this about. For example, studies by the Kendlers indicate that four-year-olds learn a reversal problem by extended trial-and-error, whereas seven-year-olds learn to reverse a discrimination in virtually a single trial.[2] The strong suggestion is that seven-year-olds can say something like "opposite" to themselves, whereas four-year-olds do not yet have the language to do this.

Suppose the concepts "liquid" and "solid" are to be taught to a young child. It seems likely that the learning situation would be something like the following: [3]

1. Show the child a glass containing water and a glass containing a rock. Say "This is a solid" and "This is a liquid."

2. Using a different container, show the child some powdered substance in a pile in a container and some milk in another container. Say "This is a solid; this is a liquid."

3. Provide still a third example of solid and liquid, using different materials and containers.

4. Show the child a number of examples of liquids and solids which he has not seen before. Ask him to distinguish the liquids and the solids. (In this example, I assume the child has previously learned to repeat the words "liquid" and "solid" readily when he hears them; they are familiar in sound.)

The characteristics of this learning situation are, first, that several varieties of the class, themselves of varying physical appearance, were used to exemplify the class to be responded to. Second, words already familiar as responses were used to guide the learning. Under such circumstances, one might expect a child to learn a fairly adequate set of concepts of "liquid" and "solid." This is tested by asking the child to identify liquids and solids from a set that he has not seen before and that has not been used in the learning.

It is also important to note two things that were *not* present in this situation. First, this is not repeated trial-and-error learning. Only three examples are used, all different. The situation is not repeated identically over and over again. Second, although there is language here, it is by no means extensive. One has not tried to teach the concepts, for example, by making such verbal statements as "A liquid is a substance whose particles move freely over each other so that its mass assumes the shape of the container in which it is placed." This characteristic of a liquid is directly exhibited, rather than being verbally described.

Presumably, much the same sort of conditions may obtain when an older student learns a new technical term. Something like this must have to be done when a student learns a concept like "point of inflection" in mathematics, or when he learns concepts such as "cell," "nucleus," or "mitochondrion" in biology, or when he learns what a "simile" is in English. Sometimes, it is true, even more extensive verbalization is used, and I shall return to this point in a moment.

Learning Principles

What is meant by learning a principle (or rule)? And how does this differ from learning a concept? It needs to be recalled here that a principle is a combination of concepts.

Principles, being combinations, can become very complex. But let us start with an extremely simple one, such as "liquids pour." What kind of learning situation would be set up to bring about the learning of such a principle? Actually, there are two possibilities, and this does not make my task easier.[4]

Possibility one is this: After determining that the concepts "liquid" and "pour" can be identified, make the statement that "liquids pour." To test the learning, give the student a liquid in a container, and say, in effect, "Show me." This technique is what is often called *reception learning,* and there is little doubt that a very large proportion of school learning is basically of this sort, as D. P. Ausubel says.[5]

Possibility two is this: First determine that the concepts "liquid" and "pour" can be identified. Then, give the student a number of different liquids in a number of different containers. Ask him to demonstrate ways in which the liquids are alike and different from solids. One thing he will do is pour them; he may also make the verbal statement, "Liquids pour." This learning technique is called *discovery learning,* and there is some evidence, though not much, that the principle learned this way is better retained and transferred than is the case with reception learning.

Regardless of the learning technique, however, the important thing to note is that what is learned is a combination of concepts, called a principle. There is no particular reason to think that there are any important formal differences between a simple principle of this sort and the great variety of more complex principles that are learned at later ages, such as principles of using adjectives, or of dividing quantities into fractional parts, or of specifying the functions of a legislature, or of relating force and mass and acceleration.

The characteristics of the learning situation for principles are, first, that the concepts of which it is composed must be previously learned. Second, the principle is either stated verbally or discovered by the learner. The acquisition of the principle is tested by asking the student to demonstrate its application to a particular case which he has not encountered during the learning.

Note particularly that the conditions of learning for a principle are *not* the same as those for a concept. Perhaps the outstanding difference is that the concepts which make up the principle must already be learned; they are prerequisite to the learning. Second, there is no requirement to illustrate the principle by two or three examples (although of course this may be done *after* the learning, for other purposes). Third, it is possible to discover a principle, since the two or more concepts which make it up may be theoretically "combined" in a number of different ways. But pure discovery, without verbal guidance, does not usually occur as a process in the learning of concepts by human beings. One could more aptly describe what monkeys do in attaining concepts as "discovery." Since they cannot be guided by language, they must go through a rather lengthy trial-and-error procedure to get to the point where they can choose the odd one or go to the middle door. If human beings had to "discover" new concepts in this way, it would take them a very long time to learn all the things they have to learn. Using a familiar word accomplishes the instruction much more rapidly. But it also short-circuits the process of discovery.

Concept-Learning By Definition

While the distinction between concepts and principles in terms of conditions required for learning seems fairly clear, there is another source of confusion between them: When people are verbally sophisticated, they often learn concepts verbally, as pointed out by J. B. Carroll in a recent article.[6] That is to say, individuals learn concepts "by definition." If a person does not know the concept "caliche," he may learn what it is by reading or hearing the verbal statement, "a crust of calcium carbonate formed on stony soil in arid regions."

It is important to note that in this kind of learning situation, a *principle* is being used to provide instruction for the learning of a *concept*. The verbal statement itself is obviously a principle, because it contains several concepts: crust, calcium carbonate, stony soil, arid, region. And just as obviously, the learner will not be able to acquire "caliche" as a concept unless he does indeed know what each of these other concepts means, that is, unless he has previously learned each of them.

There can be little doubt that many new concepts are learned in this verbal manner by literate students and adults. Lest one think, however, that this method of learning concepts is a flawless one, a caution should be noted. A concept that is learned by way of verbally stated principles may have some inadequacies. For example, if an individual visits Texas for the first time in his life after hearing a verbal definition of caliche, will he make a certain identification of this material? Or will he be somewhat hesitant about it, and tend to confuse it with something else? Perhaps everyone would agree that for learning what caliche is, nothing can quite take the place of actually observing it.

This principle of "seeing is believing" is of more than passing importance to the problem of concept-learning. It is, for example, a fundamental reason why science educators are so firmly convinced of the value of the laboratory. If the student is to learn concepts like "power," "energy," "osmotic pressure," and many others, he can, to be sure, learn them in some sense by means of definitions. But there is a danger that the concepts he learns this way are inadequate in one way or another. Accordingly, most science educators would maintain that the performing of operations, including observation in the laboratory, is an essential part of the learning situation required for the learning of fully adequate, generalizable concepts. The role of the laboratory in school learning serves to remind us of the concrete basis for learning concepts and of the potential insufficiencies of concept-learning which is based solely upon verbally conveyed definitions. This is equally true in subjects other than science. The requirement for direct observation exists in all school subjects.

Summary

In summary, it appears to be of some importance for the design of curriculum content and instructional method to recognize a distinction between concepts and principles. Different conditions are applicable to the learning of concepts and the learning of principles. Two differences that I have mentioned are perhaps of greatest importance. The first is that concepts are prior to principles and, in this sense, are simpler than principles. To learn a principle, one must have previously learned the concepts of which it is composed. A second difference pertains to verbal guidance versus pure discovery as a learning method. Learning concepts by pure discovery would appear to be an inhumanly inefficient thing to do, given the existence of language. But principles can be learned by discovery. There is some slight evidence to suggest that such a method of learning principles may be advantageous for retention and transfer, although it is likely to be more time-consuming for initial learning. Additional soundly designed research could well be devoted to this latter question.

NOTES

1. H. F. Harlow and M. K. Harlow, "Learning to Think." *Scientific American. 181*:36–39, 1949.
2. H. H. Kendler and T. S. Kendler, "Effect of Verbalization on Reversal Shifts in Children." *Science. 141*:1619–1620, 1961.
3. Robert M. Gagne, *The Conditions of Learning*. New York: Holt, Rinehart & Winston, 1965.
4. *Ibid.*
5. D. P. Ausubel, *The Psychology of Meaningful Verbal Learning*. New York: Grune & Stratton, 1963.
6. J. B. Carroll, "Words, Meanings and Concepts." *Harvard Educational Review. 34*:178–202, 1964.

VALUES IN THE CURRICULUM *

Michael Scriven

Two points are vital to the whole question of dealing with values in the curriculum, and both of them are almost completely at odds with common views about this problem. The first point is that the vast majority of value disputes are capable of settlement by rational arguments. The common slogan that "one person's values are as good as another's" is usually false and is usually an indication of insufficient training in empirical investigation or logical analysis.

The second point is that the analysis and resolution of value disputes is one of the most difficult intellectual problems that we ever put in front of the child in the course of the entire curriculum. A tremendous job lies ahead of us in developing methods and materials to teach teachers and children how to deal with this complex matter.

The Place of Ultimate Values

In disputes about what is "right," what is "better," and what "ought" to be done, the discussion frequently ends with the disputants in disagreement about the issue, but in agreement that the argument cannot be carried further. A common conclusion is that "You can't dispute basic values." Let us use the common term "ultimate values" to refer to these values that are unarguable, in the sense that no further facts or logic can be mustered to show whether they are sound or unsound.

It is possible that there is no such thing as an ultimate value. One of the best philosophers in the country once said that he had never, in the course of any debate on any moral issue, found a disputant who could not be shown, at every point, to be appealing to yet further considerations of fact or logic. The stopping-point of value-disputes, then, is very often a point of disagreement about a complex matter of fact, such as the actual effects of pornography on grade schoolers, and not a dispute about ultimate values at all.

The question of whether ultimate values *exist* is not very im-

Michael Scriven is Director of the Social Science Education Consortium's work on values in the curriculum at Indiana University, Bloomington.

* Reprinted from the *Social Science Education Consortium Newsletter 2*:1–3, 1966, with permission of the Social Science Education Consortium, Inc., and Michael Scriven.

portant, however, if it is true, as the author believes, that *the great majority* of value disputes can be settled by empirical investigation and logical analysis. The educational task is to push back the frontiers of analysis as far as possible, not to worry about whether there is a last frontier. There is an interesting analogy in the physical sciences. The status of determinism need not be settled before we agree that the right approach is to seek for causes of all phenomena with all our effort.

Education About Values vs. Indoctrination in Values

It follows from what has been said that most training of children in the realm of value disputes should have the purpose of helping them to become more skillful in clarifying issues, in verifying facts on which they believe their value judgments rest, in analyzing the soundness of the logic by which one value is based on another, and in examining the logical consistency among their values. This enormous task will keep us all busy for a long time to come, without bringing us to insoluble problems involving ultimate values. And one can only deny that this is the approach we should be taking by showing that ultimate values are encountered early rather than late in the process of tracing back the logical underpinning of everyday value disputes.

Let us take the hypothetical example of a sixth grade class discussing a particular issue about freedom of speech. Assume that, in the midst of an explosive social situation, the making of a scheduled political speech by a member of the opposition would involve a large risk of rioting and loss of life. Should the authorities prevent the speech?

A common approach, in the rare cases where this kind of material is discussed at all, is to earnestly ask the class what they think should be done. Should the sixth-graders' views on this subject be regarded as important, interesting, valid? No, no more than their views on the merits of Freudian psychology or the quantum theory. Can the teacher tell the children what the right answer is? Probably not, since her views may have no better factual and analytical basis than those of the children.

One way to begin to analyze the practical problem mentioned, where the value of life has to be weighed against the value of free speech, is to imagine what it would be like to abandon one of these values. If, for example, we abandoned freedom of speech as a value, what new institutions or system of rules would be required or possible to ensure a well-informed populace? What would be the logical consequences, for other values in our system, of abandoning the right to speak when speaking threatens life, limb, or property? What facts would be needed to assess the consequences of the change? How would it be decided whether to ban the speech? What redress for wrong decisions would exist?

The educational process suggested here has nothing to do with indoctrination in its usual sense of an effort to instill particular values or viewpoints other than by rational proof. In some contexts, indeed, indoctrination is taken to mean the instilling of particular values *plus* a resistance to rational examination of those values; sound educational policy must explicitly condemn indoctrination in that sense.

A third and perverse definition of indoctrination is sometimes encountered, according to which *any* process that affects the values held by individuals is indoctrination. By the first definition, indoctrination is nonscientific, which does not necessarily make it a bad thing. By the second definition, indoctrination is anti-rational, and therefore a bad thing for those who value rationality, as educators must. By the third definition, indoctrination is neutral with regard to rationality and morality, which may or may not be flouted by such indoctrination. Unfortunately, the term is all too often used without analysis, as a pejorative term to discourage the application of scientific methods to the study of values, and it then becomes a tool for irrational and immoral ends. Such use is irrational because it denies the use of rational methods to problems for which they are appropriate. It is immoral because it stands in the way of moral progress.

Our goal should be the straightforward development of cognitive skills for handling value disputes—not persuasion or indoctrination in the usual sense. Moral reasoning and the moral behavior it indicates should be taught and taught about, if for no other reason than that it is immoral to keep students ignorant of the empirical and logical bases behind the morality which is behind the law and the institutions which incorporate this country's virtues and permit its vices. But in addition to this intellectual payoff is the practical benefit to a society of possessing members who are skilled in making value judgments. Such a society becomes a moral community, offering important benefits to all of its members.

Values in the Curriculum

Values in the curriculum should not be a wholly separate subject, but should have the status of a pervasive substructure, like critical thinking and clear expression. Value analysis work should begin in kindergarten and continue, with problems of increasing complexity, through high school. We can begin at what may be called the level of practicality in value analysis—the evaluation of products. Then, we might go on to the area of personal problems where questions arise about behavior that is wise or foolish, sensible or not. We can talk about good and bad behavior, meaning, at this "prudence level," good or bad for you. We can then progress to the area of social problems—morality in law and politics—and finally to the level of international problems, where we come to the root question of whether or not international conflict is a domain for morality, a domain where moral judgments other than prudential ones can be given sense or made to stick.

Such a sequence suggests itself naturally, and presents many advantages. Even at the early level of the evaluation of consumer goods, there are rather sophisticated procedures and distinctions which will carry throughout the rest of the curriculum. But at that early stage, the basic moral problems do not yet need to be faced. As the student grows older and the subjects more complex, more practical ethical problems are introduced, in the course of teaching other things.

A Basis for a Moral System

As teachers and students push the logical analysis of values farther and farther, the question of ultimate values will arise more and more insistently and, eventually, perhaps even legitimately. If an ultimate value must be found, the best candidate for the position is "equality of rights." This is a value to which our schools and our nation are already politically committed, and thus has the great potential advantage of being reinforced by the prevailing mores. It is not open to criticism on the ground that appeal to it in the public schools violates the separation of church and state. Equally important, "equality of rights" is a value upon which a whole system of morality can be built, a complete rational system based on this single premise.

There is not time here to spell out the moral system that can be based on equality of rights, but one can say that it is a system very like the humanist tradition of this country, as well as much of the Christian and Buddhist traditions. Neither is there time to describe the full meaning of equality of rights, although it is essentially embodied in the provisions of our constitution and our laws on voting and due process. While there is no objection to giving "equality of rights" the temporary status of an ultimate value, a strong argument can be made for supporting this value on rational grounds, by appeal to probability, game theory and welfare considerations. As indicated earlier, it is still an open question whether any values are needed that go beyond that which is supportable by rational appeal to logical analysis.

Techniques

There are two dimensions to teaching how to handle values: the cognitive and the affective. We have been discussing mainly the cognitive side of values. In cognitive training, the methodology is that of the logician and the lawyer. In the analysis of legal systems, such questions arise as, What would be the conflicts if everyone followed this rule? What exceptions can be justified for this rule? and, What cases are subsumed under this general principle? Still other questions, the answers to which require factual materials from the social sciences, are, What would be the consequences of breaking this rule? What alternative rules might serve the same function? What is the significance of a particular custom to those who support it?

But there needs to be moral motivation as well as moral insight, which brings us to the affective side. The basic motivational training for a moral system based on equality of rights is closely connected with the training needed for understanding the positions and motives of other people. It requires seeing yourself in the other person's shoes and fostering of empathy and sympathy. Role-playing is appropriate in a great variety of historical, political and social situations. It encourages full use of materials available to support the role, and requires an active effort to understand the position of the person whose role is assumed; it is an excellent way to promote sympathy, and hence to promote moral behavior under the axiom of equal rights. Other techniques that will help to put the student into another's position are the use of graphic audio-visual materials, field experience, interviews and discussions.

Materials

With few exceptions, there should be no separate materials for value-training, just as there should be no separate subject matter. For the most part, materials should be multi-purpose. Some examples follow.

In elementary science, students could begin early to evaluate the relative merits of instruments. They could, for example, construct their own balances, and discuss with each other the relative merits of criteria of sensitivity, capacity, cost and ease of use.

Another example is the use of materials from American constitutional law. Constitutional law embodies much of the nation's moral code. It represents an attempt to create a just or moral society, and its legal aspects give good training in the study of moral analysis. Since constitutional law also reflects much of a nation's history, it provides for moral analysis an ideal entree to the schools' history offerings.

Conclusion

We need an approach to values in the curriculum which is pedagogically more explicit than at present, but not necessarily handled explicitly in a separate part of the curriculum. We should train students to assess alternative arguments about values in a consistent and intelligent way, and to push the rational analysis of values as far back as they can. Seldom if ever should a discussion of values end with the conclusion that the view of the student— or of the teacher—is as good as anyone else's. A value judgment is as good as the reasons for it, and as weak as the reasons that support alternative views.

THE KINDERGARTEN: SOCIAL SYSTEM AND LABORATORY *

Edythe Margolin

What is the place of the kindergarten in the elementary school? What can it do and what does it actually do for children? It is immediately apparent that a singular point of view cannot fully answer these questions. With the various fields of specialization and numerous perspectives or disciplines has come an enlargement of the context for analysis in examining the schoolroom and its pupils.

Edythe Margolin is Assistant Professor of Education at the University of California, Los Angeles.

* Reprinted from *Educational Leadership* 22:157–160, 1965, with permission of the Association for Supervision and Curriculum Development and Edythe Margolin. Copyright © 1965, by the Association for Supervision and Curriculum Development.

The Unspoken Pull

As a social system of its own, the kindergarten is influenced by several factors. The first factor, pertaining to space and geography, points up differences in the way these elements can function. For example, some classrooms which have ample yard space supplementing them and assistants for the teacher permit a wide range of physical activity, and a variety of materials for both vigorous and less active experiences. Where space is limited, opportunities for roaming and exploring are accordingly decreased; and where land is expensive, as it is in many urban areas, school space is of lesser proportion.

A second aspect of the social system in the kindergarten is the number of children who populate it. The amount and quality of time the teacher can devote to the children individually is related to the number of pupils in daily attendance. The "play," as adults view children's activities in kindergarten, consists in carefully designed programs which have specific purposes and functions within an educational rationale. The new kind of responsibility which a child needs to learn at school evokes some awareness that he has to count on himself. The teacher will help him with some tasks, but for the most part he has to initiate behavior or his life at school will become complacent and dull.

The number of children the teacher can observe generally and at the same time direct the heart of the activity itself requires some anticipation of the kind of interaction which might occur once the teacher presents the idea to the pupils. For this reason the activity planned for the children must be geared to the numbers who will be participating in it.

A third consideration in a social system is an awareness of rules. The kind of learning which facilitates knowledge of classroom group membership involves awareness of rules of procedure where formal type organization is concerned, and norms or general expectations where informal groups are concerned.

In the kindergarten, the formal and informal groups are not greatly differentiated. Even the description of formality and informality depends on the different kind of structuring a teacher may prefer. A wide range of formality occurs within an entire set of plans in a teacher's weekly program whether she is aware of it or not.

In a recent study of children's awareness of norms it was found that those in a permissive classroom knew less about rules than those in the more highly structured classroom (one which had a greater number of activities involving participation of the total class). The question arises as to whether it is of greater benefit to children to learn about group norms or whether it is of greater importance educationally that they perform individually in tasks of their choice.

The value of the individual in our American culture and the responsibilities which will be faced by children as they mature has led educators to decide that the democratic classroom will inculcate democratic habits and attitudes. This premise is well taken. In the kindergarten, however, where young children approach the school situation, which is for some the first time, their experience in a democratic group experience with their peers is almost pre-embryonic. The nature of children's knowledge in the direction of democracy needs to be examined.

Organization in the classroom, especially in the earlier grades, is almost completely initiated in the hands of the teacher. Where, at what time, and how certain activities will be conducted are elements which implicitly control classroom demography and the children's responses. A teacher need not be solely permissive or consistently inhibiting to children; in fact the wider repertoire of controlling behaviors she has, the greater range of possibilities she can draw upon when she anticipates a particular type to be most effective.

In any case, it appears that children's behavior in kindergarten does not become system oriented unless the teacher intervenes. Children who struggle from the core of the class are willing to stay away unless they feel the unspoken pull toward the group. They do not feel "left out" until the group becomes a strong enough organizing factor within themselves to create that kind of personal vacuum for them. It is not a "natural phenomenon." As adults we take for granted this desire to "belong" to a group, but this is not an automatic "given"; it is a developed result. Kindergarten children do not yet seem to care whether they "belong" or not.

A fourth aspect in a kindergarten social system is its range of acceptable behaviors. Because school is new to many children in the kindergarten, teachers are usually lenient in terms of behavior. Expected behavior is viewed in a relative sense such that a continuum from required, accepted, and minimally accepted may be described. For example, the teacher requires certain behavior and will not tolerate deviation from it; some behaviors are merely accepted and not commented on as acceptable or not, and some are only minimally accepted.

Certain behavior types are accepted according to duration, frequency or intensity of the act. If a child were to act physically aggressive toward his peers, the intensity, frequency and duration of the act would dictate the kind of counteraction the teacher would take. Throughout all of this, however, is the underlying idea that the offender is a child and is learning how to curb his impulses; sometimes, therefore, his behavior is viewed as testing his environment; at other times, it is viewed as a release of hostility and frustration.

A fifth consideration in the social system of a kindergarten is group goal orientation. The children do not seem to have a collective orientation toward goal attainment specific or significant to their group; classroom goals are the teacher's. The teacher plans comments in certain situations so that what he *says* the children *want* to do will in fact *become* what they want to do. It is hoped that they will begin to internalize the standards and goals suggested to them. In this case, then, the social system does not have its own goals but rather objectives which have been supplanted by the teacher who is not a part of the peer group.

A sixth aspect of concern in a social system is related to leadership patterns. These are obscure and unstable for the most part; certain children are aggressive and outgoing but they are not necessarily the ones who influence others to follow them at play. If children in kindergarten are asked who is liked by everyone, about 75% answer they don't know or will mention one child they play with frequently.

A seventh property of a social system is the means of communication which facilitates an identity for the group. When individuals interact frequently, and expected behavior and standards begin to emerge as understood among them, those predictable and accepted behaviors serve as a unifying element. The unity attributes a characteristic of identity, that is, certain behaviors are expected in this group that are not expected in others. Special significance in relation to certain gestures or expressions endows meaning to this particular group of individuals. Kindergarten children do not indicate an awareness of consensus; this is probably a result in part of their autonomy in most transactions of their affairs. The teacher may not implant consensus; this is a developmental process. It is interesting that the children do not seem to sense group agreement. They function individually.

Small Group—Large Group?

Differences in behavior which arise as a result of small group or larger group interaction suggest that both kinds of structuring have their place in kindergarten. Although some teachers are presently using both they feel guilty about it. Since the approval and continuing endorsement of democratic procedures is well known, teachers are confused when they use any procedure which seems to deviate from this. They refer derogatorily to any colleague who conducts a classroom which may resemble an autocratic one. The label carries with it diffuse notions of rigid conformity allowing few exceptions for individual deviation.

Recognition and acceptance of a wider range of teacher controlling behaviors are needed; democratic and autocratic climates need not be labeled and dichotomized to the end that we confuse kindness and harsh treatment as synonymous with or as inseparable aspects of each control pattern. Teachers may begin subsequently to think of their style of control in relation to a particular kind of activity rather than identifying control so closely with their own personality characteristics. The professional aspect of teaching emphasizes behaviors relevant to a certain role. It does not emphasize behaviors such as those involved in intimacy.

Teacher Behavior

It is easier to talk with a teacher, particularly when one is in a supervisory position, about situation and task requirements rather than his personality weaknesses in classroom performances. Defensiveness is not as prominent in such discussions. Depersonalization which gives the environment major emphasis leads to professionalization which in essence minimizes personality concomitants. A clearer and sharper differentiation between personality and role provides a greater number of specific task focuses in an unlimited number of contexts. Greater professional mileage can be gained by this kind of dichotomy than can be gained in the classification of personality qualities.

The behavior of teachers is highly visible to pupils, administrators, parents, and colleagues; it is important, therefore, that teachers know they do not need to classify themselves as permissive or restrictive. They may be one or the other and gradations between as they think the situation demands. This may relieve self-imposed pressures to meet the overwhelming prevalence of literature on the benefits of democratic classroom behavior; it can contribute vitally to their mental health.

Thus from studying the social system of the kindergarten and the freedom from consensual standards, we have noted that a wide range of alternative control patterns may be recommended to teachers. The major emphasis is on the environment, the task at hand,

and the professional requirements which proliferate the teaching role. Teachers may adapt their behavior to different patterns appropriate to the specific teaching task. Since children in kindergarten are beginning to learn how to act in a total classroom group, the teacher has to structure at times to facilitate participation in a total group setting, and at other times can permit freedom to pursue tasks individually. The teacher is not acting either democratically or autocratically; she is incorporating many control patterns and adapting to what seems most appropriate at that time. She need not feel guilty about employment of one way or another; she is exercising greater flexibility and judgment in the context of her professional role.

ENCOURAGING CREATIVE PUPIL BEHAVIOR IN ELEMENTARY SOCIAL STUDIES *

Mary Lee Marksberry

Creativity—what is it and how can it be developed? Is it a magical quality given to only a few fortunate individuals, or is it something that can either be increased or allowed to atrophy, depending upon the nurture that is given it? These and similar questions are the concern of many people in many occupations at the present time. The reason is simply that creativity, more than any other human trait, is basic to the shaping of man's future.

Creativity has been defined in various ways, but for those who are interested in its development in children and youth, one conception is generally accepted: an individual has created if he has an experience which results in a sincere, straightforward invention, new and fresh for him. It does not depend on producing a product that has never been produced before. Rather, the point is that it be first-hand for the individual, not taken second hand from someone else. Another important point is that every curriculum area offers opportunity for creative thinking and the products resulting

Mary Lee Marksberry is Professor of Education at the University of Missouri, Kansas City.

* Reprinted from *Social Education* 29:338–340, 1965, with permission of the National Council for the Social Studies and Mary Lee Marksberry.

from it. These products vary. They may take one of three forms: that of unique communications such as pictures, stories, or characterizations in creative dramatic productions; that of plans or proposed sets of operations such as plans for testing hypotheses, plans for organizing a group to gather data, or plans for evaluating an endeavor; or, that of sets of abstract relations such as the formulation of hypotheses, or the discovery of generalizations.[1]

The question of who is creative is so closely related to what has just been said that it is almost repetitive to say that psychologists are convinced that all people are to some degree potentially creative. Individuals differ in their degree of potential for creativity in various fields of activity and in the modes and expression of their creativeness. But creative thinking is made up of the same basic ingredients at all levels. Extremely creative people just have more of all or some of these ingredients. The solving of everyday problems is very likely a part of the continuum of creativity which extends from expressions having relatively little originality to those having a great deal.

Having established this much of a conceptual background, we can now turn to the question at hand: What are some principles of instruction for encouraging creative pupil behavior in the elementary social studies? Selected findings from the growing body of research in creativity can give some help.

In the first place, research has identified some of the characteristics of creative people. One study which compared the achievement of a high creative group and a high intelligence group found a relatively low relationship between the IQ metric and measures of creativity.[2] Despite the 23-point difference in IQ, and no difference in achievement motivation, there was equal superiority between the high IQ group and the high creative group in scholastic performance as measured by standardized tests. These results were replicated by another researcher with six different samples.[3]

These same researchers also found that the high IQ students were better known and better liked by their teachers than the highly creative students. Both groups (the high IQ's and the high creatives) felt that the traits the teachers valued and those predictive of success in life were moderately related, and the high IQ's

---

[1] Benjamin S. Bloom *et al.*, *Taxonomy of Educational Objectives, The Classification of Educational Goals, Handbook I: Cognitive Domain.* New York: Longmans, Green, 1956, pp. 163–164.

[2] Jacob W. Getzels and Philip W. Jackson, *Creativity and Intelligence.* New York: Wiley, 1962, pp. 24–25.

[3] E. Paul Torrance, "Education and Creativity," in *Creativity: Progress and Potential*, Calvin W. Taylor, ed. New York: McGraw-Hill, 1964, pp. 53–54.

valued these traits for themselves. There was no necessary relation, however, between the traits valued by the high creatives and success in adult life. The traits they valued were somewhat opposite to those their teachers valued.[4]

Other studies show that creative people are flexible and original, curious about the environment, open-minded, objective, indifferent toward conformity to many cultural stereotypes, willing and eager to try new ideas, willing to work long hours over long periods of time, confident in their own ability, willing to be alone both figuratively and physically, and sensitive to various sensory stimuli. They have high skill in the problem-solving abilities of comprehension, application, analysis, synthesis, and evaluation; have a wide knowledge of vocabulary, facts, generalizations, and methods in their specific fields, as well as in related and general areas; and have the psychomotor skills necessary to use the tools of their particular area of interest.

The findings suggest several principles or guidelines for encouraging creative behavior.[5]

We need to recognize that creative children tend to be penalized by the two most common criteria for evaluating scholastic aptitude— measures of the IQ test and teacher evaluations of student characteristics. Students who may potentially be the most creative, by current test criteria may be labeled "over-achievers" with all the unfavorable connotations such a term has come to suggest. We must be cognizant of this danger and avoid it.

We need to make a distinction between independence and obstinateness and between individuality and rebelliousness. Creative students may be harder to get along with but it must be recognized that their behavior likely has its roots in independence of thought. Since their values differ from the values of their teachers and less creative students, they are likely to view the world about them differently. Creative students should probably be given greater autonomy, and perhaps rewarded for behavior that fails to correspond with behavior we intended to reward.

Able students should be encouraged to work on their own interests even if it means working alone.

We should provide opportunities for discovering as well as for remembering, for playing with facts and ideas as well as for repeating them, for finding different interpretations and solutions to problems.

We need to differentiate between evaluation and censorship, between judging and prejudging.

Emphasis should be placed on discovering rather than repetition as the instructional method, and upon evaluating the ability to use knowledge rather than to give back memorized facts.

---

[4] Jacob W. Getzels and Philip W. Jackson, *op. cit.*, pp. 30–37.

[5] Some of these principles were suggested by Jacob W. Getzels and Philip W. Jackson, *op. cit.*, pp. 123–132.

We need to distinguish between creative behavior which meets standards of intellectual merit and behavior which is merely "cute." Only that which has intellectual merit should be rewarded.

A second group of selected findings from research might be classified as characteristics of creativity and the creative process.

Creativity, like intelligence, is not an entity in itself. Rather, it is thought to be a constellation of behaviors—knowledges, attitudes, intellectual abilities and skills, psychomotor skills and habits. Furthermore, these behaviors vary with different spheres of activity.

A close look at the behaviors which make up creative thinking reveals that they are the same ones involved in thinking that is termed critical or reflective. In both creative thinking and reflective thinking the intellectual abilities and skills are the ability to interpret with a high degree of accuracy, the ability to analyze, the ability to evaluate, and the ability to apply what is known. Thus the difference in creative thinking and critical thinking appears to be primarily in degree rather than in actual make-up. Creative thinking puts more emphasis on imagination and intuition and less on predetermined, correct, and conventional solutions bounded by rules and conventions.

The creative process is a problem-solving process. It is made up of a series of experiences or part processes, each of which continues what has gone on before and leads directly into other experiences so that there is a continuous merging of the whole. Each of these experiences is a problem-solving situation in itself making its contribution to the over-all creative process.

The creative process is believed by many to be made up of four stages. The first is a period of intense, routine work characterized by trial and error. It is concerned with inspection of the problem and collection of information and is called the preparation stage. The second is called the incubation stage. It is a period of quiescence out of which a new idea will come if the process is successful. The third is illumination, during which insight comes. And the fourth is verification, which is concerned with elaboration and revision.

These characteristics and two mentioned earlier—that there are gradations of creativity in problem solving and that creativity in the classroom may result in three types of products—reinforce some of the principles already mentioned and suggest others:

Learning experiences to develop creativity, like learning experiences to develop any other type of behavior, must give the learner opportunity to practice the behaviors which compose it at a level commensurate with maturational level and in such a way that he gets satisfaction from it.

Since creativity is a constellation of behaviors, learning experiences to develop it must incorporate the principles for developing these separate behaviors. We must incorporate what is known about the development of knowledges, attitudes, intellectual abilities and skills, psychomotor skills, etc.

Children should be provided opportunities to solve various types of problems (intellectual, interpersonal, and practical) in group problem-solving situations, on an individual basis, and in discussion situations.

We need to encourage original and free thinking in the problem-solving process. This can be done especially during the formulation of hypotheses and when plans are made to test the hypotheses.

We need to prepare children for the first and last stages of creativity, by teaching industry, regular study habits, intellectual skills, and critically controlled attitudes.

Since insight into a problem situation comes when the learners have sufficient background and preparation, when they are able to see the relationships in the total situation, and when opportunities for change of activities are given if they reach an impasse, the teacher needs to see that these conditions are met.

Teachers need to allow for unplanned and irrelevant happenings in the classroom so insight can be caught when it comes.

We need to be respectful of children's questions but seldom give answers which can be discovered by children themselves. The teacher's role is to help them find answers to their questions and to make the effort worthwhile by rewarding their efforts.

We need to ask provocative questions—questions which require children to interpret, to apply, analyze, and to synthesize and evaluate.

Reports, stories with a historical setting, dramatics, pictorial illustrations, murals, dioramas, panoramas, and the like (growing out of questions and problems in social studies) should be the children's own interpretations after thorough research. They should never be pattern or copy work.

Opportunities for children to make their own formulations of generalizations after careful gathering and study of facts must be provided.

The last group of selected findings to be considered here give insight into some of the forces that inhibit and promote creativity.

One report lists six inhibiting factors.[6] The first is the success orientation of the United States. This dictates that children must not be frustrated and that failures must be avoided. As a result children fear to try new things or to tackle problems that are difficult. The chance of failure with its resulting price is too great.

Second, the United States, according to anthropologists, is the most peer-oriented culture in the world. The inhibiting effects that peer pressures toward conformity exert on creative thinking have been very evident when researchers observed children, when they conducted experiments, and when they studied the creative writing of children.

---

[6] E. Paul Torrance, *op. cit.*, pp. 98–102.

Sanctions against questioning and explorations also work against creativity. The child who is constantly questioning and exploring poses a threat to many teachers in terms of the teacher's breadth of experience and in terms of smooth-running, teacher-dominated conforming classrooms. Teachers have many devices for putting the curious child in his place—insisting on one way to solve problems, insisting that every child use the same methods of study, insisting that all children complete their work within the same time limit, rewarding conformity, emphasizing giving back ready-made answers instead of answers the child has discovered for himself, and others.

Overemphasis or misplaced emphasis on sex roles is a fourth force that inhibits creativity. By its very nature, creativity requires both sensitivity and independence of thinking. Sensitivity, in our culture, is regarded as a feminine virtue and independence as a masculine one. Thus, highly creative boys are likely to appear more effeminate than their peers and highly creative girls more masculine. This results in pressures to conform to the accepted sex virtues.

A fifth force working against creativity is equating divergence with "abnormality." Although the belief once held that "genius" and madness were associated has been discredited, the belief has persisted that any divergence from behavioral norms must be corrected at all costs because it is an indication of something abnormal. The pressures of society to rid children of divergent characteristics are relentless.

Another restraining force is the work-play dichotomy in our culture. One is supposed to enjoy play and to dislike work, and something is wrong with the person who doesn't conform with this expectation. Also, there is supposed to be no playing in work. This appears to be one reason why teachers do not more frequently allow children to learn through dramatic play, through "fooling around" with maps, globes, books, and other materials and equipment, through informal discussions with their peers, and through satisfying their own curiosity by individually initiated projects.

On the positive side, biographical studies of creative people (scientists) indicate that some experiences may increase a person's chances to be creative while other experiences may decrease his probabilities. An early broad interest in intellectual things appears to be positively related to later creative performance.[7] The more creative scientists reported that they learned more about things

[7] Calvin W. Taylor and Frank Barron., eds., *Scientific Creativity: Its Recognition and Development*. New York: Wiley, 1962, p. 386.

which curiosity prompted them to study on their own than they did from classroom work or assigned homework.[8]

These findings reinforce many of the principles already given, and in connection with findings previously reviewed suggest four basic principles for providing an environment to further creativity:

1. Provide a physical environment which stimulates curiosity and invites experimentation.
2. Provide conditions where children can work with a minimal encroachment of other interests.
3. See that every individual is accepted and provided an emotional environment in which external evaluation is absent.
4. The classroom, since it is an important part of a child's culture, must tolerate deviations from the traditional and the *status quo* and permit freedom within the individual and between the individual and his environment.

In summary, if creative behavior in the social studies is to be promoted, we must put emphasis on discovery rather than repetition as the instructional method. This presupposes an informal, permissive, yet supportive classroom climate, a physical environment that invites both group and individual exploration and experimentation, many opportunities for original thinking and problem solving, honest appreciation of creative behavior that has intellectual merit, and a recognition and cherishing of individual ways of learning and responding.

THE NATURE OF TEACHING *

Hilda Taba

Teaching is much more complex than is generally assumed. The usual paradigm of teaching is a mixture of sets of scattered ideas and conceptual models and of simplistic assumptions. Neither a comprehensive theory of teaching nor a set of satisfactory con-

---

The late Hilda Taba was Professor of Education at San Francisco State College.

* This selection is Chapter II of a research paper entitled *Teaching Strategies and Cognitive Functioning in Elementary School Children*, Cooperative Research Project No. 2404. U.S. Office of Education, 1966.

[8] Calvin W. Taylor, "Clues to Creative Teaching: Developing Creative Characteristics." *The Instructor* 73:100, 1964.

ceptual models is available to describe individual teaching acts or teaching strategies and their effect on learning.

Assumptions about Teaching

Several assumptions prevail about the nature and function of teaching. Among the simplest and most obstinately held has been the idea that the chief, if not the only, function of teaching is to impart knowledge, i.e., to explain and tell. According to this assumption, effectiveness of teaching bears a direct relationship to teachers' knowledge of content areas. Evidence of this idea can be found in the practically self-teaching and presumably "teacher-safe" curriculum packages and in the emphasis on training teachers in the content backgrounds as the chief way of ensuring excellence of teaching and learning. While improvement and updating of the content of curriculum and of the content background of teachers no doubt improves teaching, it also involves the danger of a uniform curriculum uniformly and unimaginatively taught to all varieties of students and under all varieties of conditions.

Another widely accepted but equally inadequate assumption about teaching is that it consists of mastering certain special "methods," such as "methods for teaching history." Often the idea of method is narrowed still further, such as to a chronological or a topical "method" of teaching history. Acrimonious debates about the method of teaching reading consist largely of putting one method against another as the only right method of teaching a subject, such as reading. This assumption is the base of the prevailing scheme of separate methods courses in teacher training. This assumption takes for granted that there is *one* right method of teaching anything and that that method is equally effective in the hands of all teachers for all kinds of students and under a variety of learning conditions (Medley and Mitzel, 1963, pp. 85–88). However, the chief weakness of teaching modeled on this assumption is that it would be determined solely by the unique characteristics of subjects and not also by the requirements of general educational objectives, such as the development of thinking and certain values.

Still another assumption is that good teachers are born, not made. Those operating on this assumption regard teaching as a sort of mystical art, the secrets of which a few "good" teachers grasp intuitively. Such an assumption denies the possibility that teaching involves techniques and skills that can be learned by a great range of individuals, provided we can identify those techniques and skills and help teachers to master them.

Perhaps the most basic recent criticism leveled against approaching teaching as a theoretical construct is that the concepts of methods have been inferred too directly from the various partial and inconsistent learning theories, each of which postulates a different basic mechanism of learning, such as conditioning, identification, and the organization of perception and cognition. Each of these leads to a different teaching model. The first suggests that teaching is conditioning of responses by controlling the stimuli; the second, by providing models; the third, by arranging stimulus conditions to induce reorganization of perception and cognition. The confusion is further compounded by the fact that many learning theories are derived from laboratory studies, often of lower animals, in which learning occurs in tightly controlled environments that have little or no resemblance to a classroom. Page (1962, pp. 74–75) suggests that there has been a gross misapplication of behavioral sciences, especially psychological theories, and has called attention to the "verbal magic" in which both psychologists and educators engage in translating laboratory findings into educational theory. He defines "verbal magic" as a process of over-generalizing laboratory findings, such as generalizing from the reactions of hooded white rats to electric shock, to the reactions of organisms in general, and then applying the generalization to human learning in a classroom. The resulting inference would be that, since hooded white rats learn less well from punishments than from rewards, the same can be said for organisms in general or third graders in particular.

Another difficulty in analyzing teaching is caused by lack of adequate differentiation among types of learning: among learning facts, developing skills, learning to think, and acquiring attitudes. Without such differentiation it is difficult to match teaching strategies to particular types of learning. Often, therefore, principles of learning relevant to one type of learning are applied indiscriminately to all types with understandably unsatisfactory results.

Past studies of teaching which have concentrated largely on the relationship of teacher characteristics to teaching effectiveness have been rather fruitless. Getzels and Jackson conclude that, despite the importance of the problem and a half-century of prodigious effort, very little is known about the relationship between teacher personality and teacher effectiveness:

> The regrettable fact is that many of the studies so far have not produced significant results. Many others have produced only pedestrian findings. For example, it is said after the usual inventory tabulations, that good teachers are friendly, cheerful, sympathetic, and morally virtuous rather than cruel, depressed, unsympathetic and morally depraved. But when this has been said, not very much that is especially useful has been revealed. For what conceivable human interaction—

and teaching implies first and foremost a human interaction—is not better if the people involved are friendly, cheerful, sympathetic, and virtuous rather than the opposite? (Getzels and Jackson, 1963, p. 574)

The Nature of Teaching

Teaching is one of the most complex human activities. Even simple decisions, such as what questions to ask a third grader, require considering and integrating a multitude of factors as shown in the chart below (Taba and Hills, 1965, p. 48):

Considerations in Making Decisions about Teaching

The learning process

Objectives and the structure of the processes involved

Learners and variations in their capacities and readiness

Decision on Teaching Strategy

Content and its structure

Personal teaching style of the teacher

The institutional setting and its requirements

Decisions regarding teaching strategies are affected first by the nature of the content taught and by one's view of that content. To the extent that there are differences in the structures of the various disciplines, there must also be variations in the strategies of teaching them.

In addition, if teaching is addressed to multiple behavioral objectives, the behaviors implied by these objectives must be differentiated and appropriate strategies differentiated and planned. For example, attitudes cannot be "taught" in the same sense one teaches geographic principles nor yet map-reading skills.

Further criteria for formulation of teaching strategies are supplied by knowledge about the learning process *qua* process. What do principles such as generalizing in an inductive sequence, such as focusing on manageable targets and such as pacing the learning appropriately, imply in deciding what questions to ask third graders about community organization, or what research assignment in history to give fifth graders? A particularly important principle for those concerned with autonomous learning is that of involving students actively in the business of their own learning.

Still more criteria and modifications are dictated by differences among learners' abilities, cultural backgrounds, and maturity levels. Such differences require the teacher to determine ways of motivating students, or the optimum size of the steps in a sequence of learning tasks. The latter is especially important when the tasks involve conceptualization, abstraction, and other forms of thinking.

Finally, there are the considerations of whether certain teaching techniques harmonize with the teacher's personal style of teaching and with the requirements and limitations of the institutional and community setting. Even techniques that are generally the best can be unproductive if they do not fit into a given style of teaching or are inappropriate to a given school setting.

Generally, however, the above diagram suggests that teaching is a way of synthesizing into one sequence two aspects of a logical model: the structure of the content and the behaviors to be attained by the students. Too often, in current considerations of teaching, these factors are separated.

Studies of Teaching

Recently, the previously mentioned limitations of directly modeling teaching from results of laboratory studies and of inferring teaching effectiveness from the personality characteristics of teachers, or from a general list of *a priori* competencies, have begun to be recognized, and a number of studies have been conducted of normal class situations. The model for assessing teaching effectiveness is also moving toward evaluating the effects of interaction between teacher and students.

In these studies of teaching the description of teaching acts and of teaching strategies has become one of the chief tools for securing data. However, the acts selected to be described differ, as do the systems of description, both apparently as functions of what the researcher considers important in teaching. The studies of teaching tend to differ, therefore, in several important respects.

One difference lies in the range of teaching behavior observed. Whereas one set of observations may be concerned with the logic of teaching, others may focus on classroom climate, on critical thinking, or on communication patterns.

A second source of variation is the setting and the population that is being studied. For example, certain studies observe classes while they are studying a specific subject, while others cut across subject areas. Some investigators are interested in observing teaching of gifted children; others study under-achievers. Some concentrate on high school classrooms only and others investigate elementary school classrooms.

A third difference is the observational procedure itself. In one study observations may be recorded in the classroom during the lesson while in others the analysis of teaching is made indirectly by examining tape recordings, kinescopes or tapescripts. As a rule, the observational procedures used tend to be a function of the kinds of behavior under study. For example, analysis of many dimensions of a particular unit of behavior precludes the direct coding of immediate observation as the sole method of coding and requires the availability of a permanent record (Kliebard, 1966, p. 47).

Finally, the studies differ according to whether they focus on teacher or on student behavior or on both simultaneously.

In one of his earlier statements, Smith (1950, pp. 229–41) maintained that, in order to develop an adequate theory of didactics, one must first describe the behavior of the teachers. The tactics of teaching could be described later. Smith believes that such a description should cut through the verbality which now obstructs intensive analysis of teaching behavior.

Because studies of teaching show progression in methodology of recording as well as in types of behavior analyzed, the major prototypes are presented in a semichronological sequence.

One of the earliest studies by Marie Hughes (1959) analyzed teaching acts. Her study examined the effects of control and freedom in the classroom. Among the categories describing teacher acts were the following:

1. *Controlling*, acts which tell children what to do, how to go about it, and who should do what;
2. *Facilitating*, acts such as those which check, demonstrate, and clarify;
3. *Content development*, acts such as those which elaborate the structure of the problem under consideration, or build data for generalizing;
4. *Personally responsive* acts, and
5. *Positively* and *negatively* affective acts.

Hughes inferred certain qualities of teaching and a certain impact upon what the students learn from frequencies in the categories of teaching acts. For example, a large percentage of controlling acts by the teacher is considered indicative of a tendency to limit students' intellectual activity to memory and recall. A large percentage of acts designated as content development is considered to imply that mental processes other than recall are being developed.

Flanders (1963; 1966) is interested in somewhat similar categories of behavior and their effects on the classroom climate and goals. He uses ten categories to describe the behavior of teachers and students. Seven of these ten describe teacher behavior: accepting feelings, praising and encouraging, using ideas of students, asking questions, lecturing, giving directions, criticizing, justifying authority. The first four represent indirect teacher influence and the last three direct influence. Flanders' thesis is that indirect influence expands the freedom of action for the student and makes him less dependent upon the teacher while the direct influence has the opposite effect. By combining these behaviors in interaction matrices, Flanders plots the concentration of direct and indirect influence and, from the ratio of the two, infers the impact of teaching acts on students (1962a, pp. 50–62). Both of these studies catalogued teacher behavior while observing in the classroom.

Smith (1962) made the transition to the use of tapescripts as a method of recording classroom transactions. His first study was mainly concerned with teaching acts apart from their effect on learning. He classified teaching acts according to certain categories of operation: logical ones, such as defining, classifying, comparing, contrasting, evaluating, or others, such as directing and admonishing. His second study (1964) is devoted to establishing a framework for studying teaching strategies.

In the latter, "ventures" and "moves" constitute the basic elements for describing various teaching strategies. The venture is defined as a "segment of discourse consisting of a set of utterances dealing with a single topic and having a single over-arching content objective." Usually five or six such self-contained units of discourse may be found in a lesson. This definition of ventures as self-contained units assures that the teaching strategies will not be fragmented as they would be if time units were used. But such large units also constitute a source of unreliability in identification. Nine types of ventures were identified according to their cognitive import, central meaning, or theme:

1. *Casual ventures* dealing with cause-and-effect relationships;
2. *Conceptual ventures*, or the over-arching criteria for determining what is a member of a class and what is not;
3. *Evaluative ventures*, namely, the rating of an action, object, or event as to its goodness, correctness or worth;
4. *Informatory ventures*, or clarifications and amplifications of specified topics;
5. *Interpretive ventures*, namely, those dealing with the meaning of words or symbols;
6. *Procedural ventures*, attempts to disclose a sequence of actions by which an end may be achieved;

7. *Reason ventures,* attempts to reveal the reasons for action, decision, policy or practice;
8. *Rule ventures,* namely, the conventional ways of doing things or analytical relationships which may be used to guide action, and
9. *System ventures,* that concentrate on functional relations of the parts of a mechanism that produce a given end.

The move is a verbal maneuver that relates the terms set forth in a proposition to events or things. Moves are multiple. For conceptual ventures alone, eighteen types of moves are identified. Moves and ventures, combined in certain ways, make up strategies which consist entirely of abstract moves or which combine abstract moves with "instancing" moves. Smith and his associates identified two basic dimensions of strategy, namely, the treatment dimension or that of structuring the information, and the control dimension or the devices that the teacher uses to guide and to control the students' operations on the content.

Arno Bellack (1963) and his associates perceive teaching as a form of rule-governed game. Their study is essentially a description of the roles that the teacher and students play when engaged in the game of teaching and learning. The game is verbal and it is assumed that the principal function of language is to communicate meaning. Therefore, the analysis of language in the classroom offers the most promising way of studying the communication of meaning.

In the game of teaching, Bellack distinguishes four basic verbal maneuvers which constitute the first dimension of meaning:

1. *Structuring,* the function of which is to focus attention on the subject matter or a classroom procedure in launching interaction;
2. *Soliciting,* designed to elicit a verbal response, to encourage the persons addressed to attempt something, or to elicit a physical response;
3. *Responding,* which is reciprocally related to soliciting; and
4. *Reacting,* occasioned by structuring, soliciting, or responding functions.

These latter moves serve to shape or mold classroom discussions by accepting, rejecting, modifying or expanding what has been said.

The content of what is said is subdivided into two categories: 1. *substantive meanings,* such as international trade, and 2. *instructional meanings,* such as managerial statements and those concerned with assignments and procedures.

Bellack's findings (1965) are as follows:

1. The chief cycle consisted of teacher soliciting → student responding → teacher reacting; this cycle made up more than three quarters of all verbal moves made.

2. Teachers were verbally more active than students. Teachers structured the lesson, solicited responses from pupils, reacted to pupils' responses and, to some extent, summarized the discourse. The pupils responded primarily to teachers' solicitations; they did not overtly evaluate teacher statements; they evaluated the responses of other pupils only at the infrequent times when the teacher asked them to.

3. In most classes, structuring accounted for about 10% of lines spoken. Soliciting, responding, and reacting each accountèd for 20% to 30% of the lines. Summarizing was rather infrequent.

4. Regarding content, instructional meanings accounted for 25% of the discourse and approximately 75% of the discourse was specifically concerned with substantive meanings. The largest proportion of these utterances consisted of stating facts or explaining while, in contrast, analytic and evaluative meanings accounted for only a small portion of the total discourse in any class.

5. The most frequent activities were teachers' statements about procedures, assignments, and other instructional matters.

6. Teachers' behavior was characterized by a relatively stable emotional style.

The study described in this report as well as the study that preceded it (Taba, Levine and Elzey, 1964) differs from those described above in several respects:

1. This study was conducted in an experimental setting rather than a naturalistic one. This experimental setting included a newly organized curriculum plus training the teachers to develop cognitive processes in the students. (Note that Bellack did include some training.)

2. The study focused on a single target—the development of cognitive processes.

3. The study attempted simultaneously to analyze, in terms of cognitive processes, two poles of interaction: teacher behavior and the quality of student responses.

4. The study attempted to identify both the functions (in terms of behaviors sought) of the individual teacher acts and of the combinations of these acts defined as strategies, namely, the sequences, clusters, pacing, and flow.

5. The study attempted to examine a series of dependent variables. For instance, it examined the relationship of the target

objective—the levels of cognitive process—to social sciences content achievement, to intelligence, to economic status, and to reading and language ability.

Perhaps the chief distinction between the studies described above and the current study is that they generally analyzed spontaneous teaching behavior of teachers who were not specially trained to promote the behavior being studied in the students. In this study, it was assumed that the teacher had certain techniques made available through training. The emphasis was on how the teacher managed these techniques and how he combined them into a personal style of teaching.

Social Studies and Instructional Processes

*I*NSTRUCTIONAL PROCESSES ARE OF VITAL IMPORTANCE to elementary social studies education because it is through the *process* of instruction that many social studies objectives are achieved. Objectives that relate to skills and values are of particular relevance to the setting in which they are taught and therefore learned. Substantive content is, of course, important, too, for without it there could be no program at all. But the concern for content-oriented objectives without parallel concern for the manner in which they are achieved often results in programs that are out of balance and out of focus. Similarly, concern only for process and not for content does not result in a satisfactory social studies program.

Several criteria can be applied to the selection of appropriate instructional processes for elementary social studies. Through the years some have received a considerable amount of attention from the profession. Since the beginning of the child development movement in education, the nature and needs of children have figured prominently in the selection of instructional processes. Activities, materials, and procedures are selected that are consistent with the nature of childhood. The principles of child development have not always been wisely applied to classroom teaching, but few would deny that the total effect of concern for the learner has had a desirable effect on instruction. Elementary school pupils are children, not adults; they are learners rather than mature scholars; they can be interested in almost anything if it is presented to them in appropriate ways. Concern for the learner's nature and needs is not the only criterion to be applied in selecting particular instructional procedures, but it is an essential one.

The selection of instructional processes also is related to the nature of the material to be taught. The question of *what* to teach always precedes that of *how* to teach it. That is, instructional processes lack relevance when they are removed from specific understandings, attitudes, and skills that are to be learned. A good teaching method is one that enables a teacher and pupils to achieve predetermined objectives in ways that are psychologically and educationally sound. If psychological soundness relates to learner factors in the teaching-learning process, then educational soundness may be thought of as relating to the knowledge, skill, or value component to be learned.

In present-day curriculum development the methods of inquiry characteristic of the various disciplines are getting increased attention. In teaching and learning geography, for example, the study and inquiry processes should be in accordance with those of the discipline of geography. How does a geographer go about his studies? What data does he seek? What kinds of questions does he ask? What tools does he use in carrying out his inquiry? What kinds of conclusions are typically those of geographers? The same questions could be applied to the study of any of the disciplines. It is important to stress that methods of inquiry characteristic of the disciplines are not the only ones utilized in elementary social studies instruction. Indeed, in some cases such instructional approaches would be wholly inappropriate. But when combined with other criteria, they do constitute a valid consideration in selecting instructional procedures.

The type of learning task confronted by the pupil will also determine the instructional processes employed by the teacher. It makes some difference if a teacher is developing a concept, teaching a skill, or helping pupils clarify a value question. Not all learning goals are achieved in the same way, and the process of instruction must be one that will best assist the learner achieve his goal.

Finally, instructional processes may be selected because they aid in the development of certain intellectual skills. Today investigation-oriented approaches to instruction are getting much attention under the labels of discovery, inquiry, induction, and problem-solving. In order to build skills that are needed for reflective thinking and problem-solving, certain instructional processes are selected that will force the learner to apply such skills. Unfortunately the theory that undergirds these approaches is not always understood by teachers who use them, and as a result the procedures become meaningless and ritualistic. Problem-solving becomes a process of "following the five steps." Or inquiry is perceived as asking a set pattern of questions. It is more important for the teacher to know the rationale and logic along with the psychological bases for these procedures than it is for him to be able to practice them in a ritualistic way, not fully understanding what they are supposed to achieve.

Selecting and utilizing appropriate teaching processes and methods are constant challenges to teachers. Ways have to be devised to help individual children learn in group-teaching situations. The problem is complicated because of the vast amount of variation between and among pupils in their ability to learn, interest in learning, backgrounds of understanding, and preparation for learning. The articles in this section focus on several dimensions of the problems surrounding the selection and use of instructional processes.

UPDATING INSTRUCTION IN THE SOCIAL STUDIES *

Herbert G. Kariel

When asked about new developments in content and subject matter treatment, teachers generally think of the new mathematics and science curricula. These developments are directed primarily at presenting facts and aiding students to derive generalizations or, simply, teaching inductively. Equally revolutionary changes in the social sciences, however, frequently go unnoticed. Teaching inductively and using the notion of discovery are found also to be valuable in teaching the social sciences. In this approach, students either acquire information or they make their own observations about social phenomena and subsequently attempt to derive generalizations from these data.

Why is it that so little is known about these developments in the social studies? One possibility is, perhaps, that there is nothing new in the various academic disciplines from which content of the social studies is drawn—history and the social sciences, geography, sociology, economics, political science and, occasionally, psychology. This idea is patently false; never has so much progress been made in these disciplines as in the post-war years. Use of the scientific approach and the application of quantitative techniques are continually opening up new horizons.

Before further analyzing this possibility, let us consider a second one it suggests. Perhaps teachers do not know of the new developments, or if they do know of them they have no idea how they should be taught.

Finally, it may be that teachers believe that social studies is somehow inherently boring as compared with the natural sciences. Children eagerly bring bees and grasshoppers to class; they observe fish in an aquarium, or follow the transformation of polliwogs to adult frogs. What do social studies offer which can compare with the immediacy and fascination of these experiences? Can maps, dates, and place names compete with them? Are social, political and economic events somehow too removed from the child's experience, too abstract for him to comprehend?

Fortunately, we are not forced to choose among these alterna-

Herbert G. Kariel is Associate Professor of Geography and Anthropology at the California State College, Hayward.

* Reprinted from the *CTA Journal* *63*:29 ff., 1967, with permission of the California Teachers Association and Herbert G. Kariel.

tives. Probably each contributes something to the present generally low status of teaching in the social studies. Let us, therefore, consider all of them in greater detail to see what greater knowledge, better teaching methods, and improved attitudes might contribute to the improvement of instruction in the social studies.

The social sciences are changing from a period of emphasis on collection and classification of data to one of search for explanations of the phenomena studied. In most of these fields, scientific methodology has been applied to any significant degree only in the past 30 years. In essence, emphasis has shifted from finding out *what* social phenomena are in the world to discovering *why* they are as they are. Scientifically-minded geographers, for example, are no longer content with describing physical and cultural features of the earth; they wish also to understand why these features are located where they are. This involves abstracting such notions as location and distance from the physical and cultural matrix in which they are observed. These geographers ask questions such as: "Where are ports located? What are the elements common to the location of manufacturing centers? How far apart are urban places in a physically uniform region?" Similarly, many anthropologists, sociologists, economists and political scientists are seeking explanations of the phenomena which they study.

Our second question was, are teachers aware of these developments? If so, do they know how to transmit them to their pupils? Unless a teacher is aware of these developments, he can scarcely be expected to teach them. In teaching geography, for example, many teachers become bogged down in a mass of place names and descriptive statistics of the regions being studied. They neglect to ask themselves and their students *why?* Why are railroads located along the coast of a given area rather than several miles inland? Why is the population concentrated in one area while another area is virtually uninhabited? Why is timber the major product of a certain area, rather than coal, oil, wheat or fish?

Jerome Bruner, in *The Process of Education* (1960), cites an example of the use of the "discovery" approach with a sixth grade social studies class.

A sixth-grade class, having been through a conventional unit on the social and economic geography of the Southeastern states, was introduced to the North Central region by being asked to locate the major cities of the area on a map containing physical features and natural resources, but no place names. The resulting class discussion very rapidly produced a variety of plausible theories concerning the requirements of a city—a water transportation theory that placed Chicago at the junction of the three lakes, a mineral resources theory that placed it near the Mesabi range, a food-supply theory that put a great city on the rich soil of Iowa, etc. The level of interest as well as the level of the conceptual sophistication was far above that of control classes. Most striking, however, was the attitude of children to whom, for the first time, the location of a city appeared as a problem, and one to which an answer could be discovered by taking thought.

Finally, can social studies in fact be more inherently boring than the natural sciences, with the whole fascinating and complex world of human activities to be studied? The quotation above suggests otherwise. Are children not fascinated by visiting a fire station, a bakery, or factories in their community? What a discovery for a child to learn that the symbols on a map can be translated into real roads and towns and rivers! A teacher who understands and appreciates the richness and variety of potential content in social studies is far better able to communicate interest and enthusiasm to her pupils than one who is uninformed. First-hand experiences are available to her students through such activities as field trips or the study of the community.

What, then, can be done to improve the teaching of social studies? Findings of studies of the diffusion of new ideas and practices suggest that several steps are involved in the adoption of a new practice. First, the individual must be aware that the practice exists. He must then have knowledge of the practice itself, and a belief that it might be valuable for him to adopt. Given these conditions, he may decide to try it out. After trying it for a while, he evaluates it; on the basis of his evaluation he makes a decision as to whether to adopt or reject the practice.

It seems reasonable to believe that similar steps would be followed by teachers in adopting new practices in the teaching of social studies. Since each step is a prerequisite for the succeeding one, provisions must be made first for communicating information about the existence of new developments in the social sciences, then for transmitting knowledge of these developments, finally for providing opportunities to try out new methods of teaching in the classroom.

These steps have been followed successfully in the areas where change has already taken place: mathematics, science, and foreign languages. A group of specialists decided upon the curriculum content to be included; this was then transmitted to teachers in a variety of ways. By now, the new textbooks in mathematics, biology and other subjects include the new concepts. Many schools, for instance, have switched to the oral method of teaching foreign languages. The fact that changes have occurred in these fields demonstrated that change is possible if an effort is made.

Change in the social studies would require expert definition of what content should be included in the curriculum, at what grade levels various concepts should be taught, and how they could best be taught. In California, the Statewide Social Sciences Study Committee, with its advisory panels on anthropology, economics, geography, history, psychology, political science, and sociology, is currently studying the nature and treatment of social science material. The Association of American Geographers and the National Council for Geographic Education are currently co-sponsoring such a project aimed at developing a geography curriculum for junior and senior high school. Following the successful completion of these and other pilot projects, larger numbers of teachers could learn the new content and methods in a variety of ways, including television courses, summer institutes, and specially planned in-service programs.

College students in education should be exposed to a wider variety of courses in history and the social sciences, as well as to methods of teaching newer developments in these disciplines. If action is taken on all these fronts, it will not be necessary in another ten years to repeat the false statement that social studies are in the educational doldrums.

TERRITORY, LEARNER, AND MAP *

William D. Pattison

Creative, confident teaching is made possible by the teacher's knowledge of the key relationships that unify what is to be taught. An appreciation of this fact is perhaps as old as education itself, but awareness of its significance is increasing in American education. The increase may be attributed principally to efforts that have been made on behalf of teachers by representatives of many fields in bringing to light basic principles of thought for use in the schools.

As a result of these efforts at conceptual clarification, it is not all uncommon to find elementary-school teachers today who are

William D. Pattison is an Associate Professor at the University of Chicago.

* Reprinted from *The Elementary School Journal* 66:146–153, 1966, with permission of The University of Chicago Press and William D. Pattison. Copyright © 1966.

able to base their instruction in mathematics, for example, on their understanding of sets and relations between sets. Similarly, thanks to recent assistance, many teachers now interpret the economic order through the master concepts of scarcity and choice; and physical events in terms of system, object, and interaction.

To date, however, no comparable penetration to the level of fundamental conceptions has been made to improve map instruction. This statement may seem incredible, at first, to readers who are acquainted with the abundant literature on maps and mapping that has been produced for school use, especially during the past few decades. Yet, it must be granted that even the best of existing publications have stopped short of bringing into view the basic relationships that would permit a teacher to proceed with intellectual assurance in assisting the map learning process.

What is still needed is a source of guidance for the teacher, setting forth the primary principles of map instruction. One suggested form of such guidance is offered here.

The Teacher's Key

The initial requirements that must be met by anyone who wants to engage in effective map instruction are those of understanding and remembering the message in the accompanying diagram.

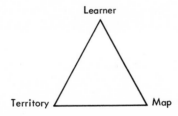

This triangle expresses the essential relationships underlying map communication. The triangle asserts, first, that a map has a basic equivalence to a territory, relating to it as a substitute. Second, the triangle tells us that the learner can enter into direct relationships with both map and territory. Third, the triangle tells us that the learner can mediate between map and territory, as a handler of information.

A territory, in the sense intended here, is more than land; it is an area, just as what we ordinarily call a salesman's territory is an area. Hence, the attributes of a given territory are to be seen as including characteristics that might not at first be anticipated: a full range of physical things and conditions, plus a multitude of intangibles, such as income levels, literacy rates, and political attitudes.

As many readers will recognize, the Territory-Learner-Map Triangle is an adaptation of the diagram known in semantics as the *Triangle of Reference, map* appearing in the place of *word*, and *territory* in the place of *referent*. As an adaptation, the triangle serves to remove the conception of *map instruction* from the isolation in which it is all too often found, and to encourage its inclusion in curriculum thinking on communication in general.

How can the Territory-Learner-Map Triangle open the way to an exploration of map learning?

The Learner's Tasks

From the Territory-Learner-Map Triangle, we can derive a specification of the tasks around which map instruction should be organized. The tasks are the two undertakings suggested by the position of the learner between territory and map: the task of taking territorial information from a map and the task of putting territorial information into a map.

In taking information, the learner generates a flow from Map to Learner in the key triangle. In supplying information, he produces a flow from Learner to Map. The first of the two tasks is map-reading, where *reading* is understood to embrace a wide range of map uses. The second task is map-making, where *making* is understood to include even simple acts of adding information to ready-developed maps.

In the contemporary language of the computer, the learner's two tasks are those of information storage and information retrieval. Storage is represented by the flow from Learner to Map and retrieval by the flow from Map to Learner. The map itself, in this view, is a computer substitute. Conversely, the computer is to be seen as an electronic alternative to the map, capable of retaining data for production in map form on command.

Mapping: The Objectives

The identification of map tasks permits us to consider, next, the purposes of the form of communication to which they pertain. We begin by drawing from the Territory-Learner side of the key triangle the reminder that the learner, in common with humanity at large, engages daily in direct territorial experience.

The learner's territorial experience extends back to the time in his infancy when he made his first attempts at locomotion, and it may be expected to continue for the duration of his lifetime. Like other experience, it assumes the form of problems to be solved. These may be stated in four questions, which are listed here with accompanying notes.

1. *Which way?* The problem expressed is one of uncertainty about *direction*. The solution lies in a determination of heading relative to landmarks, to self, or to the earth.
2. *How far?* The problem expressed is one of uncertainty about *distance*. The solution lies in a determination of physical separation relative to some standard of measure.
3. *Where?* The problem expressed is one of uncertainty about *location*. The solution lies in a determination of position in relation to some reference system, one of which is that of latitude and longitude.
4. *What?* The problem expressed is one of uncertainty about *identity*. The solution lies in a determination of the category to which the subject of uncertainty belongs. The subject is most often something physical—an observed object—but it need not be thus restricted.

Successful map instruction demands that the teacher understand the map as a means for meeting the challenge of precisely the four questions listed. Through a teacher who has this understanding, the learner can capture something of the sense of need fulfilment that was felt by early human groups when mapping made its first appearance among them and alleviated the problems that these questions define.

Fortunately for map education, the beginning pupil normally has already solved, without a map, some of the problems that have arisen in his home territory. By directing his attention to the problems that remain, the teacher is able to involve the typical learner in map use. Ultimately, through continued study, the learner gains an ability to cope with entirely strange territories, both as a map reader and as a map maker.

Mapping: The Critical Variables

If the purposes of mapping are to be found on the Territory-Learner side of the triangle with which we began, principles of no less importance are to be discovered on the Territory-Map side of the same diagram. There we encounter four relationships that are built into mapping. They are variables in that they change their character from map to map. They are critical in that the usefulness of mapped information is subject to their control. These are the four variables:

1. *Orientation.* This variable consists of the relationship between the directional system of a map and the directional system of the earth. It is a physical relationship. For any particular map, the relationship can be changed by adjusting the position of the map. When it reaches "locking position," the map is so aligned that its directions match the corresponding directions of the earth.
2. *Miniaturization.* This variable consists of the relationship between measurements of length made on a map and corresponding measurements made within a territory. It is a proportional relationship, and is usually called *scale*. Distances on a map could, conceivably, be larger than corresponding territorial distances, but practically always map distances are smaller—much smaller. We can say that the typical map "shrinks" the territory of which it is the image.
3. *Projection.* This variable consists of the relationship between the frame of reference that regulates the placement of points on a map and the corresponding frame of reference by which locations are described within a territory. It is a geometric relationship. The most convenient key to projection for any particular map is likely to be the observed "behavior" of the latitude and longitude lines that cross its surface.
4. *Symbolization.* This variable consists of the relationship between the appearance of map marks and the identity of what they stand for. It is a representational relationship in which the symbols may be words or numbers, but are usually neither. Unless the marks are obviously imitative, they require explanation, and for that purpose legends are added to maps.

From the point of view of the learner, all four variables may seem to be formidable obstacles to the fulfilment of his role as a map maker and as map reader. As in other specialized branches of education, it falls to the teacher to remove the threat involved. The recommended procedure for doing this is to lead the learner to recognize that each variable carries within itself a special opportunity for personal growth.

A Guide to Map Skills

Perhaps the most convincing way of demonstrating the value of the analysis attempted up to this point is to show that it permits an unprecedented clarity and economy in the presentation of map skills.

In the broadest sense, to judge by the learner's tasks listed here, there are only two map skills: a map-reading ability and a map-making ability. However, for map training purposes it is clear that a further breakdown is required. Such a breakdown can be produced from the lists of map objectives and of map varia-ables.

Map-reading ability divides into two groups of skills, the first of which derives from the four general objectives of mapping. This group consists of the learner's attack skills, so called because they are the abilities through which he directly attacks his territorial problems. The skills are:

1. The ability to determine *direction* from a map
2. The ability to determine *distance* from a map
3. The ability to determine *location* from a map
4. The ability to determine *identity* from a map

The second of the two groups of map-reading abilities derives from the four critical map variables. This group consists of support skills, so called because they serve to back up or support the learner's attacks on territorial problems. The skills are:

1. The ability to interpret the *orientation* relationship between a map and a territory
2. The ability to interpret the *miniaturization* relationship between a map and a territory
3. The ability to interpret the *projection* relationship between a map and a territory
4. The ability to interpret the *symbolization* relationship between a map and a territory.

Similarily, map-making ability divides into two groups of skills, those of attack and support. The attack skills, derived as before from the general objectives of mapping, are:

1. The ability to map determinations of *direction*
2. The ability to map determinations of *distance*
3. The ability to map determinations of *location*
4. The ability to map determinations of *identity*

The associated support skills of map-making derive, as in the case of map-reading, from the critical map variables. They are:

1. The ability to create an *orientation* relationship between a map and a territory
2. The ability to create a *miniaturization* relationship between a map and a territory
3. The ability to create a *projection* relationship between a map and a territory
4. The ability to create a *symbolization* relationship between a map and a territory

In our progression toward a guide to map skills, we can now take the final step, that of charting the relationship between attack and support skills. For map-reading, the result takes the form shown in Figure 1. Inspecting this chart from left to right for each attack skill, the reader will observe that the four skills supporting it are arranged in a row, with a distinction made for the particular skill whose support is most needed for solving the territorial problem under attack. In each row, this primary source of support is indicated by a white block. Secondary sources of support are indicated by dark blocks.

For map-making, the relationship between attack and support skills is charted in Figure 2. Here, again, the primary source of support for each attack skill is indicated by a white block.

The charts offer the teacher a way of thinking about what is happening at any given time during map instruction. In performing this service, the charts indicate, as well, what remains to be taught at the stage of map-learning in question.

It should be understood, finally, that a teacher must allow the strategies of map-learning adopted by a pupil to cross freely back and forth between map-reading and map-making, despite the complete separation of the two activities on the charts.

Globe Skills

A question that naturally arises is how globe learning should be thought of, in relation to map learning. For a satisfactory answer, a globe must be seen as a device that brings together two distinct aids to problem-solving. The first aid is the globe's surface image, which represents earth territory in its entirety. The image is a special form of map—a global map. The second aid is the sphere on whose surface this image appears. The sphere is a model of the earth body, and as such it is in a class apart from maps.

A globe's surface image is subject to the application of skills that are identical with those presented in Figures 1 and 2. As should be anticipated, however, the relevance of some of the

SUPPORT SKILLS ⟋ ATTACK SKILLS	Ability to interpret an orientation relationship	Ability to interpret a miniaturization relationship	Ability to interpret a projection relationship	Ability to interpret a symbolization relationship
Ability to determine direction from a map				
Ability to determine distance from a map				
Ability to determine location from a map				
Ability to determine identity from a map				

Figure 1.—Relationship between attack and support skills in map-reading.

SUPPORT SKILLS ⟋ ATTACK SKILLS	Ability to create an orientation relationship	Ability to create a miniaturization relationship	Ability to create a projection relationship	Ability to create a symbolization relationship
Ability to map determinations of direction				
Ability to map determinations of distance				
Ability to map determinations of location				
Ability to map determinations of identity				

Figure 2.—Relationship between attack and support skills in map-making.

charted items to globes has a special character. For a globe's surface to be oriented in "locking position," for example, the globe itself must be situated so that its axis is in the same plane as, and parallel to, the earth's axis. As a further example, the projection relationship between a globe's surface and the territory that it represents is peculiar in that it is one of simple correspondence, point for point and line for line.

As a spherical body—leaving the surface image out of account—a globe is helpful in solving problems pertaining to movements of the earth. The old questions—Which way? How far? Where? What?—reappear in this connection. Now, however, they express planetary problems rather than territorial problems.

To sum up, globes have a double significance for an instructional program. Their surface images call for the application of map skills. Their spherical bodies, as models that differ from maps, demand abilities that are similar to map skills, yet deserve a designation of their own, as globe skills.

Before and After

This paper proposes an interpretation of map instruction in which the two recognized activities of the learner are map-reading and map-making. To complete the interpretation, two further operations must be acknowledged.

The first of these remaining activities is observation, and the second, interpretation; or to return to the language of the computer, the first is data collection, and the second, data analysis. In computer terminology, map-making is data storage, and map-reading data retrieval. The full data processing sequence, in standard order, is collection, storage, retrieval, and analysis. In practice, this order does not always apply.

The teacher should allow ample scope for the two activities that are linked with map-making and map-reading in the data-processing chain. The opening activity—data collection—should be given a generous opportunity for development, not only because it feeds directly into the two map operations, but also because it promotes an awareness of environment, a desirable end in itself.

The closing activity—data analysis—should receive an emphasis at least equal to that accorded data collection. The teacher must realize that this is the link in data processing that is more demanding, and potentially more rewarding, than any other. It is the phase that often involves a comparison of information from two or more maps, and that rests on logical inference. Here the learner asks why, as in the question, "Why is my school located where it is?"

He is called on to explain the data that, at an earlier stage, he put into or took from a map. This is the activity that makes the learning of map skills intellectually worthwhile.

DEVELOPING SENSITIVITY AND
CONCERN IN CHILDREN *

Vincent R. Rogers

A few years ago Norman Cousins, writing on the editorial pages of the *Saturday Review,* described an incident he had recently observed at a railroad station in suburban Stamford, Connecticut:

> . . . It was Sunday evening, at about ten p.m. Some two dozen persons, among them several young men in uniform, were waiting for the express to New York.
> The door to the waiting room flew open. A woman, shrieking hysterically, burst into the room. She was pursued by a man just a few steps behind her. The woman screamed that the man was trying to kill her and cried out for the people to save her. I was standing nearest the door. The woman grabbed me, still shrieking. I tried to protect her behind me. The man tried to sweep me aside to get at her. He rushed at me, caught the woman's wrist with one hand, tore her loose and pulled her through the doorway. The woman fell to the ground and was dragged by the wrist just outside the waiting room. I tried to free her wrist. The man broke off, grabbed the woman's pocketbook, and fled on foot.
> We carried the woman inside the waiting room, sat her down, then telephoned the police. The woman's eye was badly cut; she was moaning. I looked around the room. Except for three or four persons who now came up to her, people in the room seemed unconcerned. The young men in uniform were still standing in the same place, chatting among themselves as before. I am not sure which was greater, the shock of the attack that had just occurred or the shock caused by the apparent detachment and unconcern of the other people, especially the men in uniform. . . .

The shocking thing, the truly appalling thing about the incident was not that violence had taken place; the sheer weight of population statistics assures us that a number of sick, maladjusted, vicious individuals will be among us for at least the predictable future. The

Vincent R. Rogers is Professor of Education and Chairman of the Department of Elementary Education at the University of Connecticut, Storrs.

* Reprinted from *Social Education* 31:299–302, 1967, with permission of the National Council for the Social Studies and Vincent R. Rogers.

real tragedy lay rather in the indifference, the lack of concern shown by the supposedly "healthy," "normal" individuals who coolly watched the incident with a detached complacency.

To Cousins, the incident was one more dramatic illustration of a frightening lack of man's sensitivity to the feelings, problems, and concerns of his fellow man. In his words, "What is happening, I believe, is that the natural reactions of the individual against violence are being blunted. The individual is being desensitized. . . . He is becoming casual about brutality. . . ."

History is, of course, filled with illustrations of man's inhumanity to man; today's "civilization" has no monopoly on cruelty. On the other hand, there is a discouraging lack of evidence that might link technological progress, increased literacy rates, and more efficient means of communication with an *increase* in man's sensitivity and concern. On the contrary, the willful murder of 6,000,000 human beings that has forced us to create the word "genocide" is surely an example of human bestiality unparalleled in human history. We are not at all certain, then, whether or not man is in fact becoming less sensitive to his fellow creatures or perhaps simply maintaining the discouraging level of insensitivity that history so eloquently describes. In any event, as populations increase, as society becomes more crowded and more complex, as man develops more and more deadly ways of dealing with human conflict, the need for a sincere concern for our fellow man is quite obviously increased.

It is perhaps ironic that our social scientists have concentrated for so many years on a study of the most negative types of human beings. As Pitirim Sorokin puts it, we have been cultivating "an ever increasing study of crime and criminals; of insanity and the insane; of sex perversion and perverts; of hypocrisy and hypocrites . . . the criminal has been researched incomparably more than the saint or altruist . . . the result is that our social science knows little about positive types of persons, their conduct and relationships."

Yet through the techniques of modern social science, man is now able (if he is also willing) to launch a concerted effort to develop a better understanding of Sorokin's "positive type"; what made him that way—and (most importantly) how such positive traits can be developed in others.

Empathy, Sensitivity, Sympathy, Altruism, and the Positive Type

One finds considerable confusion and overlap among researchers concerning the use of the terms "sympathy" and "altruism." One is likely to find little distinction drawn between them, and, therefore, an attempt at clarification seems in order.

Empathy, for example, is defined by Carter Goode in the *Dictionary of Education* as a state "in which the individual identifies himself with another individual or group." English and English in the *Dictionary of Psychological Terms* refer to empathy as the *"apprehension* of the state of mind of another person." One who is empathic, then, perceives another's situation and intellectually understands it. He does not necessarily share another's emotion; neither does he necessarily follow his perception with overt action.

Sensitivity is defined also as a capacity to perceive, or to perceive *and* interpret, the behavior of others. The sensitive individual, like the empathetic individual, is "aware" but does not necessarily follow his awareness with action.

Sympathy, according to Goode involves the sharing to some degree of feelings similar in kind to those of the individuals under observation. English and English also describe sympathy as a "feeling with another person" i.e., feeling his joy, sorrow, etc. Again we note the lack of any commitment to *action.* Murphy in her monumental study of sympathy in preschool children, demonstrates this experimentally as follows: Children are shown a rat in a cage. They are told he is hungry. They are allowed to observe the rat for a time. They are then asked if they would like to feed (i.e., "help") the rat. The children all expressed a desire to do so. Then they were told that they could either feed the rat or take a little toy car; they could not, however, do both. Sixteen of 18 children took the car, although all had expressed feelings of sympathy and concern for the rat.

Altruism is considered by Goode to be "the ultimate obligation of each man to achieve a selfless devotion to others." English and English see it as the "pursuit of the good of others." They also add that altruism exists whether motivated by self-interest, selfless devotion to society or by disinterested duty. Altruism, then, implies a willingness to act once one has become *aware* of the needs of others. The existence of heightened abilities to *be* aware or perceptive of the needs of others is not stated as a condition of altruism, however. In other words, one might be a rather imperceptive, insensitive individual and yet still be described as an altruist.

It seems clear, then, that the "positive type" described earlier by Sorokin calls for an eclectic term that involves elements of all of the commonly used concepts described above. Murphy suggests that "perhaps a more general term suggesting *outgoing response* or freedom from inhibition might be more appropriate." Piaget, however, cautions us that "to be sensitive alone is not to be good." For the purpose of this paper, then, we shall define Sorokin's "positive type" as *an unusually sensitive individual who possesses an active concern for the well-being of others.*

What Does Research Tell Us about the Nature of Sensitivity and Concern?

The literature dealing with the qualities and characteristics described above is exceedingly "thin" from a quantitative point of view; especially if one compares it with the voluminous literature dealing (for example) with "aggressiveness." The scattered reports that this investigator was able to uncover do, however, provide enough data to enable us to draw some tentative conclusions concerning a variety of questions. For example, neither Murphy, in her study of sympathy among preschoolers, nor Ruderman, in her study of empathy among nine- to 12-year-olds found any clear-cut evidence of sex differences or relationships. Boys and girls responded similarly in both studies, although there was evidence of uneven growth spurts at various ages.

The research dealing with the relationship between the "positive type" and intelligence is less clear. Both Sorokin and Chassell found no relationship between intelligence and morality, criminality, or altruism. Ruderman, Turner, and Murphy, in their studies of empathy, altruism, and sympathy found intelligence to be an important but not sufficient condition, i.e., one needs *more* than intelligence. Intelligence seems necessary as a means of cognitive awareness of one's social and/or emotional environment which then provides at least the possibilities for altruistic behavior.

Murphy reports examples of perceptive-altruistic behavior in very young children and also notes an increase in the number of sympathetic responses with age (31–48 months). Ruderman's research supports this conclusion, but she notes wide individual differences. Sorokin, considering the more general problem of when one acquires altruistic behavior patterns, concludes that no one age level is dominant, i.e., people may become altruistic at any stage in their lives, depending upon a variety of circumstances.

While Piaget's research indicates that instinctive or innate tendencies toward vindictiveness *and* compassion exist in human beings, he concludes that the child's total environment—his culture— is far more important in determining altruism than is heredity. Both Sorokin and Turner support this conclusion, although we know little about the specific ways in which culture encourages or discourages the growth of sympathetic-altruistic characteristics. Perhaps cross-cultural investigations such as those conducted by Clark, Eaton, Weil, and Kaplow of the Hutterites will eventually shed considerably more light on this question. Scattered data suggest that Mennonite and Hutterite communities in the United States, for example, yield the lowest quotas (or none!) of delinquents, criminals, and mentally sick individuals. Both groups exist in an environment that is pervaded with "altruistic love" in its daily behavioral patterns to a far greater extent than in typical American communities. Murphy suggests that much information concerning the ways in which altruistic—sympathetic behavior is developed may be obtained from the study of pacifist groups such as the Eskimos or Zuni.

Research related to the development of altruistic behavior through affiliation with various religious groups is scattered and inconclusive. Hartshorne and May's classic *Studies in Deceit* certainly indicates that high attendance at Sunday School, for example, does not induce a superior brand of morality in a general sense. More specifically, Friedricks concludes that altruistic behavior may be positively related to theistic attitudes, but not to mere attendance at public worship. Murphy feels that there is a possibility that "Christian patterns of kindness" increase sympathetic responses in children, but the degree of the relationship is unclear.

There is no question about the importance of the contribution of parents and the immediate family to the development of the "positive type." Studies by Isaacs and Sorokin indicate that the immediate family has had a key influence on "altruistic individuals." On the other hand, Sorokin's study of "American Good Neighbors" indicates that this group ascribes their "good neighborliness" only partially to the family; religion, formal education, and books are also listed as significant influences. Turner, while generally supporting Sorokin's conclusions, also points out that forces within our culture and society do *not* effectively foster altruism. Ruderman further complicates the picture by concluding that "empathetic ability" is related inversely to size of family, i.e., children from large families tend to be less empathetic.

One of the most interesting and, perhaps for our time, most significant insights gained from researching the development of altruism in children and adults concerns the degree to which "warm feelings" develop (or fail to develop) towards individuals further and further away from the immediate family community or national group of the subject. Sorokin asked University of Minnesota students in a sociology class to contribute to three important "causes." The first had to do with obtaining a computing machine for the class itself; the second concerned a request for help for three "impoverished" graduate students at the University of Minnesota; the third request sought "relief" for Chinese and Russian students who were dying of starvation. Although the graduate students' and the foreign students' pitiful situations were described in a most realistic manner, the class chose to contribute a far greater amount to its own "cause." Regardless of the importance or significance of the cause in terms of human values, the "closest" cause got the most money. Sorokin's study of "American Good Neighbors" also supports this conclusion, as does his study of Harvard and Radcliffe students. Wright and Rogers and Long, on the other hand, found this tendency was reversed in their studies of elementary school children's reactions to somewhat similar-situations.

A final area of investigation concerns the degree to which altruistic-sympathetic characteristics may dominate a child's personality or, conversely, the degree to which characteristics such as selfishness, cruelty, and self-gratification may dominate. That is, to what extent does a child become one or the other? How much of a "mixture" of types can he be? Havighurst and Peck defined five types of "character" ranging from the "Amoral," "Expedient," and "Conforming" types to the "Irrational-Conscientious," and "Rational-Altruistic" types. They conclude that "only rarely would an individual operate clearly and exclusively as one type." However, one type will "predominate" in the character of an individual. Murphy supports this view, reporting that while children do vary from situation to situation, they vary *within a limited range of responses* . . . it takes a most extreme attack on one child's status to elicit unsympathetic responses from her . . . they are more easily elicited from another."

Questions, Hypotheses, and Research Gaps

As one sits back and views the research in this area with some sort of perspective, a number of fascinating research possibilities come to mind; possibilities complex enough, incidentally, to keep the social scientists busily occupied for generations yet to come. One wonders, for example, about questions like these:

Since pre-school girls and boys tend to respond in a somewhat similar manner on various tests of social sensitivity, can we assume that this can be explained by the fact that our masculine dominant culture has not yet had time to make a lasting impression? What happens as these children grow older? Do boys react less sensitively than girls? If so, do boys' *perceptions* stay the same while their *overt* responses go down?

Does the tendency to give both aggressive and sympathetic responses change as the child grows older? Do his responses tend to polarize?

Arthur Jersild has said that, "Any painful occurrence that befalls someone else has meaning for him insofar as he has had the same or somewhat similar experience." One wonders then about feelings of sympathy and sensitivity among crippled, hospitalized children. Do they tend to be more sensitive to the problems of others?

Do children in *all* cultures represent a range of sympathetic and aggressive behavior, or do they only display behavior that is present among adults? The Arapesh, for example, are part of an unusually gentle culture. Would Arapesh children respond differently in some of the testing situations described above?

To what extent is social sensitivity a part of one's *total* personality? An individual may be a loving father to his children and miserable to his business associates; one may be concerned about the over-all problems of nuclear fallout and relatively insensitive to the problems of one's neighbor.

What is the effect of minority group status on the development of sensitivity in children? Are they more or less so? Might they behave gently and sympathetically toward other members of their "in" group, while behaving quite insensitively to others?

What, if any, is the effect of our more complex, relatively urban way of life on one's feelings of sensitivity? Would children living in comparatively rural environments react differently on various tests of social sensitivity than would children living in a more complex and personal urban environment?

To what extent might altruistic "models" or "heroes" affect the growth of such characteristics in children? What other ways might there be to encourage the development of Sorokin's "positive type"?

George Bernard Shaw once wrote that, "The worst sin toward our fellow-creatures is not to hate them but to be indifferent to them; that is the essence of inhumanity." While we fully recognize the complexity of the problem, we cannot help but hope that researchers will make increasing efforts to probe more deeply the qualities of goodness that exist in man.

BIBLIOGRAPHY

C. F. Chassell, *The Relationship Between Morality and Intellect.* New York: Teachers College Press, 1935.

B. W. Clark, "The Hutterian Communities." *Journal of Political Economy* *32*:357–374, 1924.

J. W. Eaton, R. J. Weil, and B. Kaplow, "The Hutterite Mental Health Studies." *Mennonite Quarterly Review*, January, 1951.

R. W. Friedricks, "An Exploratory Study of Altruism." Unpublished doctoral dissertation, The University of Wisconsin, 1957.

H. Hartshorne and M. A. May, *Studies in Deceit.* New York: Macmillan, 1929.

R. J. Havighurst and R. F. Peck, *The Psychology of Character Development.* New York: Wiley, 1960.

Susan Isaacs, *Social Development in Young Children.* New York: Harcourt, Brace & Company, 1937.

Lois B. Murphy, *Social Behavior and Child Personality, An Exploratory Study of Some Roots of Sympathy.* New York: Columbia University Press, 1937.

Jean Piaget, *The Moral Judgment of the Child.* New York: Harcourt, Brace & Company, 1932.

Vincent R. Rogers and Elizabeth Long, "An Exploratory Study of the Development of Social Sensitivity in Elementary School Children." *The Journal of Educational Research 59*:9, 1966.

Lilyan D. Ruderman, "An Exploration of Empathic Ability in Children and Its Relationship to Several Variables." Unpublished doctoral dissertation, Columbia University, 1961.

Pitirim A. Sorokin, *Altruistic Love.* Boston: Beacon Press, 1950, p. 5.

W. D. Turner, "Altruism and its Measurement in Children." *Journal of Abnormal and Social Psychology 43*, 1948.

Beatrice A. Wright, "Altruism in Children and the Perceived Conduct of Others." *Journal of Abnormal and Social Psychology 37*:218–233, 1942.

THE CULTURAL REGION—
FRAMEWORK FOR TEACHING
WORLD GEOGRAPHY *

William B. Conroy

In organizing his course and in selecting a textbook, the teacher of world geography may often overlook a vital criterion. This criterion involves the consideration of how best to divide the earth's surface into major regions, which will serve as a framework within which to develop significant generalizations about the world's peoples, their cultures, and their environments.

Geographers have devised many types of regions—climatic, landform, and agricultural to cite a few. Regardless of their differing nomenclature, arising from the fact that they summarize different phenomena on the earth's surface, any type of region [1] may be

---

William B. Conroy is Associate Professor of Curriculum and Instruction at The University of Texas, Austin.

* Reprinted from *The Social Studies 57*:71, 74–75, 1966, with permission of the McKinley Publishing Co. and William B. Conroy.

[1] Reference here is only to *uniform* as opposed to *nodal* regions. See Derwent Whittlesey, "The Regional Concept and the Regional Method," *American Geography, Inventory and Prospect*, Preston E. James and Clarence F. Jones, eds. Syracuse, N. Y.: University Press, 1954, pp. 36–37.

defined as a part of the earth's surface within which there is a substantial degree of homogeneity due to certain common characteristics within its borders, characteristics which differ from those of neighboring regions. These identifying characteristics are usually more discernible near the center of the region, and often tend to blend in with the characteristics of contiguous regions, effecting a zone of transition rather than a sharp boundary between them.

What kind of region is the most suitable for serving as a framework for the world geography course in the secondary school? The fact that this course is a part of the *social* studies, rather than the physical sciences, suggests that the selection of any type of physical region would be inappropriate for containing the kinds of ideas and generalizations that teachers are most interested in conveying to their students.[2] Of the remaining types available, the *cultural* region is the best for two reasons:

1. A primary objective of world geography is the development of cultural empathy, that is, a sympathetic understanding of cultures [3] other than the students' own. World cultural regions provide the most logical framework within which to teach generalizations and supporting descriptive details about different world cultures. Moreover, use of another type of regional framework may result in the students' making incorrect generalizations, intentionally or unintentionally, about an area. For example, use of the traditional continental framework may cause a student to make generalizations about all the people of Africa, when they are applicable only to the tribal groups of the central part of the continent.

2. In the world geography course, a variety of phenomena is considered—crops, industries, religions, governments, cities, railroads, languages, customs, people and many more. The cultural region is the most inclusive, cohesive device for organizing all this material.

It is not sufficient to decide that the type of region to be used is the cultural one. To be meaningful to both student and teacher, the earth's surface should be divided into cultural regions in such a way that the same criteria are used to identify each. Often, in textbooks at both the secondary and college level, authors are not consistent in the criteria they use to identify the uniqueness of each of their regions. In the same text, the unifying characteristic of

---

[2] Strictly speaking, physical geography should be taught not as an end in itself, but to give meaning to human or cultural geography.

[3] The term *culture* is used here in the general sense, meaning the entire way of life exhibited by a people.

one region might be a language; for a second, location around a particular water body, such as the Mediterranean; and for a third, a low level of economic development.

Because the cultural characteristics of the earth's peoples are not neatly packaged off into mutually exclusive areas, but are often exceedingly complex and interwoven, it is understandable indeed that textbook writers have difficulty in being consistent in their identification of cultural regions. It is doubtful that any perfect system can be devised. However, examination of past efforts of cultural anthropologists and geographers suggests that the following generic elements might be used as criteria for delimiting a major world cultural region:

1. A distinctive religion and/or philosophical system:
2. A distinctive social system.
3. A distinctive economic system.
4. A distinctive political system.
5. A dominant language—used in literature, law, the arts and religion.

Application of these criteria results in a reasonably logical division of the world into cultural regions. Obviously, important exceptions to generalizations arrived at through application of these criteria are present in all the regions and should be pointed out by the teacher.

The following list of cultural regions is suggested as being the most consistent with the criteria listed above,* even though all five generic elements are not present in some cases:

1. Western Europe, including all European nations outside of the Iron Curtain
2. Anglo-America (Neo-European Region 1)
3. Latin America (Neo-European Region 2)
4. South Africa (Neo-European Region 3)
5. Australia and New Zealand (Neo-European Region 4)
6. Soviet Union and Satellites
7. Oriental Complex—including the following distinct regions:
   a. India
   b. China (including North Korea and Taiwan)
   c. Japan (including South Korea)
   d. Southeast Asia (including Indonesia and the Philippines)

---

* Arrangement of the list does not necessarily indicate desirable teaching order.

8. Middle East, including the countries of North Africa and Southwest Asia in which Islam is the predominant religion.
9. Pacific Islands and Island Groups, excluding certain islands included in one of the above regions.
10. Central Africa

In the case of Western Europe, its religious and philosophical system grew out of the Graeco-Roman-Christian tradition. One distinctive characteristic of its social system is its large middle class. Its economic system has been capitalistic with a trend towards becoming more socialistic in the past quarter century. Its economy is predominantly commercial, rather than one of subsistence, with substantial activity in trade, industry and agriculture. Its political system is essentially democratic. There is no one dominant language, but two language groups—the Romance and the Germanic—each dominant in a particular part of the region. Elements of both are found in the English language.

The Neo-European cultural regions are outgrowths of Western Europe and thus have characteristics closely akin to it. However, they deserve to be treated as separate cultural entities because they are distinct, noncontiguous areal blocs and because contact with native cultures and physical environments in these areas effected differing modifications to the original Western European culture. In North America and Australia, the native culture was almost exterminated. In many areas of Latin America, contact between native and European cultures resulted in some acculturation.* In South Africa, the native culture remained intact but was subjugated to that of Europe. The Neo-European cultural regions are also modified by the fact that each drew its immigrants from a particular part or country of Western Europe, more than any other part.

The Soviet Union and its satellites are considered to be a distinct cultural region because of the dominance of the Soviet communist system—economically, politically, and socially in these countries.

The Oriental Complex actually contains several distinct cultural regions within it but because of some cultural borrowing (as in the case of Buddhism), and because of mutual problems such as population pressure, some justification may be found for the common practice of grouping them together. However, comprehensive consideration should be given to each of the regions within the complex. Southeast Asia, the fourth region listed under the Oriental Complex, is generally regarded as a "shatter belt" con-

---

* A process of intercultural borrowing, resulting in new and blended patterns.

taining elements of several other regions, elements which are not all uniform in importance throughout the area.

The Middle Eastern cultural region is dominated by Islam, and in a large segment by the Arabic (Hamitic-Semitic) language. It is a region where most of the people are supported by a subsistence level agricultural economy which is hampered by a moisture deficit.

The inhabitants of the last two regions—the Pacific Islands and Central Africa—are distinct because they are generally regarded as primitive when the above criteria are applied to their cultures.

Division of the world into major cultural regions has an added advantage. It highlights areas of cultural contact—the borders of the regions. These borders are areas where considerable friction often develops between cultural systems. The most obvious case is the Iron Curtain in Europe. Also, the dynamic quality of a cultural system can be seen by the expansion of its borders at the expense of a neighboring region. Thus, the boundary of the Islamic world, even today, moves south into Central Africa.

Conclusion

Organization of the world geography course by cultural regions, identified by the consistent application of appropriate criteria, will result in the student's developing an appropriate mental frame of reference for learning generalizations and supporting descriptive detail about the world's peoples. It follows that the teacher of world geography should select a textbook whose division of the earth's surface most closely coincides with the ten cultural regions described above, or with whatever he feels the best regionalization of the world to be.

THE TAXONOMY: GUIDE TO
DIFFERENTIATED INSTRUCTION *

John Jarolimek

Discussions of differentiated instruction in the social studies ordinarily focus on variations to be made in learning activities that the pupil is expected to perform. Most frequently the recommendations have to do with variations in reading requirements or variations in work-study activities. The teacher is advised to use more difficult reading material with the more capable pupil than with the less able one. Similarly in the case of work-study activities, the suggestion is made that the able pupil be directed toward activities that involve more independent research, more reading and elaborative thinking than his slower-learning classmate. In general, these recommendations are sound ones; but they are apt to be something less than adequate unless, in addition, careful consideration is given to the complexity of the intellectual tasks with which each of the pupils is going to concern himself.

Varying the difficulty of intellectual tasks relating to a social studies unit is a procedure that seems to have received less attention from teachers than it deserves. The hope is that if pupils are placed in reading materials of varying difficulty and are involved in varying types of instructional activities, this will, in itself, result in some differentiation of instruction with respect to complexity of learnings. No doubt this occurs to some extent. However, variations in complexity should be a deliberate and planned part of the teaching plan rather than be allowed to come about by a happy accident. In order to build such diversity in conceptual complexity into the program, one needs to begin with instructional objectives. The procedure under consideration here would hold general objectives constant, but would vary specific objectives in terms of the capabilities of individual pupils.

In an effort to plan deliberately for differentiated instruction in terms of the complexity of intellectual operations, the teacher may find Bloom's *Taxonomy of Educational Objectives, Handbook I: Cognitive Domain* [1] to be a helpful model. The *Taxonomy* classifies

---

John Jarolimek is Professor of Education at the University of Washington, Seattle.

* Reprinted from *Social Education* 26:445–447, 1962, with permission of the National Council for the Social Studies and John Jarolimek.

[1] Benjamin S. Bloom *et al. Taxonomy of Educational Objectives, Handbook I: Cognitive Domain.* New York: Longmans, Green and Company, 1956.

various types of educational objectives into six groups or categories as follows:

1. Knowledge
2. Comprehension
3. Application
4. Analysis
5. Synthesis
6. Evaluation

These are ordered in terms of an hierarchy representing an increasingly complex set of cognitive relationships as one moves from category one to category six. Behaviors in each succeeding category are to some extent dependent on an understanding of related objectives in a prior category. Sub-heads of each of the six categories indicate that they, too, are ordered from simple relationships to complex ones. Hence, children in the primary grades need not concern themselves solely with objectives in the *Knowledge* category but may make applications, analyses, and evaluations providing these are kept simple and clearly within the realm of direct experience.

It is perhaps true that the bulk of elementary social studies instruction concerns itself with objectives represented in category one—*Knowledge*. This includes knowledge of specifics, facts, terminology, events, etc. To a degree, an emphasis on knowledge is inevitable at early levels because pupils are rapidly building their cognitive structure. However, the *Knowledge* category is itself spread along a continuum ranging from a knowledge of specifics to a knowledge of universals and abstractions in a field. Pupils of varying abilities might be expected to deal with different specific objectives in the *Knowledge* category. Instruction is limiting and narrow when all pupils deal with *Knowledge* objectives pertaining only to specifics, facts, terminology, and events.

The teacher must, of course, be concerned with objectives in category one—*Knowledge*—because it is fundamental to all of the others. Particularly important would be the development of a knowledge of the terminology of the social studies. Without a grasp of the vocabulary, the pupil is unable to consider problems in the social studies thoughtfully. Knowledge of specific facts is important, too, not as an end in itself but because such specifics are prerequisite to the achievement of more complex intellectual objectives. Objectives in this category are relatively easy to teach and evaluate because they depend almost entirely upon recall of information. They have traditionally been a part of the social studies curriculum in most schools and consequently are familiar to teachers. While they are important, at the same time this does not give the teacher license to teach them in ways that are educationally and psychologically unsound.

In addition to knowledge of specifics, one finds in this category two other types of knowledge objectives. The first of these—"knowledge of ways and means of dealing with specifics"—would seem to have especial significance for the social studies. Included would be such knowledge of conventions as might be called for in the understanding of procedures in various affairs of citizenship—how a bill becomes a law, how government officials are elected, how laws are enforced, and so on. It deals, too, with trends and sequences such as knowledge of events that led up to more important events, steps in the production of goods, or the chronology associated with historical developments. The third large subhead entitled "knowledge of the universals and abstractions in a field" constitutes the highest order of the *Knowledge* category. In the social studies it would call for a knowledge of major generalizations relating to the social sciences as these are forged out of the varied experiences of pupils. An example of such a generalization would be "Man's utilization of natural resources is related to his desires and his level of technology."

The second large category—*Comprehension*— requires somewhat more complex intellectual activity than recall, as is the case in the *Knowledge* category. "Translation" and "Interpretation" are the two facets of *Comprehension* most appropriate for elementary social studies. Data gathering brings the pupil into contact with a great variety of source materials. He uses maps, charts, graphs, encyclopedias, atlases, and others. Data so abstracted must be translated into usable form for the purpose of problem solving. Literary material, when used, requires both translation and interpretation. Much of the social studies reading material is presented in highly condensed form and has within it many possibilities for interpretation and extrapolation. If pupils are to avoid making "bookish" reports, for example, they need to be able to make a translation of the material into their own everyday language. Social studies programs could be greatly enriched, especially for the capable pupil, by directing greater attention to objectives that fall into this category—translation, interpretation, and extrapolation.

The third category is called *Application*. It means essentially that the pupil is able to use what he learns; that he can bring his knowledge to bear upon the solution of problems. Numerous authors have called attention to the need for pupils to apply what they learn. Many interesting and stimulating experiences for children have resulted in situations where imaginative teachers have provided opportunities for children to apply what they have learned to life about them. Applications of learning may be represented by some classroom activity such as dramatic play, a construction, or a report given to the class; or they may include a service project in conservation, school government, or community service. Applications need not manifest themselves in overt behavior; applications may be made wholly at the intellectual level. The pupil may, for example, apply and use knowledge previously gained in thinking creatively about new problems or situations. Perhaps most of the applications that are made are of the intellectual type.

Categories four and five—*Analysis* and *Synthesis*—represent high-order intellectual processes. In the case of *Analysis*, the pupil must delve into the subject to a sufficient depth to perceive its component elements, relationships, or organizational principles. Such procedure enhances the development of concepts in depth, for the pupil is led to ever finer discriminations in what is relevant and what is irrelevant with reference to topics under study. Problems in the social studies oftentimes seem deceptively simple because an inadequate analysis is made of factors relating to them. It is only when one explores a problem in depth and makes a careful analysis of fundamental elements, relationships, or organizational principles that he appreciates the complexity of it. Many elementary pupils are ready for the stimulation that such analyses could provide.

While *Analysis* calls for the isolation of relevant data, *Synthesis* requires the bringing together of related elements and reorganizing them into new cognitive structures. In the *Taxonomy, Synthesis* is further described as "the production of a plan or proposed set of operations," or the "derivation of a set of abstract relations." For elementary social studies, *Synthesis* can be represented by the reporting of research that a pupil has conducted over a period of time. The reporting of work done on "Pupil Specialties" would be a case in point. Bright pupils find this to be an especially challenging and interesting learning experience. A capable fifth- or sixth-grade child can, through accumulated research, present an amazingly well-prepared synthesis if he has proper guidance from his teacher.

The final category—*Evaluation*—concerns itself with judgments. It assumes a considerable knowledge of the topic on the part of the pupil in order to make such judgments. To some extent it demands the use of learnings that are represented in all of the other categories. Judgments, according to the *Taxonomy*, are of two types —those based on internal evidence and those based on external criteria. Internal evidence would constitute evaluation made on the basis of clearly recognized standards with respect to internal consistency, organization, or structure. For example, a pupil looks at a map and must decide whether or not it is a correct and honest representation—rivers cannot be shown to run toward higher elevations; cities cannot be placed across rivers; colors used on the map must be consistent with those in the key, and so on. Charts, graphic material, or written reports should not contain conflicting data. A mural showing the life of the Woodland Indians should not show an Indian weaving a Navajo blanket. Judgments of this type are not especially difficult to make when one is thoroughly familiar with the material and knows what standards to apply. Judgments in terms of external criteria probably involve a level of criticism too complex and much too involved to be handled by elementary-school-age children.

It is apparent that the *Taxonomy* has much to recommend its use as a model in planning for differentiated instruction in elementary social studies. The teacher would have to become thoroughly familiar with it and with the types of objectives that might be placed in each of the categories. Perhaps the teacher would find it helpful to prepare the various categories in chart form, and in planning a unit, list possible objectives in the various categories. Use of the *Taxonomy* may also result in objectives stated more clearly in behavioral terms, as has been suggested by some authors.[2] Thus, with a knowledge of the capabilities of individual members of his class, the teacher could move pupils in the direction of those objectives that are best suited to their abilities. This would insure that all categories had been considered and that ideas would be dealt with at varying levels of difficulty.

Thus as the teacher plans his unit, he makes a careful analysis of the topic to be studied. Then he identifies specific, attainable objectives that could be classified in several categories included in the *Taxonomy*. In accordance with this knowledge and a knowledge of the pupil he teaches, he plans appropriate learning activities that make the attainment of those objectives possible. Combining this procedure with other generally accepted practices for individualizing instruction, the teacher would present his class with a highly diversified and stimulating attack on the study of problems in the elementary social studies. Certainly the *Taxonomy* deserves further

---

[2] Dale P. Scannell and Walter R. Stellwagen, "Teaching and Testing for Degrees of Understanding." *California Journal for Instructional Improvement* 3:1, 13, 1960.

investigation not only in terms of its usefulness in curriculum improvement but also as a guide to the teacher in differentiating instruction.

VALUE TEACHING IN THE MIDDLE AND UPPER GRADES: A RATIONALE FOR TEACHING BUT NOT TRANSMITTING VALUES *

Melvin Ezer

"All education, we may assume, is aimed at the transmission of values of our culture, and the development of socially acceptable attitudes [and behavior] towards problems and conflicts." [1]

"Rubbish! Not only rubbish, but . . . repulsive," exclaims Michael Scriven.[2] The reason for Scriven's rejection of this educational objective is that in the name of morality, immoral behavior is advocated. The author of this paper is in agreement with Scriven's position as it relates to value teaching in the middle and upper grades of the elementary school, and an alternative proposal for teaching values in these grades will be presented.

If there is concern with ethics, as expressed in the opening quote, then a fundamental proposition in ethics asserts that the individual has the right to determine for himself what is right or wrong concerning the basic issues of conduct. It then becomes the responsibility if not the duty of the public schools in a democratic society to inform the pupil of the alternatives available to him, to describe the modes and consequences of his behavior, and to teach him the skills that are necessary to evaluate these alternatives. The teaching of values does not give the teacher the right to force his solutions

---

Melvin Ezer is Professor of Education at Arizona State University, Tempe.

* Reprinted from *Social Education 31*:39–40 ff., 1967, with permission of the National Council for the Social Studies and Melvin Ezer.

[1] Preston E. James. "Geography." *The Social Studies and the Social Sciences.* Sponsored by the American Council of Learned Societies and the National Council for the Social Studies. New York: Harcourt, Brace & World, Inc., 1962, p. 42.

[2] Michael Scriven. "The Structure of the Social Studies." *In* G. W. Ford and Lawrence Pugno, eds. *The Structure of Knowledge and the Curriculum.* Chicago: Rand McNally & Company, 1964, p. 101.

on the children he teaches, except in so far as the information given to the children persuades them to accept his views. Underlying this position of value teaching are the assumptions that value disputes can be settled by rational means and that children in the middle and upper grades of the elementary school are capable of making their own value judgments by use of the intellect.[3]

It thus becomes obvious that it is not the teacher's responsibility to tell children what is right or wrong, but rather it is the responsibility of the teacher to raise value questions and to discuss these within the restrictions of evidence, the rules of logic, and the use of reason. The children should be given opportunities to investigate and discuss value questions under the teacher's guidance, and then the children should be allowed to make up their own minds about these vital matters without being unduly influenced by their teachers.[4]

It is at this point that the question of teacher bias is usually raised; that is, if a teacher is already committed to a value position (much in the way this author has particular enthusiasm for his view regarding the teaching of values to children) is it then possible for him to present other points of view in an objective and effective manner? The answer to this query is that children can and perhaps should be taught values by teachers who have taken a position on a particular problem or issue, because it is not only possible but quite probable that many teachers who hold particular views can present other views fully and fairly. In addition, there should be the opportunity for pupils, and supporters of other views, to make their presentations with equal zeal.[5]

Concomitant with the responsibility of presenting various points of view on value questions is the responsibility of the middle and upper grade teacher to teach children to become proficient in such skills as clarifying issues, verifying information on which values are based, and analyzing the logic inherent in the solution of problems. The teaching and attainment of these skills is crucial to the method of presenting values proposed herein.

Let us now take a value question and illustrate the manner in which it can be presented to children utilizing the format that has been suggested. Let us examine the problem presented when a decision regarding the abrogation of free speech is in question, a value that is jealously guarded. The problem had arisen in the

---

[3] *Ibid.*

[4] Nancy W. Bauer, ed. *Revolution and Reaction: The Impact of the New Social Studies.* Bloomfield Hills, Mich.: Cranbrook Press, pp. 75–76, 1966.

[5] Scriven, *op. cit.*, p. 102.

midst of an explosive situation that occurred in a suburb of Chicago in August, 1966, when tensions resulting from Civil Rights demonstrations were at their highest. George Rockwell, the self-proclaimed leader of the American Nazi movement, applied for permission to schedule a rally and speech in this community. These events could have led to rioting, destruction of property, and even the loss of life. The problem that faced the authorities and that could have been presented to an elementary school class was whether Rockwell should have been prevented from speaking.

An approach that is commonly utilized in this type of problem situation, if it is discussed at all, is for the teacher to ask the children what decision they would make if they were the authorities. In many classrooms the teachers would inform the children what the correct or right decision is or ought to be. Parenthetically, it is highly questionable whether the teacher's solution is more valid than the children's since his view may have no better factual or analytic basis than the children he is teaching. In most instances it is at these junctures that the discussion of the value question ends.

The author has stated previously that all possible solutions should be presented; in this instance, the children's, the teacher's, that of newspaper editorials, radio and television commentators, civic authorities, and so forth. These viewpoints must be examined using the skills and criteria described earlier. Additional questions must be raised and discussed—such questions as the importance of the value of free speech as compared with the value of life and property. What would the consequences be to our society if we abandoned one or both? What would be the logical consequences for other values in our society if we abandoned the right to speak when speaking threatens life or property? Who is to decide and upon what basis when speech threatens life and property? What relief for wrong decisions is available? [6]

Only after these discussions and explorations have taken place should the decisions be made, and then the children should be allowed to provide their own answers and solutions to the problem as individuals. The goal of educational process described above is to have children arrive at value decisions through rational means. It is also the attempt to develop the cognitive skills that are essential in the study of value problems.

Moral reasoning and the moral behavior it indicates should be taught and taught about, if for no other reason than it is immoral to keep

---

[6] Michael Scriven, "Values in the Curriculum." *Social Science Education Consortium Newsletter*, II, No. 1, April, 1966, p. 1.

children ignorant of the empirical and logical bases behind the law and institutions which incorporate this country's virtues and permit its vices. But in addition to this intellectual payoff is the practical benefit to a society whose members are skilled in making value judgments. Such a society becomes a moral community offering important benefits to all its members.[7]

Another question that has not yet been answered but that is most important to this discussion is the place and treatment of "basic," "ultimate," or "absolute" values. As teachers and their classes engage in the analysis of values, the problem of "ultimate" values will certainly arise. The argument about the existence of "ultimate" values is not the concern of this paper. It is of little import here, also, because the author has been attempting to demonstrate that the majority of value problems that children will confront in their public school classes can be settled by empirical investigation and logical analysis. The school's responsibility is fairly clear on this issue. It is to have the children use the processes already described to push the value "frontier" as far as possible without worrying about the last "frontier."[8]

Any discussion of value teaching must consider the affective as well as the cognitive realm, because discussions of value questions that only employ the cognitive processes for their solution may become academic exercises for the children, devoid of meaning for their own lives. In the treatment of a value question there should be emotional involvement by the child as well as insight. While as full and complete an understanding as possible of the value problem should be the first order of business and is necessary, it is, however, not sufficient. The discussion of value questions requires that the child see himself in another's position whenever possible. In short, it requires empathy and sympathy on the part of the pupil. All forms of ego-involving activities are most relevant and appropriate in teaching values.

Here again an example that actually occurred will be given in order to portray the interdependence of intellect and emotion in value teaching.

In a fifth grade class discussion concerning equality of rights (a value, by the way, to which this nation is fully committed), the various means of attaining this value by political, religious, ethnic and/or racial groups were considered. Revolution was suggested as a way of achieving equality of rights, thus raising the moral question of the "means-end" relationships. The concept of revolution was examined using Brinton's *Anatomy of Revolution* as the au-

---

[7] *Ibid*, p. 2.
[8] *Ibid*, p. 1.

thority.[9] Three revolutions, the American, Cuban, and Orwell's *Animal Farm* [10] were studied in light of the Brinton thesis. At the termination of the study, the children understood the causes of revolution and some might have even resolved the value question regarding the justification if not of revolution, *per se,* then of a particular revolution. However, it is very doubtful if the children had any empathy for revolutionaries attempting to achieve equality of rights. The problem became one of attempting to have the children feel as nearly as possible how people can be moved to revolt. To this end the following situation evolved.

One day shortly following their discussions on revolution, a "new" teacher who was to replace the "regular" teacher was introduced to the class. The "new" teacher then changed existing classroom procedures. The children who had been seated in a semi-circular grouping were separated by the "new" teacher into two groups on the basis of eye color. One group was composed of only blue-eyed children, the other group contained other-color-eyed children. Any contact between the two groups was forbidden. Two separate doors for entrance to an exit from the classroom were used, one by the blue-eyed group and one by the other-colored-eye group. Separate toilet facilities, water fountains and lunchroom tables were assigned to the two groups. The "new" teacher informed the blue-eyed children that they were to sit only in the seats at the rear of the school bus when coming to or returning from school. The blue-eyed children were made to feel inferior in other ways because their toilets and drinking fountains were located at a greater distance from the classroom and because their table in the lunchroom was in a less desirable location. Separation of the two groups was reinforced by taking the children to the playground and lunchroom using different doors for both groups and by having children use the different tables while eating their lunches. Complete and total segregation of the blue-eyed group from the rest of the class was accomplished approximately one hour after the "new" teacher had entered the classroom. It was at this point that the "new" teacher left the classroom intimating that he would return again the following day and that the "old" or "regular" teacher would now resume her role. The children reacted immediately after the "new" teacher left the classroom. They demanded that they be allowed to resume their former semi-circular seating arrangement in spite of the warnings that the "new" teacher would return. Several children suggested

[9] Crane Brinton, *The Anatomy of Revolution,* rev. and exp. New York: Vintage Press, 1965.
[10] George Orwell, *Animal Farm.* New York: New American Library, 1946.

that they act as a delegation to the principal to urge the dismissal of the "new" teacher. Other children requested permission to telephone their parents in order to be taken home and hopefully transferred to other rooms or schools. Still other children vowed never to return to school and others even suggested various means, violent and otherwise, of ridding themselves of the "new" teacher.

After further venting of feeling and some discussion of their situation, the children began to realize that they had been suggesting revolutionary measures as a means of improving their lot for much the same reasons that other groups had revolted at other times and in other places. For the first and only time in their lives these children were able to appreciate how and why people can be driven to revolt.

The children were now in the optimum position of fully understanding the causes of revolution (the cognitive realm) and of having participated in a revolutionary movement of sorts (the affective realm). They were adequately prepared to make the value judgment concerning the use of revolution as a means of achieving equality of rights. From this point it was a relatively simple matter to make the transition to a discussion concerning the "Negro Revolution."

The subtitle of this paper is "A Rationale for Teaching But Not Transmitting Values." In totalitarian countries the rigid transmission of one value system is what is taught in school, whereas in a democracy such as ours it seems proper that education, and especially the education of young children, should be concerned with teaching them not only understanding about their own culture and its values but about other cultures and other value systems as well. In addition, it is incumbent upon our schools to teach children the skills necessary to make intelligent choices among the alternatives and to create situations whereby feelings about value questions may be appreciated. The point of view presented is neither novel nor unique; however, it is one about which teachers should take a firm position.

VALUES AND THE PRIMARY SCHOOL TEACHER *

Bernice J. Wolfson

The question "Should a teacher be concerned with the development of values in her pupils?" is not a real question. Merely by the fact of living with them for the school year, she is an important influence on all they learn.

Particularly in the early school years the teacher provides some sort of model for the child. In what direction she will influence him depends on many factors, but undoubtedly he experiences the value system that she inevitably communicates through her deeds and concerns.

An observer in a classroom can infer what appear to be the values of the teacher, i.e. what is prized, important, of greatest concern. If, on the one hand, she scolds and embarrasses a child before the whole class because he has just broken a large jar of paste, it would appear that she values this property more than the feelings of this child. If she tears up a child's paper because it is not neat, she appears to be valuing her standard of neatness over the child's effort and feelings.

If, on the other hand, the teacher helps the child to see alternative possibilities and encourages him to make decisions for himself, she is demonstrating her regard for him as a person. She will be less manipulative and judgmental if she truly views him as a valued, worthwhile human being. It is apparent that as a teacher interacts in the classroom she is communicating in both obvious and subtle ways the fabric of her personal values.

Where did she get her values? Values and attitudes are learned, and also unlearned, but there is very little concrete knowledge about how this occurs. Anthropologists, psychologists, and specialists in child development have looked at the child in the setting of his culture, home, and school. It has been suggested that he assimilates the values of his society and his home as unconsciously as he breaths the air around him. Possibly he imitates the values and attitudes he experiences in his home. When he gets into the

Bernice J. Wolfson is Associate Professor of Education at the University of Wisconsin, Milwaukee.

* Reprinted from *Social Education* 31:37–38 ff., 1967, with permission of the National Council for the Social Studies and Bernice J. Wolfson.

larger society of neighborhood and school (and beyond), he may further imitate the values of those he admires. As some express it, he identifies with other individuals and accepts their values.

In all these descriptions there seems to be the assumption of determinism at work and of a lack of awareness or choice on the part of the individual. However, it is not necessary to deny the influence of the culture and family in order to recognize that human beings have alternatives. At various stages in his life, an individual may examine his feelings and new knowledge, recognize inconsistencies in his values, and revise or radically change his value priorities. He is continually valuing and re-valuing whenever he has to make important decisions.

Louis Raths [1] suggests that the process by which a person develops, reconsiders, and revises his values is one of clarification. The analysis of this process, and many examples of classroom activities found in *Values and Teaching*,[2] will be extremely helpful to teachers of all levels. Each primary grade teacher will of course need to adapt and modify the suggested procedures for use with her particular class. Initially, it would be most profitable for the teacher to try this process herself.

The influence of the teacher in value development is far from clear; but it should be evident that to the extent that her own value system is unexamined and inconsistent, she may well be providing a model that is confusing to the child. The questions she would reflect on might include some of the following:

1. Is that very important to me?
2. How did I feel when that happened?
3. What other alternatives did I consider?
4. Would I freely choose this alternative?
5. What do I mean by . . .?
6. What assumptions did I make?
7. Was this consistent with what I did?
8. Do I do this often?
9. What can I do about this idea?
10. Would I do it again the same way?
11. How do I know it's right?
12. Why did I do it that way?

(Adapted from Raths *et al.*, pp. 56–62)

---

[1] Louis Raths, Merrill Harmin and Sidney B. Simon, *Values and Teaching.* Columbus, Ohio: Merrill, 1966.
[2] *Ibid.*, pp. 112–162.

As a teacher clarifies her values, she also needs to examine her classroom actions and ask: Are they consistent with my priorities? e.g. I believe I value initiative; does my classroom encourage initiative or does it emphasize following directions?

As the primary grade teacher proceeds to reflect on and clarify her own values, she will find it appropriate to raise some of the same questions with the children. She will want to ensure appropriate opportunities for valuing. Raths and his associates express the goal as:

> . . . children who have clear, personal values. The goal, therefore, requires opportunities for children to use the processes of (a) choosing freely, (b) choosing from alternatives, (c) choosing thoughtfully, (d) prizing and cherishing, (e) affirming, (f) acting upon choices, and (g) examining patterns of living.[3]

Possibly in the primary years some children will be more ready than others to reflect and respond to questions of this sort. (In fact, Raths and his associates suggest that this may not be an appropriate technique for children "who have insufficient ego strength." [4])

There are other kinds of experiences that may encourage the child to become aware of his own feelings and the feelings of other children, to consider the consequences of alternative choices, and to engage in decision-making. Additional activities that seem to be particularly relevant are: experiencing the feelings and dilemmas of literary characters; enacting in creative dramatics or role playing the feelings, decisions, and consequences of various situations; and discussing or role playing some of the human concerns and problems that grow out of life at school.

Relatively unstructured literature and art experiences can help children keep in touch with their rich pre-conceptual feeling, which is one of the concrete referents for the valuing process. Acting out, or discussing how story characters feel in various situations is a vicarious valuing process.

Children spontaneously comment about their own experiences and feelings in relation to the story characters. They also react in terms of what other consequences might follow. In part, it is a growing awareness of the common human dilemmas that will assist a child in understanding himself and the others in his world.

Specific suggestions, descriptions, and pitfalls can be found in

---

[3] *Ibid*, p. 82.
[4] *Ibid*, p. 223.

the material written by Nichols and Williams,[5] Raths *et el,*[6] Shaftel,[7] and Wolfson.[8] No doubt each teacher will select and experiment with those approaches that seem most suitable to her.

Finally, an additional source of experience that may promote value development is a classroom that provides a wide variety of opportunities for self-selection of goals and activities by the pupils. If a child is encouraged sometimes to consider alternatives, sometimes to consider possible consequences, sometimes to explain his reasons, and often to examine his feelings, he is, indeed, engaged in valuing.

Two basic questions related to the entire discussion above are: Does it matter what values the teacher holds? Does it matter how the teacher arrives at her values?

I would hypothesize that it *does* matter what values the teacher holds, for her values influence the way she organizes and operates her classroom and the way she interacts with the children. However, more important is how she arrived at her values and if she is willing to re-examine them and to continue to engage in the valuing process.

To some extent we are a pluralistic society. Every person meets others who hold values that are different from and in conflict with his values. In addition, many of us do not continuously engage in the process of clarifying our values and we do not live the values we profess. Using Louis Raths' criteria for a value,[9] this would mean we do not have these values.

Developmental (Kohlberg),[10] therapeutic (Gendlin),[11] and educational (Raths) [12] points of view all suggest the need for attention to the valuing *process.* How we engage in valuing is significant because valuing is a crucial life-time activity.

Different analyses of the process all imply that we cannot in any

---

[5] Hildred Nichols and Lois Williams, *Learning About Role-Playing for Children and Teachers.* Washington, D.C.: Association for Childhood Education International, 1960.

[6] Raths, *op. cit.*

[7] George Shaftel and Fannie R. Shaftel, *Role Playing the Problem Story.* New York: National Conference of Christians and Jews, 1952. (Also new book in press.)

[8] Bernice J. Wolfson, "Reading About Emotions in the Primary Classroom." *Elementary English 31*:146–149, 1954.

[9] Raths *et al, op. cit.*, pp. 28–29.

[10] Lawrence Kohlberg, "Moral Education in the Schools; A Developmental View." *The School Review 74*:1–30, 1966.

[11] Eugene Gendlin, "Values and the Process of Experiencing," in *The Goals of Psychotherapy*, A. R. Mahrer, ed. New York: Appleton-Century-Crofts, in press.

[12] Raths *et al, op. cit.*

meaningful or useful sense impose our values on someone else. If I want a person to develop values that are meaningful and active for him, I cannot insist on *my* values for *him*. My values are only relevant as an example of one acting, valuing human being.

It should be stated, then, that the value assumptions implicit in this paper are generally what Dahlke [13] referred to as the Humanistic Value Orientation. His is primarily a sociological frame of reference, so I would add those assumptions about the nature of man that are developed in the more or less humanistic * approaches to psychology.[14]

It may well be that many teachers believe that their values are humanistic. However, from the point of view of social scientists, much that goes on in classrooms is stereotyped, manipulative, and based on conflicting value orientations.[15]

We are undoubtedly concerned with a problem that is of vital importance to education and indeed to civilization. Our ignorance is great and our knowledge meager, but our need to learn and to act is urgent. Our social problems, both national and international, emphasize this urgency.

Looking at the societal need, Gardner analyzed the problem as follows:

> We are beginning to understand how to educate for renewal but we must deepen that understanding. If we indoctrinate the young person in an elaborate set of fixed beliefs, we are ensuring his early obsolescence. The alternative is to develop skills, attitudes, habits of mind and the kinds of knowledge and understanding that will be the instruments of continuous change and growth on the part of the young person. Then we will have fashioned *a system that provides for its own continuous renewal.*[16]

---

[13] H. Otto Dahlke, *Values in Culture and Classroom*. New York: Harper, 1958, pp. 60–61.

* Labels are inadequate and not very meaningful. I use this one to give the general emphasis without clarifying the specific details.

[14] See Arthur Combs and Donald Snygg, *Individual Behavior: A Perceptual Approach to Behavior*, 2nd ed., New York: Harper & Row, 1959; Abraham H. Maslow, *Toward A Psychology of Being*, Princeton, N. J.: Van Nostrand, 1962; Carl Rogers, *On Becoming A Person*, Boston: Houghton Mifflin, 1961; Frank T. Severin, ed., *Humanistic Viewpoints in Psychology*, A Book of Readings, New York: McGraw-Hill, 1965.

[15] See Jules Henry, *Culture Against Man*, New York: Random House, 1963; Seymour B. Sarason, Kenneth Davidson, and Burton Black, *The Preparation of Teachers*, New York: Wiley, 1962; Donald N. Michael, *The Next Generation: The Prospects Ahead for the Youth of Today and Tomorrow*, New York: Vintage, 1965.

[16] John W. Gardner, *Self-Renewal: The Individual and the Innovative Society*, New York: Harper: Harper Colophon, 1965 ed., c. 1963.

In the last analysis, only the valuing teacher can ensure a classroom environment designed to encourage the development of the valuing process in children.

THE ROLE OF SKILLS IN ELEMENTARY SOCIAL STUDIES *

Helen McCracken Carpenter

The gentle groundswell of change that characterized social studies instruction for many decades has become in the last few years a volcanic eruption of colloquy, publication, experimentation, and reform. From all indications, the streams of educational lava can be expected to well forth at an even greater rate in the next few years. The extent to which this flow is likely to seep into the classrooms to benefit the social studies teaching and learning of the three Americans in every ten now enrolled in formal education cannot be assessed at this time. Herein lies the difficulty in attempting to take bearings on the current situation in any definite way. Analysis, of necessity at this time, involves factors that are fluid.

Skill development in elementary social studies is not at the forefront of attention in the current ferment. Of the forty projects within the national spotlight, less than a fourth deal in any way with the elementary grades and most of these focus on subject-matter content or materials. Only three touch the core of concern here, and the findings of these are not yet available. It is necessary then to look at implications of general developments in considering the function of skills in elementary social studies.

Points of Continuing Agreement

Skill development has always been recognized as an important responsibility of elementary education. In fact, the need to teach young citizens the three R's was advanced as a major justification

Helen McCracken Carpenter is Professor of History at Trenton State College, New Jersey.

* Reprinted from *Social Education* *31*:219–221, 1967, with permission of the National Council for the Social Studies and Helen McCracken Carpenter.

whenever and wherever the drive to establish public schools was underway. Concern for competence in reading, written expression, and arithmetic, now dignified as "the new math," is still central to the goals and curriculum for six- to twelve-year-olds. Achievement in these basic skills is of vital concern to social studies instruction because reading with all its varied purposes and forms—words, pictures, charts, graphs, tables, maps—parallels with increasing utility, as an avenue to learning in this field, the growing maturity of the child; mathematics supplies the foundation necessary to progress in developing a sense of time and chronology; and the expression of ideas and understandings in writing is, next to behavior, the truest yardstick of comprehension. As horizons in education widened, other skills were added to the program. Examples include the cluster concerned with locating, organizing, evaluating, and applying information; communicating orally; participating in group undertakings; listening; and observing. The relevancy of all these to progress in social studies is admitted and responsibility for fostering competence is accepted. Concern today then does not involve lack of recognition, by either teachers or administrators, of the need for skill development in the social studies program.

There is common acknowledgment also of the reciprocal relation of factors involved in the instructional situation. One helpful result accruing from viewpoints of psychologists shaping current thinking has been to highlight the inextricable relationship existing among all elements in the educational process—objectives, subject matter, method, materials, pupils—that has been obscured at different times in the past as the spotlight swung, over-emphasizing one factor and then another. The same is true within the category of objectives. The close connection of the cognitive to the affective realms—of knowledge and intellectual skills and abilities to attitudes, appreciations, and values—is manifest. Knowledge supplies the substance for the development of skills and provides standards necessary to value formation. Intellectual skills function both in the gaining of knowledge and in the process of valuing. In turn, affective elements color interpretation of knowledge and the effectiveness of skill development.

Among the several classifications of goals to which social studies teaching is directed, agreement is general that the development of skills should receive major attention. The scales tip heavier to skills than to knowledge because of the rapid rate in the obsolescence of much information today and, therefore, of the diminished transfer value of knowledge. Skills, however, represent more generalized learnings and thus are likely to be applicable continually in all facets of an individual's life. With reference to value formation, skill development weighs somewhat heavier for different reasons. The heart of the matter here concerns substantive values—the qualities of mind and character constituting moral excellence in an individual as well as concepts of ideals, customs, and institutions necessary to the good society. In a pluralistic nation like ours, social studies instruction in public schools cannot approach this area head-on. It *can* teach the process of making value judgments. Because skills are generally considered to pertain to *process* rather than to *product* of learning, skill development provides children with basic tools for arriving at their own values.

Unanimity continues also on the identification of skills that should be developed. The new social studies incorporates no categories beyond those set forth in the 33rd Yearbook of the National Council for the Social Studies.[1] Hence, on need, relative importance, and scope of skills in elementary social studies, thinking has changed little in recent years. It is in the approach to skill development involving method and organization that challenging considerations arise from the current stirrings.

Focus on Inquiry through Problem-Solving

Accelerated exploration of the nature of intellectual growth as a key to improvement of educational experiences has been a major trend in the ferment of the last decade. Perhaps the most seminal single stimulus to the movement was the appearance of Bruner's capsule-size *Process of Education,*[2] reporting findings of experimental programs in science and mathematics as well as the thinking of scholars from a variety of fields participating in the 1959 Woods Hole Conference. Renewed attention to inquiry, or discovery, as a method of learning to think is the facet of the total trend with the most pertinency in the consideration of skill development. Inquiry is considered to be the process by which a child, more or less independently, comes to perceive relationships among factors in his environment or between ideas that previously had no meaningful connection. The new understandings evolve through application and reorganization of past experiences. Insight and self-confidence grow

---

[1] Helen McCracken Carpenter, ed., *Skill Development in Social Studies,* Thirty-third Yearbook. Washington, D.C.: National Council for the Social Studies, 1963.

[2] Jerome S. Bruner, *The Process of Education.* Cambridge, Mass.: Harvard University Press, 1960.

as the child meets successfully situations of increasing abstractness and complexity; as he moves up the ladder from observation, classification, and application to generalization.

Thus the inquiry approach views the learner as an active thinker —seeking, probing, processing data from his environment toward a variety of destinations along paths best suited to his own mental characteristics. It rejects passiveness as an ingredient of effective learning and the concept of the mind as a reservoir for the storage of knowledge presented through expository instruction directed toward a predetermined, closed end. The inquiry method seeks to avoid the dangers of rote memorization and verbalization as well as the hazard of fostering dependency in citizens as learners and thinkers. Advantages of the inquiry approach are considered to be in self-direction as a motivating factor for learning and in development of a form of mental behavior essential in a democratic society. The measure of ultimate success in education through inquiry lies in the degree to which the teacher becomes unnecessary as a guide.

The parallelism of ideas such as these being examined today to John Dewey's concepts of long ago is evident. Dewey's belief in the development of reflective thinking by means of inquiry shaped the philosophy and functioning of the children's school founded at the University of Chicago in the mid-1890's.[3] In the years following, Dewey elaborated his ideas on reflective thinking and its relation to education in a democratic society [4] that Kilpatrick [5] as his disciple helped keep dominant into the Twenties and Thirties. Although the last three decades have witnessed many changes in American education, the desirability of developing citizens who are independent and skilled inquirers has been recognized in theory even though efforts to realize the goal languished. To Dewey and to leaders in the current movement, an important approach, or strategy, facilitating inquiry is problem-solving. Dewey's analysis of the mental state involved has become a classic,

> . . . *reflective* thinking, in distinction from other operations to which we apply the name of thought, involves 1) a state of doubt, hesitation, perplexity, mental difficulty, in which thinking originates, and 2) an act of searching, hunting, inquiring, to find material that will resolve the doubt, settle and dispose of the perplexity.[6]

---

[3] John Dewey, *University Record 1*:417–422, No. 32, November 6, 1896.

[4] John Dewey, *Democracy and Education*, New York: Macmillan, 1916; *How We Think*, Boston: Heath, 1933.

[5] William H. Kilpatrick, *The Project Method.* New York: Teachers College Bureau of Publications, Columbia University, 1919.

[6] *Op. cit., How We Think*, p. 116.

Although slight differences in classification of the elements involved in problem-solving exist, the pattern is essentially as follows but does not necessarily proceed neatly in the rank order given:

1. an awareness and identification stage
   Consisting of a feeling of disturbance, perception of factors involved, and clarification of the core of the obstacle
2. a data-processing stage
   Including collecting, organizing, and evaluating relevant information
3. an analytical-synthesizing stage
   Involving comparing, contrasting, inferring, speculating, and applying in hypothesis formation
4. a critical, testing stage
   Constituting probing the validity of hypotheses, reconstructing data, reaching plausible conclusions in the form of tentative principles useful in the next encounter

These ideas seem like old friends to many elementary school teachers who have long used problems as a means of getting their pupils to think critically. The current emphasis on inquiry, however, highlights interesting considerations about skills and the problems approach as a means for developing them.

Implications for Skill Development

Most important is the fact that the problems approach, as often interpreted, does not necessarily promote the goals of the inquiry method. The crux of the matter concerns the difference between inductive and deductive learning. Inquiry emphasizes the inductive process. Learning experiences set up in problem form may, or may not, call for inductive procedures, depending on the nature of the problem and what the learner is required to do. For example, if a problem is posed as "How do the religious beliefs of some people in India increase famine there?", the learner is pointed toward religion and hunger. The relationship is established; his job is to prove it with specific data. If the question is put a little less specifically, "Why does India continue to have a shortage of food?", there is no real change in the nature of the task especially if sub-problems are attached, such as, "What is the population of India?" "What methods of farming are used?" "What does India have to offer other countries in trade?" This learning experience is not designed to give pupils an opportunity to develop and test hypotheses; they are called on to proceed deductively. A corollary to this approach often is the use of materials that supply the answers organized in the same way the information is requested.

If, on the other hand, the problem is posed in a more open-ended way, such as "What accounts for problems facing India today?", and materials are provided that give data of various kinds—geographic, demographic, cultural, political—the task of finding, assimilating, evaluating, testing, rejecting, re-applying, deciding is left to the child. There is room for disagreement among pupils on the relative importance of causes and the effectiveness of possible courses of action. The learner is given the chance to draw relationships himself rather than to explain or support those made for him. The strategies employed by a child working inductively are revealing indicators of thinking style and intellectual growth.[7]

The emphasis, then, that will be dominant depends on the *nature* and *amount* of direction provided by the teacher. The need for guidance of learning, be it inductive or deductive, must, of course, be recognized. With children who are younger, less able, or inexperienced in inquiry procedures, the greater becomes the need for direction. Opportunities for structuring exist in the depth of the problems to be researched, the questions posed for discussion, the working definition used for an hypothesis, and the number of obvious cues contained in study materials provided. As pupil competency develops, the teacher can widen the horizons and plant fewer and fewer cues in the learning experience.

Gagne discusses the nature of direction as one of the conditions of problem-solving along with contiguity of the elements involved and recency of recall. He observes—

> Guidance may vary in amount or completeness, always short of describing the solution itself. At a minimum, guidance of thinking takes the form of informing the learner of the goal of his activity, the general form of the solution; this amount appears to be required if learning is to occur at all. Greater amounts of guidance function to limit the range of hypotheses to be entertained by the learner in achieving solution

---

[7] For more detailed discussion of these aspects than is permitted here, see Fannie R. Shaftel, Charlotte Crabtree, and Vivian Rushworth, "Problem Solving in the Elementary School," in *The Problems Approach and the Social Studies*, Richard E. Gross, Raymond H. Muessig, and George L. Fersh, eds., Curriculum Bulletin No. 9, rev. ed., Washington, D.C.: National Council for the Social Studies, 1960, pp. 25–47; Charlotte Crabtree, "Inquiry Approaches: How New and How Valuable?" *Social Education* 30:523–525, 531, 1966; J. Richard Suchman, "The Child and the Inquiry Process," in *Intellectual Development: Another Look*, A. Harry Passow and Robert R. Leeper, eds., Washington, D.C.: Association for Supervision and Curriculum Development, 1964, pp. 59–77; Robert M. Gagne, *The Conditions of Learning*, New York: Holt, Rinehart & Winston, 1965, Ch. 6.

. . . When these conditions are present, the learner is able to solve the problem, although the time required for this solution is likely to vary with the amount of guidance provided, as well as with certain innate capacities of the learner.[8]

The prime requisite for the teacher is the ability to distinguish between goals of various kinds and to identify the learning procedures appropriate for different ends. Important also is willingness to let pupils venture on their own, to elicit suggestions for new ways of proceeding to encourage differing opinions, and to respect pupil fumblings along the way.

Another implication concerns the relative importance of various classifications of skills. The prominence currently given to the inquiry method, with focus on cognitive skills, may seem in effect to dwarf the importance of other kinds of skills. Actually, the opposite is true because effective thinking is facilitated by competency in a variety of abilities somewhat less complicated in nature. The quest for information cannot proceed far without the ability to determine and find the kind of resource that will supply the data needed and know-how to extract the information efficiently. Similarly, the organizing skills of notetaking, outlining, and reporting are steps along the way. In addition to such work-study skills as these, proficiency with the intake skills of observing, listening, and reading is basic to effective living today. The competencies to which social studies make a particular contribution—developing a sense of place and space, and a sense of time and chronology—provide perspective for decision-making. And the need for effective group-work skills, in school and in life, is apparent. In fact, at the primary level, this category of skills may well be not only basic to but also as important as the cognitive abilities.

Nothing in the current examination of learning in relation to thought processes contradicts either the principle of sequential development of skills (although stages cannot be expected to proceed neatly) or the concept of readiness (although time is subject to re-interpretation).

The need, then, is for thoughtful design and management of the learning environment to maintain balance both horizontally and vertically among the various kinds of skills needed for effective living today—and tomorrow.

---

[8] Gagne, *op. cit.*, p. 163.

SKILLS TEACHING IN THE PRIMARY GRADES *

John Jarolimek

The term *skill* is applied to the ability to do something with some degree of expertness in repeated performances. To have a skill or to be skillful, however, is usually something of a relative matter. The kindergarten child is highly skillful in his use of language when compared with a two-year old. We would say that he is less skillful in most things he does when compared with an upper-grade pupil. Adequacy of skill development must not only take into account the expertness of performance *per se,* but the age and prior background of the learner.

When children enter the primary grades, they have already developed a number of skills. They can carry on conversations with others, follow directions, take care of many of their personal needs, play simple games; some can read. Such skills are essential for ordinary living. Left unattended and untutored, the child will improve these skills simply through continued use. The refinement of the skills the child has when he comes to school and the learning of others that are introduced as a part of the curriculum will be greatly enhanced through careful and systematic instruction. From the moment the child enters school, his continued success in the school environment will depend to a significant degree on the extent to which he is able to learn and use essential skills.

There can be no doubt that well developed skills enhance the ability to do other school-related tasks. Conversely, poorly developed skills result in arrested school progress. Pupils who are off to a poor start in their skill development in the primary grades fall farther and farther behind in their overall achievement. Eventually the deficit accumulates to a point that becomes overwhelming to the pupil and nearly impossible for him to overcome. School dropouts at the high school level invariably present histories of skill deficiencies that can be traced to the earliest grades in school. Skill competence strengthens the child's positive perception of himself, an important component of school success. The child uses skills to

---

John Jarolimek is Professor of Education at the University of Washington, Seattle.

* Reprinted from *Social Education* 31:222–223 ff., 1967, with permission of the National Council for the Social Studies and John Jarolimek.

deal with the social world confronting him, and consequently, skills contribute directly to his social competence. It would be hard to underestimate the vital role primary grade teachers play in ensuring a successful introduction of the child to the skills program.

In the primary grades it is almost impossible to separate social studies skills from the skills objectives of the total primary grade program. There is no particular reason to label certain skills as being the unique province of the social studies, providing essential skills get the instructional attention they deserve. The advantage of singling out social studies skills in the curriculum is to ensure that they *are* included and taught systematically. Moreover, skills presented in a social studies context can often be taught in a more realistic and functional setting than when presented either in isolation or in the framework of another curriculum area, as for example, in the reading program.

In the first article of this supplement, Professor Carpenter has noted that in spite of the concern for social studies revision in recent years, no new skills have been identified. Essential skills persist in their importance in modern programs even though there have been some shifts in emphasis. Uniqueness in skills teaching does not come through the discovery of some new skill but in imaginative approaches to the teaching of those that have always been regarded as important. The social studies skills with which the primary grade teacher is concerned are less complex variations of skills that continue to receive attention throughout the total program.

One large group of such skills deals basically with a variety of intellectual operations. Thinking, asking questions, using language, solving problems, interpreting stories and pictures, and making simple analyses are a few examples of skills of this type. In most cases they are related to the informational content of the program. They do not deal basically with *getting* information but with interpreting, processing, and using information. In the following example, notice how the teacher is building thinking skills with her first graders:

> The teacher selected a picture from a magazine advertising a dishwasher. The picture shows a young mother removing sparkling clean dishes from the washer while her daughter (about a six-year old) looks on. One can see a bright, modern kitchen and the landscape greenery through the kitchen window. The teacher prepared the following questions in connection with this picture:
>
> 1. Is the mother taking the dishes out or putting them in the washer?
> 2. Is this a large or small family?
> 3. Does this family have a comfortable home?
> 4. What season of the year is it?

5. What might other members of the family be doing at this time?
6. Do you think the lady is the little girl's mother?
7. Is this a city home or a farm home?

The purpose of this exercise is not to establish right or wrong answers to the questions. Indeed, it would be impossible to determine precisely the rightness or wrongness of some of them. For example, one could not be sure about the size of the family by the number of dishes used; the family may have had guests, or the dishes may be an accumulation from more than one meal. Similarly, the season of the year could not be verified by the presence of greenery because some parts of the country are green the year around. Pupils could be expected to point out these possibilities, and while they may select what they think is the most likely answer, the door should be kept open to the consideration of other alternatives. In activities of this type, it is more important to consider a variety of possibilities and have pupils give reasons why a response is plausible than to agree on a right answer. (This degree of flexibility would not be acceptable, however, in considering factual questions where correctness can be established. Factual questions serve a different purpose from those designed to encourage reflective thought.)

Other examples of intellectual skills can be developed around such situations as these:

1. Identifying sequences—What happened first; what happened next; what happened last?
2. Considering alternative solutions—Can you think of another way to do it? What are some other ways the man could have solved his problems?
3. Differentiating between fact and fiction—What parts of the story are true and what parts are make-believe. How can we find out if something is true?
4. Developing sensitivity to words—Can you think of words that make you feel happy? Sad? Angry?
5. Predicting or speculating on outcomes of situations—How do you suppose the problem was solved? What do you suppose will happen next?

Telling pupils to think or admonishing them for not thinking are not effective methods for developing intellectual skills even though such practices in one form or another are fairly common. More productive approaches call for the pupil to respond to simple questions of the reflective type that may not have a single answer but force him to consider many alternatives, predict likely consequences of each, and decide the best course of action. There can be little if any thinking if the pupil does not have to consider alternatives in situations that involve choice or decision-making.

The importance of intellectual skills, and especially thinking skills, is often overlooked in the primary grades because of the widespread belief that one gains knowledge first and then uses that knowledge for thinking purposes at some later time. As a result the development of thinking abilities of young children has not always been the concern of primary grade teachers. Children at this level were expected to build literacy and work-study skills and expand their backgrounds of information. Thinking would come later. There is no evidence to support the notion that knowledge acquisition and knowledge use in the thinking process are separate and discrete functions. In fact, the practice of disassociating a skill from its functional context is rejected as unsound practice in most other realms of skill development. It is unfortunate that it should persist in teaching pupils the most important skill of all, namely, thinking.

A second large group of skills important to the primary grade social studies involves social relationships. They include ordinary social skills needed for harmonious living and working with others, as well as those more structured skills related to instructional processes, i.e., working on a small committee, contributing to a group project, participating in class discussions, and so forth. These skills are the concern of the total curriculum of the elementary school, of course, but the social studies provide excellent settings in which to teach them because of the nature of instructional processes associated with this area of the curriculum.

The most important point that could be made in connection with social relationship skills is that they *need to be taught*. It is often assumed that all that is required are activities in which pupils can apply and practice them. Consequently, pupils are forced to learn the skills of social interaction on a trial and error basis. In the process the teacher may become annoyed, isolate those pupils who were not "cooperative," and return the others to their seats to a more formal instructional posture. While there might be times when a child should be separated from the others, no child ever learned the skills of social interaction while he was in isolation. Neither do classes learn such skills in formal instructional settings where social interaction is not allowed or is discouraged.

A third category of social studies skills has to do mainly with the use of learning resources and tools including simple map and globe reading, knowing where to go for information needed, how to speak before the class, reading signs and symbols, and other similar operations. They are commonly called work-study skills. The need for instructional attention to these skills has been generally accepted through the years. Conventional reading programs ordinarily devote some instruction to work-study skills that are relevant to social studies.

It often happens that a specific activity can be used to attack several related work-study skills. For example, a third grade class may be collecting pictures that show the way of life in another country. Such an activity might be used to promote any or all of the following skills:

1. Locating appropriate pictures.
2. Explaining or telling the class something about the picture.
3. Classifying information—placing pictures in appropriate categories such as those that show home life, those that show work people do, holiday observances, or sports events.
4. Comparing information from one picture with another.
5. Learning and using new words and concepts represented in the picture.
6. Asking appropriate questions concerning picture content.
7. Planning and arranging an exhibit, such as a bulletin board.
8. Creating and writing appropriate captions and/or explanations to accompany the pictures.

Similarly, in the selection of activities for the development of work-study skills, the primary grade teacher can attend to intellectual skills and social relationship skills as well. For example, in teaching pupils how to use the school library, the teacher will undoubtedly stress such intellectual skills as listening to directions, observing carefully, asking questions, and knowing what information is wanted. If the activity involves going to the library as a class or in smaller groups, she will also use the experience as a way of teaching or reinforcing social behavior of pupils. Finally, in the process pupils will learn something about use of the library—how it is arranged, where to look for certain kinds of books, and how to check out a book. Although we separate these skills for discussion purposes and focus instruction on specific skills from time to time to ensure learning, the whole cluster of social studies skills is highly interrelated.

To a degree skill growth is related to the developmental pattern of children. Consequently, no matter how intensively skills are taught in the primary grades, there are definite upper limits on the level of proficiency that can realistically be expected of most primary grade pupils. It is advisable, therefore, to establish reasonable criterion levels of expectation and settle for those rather than to expend an excessive amount of instructional time in order to get small increments of improvement in performance. The growth curve on skills rises sharply to a point and then levels off; perhaps the optimum performance expectancy is just beyond the point where the curve begins to plateau. If adequate instruction on skills can be assured and reasonable expectancy levels set, there will be time to spend on other important dimensions of an effective primary grade program. Skills and skills teaching, while extremely important, should not entirely dominate the primary grade curriculum to the exclusion of art, music, poetry, literature, and other learnings vital to the total development of the young child.

A STRATEGY
FOR DEVELOPING VALUES *

James Raths

This paper deals with a strategy for helping children to develop their own values. Recognition of the importance of children's values has been with us for years. "A great and continuing purpose of education has been the development of moral and spiritual values" (5). With this pronouncement, the Educational Policies Commission opened its 1957 report. As important as developing values seems to be to the DAR and the VFW; to the FBI and the HUAC, the area is even more important to us as educators, it seems to me, because of its implications for the learning process. Let me briefly spell out some of these implications.

First, Kubie (12) suggests that learning is swift, spontaneous and automatic. At times, learning is blocked—many times by what Kubie calls preconscious motives and drives. He recommends that teachers concern themselves with developing self-knowledge on their students' part to remove blocks to learning—to free children

---

James Raths is Associate Professor of Education at the University of Maryland, College Park.

* Reprinted from *Educational Leadership* *21*:509–514 ff., 1964, with permission of the Association for Supervision and Curriculum Development and James Raths. Copyright © 1964, by the Association for Supervision and Curriculum Development.

so that they may learn in a spontaneous fashion. Second, Ginsburg (7) suggests that good mental health, assumed to be a necessary condition for learning, is merely a process of living up to a set of values. Finally, several researchers, following the ideas of Louis Raths, have identified pupil behaviors associated with a lack of values (9; 11; 13; 14). These classroom behaviors, including over-conforming, indifference, flightiness and several others, it is argued, interfere with concentration, involvement, and openness in the learning process. Therefore, value development, it seems, should be one of the many central concerns of teachers.

While the area of value development has been a major concern of educators for many years, the public and many professional people, too, have had a feeling that our efforts in this area have not been too effective. The studies summarized by Jacob in his *Changing Values in College* tend to support this hunch (8). Teachers have been unable, it seems, to translate their genuine concerns about the value problem into effective patterns of action in their classrooms.

Essentially, there are four basic approaches to the development of values current in our schools. These methods include the teaching of values by the lecture method, by the use of peer-group pressure, by finding or setting examples for children to respect and emulate, and by a reward and punishment rationale. These methods are neither mutually exclusive nor exhaustive of all the approaches we use in schools, but they seem to me to be among the most prevalent in our classrooms.

Methods in Use

Perhaps the most common approach is the use of lecture methods. Teachers seem ever ready to tell students what they should believe or how they ought to act. It is easy to burlesque this method in harsh tones. Actually, it may be employed by the kindest, most sincere teachers as well as by the overly self-righteous, would-be reformers found on some school faculties. While it is possible to cite cases in which a lecture or even a "bawling out" did bring about changes in students' values, basically this method is not too successful. Attesting to this is the common cry of many teachers— "You can't *tell* those kids anything." In general, this remark has been found to be accurate.

Teachers' judgments and convictions seem, from a student's point of view, to be out of the framework of things. (Analogously, it may be akin to the feelings teachers in the field have of the "should's and should not's" of professors from schools and colleges of education.) Jones (10) has suggested a basis for explaining the ineffectiveness of the lecture method. He states that a teacher must be emotionally accepted by his students before he can contribute much to their development of self. By their moralizing and preaching, teachers may set themselves apart emotionally from their students. To the extent that teachers are not accepted by their students, it can be presumed that they will have little effect upon students' values. Students may leave the lecture all full of enthusiasm about what the teacher said, but they may not internalize what they admire and all too often they do not.

A second approach to the value development problem has been in the main popularized by exponents of the core curriculum. During a special period of the school day, students address themselves to self-evaluations and group evaluations. They are encouraged to speak freely, frankly and openly to the entire class judging their own behavior, criticizing group performances and perhaps pledging themselves to future improvements. In general, such statements are accepted by the teacher with little or no comment while other pupils are free to make suggestions, recommendations and comments.

The pressure of group approval or disapproval is a powerful force in bringing about changes in values. This method seems successful in some cases but it has some disturbing by-products. The most distressing of these is the tacit approval of the teacher of the notion that group consensus is correct or at least worthy of very serious consideration. This method, in effect, helps develop "other-directed" persons. Another disadvantage inherent in this group technique is the passive role of the teacher. In a sense, the insight, experience and skills of the teacher are muted. In their place, naive students play the dominant role in value development, and they do it quite unconsciously.

A third approach for developing students' values is one of acquainting students with examples of exemplary behavior. Instances of model behavior may be drawn from history, literature, and legend or, more directly, from examples set by teachers.

Literature for all levels of schooling has been selected for the past several hundred years on the basis of the ethical and moral lessons with which it dealt. As in other methods discussed previously, some students are truly inspired by these vicarious experiences but we have little evidence that attributes found in a student's reading are readily transferred to daily life.

Teaching values by a living example is a related tactic. Here it is assumed that "values are caught, not taught." It is argued that as teachers demonstrate values students will learn to prize these values. Surely people have been inspired by the goodness of a teacher with whom they have had the good fortune to be associated. However, teachers, especially in secondary schools, have little opportunity to demonstrate many key values. Problems that represent the real issues of life rarely present themselves in a 50-minute subject-matter period in such a way that students can observe their teacher's handling of them. It would truly be unfortunate if we had to rely on this approach as the only positive way teachers can help youngsters develop a set of values.

A fourth method deals with indoctrination and habit formation. Here it is assumed that when students are required to follow rules and regulations, when they are punished for infractions and praised for obedience, they will take on the values associated with the requirements. We are all familiar, however, with what students do when they are free *not* to obey the rules.

It is my contention that these four methods are rather ineffective. Perhaps their relative ineffectiveness arises partially because they are based on the assumption that the knowledge of ethical and moral choices necessarily leads to ethical and moral conduct. As pointed out many years ago by John Dewey (4), this assumption has little basis in fact.

Yet more important, these methods seem intent on utilizing external factors, such as lectures or peer-group pressures, to develop values. Friedenberg (6) analyzes the current problems in developing values as follows:

> . . . it is the inner discipline that is lacking; the school fails to provide a basis for it. The undisciplined behavior which sometimes results is often a sign of the anguish which results from having no core *of one's own.* [Emphasis added.]

The most promising approach would seem to be one that attempts to help each student build his own value system. This idea is supported by Allport (2) who asserts that no teaching is more important that that which contributes to a student's self. Clearly, this statement echoes the ideas of Kubie mentioned in the opening paragraphs. Are teachers able to help children in this way? B. O. Smith has said that teachers use little psychological knowledge beyond that found in common sense. What knowledge can we, as teachers, use in this area? Louis Raths has developed a teaching method designed to provide some direction for teachers who are interested in helping students develop their own value systems (15; 16; 17).

Use of Clarification Procedures

The teacher's role in this method is neither that of preacher nor that of passive listener. Instead the teacher strives to (a) establish a climate of psychological safety, (b) apply a clarification procedure. An elaboration of these procedures follows.

ESTABLISHMENT OF PSYCHOLOGICAL SAFETY

Nonjudgmental attitudes. It has been said that teachers have difficulty responding to an idea without saying, "That's good," "That's bad," or "What good is it?" To provide an atmosphere in which children will feel free to express themselves without threat of ridicule and derision, teachers must refrain from making harsh unnecessary judgments. Of course at times some judgments become necessary in situations in which the health and/or safety of students are threatened in any real sense.

Manifestations of concern. While the teacher may be nonjudgmental, it is important for him to be concerned with the ideas expressed by his students. If the concern is apparently lacking, then often the number of student ideas shared with a teacher tends to diminish. Perhaps students are reluctant to share their ideas with someone who is not interested in them. One of the most effective ways to show concern for a student's ideas is to *listen* to them. Busy teachers sometimes overlook this basic and effective technique for communicating interest to their students. Another method for a teacher's communicating his concern for a student's ideas is to *remember* them. As a teacher is able to cite a student's idea in a later conversation, the student cannot help but feel genuinely flattered and impressed.

Opportunities for the sharing of ideas. Teachers must organize their courses in such ways that children have the opportunity to express their opinions, purposes, feelings, beliefs, hunches, goals and interests, about moral issues. These attitudinal-type statements may then be examined by the child who expressed them with the teacher acting somewhat as a catalytic agent in the process. Some methods used by teachers in various researches by classroom teachers include: (a) question-answer discussion periods involving moot questions for the class to consider; (b) special written assignments; (c) role-playing techniques; (d) behavior manifestations of individuals or groups that may indicate attitudes, e.g., cheating or being tardy.

The task of finding issues that children may react to is no small problem. While our lives are filled with many, many moral and ethical questions to consider, even within our formal disciplines, it is difficult to find these issues in our textbooks, or *Weekly Readers*. Alexander (1), a textbook consultant for the New York City schools, has found that "few or no serious problems" are present in our current textbooks.

CLARIFYING STRATEGIES

Asking questions. The teacher may attempt to clarify the ideas elicited from his students by asking probing questions. The key criterion for selecting these questions is that they must be questions for which only the student knows the answer. Of course, to be effective they must be asked in a nonjudgmental manner. If a student seems seriously challenged by one of the questions, the teacher should make efforts to "save face" by accepting his bewilderment. For example, the teacher may pass on by saying, "That's a hard question for anyone to answer, isn't it?" "Let's think about it for a while and maybe an answer will come to us later." A list of questions that a teacher may ask is included below. Of course, this list is not exhaustive, and teachers may add to it as they become more fluent in the use of this procedure.

1. Reflect back what the student has said and add, "Is that what you mean?"
2. Reflect back what the student has said with distortions and add, "Is that what you mean?"
3. "How long have you felt (acted) that way?"
4. "Are you glad you think (act) that way?"
5. "In what way is that a good idea?"
6. "What is the source of your idea?"
7. "Should everyone believe that?"
8. "Have you thought of some alternatives?"
9. "What are some things you have done that reflect this idea of yours?"
10. "Why do you think so?"
11. "Is this what you really think?"
12. "Did you do this on purpose?"
13. Ask for definitions of key words.
14. Ask for examples.
15. Ask if this position is consistent with a previous one he has taken.

It is important that teachers ask these questions of students who express ideas with which they agree as well as with those students who express ideas with which they disagree.

Coding written work. Researchers have found the coding of written work very effective in value clarifying. Whenever students seem to express an attitude, belief, goal, purpose, interest, or aspiration, teachers may mark a V+ or V— in the margin to reflect this idea back to the student. This code works much like other more familiar codes we already use in our schools, e.g., WW for wrong word, or SP for misspelled word. There is one crucial difference. When a teacher marks WW in the margin, there usually *is* a wrong word. When a teacher marks V+ in the margin, it is understood that she is really asking, "Do you believe this?" or "Do you want to change it?"

Acceptance without judgment. It has been found that teachers feel awkward trying to draw the clarification exchange to a close. The verbal interaction between teacher and student is not to win an argument or to gain a debating point. The purpose of the exchange is to clarify students' ideas. It is important that teachers find a way to accept the students' ideas without communicating agreement or praise of them. In a sense, the exchange does not have an ending. Neither the teacher nor the student arrives at a conclusion. Neither is there a need for summarizing. Questions left unanswered are thought about and dwelt on by the student (and perhaps the teacher) at night before going to sleep, or during moments of quiet during the day. Some ways that have been found successful in closing an exchange are as follows:

1. Silence with a nod.
2. "Uh-huh."
3. "I see."
4. "I understand you better now."
5. "I can see how you would feel that way."
6. "I understand."
7. "I can see that it was difficult for you to decide that way."

In summary, the clarification procedure developed by Louis Raths attempts to elicit from students statements of an attitudinal nature and to clarify these statements for the student. By developing an emotional acceptance of himself on the part of his students, and asking students questions which will serve to clarify their own purposes, goals, attitudes, beliefs, etc., teachers can play an effective role in developing values in their classrooms.

This procedure can be time consuming or it may also take just a few seconds. For example, consider the following hypothetical exchange:

Student: I hate math.
Teacher: You have never liked math?
Student: Well, I did like it at one time.
Teacher: What changed your mind?
Student: I don't know.
Teacher: Oh.

Without trying to lecture the student about what he "ought" to like, without preaching about the dangers inherent in not liking math, the teacher is attempting to help the student understand his own preferences and values.

In passing, it may be appropriate to add that several researches (9; 11; 13; 14) have successfully attempted to test these ideas in classrooms in New York State and Wisconsin. Other studies are needed, of course, to test further the efficacy of this procedure. The experiences of a number of researches in this field suggest also that learning to use the process of clarifying is not easy. It is clearly a difficult matter to enter into a significant interaction with a student. The problem is much less that of identifying with a student, but one of identifying with the student's concerns, of listening, and of taking seriously what he has said and reacting thoughtfully to it.

It must be clear that teachers who apply the clarification procedure must have a tremendous respect for their students. As teachers agree or disagree with students' expressed ideas they must be able to consider them as tenable ones to hold. If teachers believe it is their role to "convert" students to a "right way" of thinking, then it seems they must basically disrespect the views their students hold now. The distinction I am trying to make is one between accepting and respecting. It would seem possible for me to respect the views of a colleague, let us say, without accepting those views. This is the spirit that I believe must dominate a teacher's conversations with his students. Of course, this statement must be modified to the extent that a student's views may threaten the health or safety of himself or society. It is my contention that such cases are rare in our classrooms. Yet there is still plenty of room for many safe differences of opinion and behavior between students and teachers.

Most of us have become accustomed to the association of teaching with changes in student behavior. Too frequently, quite without being aware of it, we look for "instant" changes. We hope for miracles on the "values front." We do not pay enough attention to the fact that it took many years for our students to learn their present almost valueless behavior, and that it may take a long sustained effort to help students to develop serious purposes and aspirations through the clarifying processes. For a free society, opportunities to clarify and to choose must be created again and again.

Norman Cousins (3) has written about his concern for the predatory quality of life in human form. He suggests that what makes our society so much like a jungle is the misfits who exert power over honest men.

There are those . . . who insist on projecting their warped ideas to the people around them. They are the agents of chaos. . . . Maybe this is what makes a jungle a jungle.

Cousins continues to say that the way out of the jungle is not just emptying it of these misfits. "There must be some notion about what is to take the place of the jungle. That is why ideals and goals are the most practical things in the world. They conquer the jungle, make men mobile, and convert humans from fawning and frightened animals into thinkers and builders." As teachers learn to develop the ideals, goals and values of students by applying the clarification procedures outlined in this paper, they may perhaps become truly "influential Americans."

REFERENCES

1. Albert Alexander, "The Gray Flannel Cover of the American History Text." *Social Education 24*:11; 1960.
2. Gordon Allport, *Becoming: Basic Considerations for a Psychology of Personality.* New Haven, Conn.: Yale University Press, 1955.
3. Norman Cousins, "Hoffa, Hegel, and Hoffer." *Saturday Review*, April 20, 1963.
4. John Dewey, *Moral Principles in Education.* Boston: Houghton Mifflin, 1909.
5. Educational Policies Commission. *Moral and Spiritual Values in the Public Schools.* Washington, D.C.: National Education Association, 1957.
6. Edgar Z. Friedenberg, *The Vanishing Adolescent.* New York: Dell, 1962.
7. Sol W. Ginsburg, "Values and the Psychiatrist." *American Journal of Orthopsychiatry 20*:466; 1950.
8. Philip E. Jacob, *Changing Values in College.* New York: Harper & Row, 1957.
9. Arthur Jonas, "A Study of the Relationship of Certain Behaviors of Children to Emotional Needs, Values, and Thinking." Unpublished Ed.D. thesis, New York University, 1960.
10. Vernon Jones, "Character Education," in *Encyclopedia of Educational Research,* Chester Harris, ed. New York: Macmillan, 1960.
11. Albert Klevan, "An Investigation of a Methodology of Value Clarification: Its Relationship to Consistency of Thinking, Purposefulness, and Human Relations." Unpublished Ed.D. thesis, New York University, 1958.
12. Lawrence Kubie, "Are We Educating for Maturity." *NEA Journal,* January 1959.
13. James Raths, "Underachievement and a Search for Values." *Journal of Educational Sociology 34*:2; May 1961.

14. ———, "Clarifying Children's Values." *National Elementary Principal 62*:2; November 1962.

15. Louis E. Raths, "Values and Teachers." *Educational Synopsis*, Spring 1957.

16. ———, "Sociological Knowledge and Needed Curriculum Research." *Research Frontiers in the Study of Children's Learning.* J. B. Macdonald, editor. Milwaukee: School of Education, the University of Wisconsin-Milwaukee, 1960.

17. ———, "Clarifying Values." *Curriculum for Today's Boys and Girls.* R. S. Fleming, editor. Columbus, Ohio: Charles Merrill Books, Inc., 1963.

CRITICISM OF CURRENT EVENTS: AN ANALYSIS *

Raymond J. Endres

The words seem simple enough: *current* and *events;* but together they are likely to evoke cries of rage from the skeptical who, infuriated by observations of current events programs, can only exclaim: "Dirty, stinking fish!" From supporters, on the other hand, come paeans of praise; these contend that the very center of the social studies is current events, a heart that pumps life's blood to the program. The truth probably lies somewhere between these extremes.

In the following paragraphs we propose (1) to review criticisms of current events programs; (2) to examine the validity of these criticisms; and (3) to propose some methods teachers in the upper elementary grades may use to help children become aware of the dilemmas they face as human beings living in the confused sixties of the twentieth century.

A Review of the Criticisms

Criticism of current events centers on the following: (1) the term itself has been made meaningless by such practices as show and tell, forced recitation, use of second-rate children's periodicals;

Raymond J. Endres is on the faculty at Bowling Green State University, Ohio.

* Reprinted from *The Social Studies 57*:8–14, 1966, with permission of the McKinley Publishing Co. and Raymond J. Endres.

(2) many teachers fail (a) to relate a current event to its historical genesis, (b) to relate an event to its geographical setting, (c) to relate an event to its psychosociological setting; (3) many teachers, in order to keep clear of entanglements, steer clear of anything controversial; (4) many teachers deal only with the superficial aspects of an event; (5) teachers lack background information and knowledge to deal with an event in depth; and (6) some teachers tend to equate the "truth" with the printed word.

The term around which the current events debate rages is "democratic citizenship," a term so broad as to be meaningless. To some, democratic citizenship as an end of instruction is perfectly consistent with their view that to educate is to liquidate ignorance. Only knowledge will allow the individual to operate as a responsible citizen; only knowledge will allow the citizen to operate in the public sector of community life for the benefit of all citizens; only knowledge will allow the human being to come to the full flower of his humanity, which is citizenship.

To others democratic citizenship is geared primarily to the development of attitudes and values, purportedly those related to life in the free society. Instruction is geared to the bent of the will. The values of the democratic society must be inculcated. The outcome of such instruction is revealed in the Boy Scout motto: "On my honor I will do my best to do my duty to God and my country."

Critics of current programs usually take a dim view of the latter position. They ask: "What is our duty to country?" They contend that many promoters of current events programs view democratic citizenship in an egregiously narrow manner. The good citizen in the narrow view obeys the law; he never challenges injustice that sometimes is the result of law. The good citizen votes; he may not recognize the issues involved in his voting. The good citizen keeps the peace; he does not realize that social injustice may emanate from the *status quo*. The good citizen supports the two party system; he does not ascertain nor can he elucidate the advantages and disadvantages of that system. In short, the "good citizen's duty" includes all those positive activities that exist on the fringe of public life and which require only minimal commitment. It's a bit like the contradictory *private citizen* concept which confuses the private and public sectors of man's activities as to which sector requires the greater autonomy, or freedom. The criticisms enumerated above will be dealt with more fully in the paragraphs to follow.

Current events programs in many classrooms are shallow. The wise teacher knows his pupils well enough not to allow them to swim beyond their depth, but depth commensurate with ability is the *sine qua non* of effective learning. Genuine understanding of current issues requires more than a cursory glance at a newspaper. Yet specialists seem intent upon developing this habit of surface reading in current events. The short synopses of news items given in student periodicals is a case in point. This treatment of news is akin to spreading sulfa powder on the surface of an ugly wound; one doesn't intend to cure the wound in this way; he *hopes* to prevent infection or insure that it won't be fatal.

Ultimately, real insight about a current event comes from an integrated understanding of the several factors leading to the event: historical, geographical, cultural. Every event has its chronological antecedents, past events leading to the current one. Only to the extent that these are known and understood will the student possess a fundamental grasp of the contemporary scene. Few current events should surprise us, unless we are ignorant of what came before. The Berlin Wall is an example. The impression given us by newspapers has been one of shock and disbelief. The answer to the question "Why?" would take us all the way back to Catherine of Russia and to the Romanoffs who followed her to the throne. We are always dismayed at man's inhumanity to man; but should we be surprised?

Events are also spatially related; that is, they are related to their geographic setting. As an example, the Angara hydro-power development complex is related to several pertinent geographic factors in the Soviet Union: (1) the topography of Siberian Russia; (2) the almost complete exploitation of available hydro-electric power in European Russia; (3) the experiments of the Soviets with long-distance transport of hydro-induced power; (4) the movement eastward of certain Soviet industries; (5) the development of the virgin steppe region and the need for irrigation and power sources; and (6) the dream of Soviet engineers and scientists to open the vast middle reaches of Siberian Russia to development through a grand diversion of naturally northern moving waters of the Ob and Yenisey to the steppe areas. It is not enough to know the 2,000,000 KWH potential of the dam at Krasnoyarsk.

Understanding of current events involves a knowledge of cultural factors. We can better understand the present Sino-Soviet rift, for example, in terms of cultural factors. We can begin by asking ourselves, does this rift have an ideological base, or is it more related to the intense national feeling of the Russian people who have had, after all, an extensive history of exposure to Russianization under the Czars? And how about the centuries-old distrust the Russians have of the Chinese, dating from the invasion and domination of the Kievan Rus by the Mongols in the twelfth and thirteenth centuries? We've heard several Russian historians and sovietologists refer to the Russian proverb: With a Chinese for a friend, who needs an enemy? A knowledge of these cultural factors is required if a current happening is to be comprehended. We must be careful, of course, that in our zeal to use our knowledge of such factors, we keep open the door to other possibilities. Some questions of politics, tradition, or the relationships among human beings have the quality of openness. Such a question, in our opinion, follows: to what extent are Soviet leaders nationalists and to what extent internationalists? That authorities disagree on this point supports this contention.

Teachers should recognize that stories in general periodicals—newspapers, weekly magazines, news summaries, and the like—do not usually reveal the background information needed to understand these events. Articles are generally brief and concise, and written in an inverted style which makes reporting in depth impossible. The article gives the reader the surface phenomena and frequently the feeling that "these are the facts." The danger in this is obvious.

Many reporters, even good ones, finding it extremely difficult to deal with the question "Why?" solve the problem by not dealing with it at all. This may be just as well. The short-term tenure of most journalists on a particular assignment does not allow them to accumulate the knowledge and insight necessary to genuine interpretive reporting. This does not alter our view that the most important question we should ask is: "Why did this event happen?"

Validity of the Criticisms

If these are the criticisms, what of their validity? Although we believe that critics are misguided in criticizing current events programs and teachers *in toto,* we do agree generally with their criticisms. There are, of course, some excellent social studies programs which include exceptional instruction in current events. The extent of the validity of the criticism is difficult to get at, however, and we base our evaluation of it on observations of programs over the past ten years. These lead us to conclude the following: (1) in general, current events instruction is weak; (2) many teachers in the social studies in the upper grades do not possess the background necessary to deal effectively with contemporary issues; (3) both children and teachers seem rather bored with the program, and at a time when the pace of history is quickening. Certainly we live in times that are frightening and frustrating; they are also exciting and energizing.

Adults, we feel, communicate to children the attitude that news and newspapers are inseparable. Many adults would be surprised if told that news is intricately tied to history, culture, geography. Some teachers suffer a similar lack and they reinforce the attitude that, to *know* the news one merely has to read the daily newspaper. Some teachers make small effort, moreover, to carry through from day to day and week to week on a story of great human significance, such as the integration story, or on one of international significance, such as arms reduction.

Periodicals developed for children do have some strengths; they likewise have weaknesses. First of all, as in most periodical literature, the publishers are interested in capturing as large a portion of the market as possible. Publishers talk about reaching the "common denominator," as one did in a recent letter to us. He meant, we surmise, that he didn't want to offend any of his readers, or more likely, the politico-cultural views of their parents. Nothing colored, nothing controversial, nothing in depth; and frequently the result is a watered-down version of the small town daily which depends exclusively on AP and UPI reports.

Using children's periodicals exclusively leads to a second weakness: teachers may be lulled into a false sense of security, that having "covered" this week's edition they've finished their job. Chances are that most teachers have a current events period, an hour or 50 minute period in which news of the week is discussed. Out comes the magazine or news sheet; each story is "read"; each story is discussed. Seldom are events of the past related to the present; infrequently are geography and history brought into the picture. In fairness, this is a weakness of teachers rather than of the periodicals, but a weakness of the program nevertheless.

After listening to some current events classes, we've caught ourselves concluding that today's children are not interested in what is going on in their world. Such, we believe and pray, is not the case. The spontaneity and curiosity of children can be great assets to the teacher if allowed to work. Some instruction leads children to surface reading. Nothing is more insidious. To take children beneath the surface of events about which they read, the teacher must possess the art of questioning. *Probe* for responses that get beneath surface considerations; *probe* to get the child to reflect, to relate his past experience and knowledge to the present; *probe* to get him to dig for understanding and to demand of the teacher more than surface generalities; *probe* to get out in the open the child's concerns about his world. A child between the ages of ten and fifteen sometimes shows a startling perception of the fundamental issues facing mankind today. Asked what he thought was the language's most beautiful word, one boy replied: *life*. "The other things don't make no difference. I just don't wanna get killed. All I wanna do is live, just live, that's all." [From an editorial, *Saturday Review,* July 20, 1963.]

Much of what passes for news is mere triviality. Any of us can easily be sucked up into the vacuity of such overblown tripe. "Names make news." How many students of journalese have heard that trite statement? We should ask: "What names?" All names are not equally newsworthy. It seems a strange perversion of the meaning of the First Amendment that editors seem forced to include in their news columns much that is merely gossip. Each of us is human, and our proclivity for little personal tidbits is sated by the daily reports of the nocturnal habits of highly paid professionals. With whom is Jenifer Tearsheet sleeping tonight? So goes the euphemistically phrased question. The importance of people in the news, we contend, is directly related to the importance of the events of which they play a part. Relatively, the President of the United States is more important in the news than Willie Mays. Even here the newspapers fail us, for they frequently report to us items of presidential performance which are little related to the great importance of the office he holds or to events which develop out of that office.

One purpose the social studies share with all education is to get the student to read better, more carefully and more critically. Fundamental to this purpose are the teacher's efforts to help children deal more effectively with their language. With the quantitative expansion of the printed word has come a possible diminution in power of much of our language. In the process words have taken on added meanings. The teacher's responsibility is to provide language experiences that will allow students to broaden their conceptual bases. This includes helping children understand the various shades of meaning and helping them assign specific meaning to a particular context. This process is called *differentiation.*

In a very real sense the end of education is the development of the power to differentiate or discriminate. The educated person's response to a given language stimulus should not be short-circuited: it should be rational rather than purely emotional. A person is exposed to the stimulus, *communist.* What is his response? If his identification-reaction is "lousy, treacherous, red," he lacks the ability to differentiate. Does a person become apoplectic when he sees certain words in print? Does he react emotionally when confronted with value-laden words—communist, conservative, birchite, fascist, socialist? The possibility of a person's having real communication with writer or speaker under these circumstances is remote.

The more experience children have with concepts in a variety of contexts, the greater the probability that their ability to differentiate will be enhanced. What is equally important, children will have the opportunity to make a commitment based on knowledge and reason. Some of them may not make such a commitment. Others, on the other hand, may come to the conviction that something or someone should never be condemned (or condoned) merely because it or he is strange and unknown to the beholder. These latter will be guiltless of the crime of xenophobia, a sin of the spirit which always looks askance at what is new, strange, or different. Children may acknowledge, moreover, that something of value exists beyond the boundaries of their province.

Possible Solutions to Current Problems

In our opinion, current events as a separate program detached from the rest of the social studies and language arts has limited value. Some teachers, however, may feel that they can have a separate program and integrate those aspects of the broader curriculum as needed. Others may want to incorporate current events into the social studies. Whether or not such an incorporation takes place is incidental to the quality of instruction possible under either organization. The good teacher will always relate current with historical and geographical factors. The integration story can hardly be separated from slavery, the slave trade, the reasons for the development of slavery in the South, abolition, Lincoln, the Civil War, Reconstruction, separate but equal facilities, and the Supreme Court desegregation decision of 1954.

In the following paragraphs we make a few suggestions which may aid teachers in their attempts to help children become more aware of their relationships to their world. The value of these suggestions may come in stimulating teachers to think critically about practices they've engaged in while teaching current events. We sincerely believe that the inspiration that comes from the imagination of the practitioner is more likely to affect the program positively than second-hand ideas.

Naming the key personalities in the news. As children pass through school they become aware of and recognize, for good or bad, those names which constantly appear in the news. In order to help them recognize the relationship of people to news of importance, the teacher may ask children to help select the top personalities in the news each week. Which names appear again and again? Why? An objective of such instruction might be to show the student that a home run by Mickey Mantle in the seventh game of the World Series in no way compares in importance to another event that may shape the destiny of mankind, such as the appointment of

Henry Cabot Lodge as ambassador to Viet Nam or the visit of Nikita Khrushchev to the Aswan Dam in Egypt.

As children develop interest they may decide to engage in a year-long study to determine the "Man-of-the-Year" in the news. Will he be Martin Luther King, Charles DeGaulle, or Mao Tse-Tung? Again, the man is incidental to the events, except as his personality may shape the course of the events. Children must be prepared to answer the question, "Why?" As children progress through this process they may decide that names are secondary to events. Thus they may move logically to the next suggestion.

Identifying the top stories of the year. As they gain insight into the events in which they are immersed because they are human beings, children may conclude, rightly in our opinion, that it is impossible to identify a single story or person as outstanding. Even given the perspective of time, the historian finds it difficult to assay events in terms of top priority. This is not to say that all stories are of equal importance. They are not. Why should the integration story, for example, be included among the top stories of 1963–64? And what are the chances it will continue to be important in the years ahead? If they are to be successful in dealing with such questions, teachers must learn to frame questions that, in effect, ask why, but in terms that allow the student to frame his answer readily. Frequently the blunt question, "Why?" is a stopper. Sometimes answers to the questions *what, when, where,* and *who* make answering the question *why* easier.

Analyzing events as they appear in the press. We would hope that teachers would always be ready to discuss questions related to the basic freedoms which most Americans are so glib to postulate, but so retarded to elucidate. Free speech and free press are certainly related. How well does this seem to be understood by editors and publishers as evidenced by the events covered most thoroughly in their newspapers? This question can serve as a starting point for a year-long discussion of news and the purpose of a free press in an open society such as ours purports to be. This can lead among upper-grade children to a discussion of how free, relatively, the press in America is; how it fulfills (or fails to fulfill) the First Amendment of the Constitution; or to what degree the press in America gives its readers those features demanded by them. Discussion can center around the extent of the advertiser's influence on editorial policy, or whether an advertising-supported news service is in the best interest of persons living in a republic.

Newspapers give so much space to top movie, TV, and sports personalities. Can this high allotment be justified? It would be interesting for children in the upper grades to study the relative amounts of space devoted to certain categories of events in their hometown newspapers. How much space is alloted to world news, local news, state news, rural news, urban news, feature stories (unknown personalities), feature stories (well-known personalities), columns giving advice (medical, lovelorn, investment, etc.), comics, editorials, interpretative columns (Lippmann, Childs, McGill, etc.).

Comparing different newspapers. Children in upper grades can compare different newspapers as to the amount of space each devotes to the several categories of news. How, for example, does the New York *Times* compare with the local newspaper in the amount of coverage given the controversial issue of aid to Viet Nam? Which paper, among several dailies, allots more column inches to international news, to national and domestic news, to editorials? How do different newspapers handle the news? Does one paper editorialize in its so-called news columns while another uses its editorial powers discreetly? Children can compare, moreover, the editorial policies of several papers through an analysis of their editorials, cartoons, columns, etc.

Discussing the special functions of various news media. As the young become more adept at interpreting the news, as their powers of discrimination develop, they can engage in other activities centered around such questions as these: Do different news media—newspapers, news magazines, television, radio—perform different functions? What is the place in America of the small town weekly, or does it have one? How does each medium function in the best interest of persons living in a democracy? To what extent should these media be protected from vested interests that may seek to exert an influence over their editorial policy? How can the individual protect himself from the power of the press if, for example, an editor uses a person's name in his columns to sell newspapers? How deep an understanding of events can we develop from reading newspapers and watching television?

Thus, in the last question, we are brought back to the fundamental problem of the need to engage in a continuing study of those immortal aspects of human activity: the unfolding of the historical drama of human existence; the battle man continues to fight, not always successfully, with the elements; man's relationship to his environment, his partnership with it; the relationship of man to man in anger, frustration, war, peace, love, and hate.

Continuing an interest in contemporary affairs. Unless the student is interested in whatever he is studying, the chances are that his learning will be limited. We start with a positive factor, the natural curiosity of man to know. Each of us wants to learn, to understand. These motives can be blunted. Sadly, they frequently are. The first requirement of a good program, whatever the subject, is a good teacher. The teacher must know his material. This requires that he read broadly, that his powers of interpretation become intensified and sharpened through reading well beyond the front page of the daily newspaper. After all, the teacher must know enough about those forces affecting man's destiny to be able to lead the child toward an awareness of them. To ask intelligent questions, we must possess knowledge. Through the art of questioning we become, like Socrates, the mid-wife of our students' ideas.

To stimulate interest and concern, the good teacher tries to assure that his discussions in class are genuine. Discussion should not be confused with recitation. More is involved in good discussion than (a) a question from the teacher and (b) a response from the pupil. In addition to discussion, sometimes to stimulate it, teachers can use quizzes, especially oral quizzes, effectively. Where is this event happening? What is happening? To whom is it happening? Why is it happening?

Identifying common concerns early. The sooner we can help children identify the central issues with which they want to deal during the school year, the sooner we can center our reading activities around these topics. Stuart Chase recently wrote an article entitled, "Bombs, Babies, and Bulldozers," in the *Saturday Review*. In this article he tried to identify the problems he considers central to life in our times. Are these—the possibility of nuclear war, the great increase of the world's population, and the geometric progression of technology and its effect on living space—the problems we would want to start with? We've already mentioned others: the slowdown of legislative machinery in the United States, the integration story, the battle of man to use his resources wisely. There are others: the changes in American agriculture, urban problems (air pollution, slums, traffic, etc.), delinquency and the rise of the crime rate.

We would not be content to take, say, three of these. Perhaps we could consider most of those mentioned. The point is that somewhere we must draw the line. There is only so much we can do in a given amount of time. And somewhere along the line stories become more trivial. We encourage pupils to read outside these areas, for another important story may break tomorrow. We keep asking ourselves and our students: are we choosing the important stories? Are we differentiating between the real and the trivial?

Helping children see the impact of propaganda on their lives. So great is the influence of propaganda on the lives of each of us, that it behooves the teacher to help children see clearly how propaganda is used. Most obvious and blatant is the use of propaganda in advertising, especially on television. Teachers must not stop at pointing out to children the techniques used in advertising: glittering generalities, name-dropping, personality identification, "plain truth," "plain folks," value identification. Propaganda can be used much more subtly than this, and it is. Propaganda, furthermore, is not necessarily an evil. It has a definite relation to doctrine. All doctrine is not evil, or life itself is meaningless. We should, however, recognize the doctrinaire when we see it.

One example of the use of propaganda: a newspaper publisher decides to go on a crusade. Whatever the rightness of his cause, he uses the columns of his newspaper to get people to identify with his value system. We do not disagree with this as a function of the press. A great many reforms have come from it. We *are* interested in getting children to see that propaganda is involved. The amount of space allotted to a particular event or series of events likewise has propaganda significance. The average man is likely to say, "Gee, if Mr. Jones (the editor) spends so much space on urban renewal, it must be important." Unfortunately propagandizing a cause is not the same as providing the reader information which he can use to make up his own mind.

Conclusion

The effectiveness of our instruction in current events or in any other subject cannot be judged by how "good" the person is after having had contact with us. A great many outstanding teachers, Gilbert Highet points out, seemed to have exactly the opposite effect on some of their students. He cites Christ and Judas as an example.

Teachers *can* hope, however. We exercise this virtue in this way: thirty years from now, when a student returns to us or we come across him in the marketplace, we expect to see a man whose *weltanschauung*, whose view of the world, has not become wizened with age, a man who has not become tightly bound to his immediate affairs, a man who can still differentiate among human affairs, picking the relevant and leaving the refuse. Our failures only stimulate us to try harder.

Investigation-Oriented Approaches to Social Studies Instruction

*I*N MODERN SOCIAL STUDIES PROGRAMS the role of the teacher has changed significantly from what it once was. Traditionally, teaching has been perceived as the process of transmitting knowledge and skills to others. The main teaching function was thought to be that of dispensing information. With this perception of teaching, pupils were not often free to inquire, reason, discover, and substantiate.

As frequently happened, the teacher became *the* primary source of knowledge. Moreover, he was often regarded as an intellectual authority figure. Such a position of power and prestige can have the effect of placing pupils in an intellectually submissive role— one that discourages an inquiring and critical attitude. Obviously such a pupil-teacher relationship did little to develop free and open inquiry on the part of young learners. On the contrary, this kind of pedagogy tended to fix pupil dependency on the teacher in the acquisition of social studies knowledge and skills. In such a setting there is little to encourage independent learning.

It is not surprising, therefore, that in recent years much attention has been given investigation-oriented approaches to social studies instruction. These approaches are founded on the assumption that much, but not all, of what the child learns in social studies can be discovered as a result of independent inquiry. The key words are *inquiry* and *discovery*. Two significant learning acts occur in applying an investigation-oriented approach: (1) the individual engages in some kind of inquiry or ideational-informational searching process focused on a question to be answered or a problem to be solved; and (2) the pupil makes a discovery, perceives a causal relationship, states a generalization, or predicts an outcome growing out of the inquiry process.

The teacher who employs investigation-oriented instruction operates differently from the didactic model earlier described. To begin with, the inquiry-discovery teacher views his teaching function as that of encouraging the pupil to find out things for himself. There is much less dependency on the teacher as the fountainhead of knowledge. The investigation-oriented teacher is quite secure in the honest admission that he does not know the answer to every question. More reliance is placed on independent thought in this classroom, and rather than using instructional time to dispense information, the teacher concentrates on the skills, techniques, and processes of investigation—that is, analysis, inquiry, hypothesis testing, generalizing, classifying, and so forth.

Inquiry and discovery are not entirely new ideas, although recent developments have provided more sophisticated techniques, thus giving new impetus to this kind of teaching. Psychologists who advocate the use of investigation-oriented instruction often claim two distinct advantages for it: (1) children tend to retain the knowledge longer when they discover it for themselves; and (2) discovered knowledge has greater transfer value. Interest in inquiry and discovery teaching strategies has also been stimulated by the current emphasis on the development of thinking processes in children.

Possibly the most cogent reason for putting the child on his own in social studies is that this appears to be a sound procedure for teaching children how to ask significant questions and work toward answering them. Although teachers are unable to teach solutions to tomorrow's problems, they are able to teach children ways in which various kinds of problems can be studied and discoveries made. Many teachers advance the hope that the child's continuing experience with investigation-oriented instruction will enable him to construct his own reusable schema for problem inquiry and discovery. Such intellectual abilities should prove useful not only later on in formal education but also, and perhaps more importantly, during his life as an adult citizen.

THE QUESTIONS ASKED: EFFECTIVENESS OF INQUIRY TECHNIQUES IN ELEMENTARY SCHOOL SOCIAL STUDIES *

Francis P. Hunkins

Introduction

Today in social studies we are after more than factual knowledge; we are striving to have pupils inquire, to investigate the various realms of knowledge. Whether objectives are stated or unstated, a prominent means of stimulating pupils' inquiring and thinking in social studies is the effective use of questions. Teachers' questions and questions incorporated in instructional materials probably are significant in nurturing the development of cognitive powers and related skills of pupils. Questions reveal operational objectives that stress, for example, the increase of pupils' knowledge of facts, of understandings, of concepts, and of pupils' skills at interpreting information and ideas. Questions reveal whether the teacher is guiding pupils in their inquiry techniques.

The classroom teacher devotes a large portion of his time asking questions (e.g., Adams, 1964; Aschner, 1961; Barr, 1928; Floyd, 1960; Stevens, 1912). Aschner observed that teachers, by their use of questions, commonly "trigger" four types of thinking activities: remembering, reasoning, evaluating or judging, and creative thinking. In designing a good question, the teacher should, according to Aschner, begin by analyzing the type of thinking to be fostered and the type of task that must be set to initiate such thinking. Questions can focus the thinking and the inquiry of pupils.

Today much emphasis has been given to making pupils inquirers. Pupils should learn how to learn, how to see relationships and build generalizations. Pupils need to engage in meaningful discovery to make them capable of assuming a productive role in society.

The usefulness of questions has long been recognized as significant in the teaching-learning interaction. However, the phrasing of questions capable of stimulating higher thinking activity, or stimulating effective inquiry, is difficult and has been among the most neglected dimensions of teaching in both research and practice.

Francis P. Hunkins is Assistant Professor of Education at the University of Washington, Seattle.

* Symposium paper presented at the A.E.R.A. National Convention in New York in February 1967. Reprinted with permission of Francis P. Hunkins.

What effects do various types of questions have on pupils' behavior? Indeed, the current plethora of information on inquiry training gives evidence that most of us are assuming that children and teachers are indeed already good questioners.

To implement the general goal of fostering thinking and inquiry, "realizable" teaching strategies and specially prepared materials must be utilized with pupils. In these strategies and materials, surely, questions must be integral elements.

Related Research and Pertinent Literature

PAST RESEARCH

Stevens (1912) conducted the first serious investigation into the role of questions. What kinds of questions did social studies and English teachers ask? She noted a dominant emphasis on memory questions in both types of classes with a larger proportion of this type of question existing in the social studies sections. From Stevens' study, several conclusions were drawn: (a) the teacher did most of the work, questioning, in the class; (b) the art of pupils' expression was smothered under the sheer number of teachers' questions; (c) individual differences of pupils received slight attention; (d) the classroom was considered primarily as a place for displaying knowledge instead of a laboratory for gaining understanding in depth; and (e) slight effort appeared to be exerted to guide pupils in becoming self-reliant and independent workers.

Stevens' work provided the empirical evidence that teachers' questions were not geared to the development of pupils' higher cognitive functions. Pupils were not being allowed or prepared for thinking, for inquiring.

A contribution to the development of a question was Yamada's work in 1913. He compared the effectiveness of telling or questioning about pictures with that of telling or questioning about objects or events from real life. Yamada concluded that the asking-questions session provided far greater range in providing information. However, the narrative or telling activities seemed to supply quality of thoughts. The position of questions in classroom discussion also concerned Yamada. He stated it was better to have a narrative session, free spontaneous report first, and, then, to engage in questioning activity. Taba (1964), more recently, seemed to be suggesting something similar in her research on children's thinking.

The next serious attempt to study the question was undertaken by Gatto (1929) who wished to discover the nature of pupils' questions in relation to various pupil characteristics and to utilize this information in the improvement of classroom procedures and study processes. Regrettably, Gatto's work is the only serious attempt to investigate pupils' questions.

Gatto's investigation revealed that memorization was the most common study activity stimulated by classroom questions. The overwhelming emphasis on memory activities was present in all curricular subjects, grade levels, and ages considered. Pupils' questions reflected the types used by teachers and types present in textbooks.

Haynes in 1935 examined sixth grade teachers' classroom questions in relation to teacher characteristics, including intelligence and experience. Questions were analyzed with reference to (1) total number asked, (2) number of factual questions asked, (3) number of questions demanding thought, (4) number of alternate questions (only two answers), (5) number of leading questions, and (6) the number of current questions dealing with topics of the day. Among his conclusions, Haynes noted a significant correlation between the intelligence of teachers and the number of thought questions asked. Conclusions also revealed that teachers with high intelligence asked more alternate and leading questions. Teachers tended to ask fewer questions as their experiences increased. However, no relationship existed between experience and the type of questions asked by teachers.

It is evident that over the years, questioning, an important feature of the teaching act, of inquiry training, and of instructional materials, has not been singled out for the attention it deserves, either in research or in speculation. Recently, however, interests have revived concerning questions.

RECENT AND CURRENT RESEARCH

Floyd (1960) studied the oral questioning activity of selected primary school teachers. His purpose was to reveal the current and prevalent oral questioning techniques of the "best" primary teachers and their classes in Colorado elementary schools. Analysis of taped discourses of thirty classrooms revealed that about seventy per cent of the oral expressions were delivered by the teacher and that 93 per cent of all questions were asked by teachers. Concerning quality of questions, Floyd observed that questions capable of stimulating thinking were employed only slightly more than six per cent of the time. Forty-two per cent of the questions asked were memory questions. Teachers' oral questions seemed to be used primarily to check the recall of facts, not to stimulate thinking, nor to guide pupils in developing effective inquiry techniques.

Adams (1964), employing a system of categories by which he

classified the questions asked by secondary school English and social studies teachers, discovered a dominating emphasis on memory questions. However, his results, when compared to Stevens' (1912) earlier conclusions, did reveal that memory questions were used by present-day teachers (both social studies and English) to a lesser degree.

These were the only two current studies that dealt specifically with questions until this investigator initiated some additional research into questions. This is not to say that interest in questions does not exist at the present time. However, questions have been considered empirically as parts of systems, whether it be teacher's verbal behavior, or inquiry training, or programed instruction.

Taba (1964) proposed specific teaching strategies .employing questions to develop thinking. A questioning strategy should provide, she urged, for appropriate constraint within a structured freedom. Questions, she affirmed, can be utilized as transition devices from one level of thought to another. They also can stimulate the formation of new conceptual schemes. Questions should stimulate and guide the direction of knowledge, she asserted, instead of providing a particular model or the end product of a search. Taba concluded that the discrimination of data is a skill that is prerequisite to performing the more sophisticated operations of inference making.

In Suchman's work (1958), the procedure of inquiry specifies somewhat the types of questions pupils ask, or should ask, but Suchman's question categories are quite broad. Also questions are not really analyzed from the standpoint of effectiveness of type. Blank (1963) dealt in some degree with this crucial problem of form and type of question in inquiry training. He studied inquiry training within the medium of programed instruction and required sixth graders to ask questions about the relevant dimensions of problems prior to attempts at solution. Analysis of data indicated that children in an inquiry training program, when contrasted with children not in such a program, asked significantly more questions on both oral and written criterion tests and participated more in class discussion with no detriment to class progress.

On the other hand, Herrick (1962) concluded from his research that the use of problem-setting questions prior to solution produced no significant increases in either rate or amount of learning. The conflicting results of Blank's and Herrick's studies preclude suggesting generalizations at this time. The foregoing results reveal that even though questions are being considered in research, no serious attention has been given to the cognitive processes that different types of questions might stimulate.

Over the years, numerous articles, speeches, and books have exhorted the merits of the question as a device for effective thinking. DeGarmo (1911), for example, asserted that excellent questioning was excellent teaching. "In the skillful use of the question more than in anything else lies the fine art of teaching; for in (such use) we have the guide to clear and vivid ideas, the quick spur to imagination, the stimulus to thought, the incentive to action" (p. 179).

Recently Loughlin (1961) equated effective questioning with effective teaching. His list of principles for questioning included (1) distribute questions so that the entire class is involved, (2) have a balance between factual and thought-provoking questions, (3) utilize both simple and exacting questions, (4) encourage responses of some length, and (5) stimulate critical thinking by asking "To what extent? How? Why? Compare." Klebaner (1964) supported these general principles by asserting that the purpose of the question must be identified by the teacher and realized by the pupil. Pupils should be made aware, he insisted, of the type of answers that different kinds of questions demand. Is this pupil awareness cultivated in our teaching of the social studies? Is it done regardless of the subject taught?

Cole in 1933 seemed to hit the mark regarding questioning when he declared that the greatest skill in questioning was manifested not so much by the teacher asking effective questions but, rather, by the teacher stimulating the pupils to formulate pertinent questions concerning the subject.

Wellington and Wellington more recently (1962) also stressed that teaching was not the teacher asking questions, but rather the teacher guiding pupils so that they asked effective questions. Carner (1963) took somewhat the same position in stressing that teachers must be cognizant of the types of thinking required before they can frame effective questions. He discussed several cognitive skills that should be nurtured by questions: sensing continuity and sequence, perceiving relationships, making inferences, drawing sound conclusions, and evaluating the validity of information.

A New Slant

The research on questions completed thus far has been primarily concerned with enumerating the types of questions employed either by the teacher or by the pupil. The teacher asks such and such per cent of memory questions. The pupils only ask a small per cent of the questions, and these mirror the memory emphasis nurtured by the teacher. This investigator, although interested in this type of data, also was curious as to the effects different types of questions would have on the thinking and achievement of pupils in the social studies milieu. Attention to this aspect of question research had not existed. In this paper, only the aspect of question influence on achievement will be discussed.

This author concentrated his attention on three types of questions: knowledge types, analysis types, and evaluation types, using as the criterion the *Taxonomy of Educational Objectives,* edited by Benjamin Bloom (1956). The null hypothesis regarding achievement stated that the use of text-type materials employing questions requiring "analysis and evaluation" will not result in differences in sixth grade pupils' social studies achievement when compared with the use of text-type materials incorporating questions requiring the recall of knowledge in relationship to pupils (a) reading level, (b) sex, and (c) the interaction between these variables.

A total of 127 pupils received text-type materials that had a dominant emphasis (more than 47 per cent) on analysis and evaluation questions. The second experimental group consisted of 133 pupils who experienced materials having a dominant emphasis (over 87 per cent) on knowledge questions. These materials dealt with specific sections of the pupils' social studies textbook.

At the termination of the four-week experimental period, it was statistically evident that those pupils who had worked with the analysis and evaluation questions had a higher degree of achievement as determined by results on an achievement test constructed by the investigator, reliability of .68 (Kuder-Richardson formula).

Several possible reasons for the higher cognitive-level questions (analysis and evaluation) stimulating a statistically higher social studies achievement among pupils may be advanced. Questions requiring analysis and evaluation can, it seems reasonable, stimulate individuals to utilize several viewpoints regarding the information embedded in the task. Pupils using such questions may have been forced to engage in intellectual activity in which they considered the various aspects of factual knowledge and evaluated the complexity, implications, and applications of this knowledge. Such mental "juggling" may have enabled pupils to know better the information with which they were dealing.

The higher-level questions employed also may have enabled pupils to think about relationships in information. Pupils, by experiencing such questions, probably evaluated information for its relevance. Drawing of warranted conclusions by pupils may have been encouraged in the process. Perhaps such intellectual activities gave greater clarity to the instructional content under consideration.

Another possible reason for the stimulation of greater achievement by the higher-level questions is that these questions presumably required pupils to think actively with information. These types of questions do not permit pupils to sit by and "receive" all that is relevant, valid, and meaningful. Pupils must "wrestle" with the information. These types of questions have the potential, it seems, to make pupils uneasy, but, also, to encourage them to probe their own knowledge and to discover meanings—to inquire.

Additional Target Problems

This investigator's research results do not mean that we can state with exactness that if one uses analysis and evaluation questions, pupils will raise their achievement levels. Indeed, we have just begun! This research on the types of questions and their influence is a beginning—a humble beginning.

Since this study is only a beginning, replication is an obvious need. Such studies would be informative and would provide additional bases for conclusions. Modifications of this author's study also can be productive. For example, the time period could be lengthened and the number of subjects increased without any drastic alteration of the investigation's format. Investigations employing samples different from the one in this investigator's research also would provide a broader base for generalization. Future research might incorporate questions with specific cognitive emphases within textual narratives and at the end of textbook chapters.

Another fertile possibility for additional study would include training some teachers in forming specific types of questions and then examining the social studies achievement of their pupils. Results obtained could be contrasted with those gathered from pupils whose teachers had not received such training. Such a study might last a year and would add clarity to points such as the following: can teachers be instructed in better questioning techniques, and does better questioning by teachers improve pupils' achievement in social studies? Further investigations should be directed to the effects on pupils of high cognitive-level questions in teacher-guided discussion as opposed to discussion where questioning had no predetermined or low-cognitive emphases. Similar studies could employ a television teacher using questions with predetermined high-level questions. Should teachers use certain types of questions in special sequences? To answer this question, research is needed. Similar research also could examine questions with regard to thinking and skill of inquiry.

What happens if pupils in a class situation are taught to form their own questions? Such instruction in the anatomy of the question might enable pupils to gain greater insights into their quest for knowledge. Such experiences make an important contribution to pupils' skill in discussion.

Do certain types of questions lend themselves better to use in certain genre of materials? What are the optimal types of questions to employ in textbooks, workbooks, filmstrips, picture sequences? Are there optimal ways of combining certain types of questions with certain materials? These questions need attention. With materials, the problem of question placement is relevant. Only scant research is available regarding this, and such research has presented conflicting conclusions.

Of course, these recommendations for further study can apply to areas of the curriculum other than the social studies. For instance, will analysis questions employed in sixth grade science stimulate an increase in achievement and greater skill in inquiry techniques? Will evaluation questions in the study of literature foster pupil understanding? Additional study can provide the empirical data needed to answer such questions.

Conclusion

Questions are part of teaching. Past research has been primarily concerned with tallying types of questions that teachers employ and has not been concerned to any appreciable degree with types of questions to employ in varying teaching strategies. We have assumed that good questions have the characteristic of spontaneous generation.

Pupils are confronted by questions in teachers' discourse, in textbooks, and in other instructional materials. An understanding of the complexities of the question is crucial to improvement of social studies education; indeed, to all of education, whether that improvement be concentrated on pupils' achievement, thinking, processes of learning, or inquiring. With further research presently held assumptions may be substantiated, modified, or discarded. This leads to the suggestion that the time is propitious to continue investigation into the realm of questions regarding their influence on pupils' intellectual growth.

REFERENCES

Thomas Howard Adams, *The Development of A Method for Analysis of Questions Asked by Teachers in Classroom Discourse.* Doctor's thesis. New Brunswick, N. J.: Rutgers, The State University, 1964.

Mary Jane McCue Aschner, "Asking Questions to Trigger Thinking." *NEA Journal 56* :44–45, 1961.

A. S. Barr, *Characteristic Differences in the Teaching Performances of Good and Poor Teachers of the Social Studies.* Bloomington, Ill.: Public School Publishing Co., 1929.

Stanley S. Blank, *Inquiry Training Through Programmed Instruction.* Doctor's thesis. Berkeley: University of California, 1963.

Benjamin S. Bloom, ed., *Taxonomy of Educational Objectives, The Classification of Educational Goals: Handbook I Cognitive Domain.* New York: McKay, 1956.

Richard L. Carner, "Levels of Questioning." *Education 83* :545–550, 1963.

Percival R. Cole, *The Method and Technique of Teaching.* London, New York: Oxford University Press, 1933.

Charles DeGarmo, *Interest and Education, The Doctrine of Interest and Its Concrete Application.* New York: Macmillan, 1911.

William D. Floyd, *An Analysis of the Oral Questioning Activity in Selected Colorado Primary Classrooms.* Doctor's thesis. Greeley, Col.: Colorado State College, 1960.

Frank N. Gatto, *Pupils' Questions: Their Nature and Their Relationship to the Study Process.* Doctor's thesis. Pittsburgh, Pa.: University of Pittsburgh, 1928.

Hubert Calvin Haynes, *Relation of Teacher Intelligence, Teacher Experience and Type of School to Types of Questions.* Contribution to Education, No. 150. Doctor's thesis. Nashville, Tenn.: George Peabody College for Teachers, 1935.

Merlyn C. Herrick, *The Effect of Problem-Setting Questions on Rate and Amount of Learning in Programming Teaching Machines.* Final Report. U.S. Department of Health, Education, and Welfare, Office of Education, Cooperative Research Grant No. 712130. Bloomington: Indiana University, 1952. (Mimeographed)

Francis P. Hunkins, *The Influence of Analysis and Evaluation on Critical Thinking and Achievement in Sixth Grade Social Studies.* Doctor's thesis. Kent, Ohio: Kent State University, 1966.

Ruth Perlman Klebaner, "Questions that Teach." *Grade Teacher 61* :10, 76–77, 1964.

Richard L. Loughlin, "On Questioning." *The Educational Forum 25* :461–462, 1961.

Romiett Stevens, *The Question as a Measure of Efficiency in Instruction.* Teachers College Contributions to Education, No. 48. New York: Teachers College, Columbia University, 1912.

J. Richard Suchman, *The Elementary School Training Program in Scientific Inquiry.* U.S. Department of Health, Education, and Welfare, Office of Education, Cooperative Research Project No. 216. Urbana, Ill.: University of Illinois, 1958. (Mimeographed)

Hilda Taba, Samuel Levine, and Freeman F. Elsey, *Thinking in Elementary School Children.* U.S. Department of Health, Education, and Welfare, Office of Education, Cooperative Research Project No. 1574. San Francisco: San Francisco State College, 1964. (Mimeographed)

Jean Wellington and Burleigh Wellington, "What Is A Question?" *The Clearing House 36* :471–472, 1962.

Soshichi Yamada, "A Study of Questioning." *Pedagogical Seminary 20* : 129–185, 1913.

THE "MODES OF INQUIRY" PROBLEM *

Bruce R. Joyce

This paper is stimulated by the "Reader Reaction" section of the December 1965 issue of *Social Education,* in which articles by Malcolm Collier [1] and Herbert Kliebard [2] respond to one by C. Benjamin Cox [3] reporting the difficulties he and his students have had identifying the distinguishing characteristics of the modes of inquiry of the various social sciences. Kliebard made a nice statement of the curricular implications of the problem Cox and his students were attacking.

"If, as an aim in developing a program of studies, one seeks to acquaint students with the basic ways of finding things out, it would be important to know whether this may be best accomplished through the study of many independent subjects such as sociology, anthropology, economics, psychology, . . . or through relatively few selected courses such as those represented by the broad fields." [4]

Put another way, if we are to attempt to help children learn how social scientists think, then does this mean that there is one generalized kind of "social science" thinking, or do the disciplines diverge markedly from one another, or, even, reveal marked and important differences within the fields?

If there is to be a coherent resolution of this problem, then a serious, cumulative inquiry into the nature of the social sciences seems to be called for. Social studies theoreticians will have to make,

---

Bruce R. Joyce is Associate Professor of Education at Teachers College, Columbia University, New York.

* Reprinted from *Social Education 30* :181–183, 1966, with permission of the National Council for the Social Studies and Bruce R. Joyce.

[1] Malcolm Collier, "A Question about Questions." *Social Education 29* :555–556, 1965.

[2] Herbert M. Kliebard, "In Search of Modes of Inquiry." *Social Education 29* :556–558, 1965.

[3] C. Benjamin Cox, "An Inquiry into Inquiries." *Social Education 29* :300–302, 1965.

[4] Herbert M. Kliebard, *op. cit.,* p. 557.

with social scientists, exhaustive investigation of the ways of thinking which characterize the field. I do not mind preaching for a moment on the importance of making this inquiry a cumulative one. There has been a great deal of careful writing on the nature of social science. Ernest Nagel's *The Structure of Science* [5] contains much on the subject. Abraham Kaplan's excellent analysis [6] of the special character of the social sciences and what they have in common brought thinking in this vein a long way, as did the books by Saveth [7] and by Cahnman and Boscoff.[8] Better known to educators is the interesting work by Philip Phenix [9] in which he raises the expert question, "Should we package knowledge as we produce it, or should we look for another structure—a way of grouping content and modes of inquiry in terms of what they will mean to the student?" Hence, he has grouped elements of language and mathematics together as "symbiotics" and elements of the sciences and social sciences together as "empirics." Many other works could be mentioned from Beard's initial effort in the early thirties [10] to the efforts by Hyneman [11] and others in this decade. Even introductory college texts on the social sciences are beginning to show an awareness of the basic premises and concepts of the fields, as, for example, Honigmann's excellent analysis of the nature of anthropological research.[12] Nearly all of the contemporary social studies projects include some statement of the nature of the field— some of these reflect interest in the social science field as a whole, of course, while others are written as if one specific discipline were the whole ball of wax.

For years, also, competent educationists have been worrying the problem. I am simply amazed at the lack of attention that is paid to the monumental series of studies that Hanna and his students have produced over the years.[13] While some of this was done from

[5] Ernest Nagel, *The Structure of Science*. New York: Harcourt, Brace & World, 1961.

[6] Abraham Kaplan, *The Conduct of Inquiry*. San Francisco: Chandler, 1964.

[7] Edward N. Saveth, ed., *American History and the Social Sciences*. New York: Free Press of Glencoe, 1964.

[8] Werner J. Cahnman and Alvin Boscoff, *Sociology and History: Theory and Research*. New York: Free Press of Glencoe, 1964.

[9] Philip H. Phenix, *Realms of Meaning*. New York: McGraw-Hill, 1964.

[10] Charles A. Beard, *The Nature of the Social Sciences*. New York: Scribner's, 1934.

[11] Charles S. Hyneman, *The Study of Politics: The Present State of American Political Science*. Urbana: University of Illinois Press, 1959.

[12] John J. Honigmann, *The World of Man*. New York: Harper, 1959.

[13] For reference see Paul R. Hanna and John R. Lee, "Generalizations from the Social Sciences," in *Social Studies in Elementary Schools*. Washington, D.C.: National Education Association, 1962, pp. 62–88.

a point of view different from that now dominating the scene, it has been honest work, and there is much there for the most careful scholar to use.

It is fairly obvious that the theoreticians in the field, the developers of the current social studies projects, and groups of social scientists have much to build on, if a cumulative dialogue can be started and maintained.

Cox, Collier, and Kliebard all suggested some of the points on which the social sciences should be compared, and I am reluctant to add yet another scheme to the growing list of ways of analyzing the structures of the disciplines. However, my own work has led me gradually to use a fairly simple system by which I try to compare and contrast the several areas of study. I generally distinguish four dimensions of the social sciences.

1. The view of knowledge held by scholars in the field. This is the *metatheoretical* dimension. It refers to the ways the scholar thinks about his field. Is he an operationist? Are deductive theories permissible? Can one attempt grand theory?

Generally speaking, I think that all social sciences—all sciences— have in common a view of knowledge that holds it to be a tentative set of hypotheses that are constantly being revised, regrouped, and reformulated as new knowledge and structures appear. To use Collier's words, "These hypotheses must be reformulated because the observers grow in ability to see, to analyze, and to hypothesize. That is what the social sciences have in common—a series of dynamic, self-developing ways of looking at man and his activities." [14] When curriculum committees ask me where to start looking for "fundamentals" to teach, I generally refer them to the constant revision of knowledge—to the view that knowledge is a set of emerging hypotheses—as the really fundamental characteristic of scholarly inquiry.

There are disagreements among the social scientists at this level, such as the differences between phenomenalists and operationists in psychology, or those among system-builders, and descriptive analysts in history.

2. The frame of reference of the discipline. Each frame of reference causes certain features of the landscape to stand out and others to recede into the distance as the scientist surveys the world. There are two important aspects to the scholar's frame of reference. The first of these is the identification of the specific domain which he studies. When the social scientists look at human behavior, they

---

[14] Malcolm Collier, *op. cit.*, p. 555.

are all trying to describe it and explain it more fully. But they do not look at exactly the same aspects of society. For example, the economist aims at the process whereby persons allocate scarce resources to their endless wants. The anthropologist sees the same process, but to him it is an aspect of culture, or a total perspective on the lives of the people. The human geographer directs his attention to the interaction between culture and physical environment, placing somewhat different stress on the same facts with which the economist and anthropologist are dealing. In each discipline direct and indirect human interaction are studied, but the slice of life which receives the greatest attention varies somewhat.

The second important aspect of the scholar's frame of reference is the system of organizing concepts in the field, or what Bruner called the structure of the discipline. These concepts serve two functions. They describe relationships among data and they also direct inquiry. For example, the economist organizes much information under the concept "division of labor." He also, studying a new economic unit, looks for the ways in which labor is divided. The domain-describing concepts of the field, with these other organizing concepts, defines the ways information is stored in the field, and they are the guidelines by which current research in the field is carried on, for they tell the scholar where to look as he commences a new study.[15] By far the bulk of any field consists of its organizing concepts and their supporting data.

3. The methodology of inquiry. This third dimension of the disciplines receives much attention as the "the scientific method." The methodology of inquiry defines what will be acceptable data, how it will be measured, quantified, manipulated with respect to the proof of hypotheses. My tendency here is to agree with Kliebard and assert, with him, that "it is fair to say that scientists as a group tend to follow a research procedure which includes observing certain phenomena under certain kinds of conditions, counting, weighing or measuring them, classifying them, and, on a more sophisticated level, trying to generalize about them and making predictions." [16] The methodology of inquiry describes the scientist at work collecting and manipulating data. His frame of reference will control this activity in terms of what will be considered important and what questions will and will not be asked. But the processes of making observations, inferring cause and effect, re-

15 These ideas are developed extensively in Bruce R. Joyce, *Strategies for Elementary Social Science Education,* Chicago: Science Research Associates, 1965.
16 Herbert M. Kliebard, *op. cit.,* p. 557.

ducing data and testing hypotheses, will be reasonably similar from area to area.

4. A language system. Every discipline has developed its own symbol system, and progression toward a common mathematical language is slower than in the physical sciences. Many of the current curriculum projects have given great prominence to the teaching of the symbol system of the discipline (as the Georgia Anthropology Project) while educationists in the past have generally preferred to have the children provide the linguistic "handles" for the concepts they form. At any rate, each discipline does have a rather complicated language system, and many terms are unique to one discipline.

Defining the social sciences is clearly of major importance for the future development of the social studies. While there is much darkness on the subject, there has been much inquiry also. We may find that examination of the several dimensions of each discipline will reveal that on some levels they have much in common (as in their view of knowledge and research methodology) whereas in some areas (their frame of reference) they have some differences and some similarities, and in others (as in language) they are at times far apart.

While the dialogue on the social sciences goes on (it is unbearable to think that it won't flourish) it is to be hoped that the voices of those, like Phenix, who see knowledge in terms of all fields, will be heard. We can also devoutly hope that there will be participation from people like Herbert Thelen,[17] who draws our attention not only to the frames of reference of the disciplines, but also to the "subjective world of the learner," for whose benefit the entire enterprise exists.

---

[17] Herbert A. Thelen, "The Curriculum and the Domains of Knowledge." *Elementary School Journal* 55:369–376, 1955.

"SEE AND SUPPOSE," LEARNING
THROUGH DISCOVERY IN THE
SOCIAL STUDIES *

Shelly P. Koenigsberg

An effort to translate into classroom activity Bruner's suggestion
for learning through discovery was tried in a seventh grade social
studies class in Englewood, New Jersey. Pupils were asked to look
at photographs and museum slides related to the unit in European
History being studied and to draw inferences and conclusions from
their observations. In this lesson, entitled "See and Suppose," each
member of the class had the opportunity "to put things together for
himself, to be his own discoverer." [1]

The lesson was tried out first with a group of representatives
from each seventh grade social studies class to test out the planned
instruction and to invite pupil comment and suggestions for teaching their classmates to "see and suppose." The try-out group was
shown a picture, from *Family of Man,* of Learned Hand dressed in
judicial robes, seated at a table with tomes before him. Told they
would be asked what they saw and what they could suppose from
what they saw, we paused to define the word "suppose." The children realized that "suppose" contained an element of uncertainty
and were told that guessing was quite acceptable as long as it could
be verified by observation. Although none of the pupils recognized
Mr. Justice Hand, they identified the man they saw as a judge on
the basis of the robes he wore. They thought their supposition was
further supported by the tomes they assumed to be law books. Some
children observed very carefully: "He's sitting on a high-backed
leather chair with tacks in it." Others supposed that the judge

Shelly P. Koenigsberg is on the faculty at Yeshiva University, New York.

* Reprinted from *The Social Studies* 57:257–262, 1966, with permission of
the McKinley Publishing Co. and Shelley P. Koenigsberg.

* The writer acknowledges her appreciation to Dr. Mark R. Shedd, Super-
intendent; Mr. John Trout, Director of Instruction; and Mr. Theodore S.
Davis, principal of Englewood Junior High School; Prof. Robert H. Anderson,
Harvard Graduate School of Education; and other staff members who were
helpful in evaluating the lesson and/or this article; and particularly to the
team of seventh grade social studies and English teachers: Miss DiBenedetto
and Mr. Teta, Mrs. Huseby, Mr. Lubben, Mrs. Pollett, Mrs. Sotnick, Mr.
Wiener, and Mr. Zeug.

[1] Jerome S. Bruner, "The Act of Discovery." *Harvard Educational Review*
31:21–32, 1961, p. 22.

was quite sad at having to sentence a man to a long prison term. When asked for validation of this assumption, the children conceded that their conclusion was unwarranted. But they did feel they could assume that he was an old man, to judge from the white hair and the lines near his eyes. One observation and conclusion was pointed out to them. Stiff cuffs could be seen protruding from the sleeves of the judge's robes. These cuffs were quite different from the lacy ones seen in pictures of men in the southern colonies in early America. We could therefore conclude that there was a fashion in men's wear.

Having mastered the first steps in "see and suppose," levels of supposition were suggested as the next step.

"You said you saw a judge with books in front of him. What can you suppose from these books?"

"They're law books."

"They might be. Let's assume they *are*. What can you suppose from law books?"

Some children assumed the ability to read, others a knowledge of printing and bookbinding. One boy said,

"Laws."

"What can you suppose from laws?"

"People who made them." Not kings or emperors, but people!

With this practice behind them, the children were shown a museum slide, "Relief of a musician playing harp, Sumerian, 3500–2500 B.C." and asked to "see and suppose" from this slide, which was identified only as a slide of Ancient Sumeria, a civilization they were studying in their social studies classes. Observations were noted and conclusions drawn. Then the children were told that this lesson would be presented to one of their classes in a few days and they were asked for suggestions in the presentation. Several of them advised that the picture shown to introduce the method of "see and suppose" be a simple one and preferably one with familiar objects so that effort could be concentrated on the process rather than on the content of the picture. The slide they had seen was considered simple enough for a beginning lesson.

The "try-out lesson" indicated that learning through discovery could be achieved, for in "See and Suppose," "the student is not a bench-bound listener but is taking part in the formulations and at times may play the principal role in it." [2] It became apparent that other purposes could be achieved as well. Pupils could become familiar with one method used by historians to gather the information contained in their textbooks. They could also be encouraged to

---

[2] *Ibid.*, p. 23.

develop an attitude toward learning and inquiry, toward guessing and hunches which Bruner considers a part of thinking and learning. In *The Process of Education,* he discusses the development of "intuitive thinking" as teachers encourage pupils to guess, to recognize the plausibility of guesses, and to verify and confirm these guesses as necessary.[3]

There was one other purpose, related to the heterogeneous grouping of seventh grade pupils in Englewood: it was thought that an examination of these museum slides in the lesson formulated was the type of learning activity in which the socially disadvantaged learner could participate on a basis of greater equality with pupils considered average and bright—in *verbal* and *book-centered* learning activities. For the try-out lesson, teachers had been asked to select one average or bright pupil and one very poor pupil, either a learning or a discipline problem. Thus a variety of pupil reactions could be observed and we could see whether slow pupils could, indeed, be interested in the lesson. Some of the disadvantaged pupils started the try-out lesson in characteristic behavior but soon became interested and made some good contributions to the lesson. One boy carried on even in the face of a friend's taunting for his participation.

The picture shown when the lesson was presented to the regular social studies class was a magazine advertisement showing a few large, brightly colored vegetables on a marbleized surface. The class was told about a game called "See and Suppose," and that they would be asked later in the period what place this game had in a social studies class. With these pupils, too, the word "suppose" was defined, the element of uncertainty pointed out, and the right to guess—based on observation—encouraged. "When we 'suppose' it's like a hypothesis in math," said one girl. The marbleized surface on which the vegetables rested provided the first opportunity to "suppose." It might be marble, but it might also be marbleized linoleum. Another object for "See and Suppose" was introduced. A plaque showing a reproduction of an Egyptian drawing was passed around the room. The children were asked to look at it, touch it, and feel it.[4]

Once the children had gained familiarity with the method—by using the photograph of vegetables—they were asked to see and suppose about the plaque. Where the photograph had elicited comments about its contents, (One girl said, "I see a picture—made

---

[3] Jerome S. Bruner, *The Process of Education,* Cambridge, Mass.: Harvard University Press, 1960, pp. 13–14, 59–60, 65–68.

[4] The thinking here was based on Riessman's discussion of "the physical or motoric style of the deprived groups," in *The Culturally Deprived Child,* New York: Harper, 1962, pp. 66–67.

up of all those vegetables.") responses about the plaque concerned the materials and tools used and the method of creating the drawing. Some of the children asked eagerly whether it was "real." Then the slide of the Sumerian musician playing the harp shown to the "try-out" group was projected on the screen.

Asked to describe what they saw, the children agreed that there was a man seated on a stool and some noted the cut of and the design on the robe he wore. Some children thought the man was playing a stringed instrument; others said that he was in the process of weaving. The pupils in two rows were asked to make suppositions based on the observation that the man was weaving, the pupils in the remaining rows to assume that the man was playing a stringed instrument. When several responses had been made by boys and girls in both groups, the opportunity was used to point out the need for careful observation and what the legend on the museum slide reported to the children.

"What can we learn when we 'see and suppose'?" was the first question posed after the presentation. The children's answers were varied. They could gather information for several school subjects through observations, but also, they could learn to observe more carefully both in and out of school. They could see the developments over a period of time, said the boy who knew how different is to-day's harp from the Sumerian. They could learn to question the experts and they could learn not to take anything for granted. That they had learned one of the methods used by historians to gather information was suggested by the teacher. It troubled some youngsters to think that the facts contained in their history books might be based on supposition; then how factual were their textbooks?

"Does 'See and Suppose' belong in a social studies class?" was the second question posed. Many children thought it did not, although it might have some place in an English class. One boy, who was concerned for the facts in his textbook, questioned the right of seventh graders to use a method he thought should be the exclusive province of older, more experienced men. Some children thought the method might belong in the social studies class. It gave them an opportunity to use their own ideas and express their own opinions. "It can strengthen thought." One youngster thought this was a new way of learning social studies. Another countered that it was a method that could be used in any class.

The seventh grade teachers of social studies and English function as a team, by which instruction is planned and reactions expressed. Their solicited opinion of the presentation—based on observation of the demonstration and discussion with their classes or pupils who had participated in the "try-out" lesson—also varied. Some thought one lesson should be devoted to pupil mastery of the operation involved and the opportunity to make a large number of assumptions. Others thought application of the technique to social studies should be immediate. After discussion with their pupils, some teachers reported that the bright students thought it all too simple to require instruction and some thought it stupid; * others thought it was fun. Some pupils reported that they liked being able to guess: "It makes people suppose more" and "It brings more thought." One youngster warned, "We may suppose too freely" and others questioned whether one slide was enough. Didn't they need to examine five or six before making suppositions about Sumerian music and musicians?

As for pupil participation, the teachers felt that most of the children were involved in the lesson either by actually contributing or by being very interested in the proceedings. The teachers of the two classes involved in the demonstration judged that the slow children "took quite well" to the lesson and that they participated to a much greater extent than had been anticipated. They had volunteered both their observations and their inferences; the quality of the conclusions drawn by some of these pupils surprised their teachers. It had been a "dull" boy who had concluded that laws presumed that people had made them.

Other reactions from teachers included these statements:

> The pupils changed their ideas of what pictures are for. They accepted the idea that pictures—and artifacts—can be useful in and beyond the classroom.
> It gave pupils a new way of looking at the same things.
> The children realized that there was a relationship between learnings in different classes, like the youngster who compared a supposition to a hypothesis in math.
> It allows for participation by the slow pupils, which many classes do not. It starts them thinking, which they *can* do.
> Reading to them from a Sherlock Holmes story, suggesting the idea of detective work, might be helpful. If they heard Holmes telling Watson about his past life the first time they met, the children would see how careful observations could be followed by warranted conclusions.
> I wouldn't want to do it constantly, but it may be a good way to start a unit.

Introducing a unit is one way a teacher could use "See and Suppose" in a social studies class. It would be particularly valuable

---

* We may assume that some children have already had practice in observation and drawing conclusions, either from discussions at home or from the efforts of previous teachers.

if a record of the class meeting were compared with observations and conclusions drawn at the end of the same unit. Or children could be asked to compare their deductions with information in the texts or library references they are using. It could be an activity for a single child, a committee, or for several committees examining different slides, pictures, or artifacts. Each could then report to the class, for criticism and discussion, their observations (how complete and accurate are they?) and their conclusions (how warranted are they?).

For large-group instruction, pupils already familiar with the techniques involved could be asked to observe several projections or artifacts and report to their next class meeting the conclusions they had drawn. Or the group could be shown a series of projections that become increasingly complex; their observations could be discussed at the next class meeting. A discussion of perception would surely result from such a class discussion. The implications for the study of history are apparent to the teacher. Additional uses of the method, or variations of the suggestions made, may well be devised by the teacher interested in encouraging pupils to learn through discovery. Used on a sustained basis over the year, such an examination of artifacts, slides, and other projections could be used to teach critical thinking skills as well as developing attitudes toward work and abilities to "put things together for himself, to be his own discoverer." [5]

This is the heart of "See and Suppose" if it is indeed to be a vehicle for learning through discovery. If the student is "to put things together for himself" the role of the teacher is to require verification of guesses, to direct thinking by the kinds of questions asked: What kind of a society produced and used these artifacts? What natural resources or trade are implied by the composition of the artifact? What attitude toward craftsmanship can we assume? What implications does division of labor have for the structure of a society? The teacher who suggests or insists on suppositions or conclusions deprives the learner of the opportunity "to be his own discoverer." The teacher can also encourage the youngster who makes bad guesses or one who won't guess at all to continue "supposing" and drawing conclusions that can be verified. When the teacher can accept the intuitive leap and a variety of logically-sup-

---

[5] The reader is referred to William H. Burton, Roland B. Kimball, and Richard L. Wing, *Education for Effective Thinking*, New York: Appleton-Century-Crofts, 1960, Ch. 7, "Inference: The Heart of Thinking," and Ch. 13, "Skill in Thinking as an Aim of Education," for a general discussion, and Ch. 18, "Teaching for Thinking: Social Studies," for additional suggested procedures.

ported suppositions, the students can learn flexibility and come to see that the rigidity of one right answer is not a high order of scholarship.

The teacher concerned in reaching the disadvantaged learner may use the method in yet another way, possibly with the help of the English or remedial reading teacher. Experience stories written with these learners recording such a lesson and/or the students' reactions to it may enhance their involvement in the learning, increase their vocabularies, and verify their understanding of what they have learned.

> Consider now what benefit may be derived from the experience of learning through discoveries that one makes for oneself,

says Bruner and he discusses at length (a) the increase in intellectual potency, (b) the shift from extrinsic to intrinsic rewards, (c) learning the heuristics of discovering, and (d) the aid to memory processing.

> Our aim as teachers is to give our student as firm a grasp of the subject as we can, and to make him as autonomous and self-propelled a thinker as we can—one who will go along on his own after formal schooling has ended.[6]

Teaching our students to "see and suppose"—to observe carefully, draw warranted conclusions and make valid inferences—is one way to accomplish our aim.

---

[6] Bruner, "The Act of Discovery," p. 23, *et passim*.

CONCEPTUAL APPROACHES: THEIR MEANING FOR ELEMENTARY SOCIAL STUDIES *

John Jarolimek

At some point in the remoteness of antiquity, man made a gigantic leap in his development that would forever separate him from all other living creatures. The similarities and differences between man and the universe of living things has been the source of some fascination through the centuries, and many explanations have been suggested for his uniqueness. Unquestionably, the unbridgeable gap between man and the rest of the animal kingdom lies precisely in his capacity to engage in high-order, abstract mental operations facilitated through the use of a complex symbol system. This is not to say that man thinks and animals do not. It is, rather, to suggest that the mental processes of animals and those of man are separated by several orders of magnitude.

Man has the amazing capacity to attach symbols to reality and thereby manipulate reality intellectually. Moreover, he can and does attach symbols to abstractions that do not exist physically at all (terms such as *tradition, colonialism, democracy*), and he can manipulate those mentally. Man's neurological system is such that it is able to classify, store, retrieve, and process a phenomenal amount of information. Because man has this capacity, he can accumulate and transmit a social heritage. He can also use his intelligence to create and invent new variations of that heritage. He can be taught to solve intensely complex social problems. He can, finally, develop and adapt a culture, something no other creature is able to do.

It is well known that lower animals can be taught or conditioned to respond to words. When trained, a dog, a horse, or a bird will react in a predictable way to a given command. Animals frequently behave in deceptively human-like ways. Because the response is often so well executed, it is sometimes mistakenly assumed that the animal engages in reflective thought, akin to that of human beings. When man responds to symbols, however, he is doing so in an altogther different way from that of a dog, baboon, or talking bird.

John Jarolimek is Professor of Education at the University of Washington, Seattle.

* Reprinted from *Social Education* 31:534–536, 1966, with permission of the National Council for the Social Studies and John Jarolimek.

He does something besides and beyond simply reacting to a sign symbol. Man associates meaning with a symbol, a meaning that goes considerably beyond a sensory impression. When man hears or sees the symbol *concentration camp*, his memory system immediately scans and sorts a vast amount of information and selects the appropriate data to associate with this symbol, thus giving it meaning. This assumes, of course, that the individual has had some prior opportunity to become acquainted with the meaning of this term. But it is not necessary for him to have personally and directly experienced concentration camps in order for this symbol to have meaning for him. He may have read about them, seen pictures of them, heard accounts of persons who had been in them, seen a movie about concentration camps, and so on. When we refer to the meanings associated with words and symbols in this way, we are defining *concepts*. Concepts may be regarded as categories of meaning. Attaching meaning beyond sensory impression to abstract symbols is what is meant by conceptual thought. It is intellectual behavior that is distinctly and uniquely characteristic of human beings.

It is doubtful if anything but the most elementary conceptual thought would be possible without a highly developed symbol system. This is so because concepts are abstract ideas and are detached from specific experiences. In order to handle ideas in this way, it is necessary to have labels or symbols to attach to them. If ideas are to be communicated, there must be common agreement on the meanings of the labels or symbols. Words provide convenient labels for concepts, and, consequently, word-symbols are sometimes confused with the concepts they represent.

Using concepts as categories of meaning makes it possible for man to establish order in all of the many thousands of specific perceptions and unique experiences he has. Concepts provide an intellectual filing system for meanings. Concept development, then, calls for the placing of information in correct cognitive categories. In developing the concept *city*, as an example, pupils must learn to differentiate a city from other political and social entities. A city is not a county; neither is it a village, nor a town, nor a hamlet. Pupils could test the validity of a vast number of statements concerning the characteristics of a city, and in so doing their understanding of the concept would be enlarged, i.e., A city has more people living in it than a village; A city provides opportunities for many types of jobs; A city must have a good transportation system; and so forth. Suppose, however, pupils conclude that "Large cities are not located close to other large cities." A test of this statement would show that there are many exceptions to it. This is not a statement that would correctly apply to all or nearly all cities. It is incorrect information.

When one includes incorrect information in a category, he then forms a *mis*conception. Pupils who learn about the English *race* and the French *race* are associating incorrect information with the race concept and are therefore forming misconceptions. It is apparent that in developing concepts it is important for the learner to have a broad exposure to the idea, encountering it in a variety of settings, and experiencing both positive and negative instances and exemplars. Concept development is largely an information sorting, discriminating process, including in the category all associations and relationships that belong and excluding those that do not.

In social studies, concepts are often expressed in the following ways:

1. as *words*—river, mountain, city, urbanism, tradition, culture, democracy, colonialism, migration, import, export, cargo, trade.
2. as *phrases*—cultural diffusion, balance of power, trade agreement, balance of payments, income tax, polar regions, representative government.

In conceptual approaches to social studies curriculum development and teaching, a great deal is made of generalizations—as organizing ideas from the disciplines, main ideas, key ideas, and so on. Sometimes they are also labeled *concepts,* although such nomenclature is not altogether consistent with the conventional and widely accepted use of the term. A generalization is defined as a declarative statement expressing a relationship between concepts or other variables and has more or less universal applicability. The statements describing cities cited earlier are examples of generalizations. Other examples that have been widely used in the social studies are: Every society creates laws; Land is used for many and varied purposes; Change is a condition of human society; Culture is socially learned.

The following generalization from geography may be used to illustrate the relationship between generalizations, concepts, and facts:

Climate is determined by sunlight, temperature, humidity, precipitation, atmospheric pressure, winds, unequal rates of heating and cooling of land and water surfaces, irregular shape and distribution of land and sea, ocean currents, and mountain systems.

This generalization has imbedded within it a number of concepts that must be understood if the statement is to make sense: sunlight, temperature, humidity, precipitation, atmospheric pressure, winds, and so forth. Moreover, each of the concepts has many specific facts associated with it that give it meaning, as for example: *sunlight*— amount, intensity, composition; *temperature*—variation, change, effects; *winds*—direction, patterns, causes; *humidity*—degree of moisture, dampness, effect on comfort. Concepts and generalizations are transferable from one setting to another. Facts, on the other hand, have no transfer value—they are useful and applicable only in their specific settings: Columbus discovered America in 1492; The Chicago fire took place on October 8, 1871; The Great Depression followed the stock market crash of October 1929. Conceptual approaches are intended to provide a framework or design for the building up of meanings from facts to concepts to generalizations.

It has long been known that social studies programs typically include an overwhelming amount of specific information. Not only is the existing fact-load heavy but the problem is additionally confounded because (1) the amount of specific information is increasing at a rapid rate due to the discovery of new knowledge; (2) specific information is ephemeral and becomes obsolete quickly; (3) the rate of forgetting specific information is known to be high; and (4) unless specifics are tied to larger ideas, it is impossible to establish functional criteria for the selection of facts to be taught. In recent years, therefore, curriculum workers in the social studies have turned ther attention to the use of concepts and generalizations as organizing schemes in an attempt to overcome the problems just cited. The basic idea is to focus instruction on a relatively few fundamental concepts that have high transfer value and that help to explain or predict social or natural phenomena. Specific subject matter is selected to illustrate particularly well the concepts under study and to permit the application of certain methods of inquiry.

In principle the use of organizing designs of the type under discussion have been received favorably by educators and social scientists alike. There is considerable agreement that the programs of the past have over-stressed learning goals dealing with the accumulation of information mostly of the descriptive type. Major curriculum revision projects of the past decade have, without exception, given some attention to an emphasis on basic concepts and generalizations. The usual procedure has been to turn to the various parent disciplines contributing to social studies and attempt to identify the core ideas from those disciplines. Numerous social scientists have been involved in the search for and identification of basic concepts from the social sciences, and several lists have been compiled. It is safe to say, however, that to date there are few very good models of social studies programs that incorporate basic concepts from the social science disciplines into functioning curriculums. Hardly any are markedly different from those of the past. Perhaps more will be available after programs now under development, such as those in Project Social Studies, are reported.

If conceptual approaches are to become the basis for elementary social studies curriculums, something more needs to be done besides simply overlaying a list of concepts from the social sciences on a traditional scope and sequence chart with some minor shifts of content allocations from one grade to another. Likewise, conceptual approaches will not contribute needed vitalization of elementary social studies if conventional methodology is employed. A substantial re-orientation to both content and method will be needed before the real values of conceptually based curriculums can be achieved.

The attention to and development of concepts necessarily suggests an instructional emphasis stressing inquiry and inductive teaching. This is not to suggest that a pupil has to discover everything he needs to know—to do so would mean that he could not profit from the accumulated wisdom of mankind. What is being suggested is that the total approach be investigation oriented—that teachers will *not* write generalizations on the chalkboard for pupils to learn or have them memorize dictionary definitions of concepts. If the emphasis on concept teaching results in practices such as these, our programs will be in a bad way, indeed. Pupils build meanings into concepts by what they themselves do and experience—through a range of encounters with concepts and through the use of a vast amount of supporting detail. Generalizations for the most part should be considered either (1) as tentative conclusions arrived at after lengthy and careful study or (2) as propositions, assumptions, or hypotheses to be tested by study and research.

It seems clear, too, that the role of the teacher in social studies instruction needs to shift from what it has traditionally been. In today's concept-based and inquiry-oriented programs, the teacher simply cannot remain the chief data source for the class. In many, perhaps most, elementary social studies classes, the teacher and the text continue to be the most important information sources, utilizing the conventional *transmitter* (teacher and text)—*receiver* (pupils) teaching model. It is obvious that there is little to be gained in re-writing curriculum documents in social studies if prevailing teaching strategies do not conform either to the philosophical base or the psychological orientation of the new program. The role of the teacher will need to shift to the extent that his behavior has to do *mainly* with stimulating, questioning, clarifying, supporting, providing feedback, guiding, and diagnosing. Because educational technology is making it possible for devices to do many tasks teachers have traditionally performed (providing information, giving assignments, correcting papers), increasingly it will be necessary for teachers to attend to those unique tasks that only human teachers can do.

In the present period of curriculum reform, it has become the accepted custom to insist that elementary teachers have a better knowledge of the subject matter relating to their teaching assignments. This assumed need is often accepted uncritically. Given the current educational climate, emphasis on knowledge of subject matter, however valid such an emphasis may be, tends to encourage traditional information-giving teaching roles.

There can be little question that the elementary teacher of today and tomorrow will need a better background in the social sciences than his counterpart did a generation ago—although not for the reasons ordinarily given. The teacher needs a strong background not to pass the information on to the pupils he teaches but to be able to know what possibilities for investigation inhere in a topic, to know what questions to ask, to know how to test hypotheses, and how to arrive at valid conclusions. The uninformed teacher may not know enough about a topic to be able to plan an extended and soundly-based investigation of it with today's informed and sophisticated pupils.

Additionally, teachers in concept-based programs need to know a great deal about the psychology of cognitive processes and the organization of knowledge itself. How do pupils learn concepts and generalizations? How can knowledge be organized to enhance learning? How can concepts be programed on a continuum of difficulty? What are the relevant concepts from the various disciplines? How does the teacher enhance and assist transfer of learnings? What concepts are particularly appropriate for slow-learning pupils? Are the same procedures for concept development equally valid for slow learners as for average and high-achieving pupils? Questions such as these must be answered before much headway can be made in developing concept-based programs that really work.

A generation ago a prevailing notion in elementary education was that process goals were more important than content goals. This was embodied in the cliché "What pupils learn is less important than how they learn it." Fortunately, we do not go around saying things like that anymore, for we have recognized that in addition to teaching pupils in ways that are educationally and psychologically sound, we also expect them to learn something of substance. There is a lesson in this for current thinking about social studies.

In the shift from traditional content-oriented, descriptive, fact-centered social studies programs to those that are concept based, there is the tendency again to assume that specific content is not especially important as long as it is representative and that it provides a good vehicle for the development of concepts. This may be a valid assumption from the standpoint of instruction. A child *can* develop such concepts relating to family life as role, status, and sanctions, for example, by studying a primitive Indian family of South America. Or a pupil *can* learn about social stratification by studying an Oriental society. But in making the selection of specific content to be used in developing concepts, it would seem important to bear in mind that there is a body of informational content that is necessary for ordinary civic and social literacy. It would be well to remember, too, that society has institutional expectations regarding social studies and elementary schools—there are some things pupils are expected to know when they complete the elementary school. Perhaps on a common-sense basis one might conclude that it is more relevant for American school children to learn something about the social forces operating in their own community than to engage in a depth study of a pre-literate society in a remote part of the world. To have social studies programs designed to build basic concepts does not mean that topics selected for study need to be unusual, unique, or esoteric. There is no reason why elementary social studies programs cannot combine the development of basic concepts *and* the building of backgrounds of functional information *and* appropriate processes of thought.

When man substitutes impulsive, emotional, and thoughtless action for behavior that has resulted from the exercise of rational, reflective, thoughtful processes, he is not behaving in accordance with those characteristics that set him apart from other animals. All of education, and particularly the social studies, should strive to enhance and promote in pupils those qualities from which man derives his humanness. This is a highly relevant concern for elementary teachers because of the nature of the child during the time he is in the elementary school. Pupils in the elementary school today will in a few years be adult citizens of their communities, holding offices, voting, serving on school boards, advising their elected officials, and making decisions individually and collectively on social and civic affairs. Conceptual approaches to social studies education, supported by compatible teaching procedures, tempered by the good sense and patience of an understanding and psychologically warm teacher, should assist pupils to learn how to come to grips with the realities of social and civic affairs in thoughtful, intelligent, and rational ways.

INQUIRY AND SOCIAL STUDIES *

Millard Clements

Although the word *inquiry* has captured the market today, interest in processes of finding things out is certainly not an innovation in educational thought. John Dewey, in his book, *Democracy and Education*, posed a challenge that has been unmet by a generation of educators:

> Give the pupil something to do, not something to learn; and the doing of such nature as to demand thinking or intentional noting of connections; learning naturally results. (1:181)

In spite of decades of fashionable talk about problem solving, learning by doing, and the recent rash of clichés about discovery methods and strategies of inquiry, there has been no great overhauling of school practice. What might we do to change this situation?

Perhaps one helpful way to think about the problem of inquiry in schools is to think of the difference between *students* and *pupils*. I think of a pupil as one who goes to authorities to find out what is in the world. I think of a student as one who wishes to establish himself as an authority about some particular situation or event. The authority of a student rests on his personal examination of materials, documents, primary sources, and statements that he has encountered.

For each of us there are places and times to be both student and pupil. But in school, there should be a formal demand that a pupil learn how to face the opportunity and the challenge of being a student.

The transformation of a pupil into a student, if it occurs, is a profound change in intellectual style. We learn most of our lives by asking questions of others: teachers and books, sadly, become

Millard Clements is Professor of Education at New York University, New York.

* Reprinted from *Elementary English* *43*:299–330, 1966, with permission of the National Council of Teachers of English and Millard Clements.

oracles of truth just as our fathers and mothers were oracles of goodness. An appeal to the authority of ceremonial knowers has a secure place in the quest for understanding, but to become a student one must learn how to put aside oracles.

The pupil mode of inquiry is to pose questions to oracles, teachers, encyclopedias, and other experts and to find his answers in what they say. In the student mode of questioning the person directs his questions only to himself and seeks to answer them on the basis of what he can see in the world.

The pupil mode of inquiry is a safe mode of inquiry: one discovers and believes the conventional views about the manners and the habits of one's own tribe, the myths that are told regarding the exploits of the past, and the contentions about the present and the future that one's own clan finds convenient to tell.

The student mode of inquiry is dangerous: one examines conventional views, myths, and hopes and seeks to appraise them in the light of reason and evidence. A student of social situations is methodologically a skeptic; such questions as these motivate his study:

1. How do people in various social positions interpret their own social reality?
2. How do people in various social positions interpret past events of their own social group?
3. What are the interesting distortions or discrepancies of perception regarding what is or has been?

A student of past events expects the histories that men write to be influenced by the lives of the history writers. A student of contemporary societies expects to find that most men in most circumstances of life find excuses or justifications or legitimations for whatever it is that they do. Very often a student of social affairs will find that people believe, quite firmly, things that are simply not the case. This discovery might lead a student to try to determine why it is that some people believe things that are demonstrably false. It might also lead him to see—to evaluate the beliefs that regulate his own life. Thus social inquiry is not an Easter egg hunt for preestablished truths; it is always an adventure, to some degree, into the unknown.

Social inquiry is methodologically condemned to:

1. Look for the difference between what men say and what they do.
2. Look for differences between what men say they hope and expect to happen and what actually happens.

3. Look for variety of interpretations of any past or present event. Expect that interpretations will be systematically influenced by the circumstances in which men live.

Thus inquiry is methodologically condemned to lead individuals to examine the circumstances of their lives, to question the values they have been taught, to become to some extent responsible for their own views.

It is here, in the secularization of thought and values, that one can find the greatest danger to the promotion of inquiry in the public schools. Perhaps our resistance to utilizing methods of inquiry in the school has social meaning. It may be our effort to avoid confronting the challenge and the danger in encouraging young people to reflect intelligently on the world in which we live. Our schools present to children an established view: it is self-assured, not ironical; unquestioned, not tentative; bland, not really human at all.

I would agree with Edgar Z. Friedenberg, when he wrote in his new book, *Coming of Age in America,* that the highest function of education

> . . . is to help people understand the meaning of their lives and to become sensitive to the meanings of other people's lives and to relate to them more fully. (2:367)

In order to seek to accomplish this:

1. We must have available in school: primary documents, a variety of interpretations of past and present events, records and artifacts that relate what has been and is going on in the world, rather than the bland, distorted texts that are now available.
2. We must develop in children the ability to evaluate interpretation; *i.e.,* to use evidence to test ideas.
3. We must nurture children's capacity to become students.
4. We must provide developing students with the opportunity to write about how they think and feel about the world in which they live. The search for clarity of expression is a central aspect of being a student.

My hope is that we in education will come to enjoy the encounter, that we will dare to be intelligent about the work we ask our young people to do. We can encourage children to act like students: they can be helped to learn the rigorous discipline of inquiry. Students can be encouraged to examine and evaluate opinions and interpretations rather than to memorize them: the somnolent reading of textbooks can be abandoned. Students can be encouraged to discover the limitations on our ability to understand our own affairs: they can learn how hard it is to develop disciplined understanding.

To pursue this enterprise, for many teachers, may be a new and rather adventurous activity: they themselves can become inquirers into their own activities as teachers. Peter Berger in his book, *Invitation of Sociology,* suggested that:

> It is very difficult to pretend in this world. Normally, one becomes what one plays at. (3:97)

I think he is right. And I find in this some hope for inquiry. If teachers will seek to face the discipline of inquiry that is part of our intellectual heritage, and if they will dare to seek to examine ideas about social affairs, then there may be some hope for inquiry in social studies.

REFERENCES

1. Peter Berger, *Invitation to Sociology: A Humanistic Perspective.* New York: Doubleday (Anchor Books), 1963.
2. John Dewey, *Democracy and Education.* New York: Macmillan, 1923.
3. Edgar Z. Friedenberg, *Coming of Age in America.* New York: Random House, 1965.

PROBLEM SOLVING IN THE SOCIAL STUDIES *

Theodore Kaltsounis

Problem solving long has been associated with mathematics and science, but today it is considered one of the leading objectives of social studies. Every authority in social studies today talks and writes at length about problem solving.

Professional books and curriculum guides stress the importance of problem solving in social studies and suggest means of imple-

Theodore Kaltsounis is Associate Professor of Education at the University of Washington, Seattle.

* Reprinted from *The Social Studies* 86:340–342, 1966, with permission of the McKinley Publishing Co. and Theodore Kaltsounis.

menting it. Professional journals publish article after article on the subject. The National Council for the Social Studies stresses problem solving again and again in its yearbooks and other publications. All emphasize the fact that problem solving is especially important to children living in a democracy, such as ours.

Why Problem Solving?

The importance of problem solving in social studies stems from two characteristics of social studies content. One of these characteristics is the fact that social studies content deals with human relationships, both formal and informal. These human relationships change and today they change very rapidly.

Such changes are inevitable and there always are reasons for them. Young people should learn to look for the reasons—why the changes occur. Then later, as adults, they will be willing to accept changes more readily, and thus to lessen the cultural lag, which is of so much concern to sociologists today. This development, if it takes place, will constitute an outstanding contribution of today's schools to the society of tomorrow.

The second characteristic of social studies content which invites problem solving is the fact that human relationships involve conflicts. Probably there never has been a time in history when persons have been involved in more conflicts than today. Certainly there never has been a time when persons through conflicts have more closely threatened the destruction of the world.

If people are to survive and live together in groups, small or large, they must be able to look at conflicts with an open mind and arrive at decisions which will motivate them to act in behalf of the general welfare. This goal is easy to state, but very difficult to achieve. Schools must start early in the social studies program and keep working with zeal in order to help citizens of tomorrow seek peaceful solutions of conflicts.

The purpose of this paper is to define problem solving, examine its status in the public schools, and, finally, offer a few practical suggestions for its development.

What Is Problem Solving?

Psychologists have done considerable research, attempting to define problem solving. Much of this research, however, has been done under laboratory conditions and the reports have been written in such technical terms that teachers have difficulty understanding them.

A number of authorities, including Richard Gross and Frederick McDonald, have conducted investigations to determine the nature of problem solving. These authorities have come to the conclusion that problem solving is a complex function rather than a single unitary function (1).

Basically, we may think of problem solving as a series of progressive steps which a person takes, as follows, when faced with a problem:

1. Initial stage, in which a person becomes aware of a problem requiring a solution
2. Data-gathering phase, in which the person familiarizes himself with the problem and seeks materials for solution
3. Hypothesis-formation stage, in which the person formulates tentative solutions
4. Hypothesis-testing phase, in which solutions are tested.

All basic textbooks in the teaching of social studies advocate similar steps in the method of problem solving. It will be noted that these are essentially the same steps as John Dewey (2) lists as steps in critical thinking. But Dewey goes on to say, "Thinking is the method of intelligent learning, of learning that employs and rewards the mind."

Do Teachers Use Problem Solving?

If problem solving is important, we might assume that teachers make it a basic method or outcome of instruction. Unfortunately, according to available research, this does not appear to be the case.

Paul Torrance recently conducted a study in Minnesota which indicates that many teachers of social studies fail to give deserved attention to problem solving (3). He based his study on J. P. Guilford's list of mental operations, which includes cognition, memory, convergent thinking, divergent thinking, and evaluation. Divergent thinking and evaluation are two exceedingly important operations in the development of problem solving.

In Torrance's study, 390 elementary teachers and 443 secondary teachers were asked to identify a specific social studies unit or course which they taught and to list the three most important objectives they attempted to achieve. The objectives were then classified on the basis of the mental operations to find out the extent to which divergent thinking and evaluation were stressed.

The results were disappointing. Of 1020 objectives, which were submitted by the elementary teachers, only 9 or 0.9 per cent were concerned with divergent thinking. Only 5 or 0.5 per cent of the objectives were concerned with evaluation. The secondary teachers submitted 1297 objectives. Of this total 30 or 2.3 per cent were concerned with divergent thinking, and only 79 or 6.0 per cent were concerned with evaluation.

"It seems obvious . . ." wrote Torrance, "that far too many teachers are concerned *only* about *familiarizing* or acquainting pupils with ideas, facts and concepts. Others seem to be concerned only about developing the *'right'* attitude, establishing behavioral norms. The concern for doing something with what is learned is largely lacking."

What Should Be Done?

To begin with, teachers should cease teaching social studies in terms of "covering ground" or pages in a single textbook. This procedure is wrong both philosophically and psychologically. It is wrong philosophically because pupils need divergent points of views regarding conflicts inherent in human relationships. It is wrong psychologically because it ignores individual differences.

An alternative plan of instruction is the unit plan—not the traditional subject-matter unit plan, but a functional activity plan. The suggested plan includes two steps: a first step in which the content is broken down into logical components and transformed into a series of related problems, and a second step in which the pupils working under the direction of the teacher attempt to solve these problems themselves.

In executing this program the teacher should direct children in the wide use of resource materials, such as trade books and fugitive materials, current event publications, maps and graphs, and audio-visual aids. She should help pupils learn to select and evaluate these resources effectively. Also she should encourage children to produce materials of their own and to dramatize materials authentically.

This kind of instruction provides opportunities for children to compare things and to discover and study relationships. It encourages them to utilize discussion and other means of communication, to analyze situations, make new discoveries, and reach conclusions or generalizations. Such instruction is based on modern theories of learning and provides for development of the method of inquiry.

Obviously, the kind of teaching suggested above requires more time and more coordinated effort on the part of the teacher. It requires dedication, adequate knowledge of what is being taught, and, most of all, a complete realization of the value and nature of the problem solving method.

REFERENCES

1. Richard E. Gross and Frederick J. McDonald, "The Problem Solving Approach." *Phi Delta Kappan, 39* :259–265, 1958.
2. John Dewey, *Democracy and Education*. New York: Macmillan, 1916, p. 192.
3. E. Paul Torrance and Janet Ross, *Improving Social Studies Education in Minnesota*. Minneapolis: Bureau of Educational Research of the University of Minnesota, 1961. Mimeographed and sent by the senior author upon request.

Social Studies for Culturally Disadvantaged Pupils

THE TEACHER SHOULD HAVE LITTLE DIFFICULTY making social studies interesting and vital for the pupil who can read, who uses language well, has had a varied and stimulating life experience, and who gets psychological support from his family. But what of the pupils who do not have these advantages in their favor? What does social studies hold for them? How can teachers present these pupils with a social studies program that they will perceive as relevant to the world in which they live?

Of all school subjects the social studies can and should be the one most important to pupils who come from disadvantaged environments, because it is through the social studies that the pupils' range of encounters with society and culture can be extended. Vicariously and directly the pupil can experience contact with cultural models otherwise unknown to him. Because of limited experience with various segments of society, these pupils are often unfamiliar with the range of life choices that are possible and available to them. The pupil who is intelligent but culturally deprived most particularly needs to understand and learn how to deal with the social forces surrounding him, for if he does not do so he is likely to be frustrated by them, and such frustration leads to hostility and aggression. Perhaps more than for most pupils, those who have experienced deprivation need to build an awareness of the social world of which they are a part and learn to understand it. Children from such environments must be provided with opportunities to move into the mainstream of American society. The elementary social studies program can and should materially assist in this process.

It is fair to say that social studies programs for pupils from disadvantaged environments have not been innovative or imaginative. In most cases they represent minor modifications of the programs for all pupils. In general, somewhat the same learning goals are sought, materials of instruction and teaching strategies follow conventional models. For example, reading is important for information-getting for all pupils. In the case of disadvantaged pupils, however, reading skills are typically inadequately developed to handle the usual reading tasks that confront the learner in social studies. Therefore, the material is rewritten at a more simple level or other material is selected that is simpler in conceptual load, vocabulary, and/or structure. If the pupil still cannot read the passages, they may be recorded on tape and the child listens to them. These are procedures that are most often recommended and are familiar to most teachers. The question should be raised, however, as to whether or not these are sound procedures to use for information-getting with disadvantaged pupils. It may be that such information packages as texts and recordings are not at all appropriate and that more fundamental forms of information-getting should be used.

The problem of program relevance is one that is bothersome in working with children from all segments of society, but it needs special attention in working with pupils from disadvantaged environments. Often there is little in the conventional program that seems important or vital to these children because it is too far removed from their world of reality. This is not to suggest that the total social studies program for these pupils must grow out of their immediate surroundings and their own personal experiences. However, unless the pupil perceives what he is being asked to learn as having some meaning and value to him, the program cannot possibly succeed.

The problem of deprivation exists everywhere. It is found in the rural sections of the nation, in the slums of the large cities, in the towns and hamlets throughout the land. In recent years there has been an increased awareness of the magnitude and extent of this problem, and as a result tremendous amounts of money and energy have been allocated to the improvement of educational opportunity for disadvantaged pupils. Whatever the success of such programs has been to date, there can be little doubt that these investments in human resources will pay large dividends to society. It is only through education that pupils who are victims of deprivation can be converted into contributing and responsible citizens of this nation.

In the articles that follow the authors have provided valuable assistance to teachers in working with disadvantaged pupils. It is in this area of American education that can be found some of the greatest challenges to teachers today. Also it is the area in which the richest rewards both to individuals and to society as a whole can be found.

WHO ARE THE SOCIALLY DISADVANTAGED? *

Robert J. Havighurst

In all of our big cities, and in many smaller cities and rural counties, educators are trying to find better ways of teaching a group of children and youth who are variously called "culturally deprived," "intellectually deprived," or "socially disadvantaged." This is a major movement, which enlists a large amount of money and time of skilled teachers, and also a considerable amount of research effort.

There is consensus that this group of children and their families present a great social problem, perhaps the greatest of our domestic social problems. It is important that the problem be seen clearly.

Different writers and different workers in this area have defined the target group somewhat differently. The group is sometimes (and frequently enough to cause confusion in the minds of readers) described as all children of manual workers. But few if any educators care to call this large working-class group, some two-thirds of the child population, "socially disadvantaged."

A more useful definition of the "socially disadvantaged" can be arrived at in the way that is demonstrated in this chapter. Children with social disadvantages have always been present in any society, but probably the numbers are unusually large in the present American society, due to the urbanism of this society and to changes in the labor force which make it difficult for youth aged 16 to 20 to find employment.

The question which gives title to this chapter may be answered in various ways. One way is to illustrate by describing some cases of social disadvantage.

Suppose we observe two mothers riding with their 4-year-old children on a bus. The mothers want to teach their children to sit properly on a bus seat, while the bus starts and stops suddenly.

Case A
Mother: Hold on tight to your seat.
Child: Why?
Mother: Hold on tight.

Robert J. Havighurst is Professor of Education at the University of Chicago.

* Reprinted from the *Journal of Negro Education* 34:210–217, 1964 Yearbook, with permission of Howard University and Robert J. Havighurst.

Child: Why?
Mother: You'll fall.
Child: Why?
Mother: I told you to hold on tight, didn't I?

Case B

Mother: Hold on tightly, darling.
Child: Why?
Mother: If you don't you will be thrown forward and then you'll fall.
Child: Why?
Mother: Because if the bus stops suddenly you'll jerk forward and
        bump against the seat in front.
Child: Why?
Mother: Now hold on tightly, darling, and don't make such a fuss.

The first thing that strikes the observer of these two cases is that the mother in Case A does not try to explain to the child. Thus the child does not have an opportunity to learn the "why" of things, and if this kind of situation occurs again and again, the child may lose the habit of asking *why?* The next thing is that the vocabulary in Case A is more restricted than in Case B. Thus the child does not get practice in extending his vocabulary. Perhaps the next thing that will be noticed is that there is a difference in the *relation* between child and mother in the two situations. In Case A the mother asserts her authority through categorical statements. She does not really try to explain why the child should hold on tight, but *orders* the child to do so. The mother's authority is invoked almost at once, with the result that the natural curiosity of the child is pushed back, and the child is learning *not* to think for himself. In Case B the mother attempts to satisfy the child's curiosity with explanations. Although she finally resorts to her authority, she has first given the child a chance to learn about the world in a relationship which permits him to challenge authority with his questions.

The child who experiences language and social relations of Case A during his early years is likely to develop a different kind of mind than the child who experiences language and social relations of Case B. The child in Case A is socially disadvantaged when compared with the child in Case B.

Disadvantaged for What

Disadvantage is a relative term. When we speak of a child as being *socially disadvantaged* we mean that he has a disadvantage relative to some other child for some kind of social life. As the term is used in this book, it means disadvantaged for living competently in an urban, industrial, and democratic society. The socially disadvantaged child is one who is handicapped in the task of growing up to lead a competent and satisfying life in the American society.⌋

Consider, for example, Michael, who is a 10-year-old boy living in an ordinary town. His father is a truck driver, and makes a good income, though he must be away from home frequently for days at a time. Michael's mother stays at home and does her best to give her three children a good start in life. She looks after the children faithfully, and wishes they had enough money to rent a house in a "better" part of town where the neighbors had nicer children and there were not so many Saturday night fights and Monday morning hangovers.

When Michael was 7 years old he was put into an experimental second grade class consisting of 18 children who had failed the first grade by not learning to read at the proper grade level. Instead of making them repeat the first grade, the principal put them all in one class with a teacher who volunteered to work with them, and with a social worker who spent a day a week visiting the homes of the children. Michael had an IQ of 97. He began to read by Thanksgiving of the second year, and soon was reading at a second grade level. He liked especially the trips his group took to the public library, where the children's librarian read to them and encouraged them to borrow books and take them home. Michael read about 20 children's books by the spring of the year. But he forgot to return his books on time, and one day his mother received a post card telling her that there was a 16-cent fine for overdue books. She sent Michael to the library with the money, but told him, "Don't you ever go near that library again. They didn't have a right to fine you."

To Michael's mother, a fine was a bad thing. She associated it with the punishment some of her neighbors suffered when they got drunk and had a fight at a nearby tavern and were arrested and fined "for being drunk and disorderly." She was raising her children to avoid this kind of life, and she did not think Michael was guilty of a crime by keeping the library books too long.

Michael got along fairly well in school; his grades were average, and he was a good boy. One day, when he was in the fifth grade, he was playing after school, and he spied the social worker who used to visit his home when he was in the experimental second grade. He greeted her, and said, "Miss Jansen, please come to my house and see my books." He took her into his home and showed her a set of Britannica Junior books. "These are all mine," he said. "My dad pays five dollars a month for them." The social worker said, "That's wonderful, Michael, and do your folks read to you from these books?" "Oh, no," said Michael, "they don't like to read much, and, besides, they said that these are my books, for me to read. Of course, I can't understand everything, but I've been reading about the animals of the world."

Just then, Michael's mother came in and greeted the social worker warmly. "We'll never forget how much you helped us when Michael was in the second grade," she said, "and don't you think these books are wonderful?"

This was a case of social disadvantage, and illustrates the fact that parents may take very good care of their children in an emotional sense, but still deprive them of a good intellectual start in life. This mother and father simply did not *know* how to help their children do well in school. In spite of their good intentions, they deprived Michael of the use of the library, which might have been a major intellectual resource for him, and then they splurged by getting him a children's encyclopedia but they did not set an example of reading, and they did not read to him or help him learn to read.

Who Are the Socially Disadvantaged?

The socially disadvantaged children may be defined and described in three ways: in terms of certain family characteristics relating directly to the child; in terms of their personal characteristics; or in terms of the social group characteristics of their families.

FAMILY CHARACTERISTICS

Compared with other children whose families give them average or better advantages for getting started in modern urban life, the socially disadvantaged child lacks several of the following:

A family conversation which: answers his questions and encourages him to ask questions; extends his vocabulary with words and with adjectives and adverbs; gives him a right and a need to stand up for and to explain his point of view on the world.

A family environment which: sets an example of reading; provides a variety of toys and play materials with colors, sizes, and objects that challenge his ingenuity with his hands and his mind.

Two parents who: read a good deal; read to him; show him that they believe in the value of education; reward him for good school achievement.

Bernstein (1) has studied the language behavior of families that relate to the intellectual development of their children. He distinguishes between two forms or *types* of language. (These language types are statistically related to social class, as will be pointed out later.) One form of language is called *restricted* and the other form is called *elaborated*. A family which employs restricted language gives a child a language environment characterized by:

1. Short, grammatically simple, often unfinished sentences with a poor syntactical form stressing the active voice.
2. Simple and repetitive use of conjunctions (so, then, because).
3. Little use of subordinate clauses to break down the initial categories of the dominant subject.
4. Inability to hold a formal subject through a speech sequence; thus a dislocated informational content is facilitated.
5. Rigid and limited use of adjectives and adverbs.
6. Constraint on the self-reference pronoun; frequent use of personal pronoun.
7. Frequent use of statements where the reason and conclusion are confounded to produce a categoric statement.
8. A large number of statements/phrases which signal a requirement for the previous speech sequence to be reinforced: "Wouldn't it? You see? You know?" etc. This process is termed "sympathetic circularity."
9. Individual selection from a group of idiomatic phrases or sequences will frequently occur.
10. The individual qualification is implicit in the sentence organization; it is a language of implicit meaning.

On the other hand, a family which employs an *elaborated* language gives the child a language environment characterized by:

1. Accurate grammatical order and syntax regulate what is said.
2. Logical modifications and stress are mediated through a grammatically complex sentence construction, especially through the use of a range of conjunctions and subordinate clauses.
3. Frequent use of prepositions which indicate logical relationships as well as prepositions which indicate temporal and spatial contiguity.
4. Frequent use of the personal pronoun "I."
5. A discriminative selection from a range of adjectives and adverbs.
6. Individual qualification is verbally mediated through the structure and relationships within and between sentences.
7. Expressive symbolism discriminates between meanings within speech sequences rather than reinforcing dominant words or phrases, or accompanying the sequence in a diffuse, generalized manner.

8. A language use which points to the possibilities inherent in a complex conceptual hierarchy for the organizing of experience.

A child who has learned a *restricted* language at home is likely to have difficulty in school, where an *elaborate* language is used and taught by the teacher; and the difficulty of the child is likely to increase as he goes further in school, unless he learns the elaborate language that is expected in the school. On the other hand, the child who has had experience with an elaborate language from his earliest years has a relatively easy time in school, because he must simply go on developing the kind of language and related thinking which he has already started.

PERSONAL CHARACTERISTICS

The family environment with the characteristics just cited tends to produce children with certain personal deficits. Martin Deutsch (2) has studied such children with techniques of the experimental psychologists, and he finds them to have inferior auditory discrimination, inferior visual discrimination, inferior judgment concerning time, number and other basic concepts. He finds that this inferiority is not due to physical defects of eyes and ears and brain, but is due to inferior *habits* of hearing and seeing and thinking. Presumably, the family environment of these children did not teach them to "pay attention" to what was being said around them, or to the visual scene. Then, when they came to school, their school performance suffered because they had not learned to "listen" to the teacher and other important people or to "see" the things they are shown in the school.

SOCIAL GROUP CHARACTERISTICS

We introduce the social group characteristics of socially disadvantaged children last so as to avoid giving the impression that there is a hard-and-fast relation between socio-economic status, or some other group characteristic, and social disadvantage for the child. While there are statistical relations and very important ones between socio-economic status and social disadvantages of children, there are so many individual exceptions to the statistical generalizations that any educational policy aimed at identifying socially disadvantaged children should avoid reliance upon general socio-economic characteristics as the decisive criteria.

Above all, it is important to avoid the error of saying that all children of working-class families are socially disadvantaged. Approximately 65 per cent of the children of this country are living in working-class homes. That is, their fathers or mothers do manual work for a living. The great majority of these families give their children a fairly good start for life in an urban industrial democratic society. Their children are adequately fed and clothed. They are loved and protected by their parents. They learn to respect teachers and to like school. They do fairly well or better than that in school.

While working-class children as a group are somewhat different from the children of white-collar workers, it would not be reasonable to say that the working-class children are socially disadvantaged or culturally deprived. Working-class children as a group score slightly below children of white-collar families in intelligence tests; they fall slightly below on tests of school achievement; they attain somewhat less formal education. But the differences are relatively small, and become even smaller when the socially disadvantaged children are removed and the majority of working-class youth who remain are compared with white-collar children.

Most working-class families participate fully in the American mass or core culture. This is certainly not a culture of deprivation. While the differences between the upper working-class and the middle-class are real and they are interesting, these differences should not be described in terms of social advantage or social disadvantage. The great amount of movement of people across the boundary between these two classes as they grow up is evidence that the differences between these two classes are not fundamental ones.

Who, then, are the socially disadvantaged when we attempt to describe them in terms of observable social groups? They are groups with the following characteristics:

1. They are at the bottom of the American society in terms of income.
2. They have a rural background.
3. They suffer from social and economic discrimination at the hands of the majority of the society.
4. They are widely distributed in the United States. While they are most visible in the big cities, they are present in all except the very high income communities. There are many of them in rural areas.

In racial and ethnic terms, these groups are about evenly divided between whites and nonwhites. They consist mainly of the following:

1. Negroes from the rural South who have migrated recently to the Northern industrial cities.
2. Whites from the rural South and the Southern mountains who have migrated recently to the Northern industrial cities.
3. Puerto Ricans who have migrated to a few Northern industrial cities.
4. Mexicans with a rural background who have migrated into the West and Middle West.
5. European immigrants with a rural background, from East and Southern Europe.

Altogether, these groups make up about 15 per cent of the United States population. Since they tend to have large families, their children make up as much as 20 per cent of the child population. Not all socially disadvantaged children come from these groups, but the great majority do. Not all children in these groups are socially disadvantaged, but the great majority are.

How Many Are Socially Disadvantaged?

There is an infinite graduation of social advantage-disadvantage, and therefore any quantitative estimate of the number of socially disadvantaged children and youth must be a personal rather than a scientific statement.

The writer would place the number of socially disadvantaged children at about 15 per cent of the child population. One basis for this estimate is the proportion of unemployed, out-of-school youth between the ages of 16 and 20. These young people have been relatively unsuccessful in school and in the labor market. The great majority of them come from the social groups listed above. There are about 11 per cent of boys and 17 per cent of girls in this group. The boys are clearly maladjusted to society. Some of the girls are not; they are simply doing what girls have done for a long time, helping out at home while waiting to get married. But these figures place a minimum on the numbers of socially disadvantaged youth. There are a few others who have jobs which are below their capacity or are disadvantaged in other ways—enough to bring the total up to about 15 per cent.

Since these children and their families tend to concentrate in the large cities, while upper-income people tend to move out from the cities to the suburbs, the socially disadvantaged children are in big cities in larger proportions than 15 per cent. Probably *30 per cent of the children* in such cities as New York, Chicago, Philadelphia, Washington, Detroit, Cleveland, and Baltimore fall into the socially disadvantaged category.

Do the Socially Disadvantaged Have Special Advantages?

In discussions of education for the socially disadvantaged there is a good deal of sentimental talk about the "valuable" or the "positive" characteristics of the cultures from which these children come, and about the desirability of developing school programs that allow the child to profit from these positive qualities.

It is said that this kind of child is "physically oriented"—that he likes action rather than words. It is said that he has non-language skills that can serve him for learning. It is said that he can perceive (see, hear, and smell) in superior fashion. It is said that he has more of certain kinds of creativity. It is said that he has a different "mental style" from that of children who do well in the ordinary school.

This set of propositions is conceivably correct. The child growing up in a rural culture certainly gains some skills that are likely to be more highly developed than they would be if he grew up in a city. Every culture has characteristics that are positive in its own situation. For example, in a study of Hopi Indian children of the American Southwest, it was found that their drawings were superior in many ways to the drawings of American white children. A university art teacher made systematic comparisons of the drawings and found that, according to his own criteria of good children's art, the Hopi drawings were superior to those of Midwest white children of the middle-class. Yet the same Hopi children were inferior to Midwest children on a verbal test of intelligence. Thus one might make use of this positive quality of the Hopi children in developing schools to fit them for participation in the surrounding American culture.

However, there is substantial doubt that the socially disadvantaged children in our big cities have *any* positive qualities of potential value in urban society in which they are systematically better than the children of families who participate fully in the mass culture. The writer does not know any comparative study which shows American lower-lower class children to be superior in any positive respect to American upper working-class or middle-class children. As a group they are inferior in tests of spatial perception, for example, as well as in tests of vocabulary and arithmetic. It is true that the difference between the socially disadvantaged and the mass culture majority is less on tests of certain non-verbal skills than on tests of more verbal and abstract abilities. This fact might suggest that the socially disadvantaged could learn more rapidly and efficiently if they had more concrete experience on which to base their vocabulary and their reasoning skills. This is probably true, but it does not argue for a difference in "mental style" and therefore a difference in school curriculum. It argues for more building of "readiness" for reading and arithmetic in the pre-school and primary grades.

Conclusion

The *socially disadvantaged* children can be defined and discovered at an early age. While social disadvantage and social advantage are concepts which shade into each other, it is possible to make working distinctions which are a basis for identification of some 30 per cent of the children of the big cities as socially disadvantaged. These are not necessarily working-class, or lower-class children. The majority of children of working-class families are not socially disadvantaged as the term is used in this discussion.

The socially disadvantaged children tend to come from families that are poor, and that are recent immigrants to the big cities. They are a group that need special attention in the schools and special help to assist them to overcome the disadvantages conferred on them by their families.

REFERENCES

1. Basil Bernstein, "Language and Social Class." *British J. Sociol. 11*:271–276, 1960.
   Basil Bernstein, "Social Class and Linguistic Development. A Theory of Social Learning," in *Economy, Education and Society*. A. H. Halsey, J. Floud, and C. A. Anderson, eds. New York: Free Press of Glencoe, 1961.
   Basil Bernstein, "Social Class, Linguistic Codes and Grammatical Elements." *Language and Speech 5*:221–240, 1962; "Elaborated and Restricted Codes: Their Origins and Some Consequences," *American Anthropologist,* 1964.
2. Martin P. Deutsch, "The Disadvantaged Child and the Learning Process," in *Education in Depressed Areas,* A. Harry Passow, ed. New York: Bureau of Publications, Teachers College, Columbia University, 1963.

UNDERSTANDING THE LANGUAGE OF THE CULTURALLY DISADVANTAGED CHILD *

Eddie G. Ponder

Introduction

The urban schools of our country are faced with a sizeable number of school-age children who are considered educationally and culturally disadvantaged.[1] This presents a challenge to the public schools which try to provide an effective educational program for the boys and girls of this segment of the population. There is evidence, however, of a wealth of untapped resources among disadvantaged children. Because their self-images, motivations, and cultural horizons are very low, they are prevented from achieving at a level commensurate with their ages and abilities.

Phenomena Regarding the Oral Language of Disadvantaged Children

Lack of verbal symbols for common objects and ideas—Speech patterns which cause frequent misunderstandings in oral communication.

The above statements, extracted from one of the first reports of the Milwaukee Great Cities Study,[2] are indicative of findings and impressions of many school psychologists relative to the oral language productions of the majority of disadvantaged children. One has to take into account, however, that the standardized tests available and used are mostly standardized outside the experiences and language of these children. Most standardized instruments used to measure the language of the disadvantaged child do not tap the kind and quality of language that he possesses. His patterns of

Eddie G. Ponder is on the staff of the Institute for Developmental Studies, New York University, New York.

* Reprinted from *Elementary English* 42:769–774 ff., 1965, with the permission of the National Council of Teachers of English and Eddie G. Ponder.

[1] The terms culturally and educationally disadvantaged are used interchangeably with urban disadvantaged, socially disadvantaged, disadvantaged, culturally deprived, experience poor, educationally underprivileged, children with limited backgrounds, and the disaffected.

[2] Milwaukee, Wisconsin Board of School Directors, "Orientation Classes for In-Migrant—Transient Children, Report I, Part I," October, 1961.

speech, usage, and pronunciation do not, for the most part, approximate the standards of language expected by the school (commonly referred to as school language).

The oral language of the disadvantaged child is usually on the "vulgar" level. The "vulgar" level is used here to denote a language category of the people or the crowd (vulgus). In addition, the "vulgar" level is usually designated as the lowest level of language. The common man without adequate educational experiences speaks mostly on the "vulgar" level.

The oral language habits of disadvantaged Negro and white children coming from the same region are similar. In working directly with children and parents from the two racial groups, one can easily discover many similarities in language usage, oral expression, and sentence sense. There are, of course, some differences. The differences, however, are of degree, not kind.

Following are some samples of the oral language (along with comments) of socially disadvantaged children. The first two samples selected for use have been extracted from the final report of the Milwaukee study on Orientation Classes for In-Migrant—Transient Children.[3] The third and final sample was selected from an actual classroom discussion in one of the Milwaukee Orientation Classes for In-Migrant—Transient Children where a tape recorder is familiar equipment and was used to record this session.[4]

Sample I
  An Original Play
  Students used the tape recorder in putting this play together.
  Boss: Hey you, boy, come here (menacingly). I thought I asked you for two bales. You got a bale and a half here.
  Worker: Yes sir, you did and I'm trying to pick the rest of it.
  Boss: I hear you been playing and loafing out there in the field.
  Worker: No sir, that ain't so. I been working hard.
  Boss: You—yeah you, come here. You the one who told me this boy was playing and laughing stead o' doing his work?
  Worker Yas sir, and he keeps the rest of us from doing our
  #2:   work.
  Boss: I reckon um have to give you a beatin'. Kneel down. (Boss lashes worker on back.) Now get up. You got a woman?
  Worker: Naw sir, I ain't married.

---

[3] Milwaukee, Wisconsin Board of School Directors, "Orientation Classes for In-Migrant—Transient Children, Final Report," March, 1964.

[4] The comments following the language samples are a result of staff conferences on selected children enrolled in the high school orientation class. The author wishes to acknowledge the professional services of Mrs. Dorothy Carter, Teacher of the class, Mrs. Lottie Porter, Project Social Worker, and Mr. Hoyt Harper, Project Psychologist.

Boss: Boy, go get yourself a woman. Maybe you'll work better and get them bales picked.

Worker: (Student goes off stage, selects a girl.) E. says, "I don't want to be in that old play, Mrs. Carter." Other students urge E., "Aw go on, E." E. and worker go to field.

Worker: Bossman, this is my wife.

Boss: You got any children old enough to work in the field?

Wife: No sir, they're in school.

Boss: Send them out here to help this good for nothin' man of yours.

Wife: (Resolutely) They're staying in school.
(as they leave the field) I don't care whether he ever gets his cotton picked. My children are gonna stay in school, even if I have to leave Mississippi and go to Milwaukee and live with my sister. The children will have a chance up there.

One can readily see how environment helps to shape an individual's attitudes and values. Fortunately, special personnel providing social and developmental histories as well as psychological evaluations were available to the teacher in her efforts to try to understand her students through their use of oral and written expression. In this play, it is interesting to note the male acceptance of the Southern social system from which they came. Too, the teacher observed that the boys laughed as they played these roles and expressed no resentment toward the social system portrayed. (They didn't even react to the name, *boy*.) On the other hand, the girls did not like the image portrayed. Also, it appears that the female values education. The play seems to suggest that immorality, values, and attitudes often thought of as being *inherently* associated with lower-class status (and sometimes racial minority groups) can be and are influenced or conditioned by authority figures of a supposedly higher social order. In addition, this play seems to support the notion that disadvantaged families are migrating from rural impoverished circumstances to the urban zone to better themselves. The extended family is most often crucial in this regard.

Sample II
When mama and papa died, my brother sent for us to come live with him. He can't read and write and he's so ashamed. He ain't never had no trouble on his job tho'. He wants to give us a chance to finish high school. My sister-law is nex' to the angels—she's so good to me and my little brothers. There's a baby in the house that loves me so much— I don't know why because I'm only his aunt, but they all say he looks just like me. I do love that little baby.

This sample seems to suggest strong family ties which facilitate the social system of the extended family. Moreover, one can sense the value of education which the family holds even though the male head of the household appears to lack a positive self-image because of his inability to read and write. Nevertheless, there seems to be a sense of pride in the work of the male as well as love of family. Note also the poetic quality of the line, "My sister-law is nex' to the angels."

Sample III

William: Will you have seven years of bad luck if you break a mirror?

Scott: I broke mine and that was bad luck enough cause it was brand new. But, I'm gonna buy me a new one. Bad luck just comes—you don't have to break nothing—But you got to make good luck by working hard and saving—getting an education.

This dialogue between two students indicates adequate language to express interesting ideas, aspirations, and philosophy of life.

The samples contained language of Negro and white students. Was it possible to determine racially one from the other?

The Cratis Williams' studies on Southern Appalachian speech also indicate regional characteristics which are interracial. Further, Williams asserts that words, more particularly verb forms and even diction, when examined comparatively, reveal little that is confined only to Appalachia.

Following is a selected list of some of the most common verbs used in mountain speech which was developed by Williams: [5]

Present	*Past*	*Past Participle*
(ask) ax	axt	axt
bring	brung	brung
burst	busted	busted
drive	driv	driv
fight	fit	fit
hear	heared	heared
reach	rech	rech
see	seed	seed
sneak	snuck	snuck
take	takened	takened
teach	teached	teached

Although the above list does not indicate acceptable verb forms in our culture, it, nevertheless, displays verb forms with certain

---

[5] Cratis D. Williams, "Verbs in Mountain Speech," *Mountain Life and Work.* Berea, Ky.: Council of the Southern Mountains, Inc., Spring, 1962, pp. 15–19.

systematic characteristics. While the verbs in the past tense and past participle are at the "vulgar" level, they are within the framework of regional speech which is fluent and meaningful. There are many positive aspects of mountain speech. It is colorful, metaphorical, lyrical, rhythmical. Frazier [6] asserts that the great mass of children we consider poorly languaged actually have quite a lot of language. Therefore, Frazier argues, if we let them, they can talk a blue streak about the things they know how to talk about. Thus, it would seem reasonable to suggest that we need to understand and learn the language which the disadvantaged child brings to the school situation if we are to "take him where he is."

Some of the language of the disadvantaged child may be less fluent. For example, these children often answer with a nod or one-word reply for fear of not being able to answer correctly in the school culture. On the other hand, generally speaking, the child is from a home where the parents are educationally and culturally disadvantaged, thereby affording little opportunity for the development of his oral language. Moreover, the child is usually from a large family living in a crowded, noisy apartment. The noise, however, does not represent meaningful stimuli.

The extended family is not uncommon in the family structure of the disadvantaged child. Uncles, aunts, grandparents, cousins, and sometimes very close friends are a part of the family structure. It would appear that the disadvantaged child has only advantages regarding language development with so many people around. The extended family structure, however, may cause serious discontinuity in the language development of the child. He learns language from the many people around him, likely speaking in varied pitches and accents. Lost in the shuffle of so many people, often in a crowded space, the child has limited opportunities for help in learning to label the objects in his environment. His opportunities for enrichment within and outside the encapsulated, socially impoverished environment are also limited.

Allison Davis [7] stated that one night he attended a movie on Chicago's Southside to gain further insights into the language of disadvantaged adults. He sat behind two women who were engaged in a lengthy discussion trying to label two animals (rhinoceros—hippopotamus) which had been flashed on the screen in a zoo scene. Davis discovered (1) that these women were born and reared in the South, (2) that they had never been to a zoo or circus because

---

[6] Alexander Frazier, "Helping Poorly Languaged Children." *Elementary English*, February, 1964, pp. 149–153.

[7] In an address at the New York University sponsored conference, *Integrating Diversity Through the Curriculum*, December 1, 1963.

being Negro in their previous locale of the South prevented them from attending, and (3) that the women had not become acquainted with these animals in their sketchy educational or experiential backgrounds. This illustration by Davis would seem to support the notion that the disadvantaged child is the product of a disadvantaged family in which his opportunities for learning to label, including feedback regarding labeling, are limited.

These boys and girls pass innumerable resources and objects going from school each day (also in their travels about the community) without the slightest idea as to how to label them. They label them as *a thing, do hickey,* or *somethin' out yonder.* These seemingly crude labels, however, serve an important function in the communication system developed in the disadvantaged populace.

Many idiomatic expressions uttered by the disadvantaged child and his parents seem to baffle the more affluent speaker and often obstruct communication. For example, in some disadvantaged neighborhoods, "I don't care to," can mean "yes, I'm willing," according to the intonation of the speaker. Whether the disadvantaged child utters "twice out of sight" (go around two mountains) in the Kentucky hills or "gwine to tote this poke of 'taters' " (going to carry this bag [sack?] of potatoes) in Mississippi, his oral language is highly clear, understandable, and completely acceptable in his particular social milieu.

Should We Try to Change the Language of the Disadvantaged Child?

It seems of paramount importance that we accept the language of the disadvantaged child. To be "accepting," however, does not indicate a reluctance to "build on" or improve the language habits and skills of the disadvantaged child for fear of alienating him from his family and/or peers in the socially impoverished environment.

Disadvantaged parents want their children to improve educationally. In fact, they realize the necessity of a good education. They are perplexed, usually, as to means by which to attain educational ends. Yet, it should be realized that many racial and ethnic groups which presently enjoy high cultural and social positions in the social stratification of our society are descendants of disadvantaged parents and depressed neighborhoods.

There is also concern that it is futile to try to teach the disadvantaged child "correct" language skills because he returns to the impoverished environment only to revert back to his "incorrect" usage of the language. It should be stated that the intent to improve the language skills of the disadvantaged child should not be to train him *only* for a given higher level of language. Rather, he should be made aware of other levels of language, especially as they relate to actual occupational situations in our society. Thus, if the disadvantaged child subsequently becomes verbally mobile, to what degree is his reverting back of importance? Is there a correctness to our language? Tomlinson [8] states that in helping children achieve social standards of language, the teacher should keep in mind that these standards do not deny certain regional characteristics of tone, accent, rhythm, and idiom. Might we think of acceptable ways of expressions for *given* situations as we work with disadvantaged children (and, indeed, all children)?

Can We Change the Language of the Disadvantaged Child?

While it is important to try to assess the amount and quality of the language possessed by disadvantaged children, it is equally important to try to assess their language deficiencies. This will facilitate the establishment of a "communicative" benchmark from which to build more acceptable language usage. Research indicates some interesting findings relative to the language of the disadvantaged child: paucity of language, shorter sentences in speech, poorly structured speech syntactically, and language related to social class.

Cutts [9] states that the utterances, huh—uh . . . huh . . . nuttin . . . naw . . . wuh? . . . cuz . . . unhunh . . . sho! and other *strange noises* [italics mine] that take the place of standard American English reflect the impoverished language background of underprivileged children.

John [10] reports that several studies indicate that children from lower-class backgrounds rely on shorter sentences in their speech than do their middle-class agemates. She further reports from her summary of studies that children from lower-class circumstances have a more limited vocabulary and poorer articulation.

Deutsch,[11] reporting on some of the basic research at the Institute

[8] Loren R. Tomlinson, "Accepting Regional Language Differences in School." *Elementary English 30*:420–423, 1953.

[9] Warren G. Cutts, "Reading Unreadiness in the Underprivileged." *NEA Journal 52*:23–24, 1963.

[10] Vera P. John, "The Intellectual Development of Slum Children: Some Preliminary Findings." *The American Journal of Orthopsychiatry 33*:813–822, 1963.

[11] Martin P. Deutsch, "The Disadvantaged Child and the Learning Process," in *Education in Depressed Areas*, A. Harry Passow, ed. New York: Bureau of Publications, Teachers College, Columbia University, 1963, pp. 163–179.

for Developmental Studies, postulates that the lower-class home is not a verbally oriented environment. Moreover, he reports that from observations of lower-class homes, speech sequences appear to be temporally very limited and poorly structured. Thus, Deutsch argues, it is not surprising to find that a major focus of deficit in the children's language development is syntactical organization and subject continuity.

Newton [12] states that the opportunities for language development are stretched on a continuum and the economic "have nots" are often the verbal "have nots" as well.

This brief look into research on language development of disadvantaged children is helpful in providing a frame in which to understand the nature of their language deficiencies. It facilitates the development of an instructional program to more adequately meet their needs. For example, special tapes may be prepared to develop attentional or listening skills. These skills are important first steps with respect to language development. Too, a sequential program may need to be planned which begins with attentional or listening skills and moves to such higher levels as the labeling of objects, and the labeling of similarities and differences in objects and functions of objects. While this example indicates how language may be developed, it also has implications for the development of other skills.

Conclusion

In conclusion, it seems of paramount importance that the language spoken and written by the disadvantaged child be understood by the teacher in order to (1) facilitate meaningful communication and (2) provide a starting point from which to build on the language which he does possess.

The teacher will need to develop good rapport with the children and provide a positive classroom climate in order to free them to express themselves orally. Moreover, good classroom climate will help the teacher gain better opportunities to help children develop "other ways" of speaking and using the language. When good classroom climate exists, children can often be heard to say "I know better than that," or "That sounds like me."

Understanding the language of the disadvantaged child is not as difficult a task as is often assumed; the teacher's attitude and

---

[12] Eunice Shaed Newton, "Planning for the Language Development of Disadvantaged Children and Youth." *The Journal of Negro Education 39*:264–274, 1964.

the understanding with which he approaches the task will determine to a large extent the degree of difficulty. Moreover, the teacher's awareness of the individual needs of his children will determine the kinds of activities and program to be provided in the classroom. It is quite likely that the approach in helping the disadvantaged child develop language facility is applicable for use with advantaged children. The teacher will in both cases plan his instruction around the language strengths and the language needs which the children bring to the school situation.

REFERENCES

1. John B. Carroll, "Language Development," in *Encyclopedia of Educational Research,* 3rd ed., Chester N. Harris, ed. New York: Macmillan, 1960, pp. 744–750.
2. Werner Cohn, "On the Language of Lower Class Children." *School Review 67*:435–440, 1959.
3. Warren Cutts, "Reading Unreadiness in the Underprivileged." *National Education Association Journal 52*: 23–24, 1963.
4. Martin P. Deutsch, "The Disadvantaged Child and the Learning Process," in *Education in Depressed Areas,* A. Harry Passow, ed. New York: Bureau of Publications. Teachers College, Columbia University, 1963.
5. Alexander Frazier, "Helping Poorly Languaged Children." *Elementary English 41*:149–153, 1964.
6. Vera P. John, "The Intellectual Development of Slum Children: Some Preliminary Findings." *The American Journal of Orthopsychiatry 33*:813–822, 1963.
7. Milwaukee, Wisconsin Board of School Directors. "Orientation Classes for In-Migrant—Transient Children, Report I, Part 1," October, 1961.
8. Milwaukee, Wisconsin Board of School Directors. "Orientation Classes for In-Migrant—Transient Children, Final Report." March, 1964.
9. Eunice Shaed Newton, "Planning for the Language Development of Disadvantaged Children and Youth." *The Journal of Negro Education 33*:264–274, 1964.
10. Loren R. Tomlinson, "Accepting Regional Language Differences in School." *Elementary English 30*:420–423, 1953.
11. Cratis D. Williams, "Verbs in Mountain Speech," in *Mountain Life and Work.* Berea, Ky.: Council of the Southern Mountains, Inc., Spring, 1962, pp. 15–19.

EDUCATION FOR THE CULTURALLY DEPRIVED: BUILDING ON PUPIL EXPERIENCE *

Dorothy M. Bryan

The problem of education for the culturally disadvantaged, though not a new one, has only recently begun to receive the attention from the general public that is so urgently needed. It is a serious problem and one that is expanding with alarming rapidity. Where in 1960 one out of every three children in America's large cities was culturally deprived, current studies indicate that by 1970 the figure will be one in every two.

Much of the current literature on the culturally deprived contains studies carried on in the slum areas of our large metropolitan cities. But the deprived can be found, not only in big cities, but often right in our own communities. This is a fact that many of us, including teachers, often fail to recognize. My own work with disadvantaged children has been carried on in the southeastern part of the country in a city with a population of only 80,000 people. The study here presented was made in an integrated school and involved a third-grade class of boys and girls from what is commonly termed "slum backgrounds."

Perhaps the characteristic that most often identifies the culturally deprived child is a poverty of experience. I believe that too few teachers recognize the importance of experience as related to learning. A teacher of the disadvantaged should be aware of the lack of direct, or first-hand, experience of her pupils. To understand the difference in the backgrounds of experience between the child from the slums and the child from the "other side of town," one must realize that many slum-dwellers have never ventured beyond their immediate neighborhoods. Often the slum child has no conception of life beyond his home, the street on which he lives, and his school —with the possible exception of some knowledge of the world of television. For many such children, a fear of embarrassment and a feeling of insecurity prevent them from seeking new experiences outside their own neighborhood.

Dorothy M. Bryan is an elementary school teacher in the Durham City Schools, North Carolina.

* Reprinted from *Social Education* *31*:117–118 ff., 1967, with permission of the National Council for the Social Studies and Dorothy M. Bryan.

It was with all these considerations in mind that I set out to determine just how limited the experiences of my 22 third-graders were. Through written questionnaires administered to the children, and through discussions in reading groups and in class sessions, I was able to determine words and concepts with which they were familiar.

Before turning to the results of my study, a word about the extent of deprivation existing among my 22 students may be in order. Ten of them were obviously ill-clothed; nine could not afford to pay the minimal school lunch cost and were given free lunches. Fourteen did not own a toothbrush! Eight of the children came from families on relief, and eight of the fathers were unemployed. None of the fathers was a member of a profession, or even held a "white-collar" job. In three of the families, there was no man who could fulfill the role of father, and not all who did assume the role were married to the mothers. With such cultural backgrounds, it may not be surprising that more than a third of my third-graders had already repeated at least one grade.

Perhaps one of the most significant findings was the poverty of travel experience of the children. In regard to points of interest in their own city, I found that only four had ever been on a tour through a cigarette factory—and this in a city whose factories produce one-fifth of the nation's cigarettes and through which factories hundreds of visitors are conducted on daily tours. Only six indicated that they had ever been inside the magnificent chapel of the local major university; only 13 had checked out books from the public library; only 11 had visited the Children's Museum. Fourteen had been inside a bank, and five had participated in YMCA activities.

A further picture of the lack of travel experience of these children is reflected in the small number of those who had been to places quite familiar to most of the city's middle-class boys and girls: a concert, 3; summer camp, 4; a zoo, 6; mountains, 6; a circus, 8; a football game, 8; a museum other than the local Children's Museum, 9; a baseball game, 12; a beach, 15; a restaurant, 17; and 7 had stayed overnight at a hotel.

Only five children had even been out of the state of North Carolina, and one of these had traveled only as far as Virginia. One child came to Durham from California, and one each had visited Washington, D.C., New York, and Texas.

Television sets were in the homes of all but three of my students. Although television has probably done more than any other single factor to increase the vicarious experiences of disadvantaged children, my findings showed that the children looked mostly at cartoons and westerns. When asked to select their favorite TV program, "Daniel Boone" and "Man from U.N.C.L.E." were chosen most frequently, with cartoon programs rating the second highest choice. Only a small fraction of the class ever watched any of the educational programs, such as "Animal Kingdom" or "Young People's Concerts."

We are apt to assume that all eight- or nine-year-olds know how to use a telephone; yet only eight of the families of my third-graders had telephones in their homes. Out of the 22 families represented, only six took a daily newspaper. Twelve children reported that they had magazines in their homes, an encouraging observation until I learned, on further investigation, that five of the 12 were of the love-story or movie-star variety.

One of the greatest problems in interesting underprivileged children in reading is the lack of books in the home. Eight of my students reported that they did not own a single book. Four others estimated the number of books they owned to be less than ten. Only one child indicated that he had a large number of books which which he could call his own.

One of the most common experiences shared by the group was that of helping at home. Among the chores most often performed were washing dishes, bringing in wood or coal, and sweeping the floor (no one ever mentioned a vacuum cleaner). Fourteen of the students indicated that they often had to take care of younger brothers and sisters.

All of the group reported some experience with pets. However, with the exception of one boy who owned a parakeet, dogs and cats were the only ones mentioned. Many of the children had had to give up pets because of having moved into low-cost government housing where pets were forbidden.

When I asked what foods the children were familiar with other than those served in the school lunchroom, I found that squash and turnip were in nearly everyone's diet, but only six had eaten dates; only three had ever eaten chow mein; only two had ever tasted broccoli; only one knew what asparagus was, and no one had ever eaten or even heard of cauliflower. I was surprised to learn that 16 ate pizza quite often.

During the several years I have worked with disadvantaged children, it has become my firm conviction that the only way we can ever reach the culturally deprived is through adapting the curriculum to their everyday experiences. One place to begin is to provide them with more meaningful books.

One of the most glaring discrepancies I found between the stories in the school books and the real experiences of the children was that in so many of the stories "father" was forever going off to work or coming home from work. Yet for half of my class, father did *not* go to or come home from work. Add to this the fact that even with the other half of the class the parent's employment is often erratic; it is easy to understand why the children had difficulty in grasping the concept of family life where the father had steady employment.

Although there are some books now being published that deal with experiences familiar to disadvantaged children, their use is not sufficiently widespread. Illustrations almost always show white, middle-class people living in middle-class homes and wearing middle-class clothes. My pupils asked why father always wears a suit in the pictures. There are few situations in any of the reading books which picture men working at unskilled jobs. Yet these are the only jobs with which my pupils were familiar.

In answer to the question, "What do you want to be when you grow up?" only six children aspired to an occupation that would require any higher education. Two each indicated they would like to be teachers and nurses; a Negro boy was the only one who desired to become a scientist; and one of the slowest learners in the group hoped someday to be President.

One of the most common settings used as background for stories is the farm. Five of the readers I used last year contained a unit of farm stories. The authors seem to assume that all children have a knowledge of farm life and animals within their experience. Yet I have had children in my classes who could not tell a cow from a horse. Another concept which the reading books attempt to develop is that of a zoo. One book contained a whole unit of stories concerning a zoo, one of which concentrated on a cockatoo—a bird totally unfamiliar to my entire class. As indicated earlier, only six of my 22 children had ever been to a zoo. The remainder of the class evidenced no accurate conception of a zoo whatsoever. They seemed to visualize the animals, one to a cage, shut up in small cages as in circus pictures. Although a movie on the zoo was of some help, except for the six with actual experience, few of the children could even imagine the actual expanse of a large zoo with natural habitats provided for the animals.

Stories could and should be written about experiences that disadvantaged children share. Every child in my class was at least an occasional visitor to the local community center. Yet not a single story in any of the books read in our school used a community center for a setting.

The high point of the reading program in my third grade this past year came the day we read "The Babe," an excerpt from a biography of Babe Ruth for young readers. The story revealed that as a small boy, George Herman Ruth had no real home. He spent much of his time on the streets and was nearly always hungry. From the first words of the story, the identification of the children with this boy of the streets was almost tangible. Seldom have I seen so many eyes alight with real interest as when they read and reread about someone so much like themselves. Why cannot special reading books for children of this age and background be made up of stories about other heroes whose lives and problems they can understand?

Another area in which the curriculum for the disadvantaged child must be enriched is that of visual aids. We cannot assume that all children have had the experiences needed to understand what are to us common concepts, and we must develop these concepts through pictures, motion pictures, filmstrips, use of overhead projectors, etc. I have found it necessary to use twice as many visual aids with these children as with children from middle-class homes.

It is well known that direct experience is far more valuable than vicarious experience. We need to take culturally deprived children out of their neighborhoods and help them to feel secure in all areas of the city. These children should participate in a large number of field trips at all grade levels. Yet I fear that the truth is they are taken on fewer field trips than children in average classrooms.

In Durham, some of the places which could be visited in an effort to enlarge the horizons of children from slum areas are the newspaper office, Duke University, North Carolina College, the Children's Museum, Duke Gardens, the bus station, the airport, the Jack Tar Hotel, and the Y.M.C.A. Other places where children could gain insight are the water plant, the police department, and the fire department. And within a short distance are farms and factories of many kinds. I am confident that arrangements could be made for the children to attend desirable concerts, plays, and motion pictures either free of charge or at greatly reduced rates.

Another area in which I think definite headway could be made even in the lower grades is in arousing an interest in various occupations. Culturally deprived children must be educated to understand that employment is desirable. We can familiarize them with different types of occupations to which, hopefully, they may one day aspire. Most disadvantaged children have never been inside a business office. It is of prime importance that these children gain an awareness of the fact that with determination and hard work, college and a professional career can become a reality for them, as well as for the culturally advantaged. Unless, through the school, we seek to remove the educational apathy which surrounds most children from slum areas, they will, in years to come, merely add to the welfare rolls.

Not to be overlooked in this endeavor is the possibility of exploiting to the fullest the experiences culturally deprived children already have. We need to start where these children are, capitalize on the positive aspects of their culture, and move out from there to broaden their experiences and their perspectives.

In retrospect, it is my contention that when we come up with teaching materials that are within the experiences of disadvantaged children, when we exploit fully the limited experiences they have had, and when we seek to provide more meaningful first-hand experiences for them, we will do a better job of educating these young people to be more useful citizens and to take their proper place in society.

EXPOSE—DON'T IMPOSE *

Joseph D. Lohman

While America is proud of her cultural diversity—of having many differing ethnic and racial stocks following many different customs —the pressure for basic conformity has worked to diminish this diversity. Such pressure frequently leads to unfortunate or even disastrous conflicts and rarely solves the basic problem of existing cultural differences.

So completely are we submerged within our own values that we have difficulty in realizing that those habits which are different from our own, particularly if they are annoying to us, may have a coherency and an integrity of their own.

The school contains a number of built-in value conflicts. First, there is a conflict between teachers and students because of difference in age. Teachers bear adult values, while students are representatives of current student subcultures with their own habits and norms.

Joseph D. Lohman is Dean of Criminology at the University of California, Berkeley. Dr. Lohman has written on this topic at greater length in a chapter of *Cultural Patterns of Differentiated Youth: A Manual for Teachers in Marginal Schools*, prepared under Grant No. 63228 of the U.S. Department of Health, Education, and Welfare. Copies of the book are available for $3 from Dr. Lohman's office.

* Reprinted from the *NEA Journal* 55:24–26, 1966, with permission of the National Education Association and Joseph D. Lohman.

The conflict, however, which is most relevant to our interests is that which occurs because teachers are the ones charged with transmittal of our cultural heritage. Students are part of the contemporary culture of their particular community, and if this community is a culturally diverse one, the natural conflict becomes the more complex.

Because the school is representative of the mainstream of American values, most teachers naturally tend to enforce middle class values and manners.

By "middle class" we mean the mass of American society that places a high value on a stable family life, regular employment, and on education and social and professional achievement. For purposes of this article we will define the "lower class" as that population group who are blue collar workers if employed; who place importance on toughness, excitement, and "conning activities"; and whose family life is unstable and often mother-centered because there is no responsible male present.

Young people from lower class groups are insulated from middle class values and are at odds with them; their early years have shaped their interests and social contacts in a strong pattern that is not easily broken.

Changing of values by talking about them in the classroom is a high goal and a difficult one for teachers. Value change comes about slowly and usually through complex incentives, including the emulation of models. In this respect the teacher is as important in character building as he is in teaching his subjects. He can be a great inspiration to his students, especially to those who have not had a stable model in their homes. Although the fruits of the teacher's labors may not be readily apparent at the time, the teacher may often have more impact than he believes, and subtle changes may appear in the student years later, as a result of the efforts of effective teaching.

One approach to changing values would be to launch a program to point out to this group of alienated students the specific middle class values and skills that are necessary for their survival in the economic order, and to emphasize that their command of these will help them in the future without threatening or violating the primary values of their family and community.

For example, certain instrumental skills of know-how and communication must be mastered by all young people, including those of the lower class, in order to find a place in today's economic and social order. The first one of these is reading. Teachers experience great frustration because so many students are years below their grade level in reading.

Another point of know-how is how to ask questions in an acceptable manner. Many students appear to ask questions in a belligerent or purposefully naive manner. Often the teacher is annoyed and does not answer because he feels the student is simply acting out or testing him, when in reality the student does want to ask a question but does not know how to communicate in a socially acceptable way.

Communication by word and gesture is difficult for children who come from homes where such skills are not naturally transmitted in the course of life. For example, a study of slum families in New York revealed that in one-half of the families contacted, the children do not eat with their parents or have opportunities to talk to them except about elementary matters of physical necessities.

The togetherness of the middle class meals gives the children opportunity to converse with their parents or to listen to abstract conversation. In fact, much of the social, educational, and cultural tradition that a middle class child learns is gained in conversation over the meal table.

In this area, teachers could try to supplement the verbal skills of lower class students by instruction in socially acceptable forms of communication and gesture—for example, that one should look directly at a teacher or potential employer when speaking to him to convey sincerity of purpose. Niceties of speech seem elemental to most of us, but many a job has been lost, or a question or plea for needed aid refused, because the seeker did not know how to ask his question or present himself in an acceptable way.

Many lower class youngsters are also unaware of the importance of promptness and of reliability in keeping appointments. Many such children come from families where there is no father and the family lives on welfare, or where the father is unemployed. In such cases, there is frequently no regular schedule for rising in the morning and for holding communal meals. The importance of living on a time schedule is not emphasized, and the school or some similar agency needs to teach the children promptness and conscientiousness in meeting appointments.

Children from disadvantaged homes have other habits which are annoying by middle class standards, but are not potentially harmful to economic survival. These, school personnel might try to understand and accept, even though the habits are unpleasant or even shocking. Weird speech forms could be accepted if they are not objectively obscene; bizarre hair styles and clothes could be tolerated if they do not go beyond the limits of legally defined indecent exposure.*

---

* Reader comments or suggestions on this point will be welcomed for possible use in an article on students' dress and hair styles.

Teachers need to realize that such habits and manner of dress are probably a youngster's badge of status and membership in his peer group. Many of the students we call culturally disadvantaged have weak or strongly negative self-images and bolster their self-esteem in ways that are alien to the middle class. The more flamboyant their dress, the greater their sense of belonging.

For teachers to understand and to try to accept, even though disapproving, the behavior and trappings of this subculture is perhaps the most difficult but the most potentially productive way to react.

In considering the conflict between the middle class school and the lower class student, this discussion has dealt with the methods by which change can be brought about in the student, the extent to which such change can be expected, and the kinds of lower class behavior which the school might tolerate without a loss in the learning situation.

There is another direction in this relationship between differing classes and their ways of living. While it is necessary for the lower class group to be exposed to middle class values, to adapt them and sometimes even adopt them for their own survival in the dominant society, it is also necessary for middle class school personnel to become exposed to the values and ways of life of the lower socioeconomic group. The very insularity of the middle class person, his ability to live his life almost totally among others like himself, often gives him the feeling that his way is *the* way, the *only* way, and that all others must be converted to it.

Little real education can take place in a situation where there is no trust, no rapport, no understanding between the teacher and the students. In this context "teacher" may be expanded to mean the school as an institution, and "student" expanded to mean the community of families of students. This trust, rapport, and understanding cannot result if all interaction, or rather action, between these groups is in one direction.

While there seems to be general agreement that the adoption of certain values of the dominant middle class culture is necessary for survival in this society, such adoption cannot be forced. Perhaps an effective approach might be: Expose, don't impose.

If school personnel can open the doors for their students without attempting to push them through, if they can sincerely convey to these students that there are different values which may be of practical help to them without intimating that their present values are worthless, if the school can allow the student to take what he wants without insisting that he take everything, then the student may be able to accept some of the school's values.

The ability to adopt certain middle class values such as those already discussed—punctuality, ability to communicate verbally in reading and in writing—in order to achieve certain practical ends, while still retaining roots in and identification with the original subculture, has been compared to owning and wearing different kinds of clothes.

One puts on a suit for certain occasions, sport clothes for another. Similarly, one may use different language and behavior at certain times and still slip back into other language and behavior for other parts of one's life. In order to help a student to accept more than one set of values, the school personnel must be ready to accept some elements of the student's set of values.

If a teacher received a teaching assignment in a foreign country, he would thoroughly prepare by reading and by meeting with people who had been there and, if possible, with natives of that country in order to learn as much as possible of the culture ahead of time. He would undoubtedly feel that one of the main values of his stay in this other country would be the experiencing, at firsthand, of this other way of life.

Effective working with a subculture within one's own country requires much the same approach. To begin to know and understand others requires a knowledge of the forces that have shaped them. The exchange teacher would undoubtedly study the history of the country he is visiting, and yet most school personnel see no need to learn the history of minority groups in this country—a history they would have to make a special point to learn, since it has so often been either ignored or distorted in our history books.

The middle class teacher who studies his students' subculture may be surprised to find many positive elements (an absence of self-blame, for instance), some of which he might even want to incorporate into his own values. More likely, he will reject this other mode of life for himself, but he may be able to see how it meets the special circumstances of other people. Even if he rejects the elements of the subculture completely, the knowledge which he has gained would enable him to better understand his students and to develop ways of teaching more in line with their ways of operating.

It is the actual or implied criticism of his way of living, his home, his very being which so demoralizes the non-middle class student, especially if he is from a minority group. For example, the common reaction of the school to the language of the subculture is to look upon it is ungrammatical, undesirable, and to be totally wiped out if possible. To the student, his language is an integral part of his culture—his very being—and an attack on it is much more than an attack on his conversation; it is an attack on his own worth. Small wonder he so often reacts with sullenness, resentment, defiance.

If the teacher really listens, he will find that this language of the students is extremely inventive and that it communicates in an effective, down-to-earth fashion.

If the teacher can let the students know he appreciates the positive aspect of their language, they will be more willing to learn the school's language. If their language is not regarded as totally worthless, they will be more able to see the need for using the middle class language pattern at times.

Other differences can be handled on this same basis: that some things are necessary for the student to know for his own benefit and not because the school is attempting to displace his "inferior" way of life with its "superior" one.

Langston Hughes' poem "Motto" succinctly summarizes this value of knowing more than one way of life:

> *I play it cool and dig all jive.*
> *That's the reason I stay alive.*
> *My motto, as I live and learn,*
> *Is: Dig and Be Dug in Return.*[1]

This applies to students and to school personnel alike.

A CUSTOM-TAILORED CURRICULUM *

John I. Goodlad and
Madeline C. Hunter

Today hundreds of thousands of children in big cities dwell in harsh environments. These children began life with handicaps that never will be overcome unless deliberate steps are taken to remove them or to compensate for the disadvantages.

---

[1] Copyright © 1951 by Langston Hughes. Reprinted by permission of Harold Ober Associates Incorporated.

John I. Goodlad is Dean of the Graduate School of Education at the University of California, Los Angeles. Madeline C. Hunter is principal of the U.C.L.A. elementary school and also principal, Los Angeles City Schools.

* Reprinted from *The PTA Magazine* 59:8–10, 1965, with permission of the National Parent Teachers Association and John I. Goodlad and Madeline C. Hunter.

We are not going to talk about changing the immediate economic and social lot of these children, crucial though this need is. We are concerned here with how schools can be conducted so as to give all children a chance to struggle somewhat more successfully and satisfyingly in a world of a decreasing number of "second chances."

To be in a nonreading family, in which the spoken language is parochial, is to be handicapped in learning to read. To read haltingly by the age of nine or ten is to carry an added burden into all the school's activities, to become a learning cripple. This means that most paths to self-fulfillment will be blocked and the self-renewing society denied a valuable recruit.

Children in harsh environments do not differ in kind from other children. They learn to communicate, to conform to models of behavior, to develop characteristic ways of coping with frustration, to respond to systems of reward and punishment. Like children everywhere, they differ in how well they succeed in attaining behavior they consider important. But unlike children in suburban communities, they are sharply restricted in the range of alternatives from which to choose. Education for them must be more than a reflection of the life they lead; it must be a revelation of alternative patterns for a life worth living.

If schools in general were adequate, those for children in harsh environments would not need to differ from other schools. Whatever changes are needed to make all schools more nearly adequate are needed still more sharply for disadvantaged children. Adequate schools—the schools emerging today in the promise of a better tomorrow—have the following characteristics:

—Educational decisions are based on diagnosis of the individual child; in effect, education is tailor made.

—Expectations for each child arise out of continuing diagnosis, not out of arbitrary conceptions of appropriate work or performance at a certain grade level.

—Grade standards and labels are swept away and replaced by more realistic descriptions of each child's actual performance. The school becomes nongraded.

—Additional resources supplement the limited resources of a single teacher in a self-contained classroom. Teams of teachers with specialized abilities come together to diagnose needs and to plan for better learning.

—The curriculum is stripped down to reveal the bare bones of human knowledge and processes of learning. It draws on the life the child knows and provides direct experiences he might otherwise never know.

—Teaching is a response to what each child is ready for rather than an imposition of identical experiences upon all.

Free the Teacher, Free the Child

The first two steps toward getting the schools we need are the most difficult. They must be taken simultaneously. First, teachers must be freed from the arbitrary expectations that have made schools what they have been and largely still are. Teachers must come to ask, "What is this child ready for?" and not "Is this child ready for school?" Next, the school environment must be reorganized to provide something for every child.

Children entering school differ by as much as four years in their readiness to profit from what is traditionally thought of as first-grade work. One may behave like an eight-year-old in some ways, another like a four-year-old. It is folly to expect like performance from all children. It may be tragic to insist on it. But such expectation and such insistence are implied by the graded school.

Children in harsh environments differ markedly, too, in their readiness to profit from a graded school. But on the average their attainment and readiness are skewed sharply downward—as much as two and three years below those of children in many suburban communities. To expect first-grade performance from them is sheer madness. That expectation alone can maim beyond repair a child's already wounded concept of himself.

A child-centered nursery school can and should enable a child's self to unfold at the age of three or four. But even if a child has been kept out of school until the age of five or six, there is no cause for weeping and wailing. Much can yet be done, if the child's needs are properly diagnosed and prescribed for and if the school structure provides the alternatives needed to fill the prescription.

The structure of the school must permit—in fact, encourage—the teacher to provide the child already turned six with some four-year-old activities and some five-year-old activities. This is the essence of nongrading. Nongrading encourages careful diagnosis and invites teachers to search for appropriate alternatives. The school must not prescribe all first-grade work for six-year-olds who have lacked nursery school experience. Grading discourages diagnosis and sharply limits the alternatives from which to prescribe.

At the end of each school year a critical decision must be made. Where is the child to be placed for the most productive activity next year? Commonly, placement is determined almost entirely by the organization of the school. The child is ready for the work of the next grade and so is promoted, or else he is not ready and so is retained for an additional year. This is primitive decision-making, bearing little relationship to the developing child. How is the child coping with his parents' expectations? What preoccupations are contaminating his awareness of the environment? With what other children should he be associating? What teacher can best help him in his present stage of development and in the taking of new steps? Only after carefully answering questions like these should the next year's placement be made.

Often the attempt to provide the needed environment severely strains the resources of a single teacher. For instance, a person highly skilled in reading or in speech therapy may be needed. Perhaps the child needs to alternate between rapidly paced and slowly paced learning. To meet these varied demands only a team of teachers may be adequate.

Within a flexible school structure, individualized instruction comes naturally. This does not mean different instruction and activities for every child, but those *appropriate* for every child. If individualized instruction is to work, the teacher must be able to make critical decisions that will insure the necessary "fit" in the education of each child. Such "custom tailoring" is especially essential for those who begin with an environmental handicap. These are some of the decisions a teacher must make. How large should a particular instructional subgroup be? What are the appropriate learning opportunities within that group? What kind of teaching will best help each child accomplish the task for today?

Fabric and Fit

This is a far cry indeed from dealing out the graded spellers, math books, and readers, and teaching from them on only one or two levels of instruction. Such a technique is boring to the fast learners, frustrating to the slow, and inefficient and ineffective for all. We know enough these days about the learner and the learning process not to tolerate, much less condone, such "instruction" in our schools.

When a teacher begins individualized instruction, he first determines the child's educational latitude and longitude, so to speak. In much school learning each new task is based on previous tasks. Hence it is important to complete one task before taking up the following one. For example, reading requires a combination of many previous learnings, such as perceptual skills, communication skills, and ability to work with abstract symbols.

The traditional first-grade reading program is built on assumptions about what a middle-class, Caucasian six-year-old has already learned. These assumptions contain all the errors of averaging. As a result, we have frustration and failure even in the group for which the program was designed. But when the program is applied to a six-year-old for whom none of the assumptions is valid, damage is a great deal more serious. The typical first-grade program is a gross misfit for many children. It offers dramatic proof that it is useless to build a program that does not call for an understanding of the individual learner.

Is it wise to delay the disadvantaged child's entrance into school? No, because this only leaves him longer in the handicapping environment. It's equally wrong, of course, to place him in an inappropriate educational environment. To prescribe appropriate educational opportunities for a given child, we must measure his position on the learning scale.

After the educational diagnosis has been made, the school is ready to determine the size of instructional groups for each activity. When an assignment permits wide variation in performance, it can efficiently be scheduled for the entire group. But when the learner's response must be more specific, the instructional group must include only children capable of this kind of response. For example, the whole group may well listen to a story. But a first-grade reader is effective only with those children who have completed the necessary prior learnings.

Educational systems should see that teachers have enough free time to custom-tailor learning opportunities for each child. Children whose environment lacks certain educational riches need compensatory experiences, not lamentations over their poverty.

After diagnosis and prescription for the learner comes provision of the necessary alternatives in the educational environment. This step creates the pharmacy in which prescriptions can be filled. The teacher is the trained professional in whose hands rests the ultimate success of this part of the educational venture.

Watching It Work

Freed from arbitrarily imposed standards and expectations, the teacher can now implement the diagnosis. If he is provided with the additional resources of a team of colleagues, this task will be accomplished more effectively. Important too is the professionally trained teacher's ability to apply the basic principles of human learning to children's day-by-day education. In fact the sound application of our rapidly expanding knowledge of how children learn is the essence of good teaching. Ill-judged or ignorant application slows down even the most eager learner—and makes a fatality of the disadvantaged one!

Consequently in the teaching-learning process decisions must continually be made, some of them minute by minute, so that the child's desire to learn will remain at the highest level. Ideally the learner actively participates in the learning process. He clearly perceives his objective and knows to what degree he is achieving it. He distributes his practice wisely. And he experiences appropriate reward for his effort.

The over-all objective of the entire educational program is to enable each child to apply and use what he learns. Teaching a child to read is only a necessary step in developing a learner who *does* read. In this way a custom-tailored educational environment is in itself an essential step in improving the harsh community environment of many children.

A child's initial handicapping environment, then, need not be forever crippling. Educational systems need not remain forever inflexible. Needed alternatives in educational practice can be found. And education for all children need not remain a dream.

Educators in America now possess the knowledge to create equal educational opportunity. Courage and freedom to apply that knowledge can indeed transform the vision of our forefathers into reality for all children.

DIFFERENTIATING INSTRUCTION FOR DISADVANTAGED STUDENTS *

Daniel U. Levine

Most teachers and administrators believe that instructional practices should be modified in accordance with the needs of students. Attempts to individualize instruction usually include differentiating the content of materials and varying the way materials are presented in the classroom. Attention is sometimes given to more global differences in the ways educational goals can be pursued in a given instructional setting. At one end of a continuum the ideal educational approach can be conceived as the organization of in-

Daniel U. Levine is on the faculty of the College of Education at the University of Missouri, Kansas City. He is also Associate Director of the Center for the Study of Metropolitan Problems in Education.

* Reprinted from *The Educational Forum* 30:143–146, 1966, with permission of Kappa Delta Pi, an honor society in education, and Daniel U. Levine. Copyright © 1966.

struction based on and leading to self-directed inquiry. At the other end of the continuum the ideal approach is conceived as the detailed structuring of instruction to accomplish objectives defined with reference to specific subject matter and easily tested skills. Because these approaches represent contending philosophies of education, most educators eventually become committed, emotionally and intellectually, to one or the other. A person with an implicit or an explicit attachment to a pervasive philosophy of education will have trouble recognizing situations in which relatively unambiguous considerations make a competing philosophy more appropriate. In a sense, we are confronted with a dilemma in which our allegiance to a particular philosophy (which defines individualized instruction as desirable) interferes with our attempts to individualize instruction by analyzing the advantages and disadvantages of competing approaches in each instructional setting. This dilemma has become most acute in connection with the unusual learning problems of a very special population among our students: those who are socially, economically, and culturally disadvantaged.

There are many possible ways to structure the classroom learning environment. If we are sincere in the belief that no one standard approach is suited to the needs of groups of students differing greatly in previous experience, then we must identify, if only crudely, the particular learning environment which best matches the developmental level and the behavioral characteristics of any given group of students. More specifically, there is good reason to believe that practices which are appropriate in working with middle-class students are inadvisable when working with disadvantaged youngsters. Students who live in underprivileged and disorganized communities need unusually intensive guidance and supervision, so much so, in fact, that classroom approaches almost universally recommended in educational psychology textbooks will not work in inner-city schools. This is not because disadvantaged youngsters are inherently less able than middle-class youngsters to handle the "relaxed" and relatively unstructured classroom atmosphere rightfully extolled in the textbooks, but because child-raising practices in low-income families negate the likelihood that the children of the poor will perform well in such an atmosphere.

Melvin L. Kohn has summarized several of the relevant social class differences in child-rearing values as follows:

> . . . working-class parents value obedience, neatness, and cleanliness more highly than do middle-class parents, and . . . middle-class parents in turn value curiosity, happiness, consideration, and—most importantly—self-control more highly than do working-class parents. We further found that there are characteristic clusters of value choice in

the two social classes: working-class parental values center on conformity to external proscriptions, middle-class values on *self*-direction. To working-class parents, it is an overt act that matters: the child should not transgress externally-imposed rules; to middle-class parents, it is the child's motives and feelings that matter: the child should govern himself.

. . . the differences between middle-class and working-class parental values are probably a function of the entire complex of differences in life conditions characteristics of the two social classes.[1]

Not trained to work in a self-disciplined style which leads to success in a "progressive" classroom, disadvantaged students quickly exceed the boundaries teachers assume pupils will observe as a matter of course. Inexperienced in planning activities directed at long-range goals, disadvantaged youngsters are at sea when teachers attempt to "recognize" their human dignity and individuality by allowing them great discretion in deciding how to proceed in the classroom. Unprepared for situations in which they are asked for preferences rather than told what to do, disadvantaged youngsters are overwhelmed by the freedom imposed by the teacher who has been taught that children respond best when rules and expectations are flexible and self-defined. Such children should not be expected to handle all at once a confusing excess of freedom and the terrifying range of choice which is its necessary corollary. They are likely to respond more satisfactorily to regularity and pattern in classroom activities. Definite rules should be introduced and enforced at the very beginning of the school year. The teacher should stand ready to provide close direction at every stage, no matter how small, of each classroom activity.

Assignments and learning activities necessarily will be more highly structured in classrooms serving disadvantaged students than in classrooms constituted by pupils who have been encouraged at home to seek independence and self-direction. The structuring of learning experiences fortunately does not require that pupils be excluded from participation in the definition of rules or that teachers be any less fair and sympathetic or assignments and presentations any less imaginative than is desirable in all classrooms; attention to these instructional goals is as important, if not more important, in inner-city schools than in schools serving more fortunate youngsters.

---

[1] Melvin L. Kohn, "Social Class and Parent-Child Relationships: An Interpretation," in *Mental Health of the Poor*, Frank Riessman, Jerome Cohen, and Arthur Pearl, eds. New York: Macmillan, 1964, pp. 163, 165.

The long-range goals in working with disadvantaged youth are, of course, identical to those to which we are committed elsewhere: to develop students who can think for themselves and who are skilled in the self-directed management of meaningful learning experiences. Such an orientation is developed slowly, by degrees, even with children whose environment includes every educational advantage parents can provide. It is unrealistic and, indeed, harmful to expect the children of poverty to meet such an expectation before they have been exposed to many years of carefully-supervised instruction which gradually liberates their undeveloped capacity to study and to learn.

At the present time inner-city classrooms organized to provide highly-structured and clearly-patterned activities congruent with the special circumstances and problems of disadvantaged students are difficult to find. Typically, the inner-city teacher, with high hopes and admirable motives, attempts to organize her classroom in accordance with the optimistic philosophies expressed in the textbooks used in teacher training courses. The pupils, bewildered by the absence of unsophisticated supervision they are accustomed to expect from adults, thereby are set loose to work their wills. The situation quickly moves beyond the control of the teacher. The teacher and/or the administration proceeds to overcompensate by clamping down with extreme regimentation and heavy-handed discipline. The school itself increasingly resembles a jail, with predictable reactions from its inmates. As a consequence, gradual growth in self-control is unlikely to take place among the pupils.

Whether many inner-city schools introduce the highly structured learning experiences most appropriate in working with disadvantaged youngsters will depend on the strength and resolution of administrators and teachers. The pressures of public opinion are likely to favor the implementation of less suitable policies. Public opinion concerning education, after all, is primarily middle-class opinion. The demands middle-class parents will make of the schools during the next few years are fairly predictable. As more and more students begin to compete for openings in the nation's colleges, pressure on elementary and secondary school personnel to tolerate no "nonsense" in the classroom will grow still more stringent. More middle-class parents will accept the seemingly reasonable idea that instruction be organized so as to reward only unusually distinguished achievement, hoping, of course, that this will produce a ticket of admission to college for their son or daughter. In an elitist atmosphere generated by a pervasive concern for college preparation, it will be easy to lose sight of motivation, inquiry, and individualized instructional arrangements for disadvantaged students as legitimate concerns in the public schools.

A growing minority of middle-class parents, however, will support an opposite position favoring the elimination of school practices which make their school-age children tense and overburdened. As the crisis over college enrollment intensifies, parents whose children are only average in ability cannot afford the "luxury" of any policy they believe might somehow lower academic standards in their local school; therefore parents enlisting in the "reduce the pressures" camp will be mainly those whose children are unusually high in ability and initial motivation to learn. In the past year a trend toward the publication in influential newspapers and periodicals of articles critical of extreme competition for grades and of the increasing quantity of homework assigned in high-prestige schools has already become evident.[2] Since the advocacy of an across-the-board relaxation of school requirements coincides with the personal views of many teachers and administrators, educators will be tempted to manipulate the support of this influential segment of public opinion to reverse the current retreat from the free and easy classroom atmosphere recommended in the "progressive" philosophy of education. Such a retrenchment is desirable in schools populated mainly by middle-class students; the obvious danger is that inner-city schools, too, will be swept along and recommitted to the relatively unstructured organization of learning experiences which has proved disastrous in teaching students from disadvantaged communities.

The polar pressures generated by warring middle-class factions are unlikely to contribute to the synthesis of instructional arrangements appropriate to the needs of working-class children. Neither an overwhelming dedication to preparation for college (viewed as the simple-minded accretion of factual information) nor a rededication to the emotional equilibrium of the child (viewed as liberation from control imposed by adults) is likely to produce the complicated interweaving of firm yet sympathetic supervision, imaginative subject-matter, variety in the ways materials are presented, regularity and consistency in the scheduling and conduct of learning experiences, and strong emphasis on the development of basic learning skills which is needed to stimulate improved academic performance from disadvantaged students. Initiative in

---

[2] Washington journalist William S. White, for example, recently devoted a column to the heavy load imposed on his teen-age daughter. He pointed out that while adults increasingly treasure and guard their leisure time, school requirements systematically deprive students of the time for constructive non-school activities.

planning and implementing an educational philosophy specifically directed at the needs of disadvantaged youngsters can be carried out only by professionals who understand what is at stake and have the courage to insist that it deserves the highest priority.

CULTURALLY DISADVANTAGED CHILDREN CAN BE HELPED *

Lessie Carlton and Robert H. Moore

People often assume that culturally disadvantaged children cannot make normal progress in school unless conditions in their homes are improved. We believe that this assumption is false, that the school can bring about normal learning progress by providing effective learning experiences, developing a favorable classroom climate, and fostering positive self-concepts.

To determine the validity of this belief, we conducted a study (and a recent corroborative follow-up) in which teachers of culturally disadvantaged elementary children used self-selection and self-directive dramatization of stories by pupils to teach reading.

Classes in each of the first four grades of a school in a very old area of Joliet, Illinois, made up the experimental group. Of the total school population of about 500 children, 85 per cent were Negro and 5 per cent Puerto Rican and Mexican. Children moved in and out of the community often and very few school records were available. The economic level of the community was low, and pupils frequently came to school crying because of cold and hunger. Since the school had no lunch program, many children remained hungry all day.

We found most of the children to be emotionally unstable. They talked incessantly, but rarely to anyone in particular. If a pencil fell on the floor, they would often shout "Thief!" and accuse someone of taking it. They hit each other. They tattled. They moved continuously.

Lessie Carlton and Robert H. Moore are on the faculty in the Department of Education and Psychology at Illinois State University, Normal.

* Reprinted from *NEA Journal* 55:13–14, 1966, with permission of the National Education Association and Lessie Carlton and Robert H. Moore.

The study reported herein was supported as Cooperative Research Project S-190 by the Cooperative Research Program of the U.S. Office of Education.

Although we recognized the possibility of obtaining inaccurate results, we administered reading achievement and mental maturity tests to all the children in both the experimental and the control groups. A large percentage in both groups had low intelligence-quotient scores, and the majority were much below their grade level in reading achievement.

Three women and one man taught the experimental groups. All four had studied the techniques of self-directive dramatization, and two had taken part in a similar study with classes made up largely of middle-class white children. One teacher had taught two years in a school which used basal reading books and three reading groups. Another was a beginning teacher.

The teachers of the control group had more experience teaching the culturally disadvantaged than the teachers of the experimental group and had been in their present positions longer but they had not studied techniques of self-directive dramatization. During the study, they gave reading instruction chiefly through the traditional use of a basal reader and mainly in formal whole-class or small-group instruction. No special teachers worked with either the experimental or the control group.

Matches for each pupil in the experimental group were selected from other classes in the same school and from classes in another elementary school with a population of similar racial makeup and socioeconomic level.

To provide for the needs and desires of all the children in the experimental group, books on many different reading levels were made available in the classroom. As a preliminary step to self-directive dramatization, the children selected their own stories and read alone. Gradually they began to work in pairs and in small groups and to take turns reading to each other.

The groups were formed according to each child's preference for a story to read and dramatize. After the children in a particular group had read the story cooperatively, they agreed upon which character each would portray in the complete dramatization. Generally the groups selected different stories and stories on different reading levels. The groups all read their stories at the same time but took turns in dramatizing them. The dramatizations were spontaneous and completely unrehearsed.

Self-directive dramatization was employed in this study not only to find out what gains children would make in reading but also to see if pupils' self-concepts would change. We assumed that a change from a negative to a positive self-concept would contribute to progress in reading.

On the supposition that a child's behavior reflects his concept of himself, we made up a checklist of thirty-one questions dealing with different behaviors. Before the beginning of self-directive dramatization, teachers of the experimental group observed each child in relation to these questions and recorded the observations. At the end of the year, teachers checked the questions again to see what gains each child had made.

Typical checklist questions were:

1. Does the pupil refuse to do things because he thinks he does not do them well enough?

2. Does he try to have the attention of the teacher at all times?

3. Does he often fail to finish what he starts?

4. Does he do things to attract attention—make faces, talk loudly, try to "steal the show"?

5. Does he show signs of being jealous (of a child's new clothes or praise given another pupil, for example)?

The number of checks before and after the use of self-directive dramatization in the classroom led to the inference that desirable changes did occur in the self-concept of the pupils. The following are the number of checks for the children of each grade before and after the self-directive dramatization.

	Grade 1	Grade 2	Grade 3	Grade 4
Before	519	480	318	558
After	204	82	104	105

After participating in self-directive dramatization, many of the children were able to sit together without hitting each other. Intermittently, they still talked at the same time, but not excitedly and unceasingly. They were also a bit more willing to take turns. In various ways, they showed that they felt more kindly not only toward their classmates but toward the adults who worked with them. One child wrote this letter to us:

"You are kind to us. Our teacher is kind to us. You bring us books that we like. Be careful on the highway when you come back to see us."

Children who had refused to have anything to do with reading at the beginning of the school year now often preferred reading to going outside to play, especially if they could find someone to sit near them and listen to them read. This was a great change from the early part of the school year when a boy threatened one of the investigators with his fists for offering to help him read.

Now, too, the children talked with visitors or strangers who came to the school. They smiled occasionally and had lost much of their look of fear, hostility, or suspicion.

In all four experimental groups, the mean gains in reading exceeded those of the control groups. In addition, the gains of all the experimental groups were greater than would be considered "normal" for the length of time involved. For example, the first graders in the experimental group gained more than one year in reading over a period of about three-and-one-half months. The gains for the other grades were made over a seven-and-one-half month period.

The first two columns of the table below show the mean reading grade scores for each grade of the experimental group before and after the experiment; the last two columns show the mean gains of the experimental and control groups.

	Mean for *Each Grade of* *Experimental Group*		*Gain of* *Experimental* *Group*	*Gain of* *Control* *Group*
	Before	*After*		
Gr. 1	0.58	1.71	1.13	0.24
Gr. 2	1.26	3.13	1.87	1.25
Gr. 3	2.17	3.35	1.18	0.79
Gr. 4	3.39	4.24	0.85	0.43

The results of the reading tests seem to confirm our belief that culturally disadvantaged children can learn if good teachers supplied with appropriate materials employ the best possible methods of teaching.

Among these methods, self-directed dramatization seems to be particularly effective for a number of reasons. On the basis of the study, we feel that it can contribute to the improvement of self-concept of pupils and can help develop their skills in reading. It provides pupils with a chance to express themselves in the guise of somebody else and gives them a chance for physical activity—almost a necessity because these deprived youngsters are inclined to be excitable, restless, and unable to concentrate on desk work for any length of time.

In short, our study suggests that the technique of self-selection and self-directive dramatization of stories may prove to be a major means of upgrading the educational level and improving the personal and social adjustment of culturally disadvantaged pupils.

CHILDREN LOOK AT THEIR
OWN BEHAVIOR *

Ronald Lippitt, Peggy Lippitt,
and Robert S. Fox

Children today are avid consumers of technology. Chances are that the small boy in the third row, fourth seat knows more about the second-to-second preparations for a space shot than he does about the day-to-day work of his father at the office or plant.

Youthful enthusiasm for technology need not be limited to the race for the moon, however. It can also provide motivation for learning about matters much closer to the child's everyday world. In Michigan, for example, children are learning about the ways people behave toward each other in much the same way the children might learn about the behavior of a space ship in orbit.

In the Michigan Social Science Education Project, elementary school teachers, assisted by curriculum specialists and behavioral scientists from the University of Michigan, are introducing their pupils to some of the scientifically accepted methods for studying human behavior, particularly everyday behavior experienced by the pupils in their classroom life. Begun two years ago, the Project involves several first through sixth graders in the university town of Ann Arbor and in industrial Willow Run, as well as the pupils at the University of Michigan Laboratory School.

The methods and techniques by which the children study human behavior are, of course, simplified to fit their various levels of comprehension. Nonetheless, the children are able to acquire useful information about themselves, about their own reactions to situations, about interpersonnal relationships in the classroom, and about scientific method.

"Friendly and Unfriendly Feelings" is the title of one of the units introduced in the curriculums of the three participating school systems. In this unit, the children are encouraged to look objectively at their own human relations. Although the children acquire a

Ronald Lippitt is Professor of Psychology at the University of Michigan; Peggy Lippitt is affiliated with C.R.U.S.K. of the Institute of Social Research, University of Michigan; Robert S. Fox is Professor of Education and Principal of the Campus Laboratory School, University of Michigan, Ann Arbor.

* Reprinted from the *NEA Journal 53*:14–16, 1964, with permission of the National Education Association and Ronald Lippitt, Peggy Lippitt, and Robert S. Fox.

surprising amount of knowledge about what behavioral scientists
have learned about emotional behavior, the emphasis in "Friendly
and Unfriendly Feelings" is on methodology—the children learn
to use the scientific method as an inquiry procedure, as a way of
asking and answering questions.

The learning techniques presented during this and all the units
depend on the pupils' grade level and, to some extent, on the
teacher's ability to work with a particular method. So far, the
teachers have succeeded with learning procedures that incorporate
role playing, unfinished stories, simplified interviewing and observation techniques, pupil-made graphs and charts, and group projects. The lecture-by-teacher method is rare; participation by the
children is stressed.

Before the children begin the unit, they are given an orientation
to what "behavior" is as an object of study and to ways of exercising their scientific curiosity.

How objectively the children are able to observe behavior is
perhaps best illustrated by the experience one mother had with
her little girl who was in the third grade last year. The girl was
having trouble getting to sleep one night and she asked her mother's
advice.

"Think about something interesting," said the mother.

"I'll think about behavior," said the child.

The mother, concerned, asked her daughter if she were having
trouble at school. "Oh, no!" was the reply. "Don't you know that
all actions *are* behavior?"

The purpose of the orientation is to build children's ability to
differentiate between scientific observation and a value judgment.
In the long run, this ability helps them to articulate and share more
intelligently the many different values they have. The atmosphere
of tolerance and trust in which the children learn encourages them
to question and examine their own values and to develop some
new and more positive attitudes toward their classmates, teachers,
and families.

After the orientation period, the children undertake specific
study projects. A third grade teacher, for example, may present
his children with the problem of what makes people become angry.
He may choose to begin with one of the laboratory exercises described in a special guide designed by some of the experienced
teachers and scientists involved in developing the "Friendly and
Unfriendly Feelings" unit.

Each exercise is designed to present a specimen of behavior
which the children can examine and from which they can draw
tentative hypotheses. For example, one exercise involves a stan-

dardized role-playing scene in which conflict develops over children taking turns.

In this case, Jim refuses to let Jack have the bat in a game of rounders. Jim says that he is not finished batting. When Jack tries to grab the bat from Jim, Jim pulls it away. Jack then hits Jim in the face.

The children observe the role-playing scene as members of observation teams. One team is given the task of collecting data on the different feelings exhibited by the actors. Afterward they tabulate the data on a chart showing how often feelings of friendliness or unfriendliness were revealed in the scene. Another team is assigned the task of observing one actor. Afterward they will be asked to make a team report on how that person reacted.

The teacher assigns the observation tasks on the basis of what the unit builders think the children should learn from the experience. The guides also include criteria for evaluating the experiences.

In the case of the children observing Jim's reaction to relinquishing his turn, they might study the accuracy of their report by comparing their independent observations. The scientists call this reliability of observation.

As the children become more adept at observing simple interactions between people, they are able to draw some conclusions from the sequences of behavior they see. For example, they may be asked to interpret "Why did Jack hit Jim?"

At this point, the children's answers involve no assigning of right and wrong in the situation, only *why* the action happened. Once they can describe and explain the action, they can seek ways of resolving conflicts with more desirable results.

In the final part of the unit, the children learn to draw parallels between the kinds of forces influencing the behavior witnessed in the laboratory exercises and the forces operating in their own minds. This ability helps them to evaluate their own behavior and to find ways for making it more rational and more effective.

Thus far, the children have shown a surprising ability to understand basic principles of human relations and to use intelligently the methods and techniques of the behavioral scientists. Boys and girls from the third grade up have learned to read and construct data charts. The children also read with understanding summaries of some experiments mentioned prominently in professional journals.

In the sixth grade last year, pupils developed skill with interview techniques. The subjects for their interviews were first graders; the purpose was to compile an inventory of attitudes toward older children. The thoroughness and objectivity represented in some of the final reports show a real grasp of the scientific approach.

Perhaps the greatest difficulty in the Project has been to orient classroom teachers to the subject matter and the teaching techniques involved. The Project staff discovered that some teachers had little college preparation in the behavioral sciences and thus had trouble in differentiating between a value judgment and a scientific analysis.

Some teachers were also unable to restrain themselves from exercising an undue amount of control over their classes. In order for the children to study human behavior, they needed the opportunity to engage in social interaction themselves. This could occur only when the teacher was willing to permit a good deal of pupil participation and interaction.

To remedy these difficulties, visiting teams composed of experienced classroom teachers, college educators, and behavioral scientists meet with the teachers early in the school year to explain the methods and assumptions underlying the Project. The visiting teams also conduct weekly, voluntarily attended seminars during the school year. In addition, tape recordings of classes conducted by teachers with backgrounds in the behavioral sciences are available to less experienced teachers.

A basic assumption underlying the Project is that having the children study human behavior rationally will make a significant difference in their attitudes toward their teachers and other adult authorities, in their concepts of such ideas as cooperation and competition, in their understanding of themselves, and in their appreciation of differences in others.

Since the Project began, several teachers have noted a marked decrease in traditional anti-teacher feelings, particularly among disadvantaged pupils. They have also noted positive changes in their pupils' concept of cooperation. Prior to the Project, many of the children regarded cooperation as nothing more than helping each other to cheat on tests—to "beat the system," so to speak.

The children's enthusiasm for the Project, as evidenced by the high degree of participation and skill they exhibited at all elementary school levels, has strengthened the staff's belief in its feasibility and appropriateness. Furthermore, the children are discovering that there is no subject more exciting to study than the behavior of themselves and others.

Learning Resources For Elementary School Social Studies

*T*HE INCREASED QUALITY AND QUANTITY of instructional materials coupled with modern teaching strategies are producing a shift from the traditional "audiovisual aids" approach to the more comprehensive and efficient *learning resources* concept. This broadened concept of media is predicated on the assumption that if effective learning is to be promoted, the child must have easy access to a wide range of learning resources. In applying this principle, therefore, an array of media is brought to the classroom. Naturally, use is made of the conventional materials such as books, motion pictures, filmstrips, and study prints. But beyond these, other educationally valuable media are used, including some newer and more exotic innovations such as simulation and gaming, programed instruction, multimedia kits, and computer-based instruction. Multisensory-assisted learning is especially worthwhile in social studies because of the abstract and complex learnings in this field.

As the learning resources idea flourishes in the schools, it can be expected to cause changes in the methods of housing, distributing, and utilizing educational media. It will become imperative to streamline the distribution-utilization system in order to close the gap between pupil need and availability. With this in mind a number of elementary schools across the nation have already converted libraries into learning resource centers. Collections of books and other printed materials have been augmented by the addition of other learning resources. Thus, with ready access to all needed learning materials, the pupil can be expected to shoulder greater responsibility for selecting resources than he does now. With utilization on an immediate and highly individualized basis, he will no longer need to wait for nor depend on the teacher to present a particular resource to the entire class before he can make use of it.

Learner-centered use of resources will present teachers with some new responsibilities, too. One of the most important of these is to assist in selecting good items for the school collection. Unlike a generation ago when his counterpart faced a barren desert of materials, today's elementary teacher confronts a bumper crop. Great claims are often made for the value of new instructional materials. However, solid evidence to support such claims is frequently lacking. The problem is the plethora of materials and the resultant necessity to separate wisely the wheat from the chaff. Quite obviously the classroom teacher needs to be involved in making such choices.

Materials must be selected with care so that they not only instruct but instruct appealingly. With disturbing regularity, investigators have directed attention to the indifference with which many youngsters regard elementary social studies. The source of objection is not the content *per se*, but the manner in which the content is taught. One effective approach toward vitalizing social studies instruction is through the use of carefully selected and wisely used instructional media. Media that provide information in a clinically sterile and uninteresting way cannot be expected to contribute positively to increasing the appeal of social studies.

The essays that follow provide an overview of current thinking regarding the use of learning resources in elementary social studies. The technology of education is producing new and exciting innovations in media at a rapid pace. These new resources along with improvements in the old ones should materially assist the teacher in his work and enhance the learning of the pupils who use them.

SELECTING AND USING COLLATERAL MATERIALS IN SOCIAL STUDIES *

Val E. Arnsdorf

Teachers' complaints about instructional resources for social studies have changed in substance during the past two decades. While there is a continuing concern regarding quantities and varieties of materials available, the complaints are fewer and are being overshadowed by concerns for quality. This condition is not unique to the social studies curriculum; rather, it tends to be a characteristic of most instructional areas. Most teachers will agree that during the last decade the quality of instructional resources, including textbooks, has greatly improved, but with qualitative changes and a rapidly multiplying supply of available materials, the teacher's problem of selection has grown increasingly acute.

Teachers may search for relief from this problem, but there seems to be no immediate escape. The involvement of the teacher as a decision maker determining which materials shall be used to contribute to the program under her direction should not be reduced. This is a responsibility that cannot be delegated, although the task is one that can and must be handled cooperatively, using the advice and knowledge of others.

Which materials are selected or recommended for the social studies curriculum might not be the most significant issue. A material's value is basically dependent upon its role and use in the hands of the teacher and pupil. Citing the outstanding characteristics of a paperback, pamphlet, document, map, or chart may be helpful. The clear type, direct presentation, related illustrations, controlled vocabulary, distinctive shadings, and pedigree authorships cannot be regarded as conclusive evidence of an effective contribution to the educational program. The worth of any instructional resource must be viewed in terms of several interacting variables. To praise or condemn materials produced in 1867, 1907, or 1967 from one coast to the other, here or abroad, is unproductive. To look at how collateral materials, with their limitations and strengths, could contribute to the achievement of the purposes of a program should be helpful.

Val E. Arnsdorf is Associate Professor of Education at the University of Delaware, Newark.

* Reprinted from *The Reading Teacher* 20:621–625, 1967, with permission of the International Reading Association and Val E. Arnsdorf.

Criteria for the selection and use of collateral materials in the social studies need to be developed in terms of (1) purposes of the social studies instructional program, (2) the students engaged in the program, and (3) the instructor. Each of these variables is in itself important and each becomes increasingly important as it is viewed in its relationship to the others.

Social Studies Purposes as Criteria

The purposes of the social studies curriculum include development of the student's understanding of social science concepts and his proficiency in the use of selected skills and tools. Supportive materials are available for each of the contributing social science disciplines from the primary grades through high school. Some improvements are noted in recent materials; however, old limitations persist. Recent publications give more emphasis to generalizations from the social sciences, with an associated reduction of isolated factual information. Differentiation between relevant and irrelevant data has not yet taken place in most collateral materials, resulting in some student confusion.

Three serious problems are readily noted. The tendency to overgeneralize and oversimplify cause and consequence continues. The complexities of the social sciences and the multiplicity of causes and possible consequences are widely recognized. Yet, children are still directed to read through materials in which rainfall, mineral resources, and location are given as the causes, and vegetation patterns, cities and climate, respectively, are the singular consequences. This simplification of cause-effect relationships does eliminate problems, although the ideas, if tested, would be impossible to substantiate. One-to-one causal relationships seldom exist in the social sciences except in materials prepared for the student. Granted it may be easier to suggest a singular cause for an exploration or a singular consequence for a war, but such simplification sacrifices authenticity and contributes little to the purposes of the social studies program.

The second problem, perhaps more serious than the first, is the treatment of skill development and thought processes in collateral materials in today's supermarket of educational supplies. A quick survey of the wide range of materials reveals an unfortunate striking similarity. That is, the printed page's major function seemingly is to present to the reader conclusions, generalizations, and concepts accompanied on some occasions by supportive factual information. Opportunities or situations permitting the student to engage in thought processes other than memorization are still too rare. Equally scarce are materials engaging the pupils in systematic skill development in the use of social science tools and methods of inquiry. (*The Sciences of Mankind,* by Jane Werner Watson, Golden Press, 1960, is a rare exception; it helps the pupil to understand the role and tools of the social sciences and man's problems.) The pupil becomes thoroughly and rapidly aware of what is known, but at the same time he is protectively shielded from an introduction to the processes of how we know.

The third and most vital problem is difficult to explain and understand. Central to the social studies is "man." His treatment in several sources suggests that man does exist. Little more is added. Man is identified, studied, and questioned in an impersonal manner not unlike the impersonal discussions of crop lands and climatic or mineral resources. Approximately 700,000,000 Chinese or 226,000 Alaskans are too often treated as things or fictional characters from another galaxy or planet rather than as men, women, and children who eat, work, play—persons who live in organized societies with values and value systems that may differ from our own.

Collateral materials selected for the social studies will contribute to the learner's achievement of the purposes of social studies education when the human element is given proper recognition. The proper study of mankind-is-man is long overdue in this curriculum area and its materials.

The Learner and His Characteristics as Criteria

Criteria relative to the inherent and acquired characteristics of the learner could be developed into an extended listing. Generally they are, or should be, readily recognized and applied by the teacher. A magazine, chart, brochure, trade book, or document will be suitable for only selected pupils, depending upon the purpose that item is to serve within the parameters of the program. There are no magical aids available today that serve all purposes and all pupils, regardless of what claims are made by the author or publisher. Expecting each pupil to arrive at the same interpretation from a passage, page, chapter, chart, or map is a failure to recognize the varied levels of skill development, interest, motivation, background, and intelligence of individual learners in even the most homogenous classroom.

Pupils' understanding and acceptance of the purposes served by the collateral materials are fundamental. An eighteenth-century newspaper's account of early Philadelphia may provide one learner with descriptive data about industrial developments of the era; for another the account may be a basis for the study of cultural change; for a third learner it may provide interest for a study of persistent issues that confront man. Each learner requires specific skills appropriate for the task involved. Time and study habits will vary with interpretations, differing from pupil to pupil although a single source is employed.

Even though knowledge of children's reading abilities is extensive, numerous questions remain unanswered. Inquiries must be conducted and decisions made by the teacher with inadequate evidence in attempts to determine how the nature, difficulty, and frequency of social science concepts presented in the materials influence the pupil's comprehension. Among other factors in need of consideration are the pupil's flexibilities in vocabulary recognition techniques and other related reading skills involved in social science concept development.

The Teacher Factor in the Criteria

Whether the teacher is the most important component of the three factors involved—purposes, pupil, teacher—is an issue that can lead to an endless discussion. The teacher's role is a dominant one, demanding in its responsibilities, with each teacher engaged in the making of critical decisions to select, use, and appraise the effectiveness of instructional resources included in the school curriculum. Criteria used in the selection of collateral instructional resources in social studies must therefore focus on the teacher.

Horn's statement that there is "no other single aspect of instruction that makes a greater contribution to the improvement of reading than does a well planned assignment" is as significant today as it was three decades ago * in bringing the curriculum, pupil, and teacher together. And it goes unheeded too frequently in today's classroom. The teacher's knowledge of the instructional resources and the learner is implied in the statement. Ideally the teacher should be able to guide the learner to appropriate sources for data pertinent to the issue 'in question. Sources recommended by the teacher should reflect her knowledge of the pupil's characteristics—his interests, study habits, reading abilities, and goals. Her knowledge of the materials should include: an understanding of the era, region, and social sciences involved; the nature and

---

* Ernest Horn, *Methods of Instruction in the Social Studies*. New York: Scribner's, 1937, pp. 202–203.

number of concepts presented; manner of presentation; skills and abilities required to comprehend the concepts; and the potential contribution of the materials to the learner's development.

These are monumental charges for any teacher. Nevertheless, the success of the social studies program is dependent upon the degree to which these responsibilities are accepted and met.

In a recent widely distributed weekly newspaper for elementary school children, a comprehensive analysis of two states was presented. Facts given to the students included area in square miles and population. How meaningful to a nine- or ten-year-old are selected informational items such as: 586,400 square miles, 483 times larger, population 859,488 (1960 census)? A teacher using the instructor's edition, assigning the exercises and maps for directed study, would conduct a lesson with little impact and considerable frustration potential. The fact that "man" in comparing the states was reduced to numbers is one consideration. The magnitude of the numbers, the computations, mathematical comparisons, vocabulary, and map skills involved in the two-page exercise demand an array of competencies. A pupil unable to use a scale of miles, visualize a square mile, interpret abstract symbols, or one otherwise limited in his geopolitical knowledge of the fifty states, would find most of the questions out of range, and those within range could be answered from simple recall projections questionably selected for study. An effective teacher could depart from the guide, restructure the exercise, and prepare new materials if time would permit.

How the teacher would see this and other news items from the pupil's weekly paper as part of the total social studies program is critical. She needs to use the purposes of her program as a basis to determine whether an instructional resource will be included. Neither money nor time will be wasted if an entire issue is not read by all pupils.

Decisions concerning which materials to use and how to use them must be carefully made by the teachers and pupils. Shortcomings noted in resources may be used to advantage in sound instructional practices to develop the learner's ability to read analytically, generating his own thoughts and conclusions based upon evidence found in available materials. Instructional resources, increasingly abundant in number and kind, have value basically in terms of how they are used by the teacher and pupil to achieve the purposes of social studies education.

Reading a descriptive account of the Tuareg might be directed toward several goals. For some, attention might be directed at the impact of technological changes on a society; another might read to better understand man-land relationships; another's goal might be to investigate the ways man meets his basic needs for food and water; another could direct his attention toward a comparative study of family organization; while still another could consider the roles of children in different cultures. There would thus be a commonality in the purposes for the total group and, at the same time, a differentiation accorded to the more specifically identified needs, abilities, and interests of the individual student. Skills required by the learners would vary, along with the expected level of understanding to be attained from the study. The use of multiple approaches to the study of a selected resource or of a single approach to the study of multiple resources should help the learner and teacher develop a better understanding of the complexities of man's behavior. Simplified answers explaining cause and consequences rarely exist. Materials supportive of that position contribute little to the student's development, and more often serve as deterrents through the development of erroneous concepts and stumbling blocks that need to be corrected later. Materials need to provide opportunities and challenges for alternate positions and tentative conclusions for the consideration of teachers and pupils.

One relatively simple question demands an answer from the teacher. With a satisfactory response she should be able to proceed with her instructional program. The question is, "What difference will this material make in the student's development in the social studies program?"

LEARNING RESOURCES FOR INDIVIDUALIZING INSTRUCTION *

Huber M. Walsh

There are several reasons why teachers equipped with proper learning resources can meet individual learning needs in a superior manner. First, instructional materials make it possible for the classroom teacher to "stretch" his time. When resources such as auto-instruction media are utilized to perform certain routine in-

Huber M. Walsh is Professor of Education at the University of Missouri, St. Louis.

* Reprinted from *Social Education* 31:413–415 ff., 1967, with permission of the National Council for the Social Studies and Huber M. Walsh.

structional tasks like drill, the teacher is freed for other tasks demanding more creative, human teaching. Second, children *do* have different learning patterns and these necessitate the use of various instructional vehicles to "reach" them successfully. Books and other printed materials are the most effective keys to understanding for some pupils, but individual learning patterns may make viewing a motion picture, hearing a tape recording, or working with self-directed programed materials more profitable for others. Most pupils will require all of these and perhaps others in combination. The point is, we have yet to discover a universal skeleton key in teaching children. No single best way to reach all pupils exists; hence, the need is created to find and to use the right material(s) tailored to the particular needs of particular individuals. Third, good instructional materials seem to have built-in child appeal—a kind of intrinsic glamour and fascination that tends to intrigue youngsters. At least in the beginning, they find most new media attractive and, consequently, are motivated to use them. This phenomenon tends to vitalize social studies instruction and make it more enjoyable. Fourth, certain of the learning resources now available are well suited to individualizing instruction in the fullest sense of the term. That is, these devices can provide instruction on a fully self-directed basis allowing the child to investigate and discover on his own when there is no teacher present to assist him. Innovations in technology have simplified equipment operation to such an extent that pupils can use machines easily. Such refinements have made it possible for children to use motion pictures and filmstrips at home evenings and week-ends as their own private tutors.

Reviewed below are several new resources that hold the promise of being quite useful in "reaching" children of varying abilities in social studies—the slow learner, the culturally-disadvantaged child, the non-verbal youngster, the retarded reader, the gifted learner, and others. An attempt has been made to focus on salient new developments that provide refreshing, innovative approaches to individualized instruction. Most of these are already available to the classroom teacher; others, however, are in the developmental stage and will become available later on.

8mm Cartridge Projector. Because of its compactness, lightness, and simplicity of operation, the 8mm cartridge projector is particularly valuable as a tool for individualizing instruction. It can be used easily by youngsters in the classroom or at home for independent study because the problem of threading film is eliminated. Film is housed entirely within a plastic case and formed into a continuous loop making rewinding unnecessary. Using the projector is as simple as inserting the cartridge, turning a switch, and making minor focus adjustments.

A variety of film loops germane to elementary social studies is available, with most designed to teach a single concept. The ordinary film runs for about four minutes, then repeats itself as many times as desired. This continuous presentation feature makes this a particularly valuable resource in meeting the needs of individuals requiring more than the usual amount of repetition for concept mastery. Such children, on their own, can view and review the film as many times as is necessary to fully grasp the idea. Inasmuch as present-day film loops are without sound tracks, the ideational presentation is exclusively visual, with very slight use being made of printed captions. Thus these films are advantageous for slow readers and pupils with restricted language backgrounds such as those coming from culturally-disadvantaged environments.[1]

The Multi-Media Kit. Multi-media kits are rather complete learning-resource packages containing a wide variety of audio and visual media, printed materials, artifacts, and other learning tools related to various social studies units. They will be particularly welcome in those classrooms where a wide diversity of individual learning needs exist. Each kit contains something beneficial to and usable by almost every child, whether he learns best visually, aurally, or tactually.

The use of kits simplifies the often vexing problem of instructional materials procurement, for it is far simpler for the teacher to procure one package containing an array of media than to have to order each item separately. Its most important contribution, however, is that it provides excellent resources for the individualization of instruction. In a multi-media kit on Mexico, for instance, one would have at hand the following resources: (a) information brochures on Mexico City (these appropriate for use by gifted children) ; (b) filmstrips with accompanying records (these could be used for research by average children) ; (c) photographs (slow readers could use these to advantage) ; (d) a collection of Mexican toys and other artifacts of the culture (non-readers and non-verbal children could make discoveries from studying these articles).

Multi-media kits to be used in cross-cultural studies are commercially available,[2] and, in addition, some school districts have

---

[1] For additional information, contact The Technicolor Corporation, 1985 Placentia Avenue, Costa Mesa, California 92627.

[2] For further information, contact International Communications Foundation, 870 Monterey Pass Road, Monterey Park, California.

begun to develop their own multi-media kits for social studies teachers.

Programed Materials. The ever-expanding array of programed materials for social studies instruction is an additional resource useful in meeting individual learning needs. Though many of these are intended for total-group use, perhaps their most significant contribution to learning is made when they are used to individualize instruction on a single-pupil basis. Programed materials become particularly valuable for reviewing, reteaching, and re-inforcing knowledge already presented by the classroom teacher. Used in this way programed materials do not supplant human teaching, but instead provide a way to meet special needs of a given learner without necessitating the expenditure of a disproportionate amount of the teacher's time.

One new set of programed materials provides instruction in map and globe skills. This kit, like the two described immediately below, uses very much the same color-coded, sequential approach as is used in the SRA Reading Laboratory Materials. The map program consists of materials to teach basic concepts, study-exercise materials, and self-checking devices.

A recently introduced organizing and reporting skills kit is a program designed to provide instruction in reporting, note-taking, and outlining. Its companion set of materials is a graph and picture skills program intended for the upper-elementary grades. Skills in interpretation and application of graphic materials such as photographs, editorial cartoons, diagrams, charts, and the like are included.[3]

A study skills library will answer the need of many pupils for individualized instruction in social studies reading skills—especially those needing remedial instruction. Comprised of seven different sets of materials, the library encompasses reading levels III through IX. Within each is a series of sequential lessons predicated on a self-directed reading exercise followed by a self-checking activity. Individual lessons are designed to teach such specific skills as interpretation, judging relevancy and significance, verifying accuracy, and finding and organizing ideas.[4]

Automatic Projection Center. A fascinating new idea that is destined to capture the imaginations of creative social studies teachers is the Automatic Projection Center. Capable of a myriad variety of multi-media presentations, the device consists of two

---

[3] For additional information on these three programs, contact Science Research Associates, 259 East Erie Street, Chicago, Illinois 60611.

[4] For additional information, contact Educational Development Laboratories, Huntington, New York.

sound motion picture projectors (16mm and 8mm); three slide projectors, and a stereophonic tape recorder.

The heart of the center is a punched paper tape that programs the presentations. Equipment is started, paused, stopped, and reversed on command of the tape. Slide projectors may be programed to operate individually, to project in 1-2-3 order across the screen to illustrate a step-by-step process; or all three may be used in concert to produce a cinemascope-like, wide-screen panoramic view. Inclusion of the 8mm projector makes it possible for teachers to augment commercial film presentations with their own inexpensively-made films. The flexibility of tape programing produces almost unlimited possibilities for individualizing instruction. Using the same projection materials, for example, one program can be prepared appropriate to the learning requirements of the gifted learner; another can be made for slow learners; and yet another can be developed for use by average pupils. Though the same instructional media are used in each case, such factors as order of presentation, and provisions for repetition and review are varied according to need differential. Although the APC is not yet commercially marketed, its components and plans for its construction are available.[5]

World Affairs Reports. Teachers searching for resources in current affairs for use with above-average pupils may find what they are looking for in a new series of materials entitled *World Affairs Reports.* Though created for use in secondary classrooms, these materials appear equally well suited to limited, specialized use in the elementary school. A typical set of materials consists of a 25–30 minute sound tape presentation containing on-the-spot recordings of news events as they happened (these made in cooperation with United Press-International); multiple copies of a programed textbook to complement the tape and teach additional information; and a guidebook for the teacher. Kits are to be issued on a monthly basis, and future topics will focus on "The Negro Crisis," "Russia vs. China," and "The Poor." These materials seem particularly well suited for individual use by elementary children as self-tutoring devices. In some cases, however, there may be advantage in using them with small groups of advanced pupils.[6]

Project Discovery. A new departure from customary materials utilization and a noteworthy venture in individualizing instruction is underway at Mercer School in Shaker Heights, Ohio. There pupils

---

[5] For additional information, contact Eastman Kodak Company, Rochester, New York 14650.

[6] For further information, contact Behavioral Research Laboratories, Ladera Professional Center, Box 577, Palo Alto, California 94302.

take home projectors and films for independent study with much the same ease and regularity that their elementary-school counterparts elsewhere take home their books. This began over three years ago when the school was designated as the pilot unit for Project Discovery—a cooperative effort by manufacturers, school districts, distributors, and universities to investigate the effects of saturating an individual school with audiovisual materials and equipment. An important aspect of the total concept is to facilitate pupil investigation and discovery by expanding the scope of research tools available to the child for independent use.

Each classroom is equipped with both an automatic motion picture projector and an automatic filmstrip projector. Pupils begin to learn to operate these in the second grade and by grade three all but a few can operate them with facility. Adjacent to the school's 12,000 volume library is the film center in which are housed over 1,000 filmstrips and upwards of 600 motion picture films. All materials are clearly labeled and easily accessible to the child user. The center is outfitted with several projectors and headsets making it possible for several pupils or small groups to study motion pictures simultaneously without disturbing one another. The center is available to children before, during, and after school.

An individual with a topic he wishes to investigate may consult a special card catalog to identify the projection materials germane to his research area. Once materials are located, the pupil may view them either in the film center or in his classroom. He may elect to check out the films and necessary projection equipment (with the assistance of parents) for overnight or over the week-end study at home.

Teachers and pupils are enthusiastic about this effort to reduce the usability gap by facilitating self-directed pupil utilization of audiovisuals. Moreover, teachers appreciate having at hand a basic collection of materials ready for immediate use rather than having to guess at future needs and having to order items months in advance of their use.

In addition to Shaker Heights, the project is currently in operation in other cities across the nation in a variety of socio-economic settings. Quite possibly this effort may herald the coming of learning resource centers to the elementary school. Such centers would represent an expansion of the conventional school library into a full-fledged instructional materials center providing a total spectrum of printed and non-printed resources immediately available to both pupils and teachers.[7]

---

[7] For further information, contact Encyclopaedia Britannica Films, Inc., 1150 Wilmette Avenue, Wilmette, Illinois 60091.

Computerized Programing for Individualization. A future possibility more than a present-day actuality is the prospect of using automated data processing to aid teachers in individualizing social studies instruction. For example, given data on what a pupil learned yesterday, on his learning needs for tomorrow, and on his optimum learning pattern, data analysis could be used to identify the most promising learning activities and resources to be used with that particular child. For one, this might indicate an individualized session with some kind of electronic teaching device; for another it might mean a small-group work session with the classroom teacher, or perhaps the beginning of some kind of construction project. For others additional work in textbooks might be prescribed. One type of learning resource would be suggested for the gifted, another for the average, and a different one for the slow reader, and so on, accommodating each according to his special needs.

Study-Print Packages. A review of new learning resources for individualizing instruction would be incomplete without at least brief mention of the new packets of study prints becoming available. The typical set contains a coordinated collection of large, full-color photographs centered about a topic or theme such as "Life in the Heart of the City." Although they are good media to use with all pupils, they are especially appropriate to the needs of the slow learner, the retarded reader, and the non-verbal child. Slow learners, for instance, can use them for independent research, recording on tape the information discovered from carefully studying the content of the pictures.[8]

The innovations described are illustrative of new resources becoming available to individualize instruction in social studies. In the final analysis, however, it is not the addition of more hardware to the classroom that will, in and of itself, effect greater individualization of instruction any more than the addition of more hardware to the kitchen produces gourmet meals. Indeed, the critical factor is not a mechanical but a human one. The key point is *how* these media are put to work in individualizing instruction by the classroom teacher. And so, in a very real sense, the most important single resource in individualizing instruction still is the creative teacher.

---

[8] Further information on Study-Print Sets can be obtained from producers such as Silver Burdett Company, Park Ridge, Illinois; and Society for Visual Education, Inc., 1345 Diversey Parkway, Chicago, Illinois 60614.

INNOVATION IN THE SOCIAL STUDIES:
THE 8mm SINGLE CONCEPT FILM *

Leonard W. Ingraham

One problem has long plagued the social studies teacher who uses motion pictures or filmstrips in the classroom. How do I cope with the usual 18- to 50-minute film or 40- to 60-frame filmstrip in the 40-minute classroom period . . . if a lesson is to be taught? At what specific point in the film is the concept reached toward which the lesson is aimed? When do I stop to establish this concept? Do I continue showing the rest of the film? Do I create a "cinematic point of no return"? Can I fulfill the objectives of this lesson by so staccato a technique? Is this showing to be purely amusement or is it a teaching device? Why not an audio-visual tool which alleviates this problem? Why not a motion picture which *does* present a "single concept"?

The answer is here and now. There is just such a tool. This exciting new goal has been reached in the area of instructional materials for teachers of the social studies—*the single concept 8mm silent film.* The answer has come for those communications specialists who have urged the utilization of only those portions of projected materials which serve a specific instructional purpose. The means is now provided for the implementation of the conceptual approach to teaching and learning as conceived by the researchers in social studies curriculum.

The single concept 8mm film concentrates upon and presents, in a two- to four-minute period, a single idea, or concept, specifically film-oriented. This single idea is planned to be integral to a lesson. It is presented on black-and-white or color loop film, with no audio portions, and may or may not be captioned.

This motion picture also fulfills the requirement of a means to achieve the "planned experience" so vital to a social studies lesson if specific concepts are to be achieved—if "teachable moments" are to be reached—if concepts are to be implanted.

Today's explosion of knowledge has made it almost impossible to cope with the ever-expanding plethora of factual data in history and the social sciences. All of the curriculum revision projects in

Leonard W. Ingraham is Acting Director of the Bureau of History and Social Sciences, New York City Board of Education, New York.

* Reprinted from *Social Education* 30:91–92, 1966, with permission of the National Council for the Social Studies and Leonard W. Ingraham.

the social studies have recognized this problem and have proposed the selection of basic concepts, understandings, generalizations, or large central motifs around which learning can be organized.

Our young students must be helped—not spoon-fed—to derive meanings from the facts with which they are presented. The concepts will *not* be taught as facts merely to be committed to memory. They must emerge from their studies as illuminating ideas or analytic findings. Although facts will still be learned, they will be used to build understanding of major concepts, in the context of a systematic conceptual approach. The methodology to be employed may be inductive, as the student learns how to find out things for himself through *inquiry and discovery.*

For the social studies the 8mm single concept film, when properly structured, can provide understanding of concepts and generalizations, as facts and ideas are visualized and illuminated. We see all of the directional signs in social studies pointing toward this single concept film as the proper avenue of approach toward rounding out the "packet of instructional materials."

The focus of these single concept films will be upon the ability of the student to extract the presented facts, and to develop both insight and critical judgment. They will attempt to achieve sequential cumulative stores of information for the student in this conceptual approach, to develop skills, to encourage him to think as he views, to ask a question as it arises and to have it answered on the spot.

Geared, as it is, toward a broad grade level—from kindergarten through grade 12—the single concept film will offer concepts which are not restricted, but will readily fit into the established curriculum, however sophisticated the viewers may be. Its unique contribution to teaching lies in its inherent qualities: It provides the motion which the filmstrip lacks; the motion may be stopped by "stop-frame" clutches for safe still-picture projecting; it does not depend upon sound; it permits commentary and questions by both the student and the teacher during the viewing. The film can show relationships, cause and effect, permit further inquiry and discovery. It will undoubtedly provide deeper understandings, for it allows for the "open-ended" discussion—the "to-be-continued-in-our-next-lesson" technique. All of this can be carefully planned and structured by the producers working in conjunction with the educational specialists.

What additional assistance does the eight millimeter film offer to the teacher? It may be viewed by the class more than once, even during the regular class period. It may be used for individual or small group self-study. A specific skill can be taught or it can become the material for a specific instructional purpose, as it fits into the multi-faceted methodology, including team-teaching.

Perhaps the most outstanding feature of this new instructional tool is its new design and size. The 8mm film is packaged in a cartridge which fits a simplified projector requiring no threading whatsoever and no rewinding. One such is the Technicolor Magi-Cartridge. A five-year-old can be taught to operate and show the film within a few minutes. The picture quality is good and the cost is low for both film and projector. (Projector, less than $50; film in cartridge, from $7 to $15). These projectors and films, easy to show, low in cost, accessible to both teachers and students, will come to be known as the "paperbacks of the film world"! Now the films will come out of their central film libraries and into the classroom to be used as needed, even on the spur of the moment, at the will of the class or teacher.

Single concept projectors and films have already been purchased by many schools for classroom use in physics, biology, physical education and industrial arts. Professor Louis Forsdale, Director of Project in Educational Communications of Horace Mann-Lincoln Institute at Teachers College, Columbia University (and a pioneer in the 8mm field) has indicated that there are now 1600 silent 8mm single concept films commercially available in the aforementioned areas. However, relatively few have been produced for the social studies. Many will be forthcoming in the near future. Dr. Forsdale, in a recent address on "The Promise of the 8mm Film," predicted that ten to twenty thousand silent loop films will be made available within the next decade.

As with the early materials available in programed instruction for the social studies, some of the 8mm single concept films are good and many are very bad indeed from the technical and content point of view.

At Michigan State University, a Single Concept Film Clip Project has been established which may be compared to the National Council for the Social Studies' Teaching Films Custodian Committee. However, at the Michigan State Project audio-visual specialists are screening educational and instructional films, already produced, to search out a basic library of single concept films. The NCSS group has done this for only 35mm commercial films and some television programs. Two commercial producers—Modern Learning Aids, Inc. and International Communications Foundation —have 8mm single concept films in the social studies now available on the market. (See Appendix for sources.) Schools, teachers, and students have produced their own 8mm single concept films to meet the current demands, which will grow increasingly greater in the immediate future.

Innovation and the use of multi-media approaches are the keynotes of the new social studies curriculum. But it is not necessary to wait for the ultimate refinement of equipment and procedures. Imaginative supervisors should place 8mm single concept films and means for using them in the hands of inventive teachers and say, "Go—gain experience, explore, fire the imaginations of your students, try out the new approaches to inquiry and discovery in the social studies."

C. P. Snow, writing about 8mm films stated: "I believe we are about to see an application of narrow-gauge films to education and industry which will be as revolutionary as the paperback has become in publication and which will come more speedily.[1]

"What is the great contribution to be made by the 8mm single concept film?" may very well be the critical question posed by the social scientists. The answer must necessarily focus upon its unique ability to transform the motion picture from the most difficult to the simplest-to-use of all pictorial media. *Newsletter of 8mm Film in Education* reports that the 8mm film is the only presently available vehicle, cheap enough, good enough, and simple enough to make the motion picture accessible to the average teacher in the average school. It concludes by stating, "And it [the 8mm single concept film] can do it . . . has already begun to do it . . . now."

The social studies teacher, too, must begin to use the 8mm single concept film *now*. The "explosion of knowledge" must *not* be allowed to become an atomic bomb of destructive confusion, but rather a meteoric shower of increased educational riches.

Appendix

Sources of Information

Newsletter of 8mm Film in Education. Project in Educational Communication of Horace Mann-Lincoln Institute of School Experimentation. Teachers College, Columbia University, New York 10027. Published periodically. Issues: No. 1, March 1965; No. 2, June 1965; No. 3, Fall 1965.

Louis Forsdale, ed., *8mm Sound Film and Education.* New York Bureau of Publications, Teachers College, Columbia University, 1962.

---

[1] Mathew B. Miles, ed., *Innovation in Education.* New York: Bureau of Publications, Teachers College, Columbia University, 1964, p. 21.

James L. Page and Elwood Miller, "A Major Breakthrough in Film Use?" *Audio-Visual Instruction* 10:318–319, 1965.

Source Directory, Educational Single Concept Films. Technicolor Corporation, 1985 Placentia Ave., Contra Mesa, California 92627.

Gateway Film Productions Ltd. 470 Green Lanes, Palm Green, London, N 13, England.

International Communications Foundation, 870 Monterey Pass Rd., Monterey Park, California.

Modern Learning Aids, Inc. 1212 Avenue of the Americas, New York, New York 10036.

IDEAS AND OBJECTS: THE ARTIFACT KIT *

David G. Menser

Teachers and students alike know that history teachers are very wordy. Dealing so much in words, both written and spoken, we are like the man who painted himself into the single remaining corner in the room. Our paint is the sticky goo of too many words. Like the man in the corner, our dilemma is painful. We have tried desperately to contrive props and walkways to escape.

The whole range of audio-visual materials available today is an attempt to find a way out of the word prison. In the hands of a skillful teacher a filmstrip can hold attention much better than words alone, bringing details of technology, costume, and architecture to the class. Through films a class can visit Williamsburg, Monticello with its many wonders, or stand by Concord Bridge. A record can capture some of the flavor of putting to sea. Surely "The World Turned Upside Down" speaks the feelings of the British at Yorktown. Yet all of these are flat. They have no dimension. They cannot be touched or held.

More serious than the lack of size and shape, films and records lack a time dimension. They are not old. The things that they show are not the same as they were. The colors are too bright. The grass is too well trimmed. The new techniques help in many ways, but they, like words, have no dimension.

David G. Menser is a history and government teacher at the Mount Pleasant Junior High School, Wilmington, Delaware.

* Reprinted from *Social Education* 30:343–345, 1966, with permission of the National Council for the Social Studies and David G. Menser.

Many museums have attacked the bars of the word prison. Most have education departments. They are eager to cooperate with the schools and to share their collections. For example, the Marine Historical Association of Mystic, Connecticut, sends out wooden chests containing many artifacts of nineteenth-century whaling. Colonial Williamsburg plays host to thousands of children each year in a well organized and enjoyable educational experience. But, of necessity, the museums have had to rely on people coming to visit them. This leaves the majority of teachers where we found them— in the corner. The teacher who could not go to the museum now or ever is left with the current audio-visual aids and words.

Last winter the American Studies Research Project, a part of the Wemyss Foundation, decided to design and build teaching kits:

> We are anxious to develop teaching kits which would bring a third dimension reality to the history class. They would include artifacts (especially those used in America between 1800 and 1830) telling how men lived and worked in the young Republic.
>
> . . . hand tools and nails from which America was built; pieces of textile and homespun by which men were clothed; samples of the food on which they were nourished.

Starting with this general idea, a kit research team composed of a director, an anthropologist, and three high school history teachers was established. Working under the supervision of Marshall Fishwick, the team assembled five kits: a peddler's kit, a Civil War soldier's kit, a covered wagon kit, a technology kit, and a seaman's kit. Each has its own container so that it is easily portable. Each can be reproduced in limited quantity.

Before the work could begin, several questions had to be answered. The answers were worked out by the team. Four tests were established. The answer in each case had to be "yes" before an object could be included in a kit. Is the artifact authentic? Would a sailor have had one of these? Nothing was to be included that could not be documented.

Does the object illustrate a teaching point? Here the difference in the museum and kit approach begins to show. In the kits the point to be illustrated was decided and then the object tracked down. We had no collection to draw on.

Is the artifact unique? A student's attention is most easily attracted by things that are different. Some early sailor's tools are unique enough that many students have never seen them. A palm and a fid (a tool used in splicing rope) drew nothing but blanks from a ninth-grade class. Yet both tools were bought in a well known marine store in their own city. These objects made in 1965 are the same as the fid and palm made in 1765. Not only are the tools unique, the teaching point is there. Today these are the tools of the yachtsman. Today's leisure was yesterday's toil.

Is the object available? It defeats the whole purpose of the kit if the objects in it are so rare that teachers and students are constantly worried about breaking them. No amount of talk will convince a boy that the Civil War musket he is holding is for real if he is constantly being admonished to treat it as though it were an egg from a whooping crane's nest. He must feel its weight, shoulder it, sight down its barrel, and aim over its sights at someone. It helps if it goes bang. Only then can the student really identify what he has in his hands with the musket of the lad of Gettysburg or Fredericksburg.

Touchability is the heart of the matter. Where it was possible, the teams used objects that could be used and handled the way they were intended to be used. In two kits there is a piece of hardtack. Our students can touch and taste it. An old fashioned ax, were it included, should have a log for chopping.

Touchability presented a problem that had to be answered before assembling the kits could begin in earnest. Does the kit include antiques, facsimiles, reproductions, or all three? In the end, the teams decided to use only antiques and facsimiles. To bring in reproductions would have let in an *ersatz* quality that nobody wanted.

It was not difficult to define antique—something made during the period. The kits needed some antiques or they would not have the time dimension that was part of the original plan. It was equally obvious they could not be made completely of antiques. Availability, ease of replacement, and cost were all factors to be considered.

Facsimiles eased the problem. A facsimile is an artifact made in the same way as it would have been made in the past. The seaman's kit includes a set of checkers cut from the top of a discarded leather boot. They were made this summer using the same materials that a sailor used to make a set of checkers now in the Smithsonian Institution.

There are two advantages to be gained from the use of facsimiles. They help to keep down cost and they can be easily replaced if they are accidentally broken. A clay pipe bought for fifty cents and then covered in a sailor's stitch, says just as much about a sailor's humanity and ingenuity as an antique pipe. If broken, it can be replaced. Students can make facsimiles themselves. In this way, they can participate in history. Facsimiles lack only the patina of age. Too many facsimiles can make a kit as phony as the too bright colors of the well trimmed grass at the Bridge.

My project was the sea chest. It is a composite; no single sailor would have had all the things in it. I had hoped to be able to assemble the things that a boy would have had when going to sea for the first time. I gave this up, for in limiting the kit, many useful and interesting artifacts would be left out. The kit illustrates traits that were found in many of our early seamen.

I wanted to emphasize that these seamen were human beings. They were alive; they chewed tobacco, played an occasional game, and had aches and pains. They had certain skills and used particular tools that were peculiar to their work. I wanted to show how the American was different from his European counterpart with his class mobility. I felt it was important to capture some of the discomfort that one feels in the fo'c's'les of ships like the *Constitution*.

The task of finding what belonged in a sea chest took me to many museums. Everywhere I found people eager to help. Mystic furnished details on chests and clothing. New Bedford's library has an excellent collection of old ships' account books. There are many curiosities of the whaling trade on Nantucket. The Peabody Museum at Salem provided valuable advice and several antiques. The libraries in Washington as well as the Smithsonian, cooperated in opening non-public rooms and collections.

Once the research was done, I began collecting artifacts for the kit. I had never really gone antiquing. The kit was not to be a treasure chest. The criteria for inclusion at the beginning of the summer remained. Did the artifact say something? Was it accurate? Was it available? Since cost was a fact of life, some interesting and illustrative objects could not be included. There is no clothing in the chest. A sailor's clothes belong in the chest, but to have had accurate reproductions would have cost as much as all the other items in the chest together. Clothing just does not say that much. On the other hand, an antique quadrant accounted for almost half of the cost of all the artifacts. For what it says of hopes and dreams, it was worth the cost.

The last task was to prepare a teacher's manual to go with the kits. In the manual is a description of the objects in the box. No teacher could be expected to know why some things were included and others were not. Each manual contains background information for the teacher who uses the artifact kit. At the end of each manual is a bibliography including fiction and non-fiction, records, films, and filmstrips. There is also a list of suggested student projects.

What happens now is anybody's guess. It was somewhat humbling for me to be told after presenting my kit to a group of local teachers that "this is nothing new. I've been doing this with my classes for 18 years." We don't claim that the artifact kits will make anyone an inspired teacher. They are not an aluminum cat-walk to climb out of our corner over the wordy paint on the floor. They are more like an open window letting in a breath of fresh air to clear out some of the fumes.

THE ROLE OF READING
IN THE SOCIAL STUDIES *

Paul A. Witty

During the past decade, there has been widespread criticism of reading methods and materials of instruction used in our schools. It has been shown that some of the criticisms are unjust. Children are, on the whole, reading better and more widely than ever before. However, some of the criticisms are valid and merit the serious consideration of teachers and administrators. It has been clearly shown, for example, that permanent interests in reading are *infrequently* developed in children and youth. Far too many people who *can* read do not choose to read books. They have failed to develop a strong interest in reading.

Not long ago, The American Institute of Public Opinion reported a poll in which six out of ten adults questioned stated that the last time they had read a book other than the Bible was a year or more ago. Moreover, one out of four college graduates had not read a book during the last twelve months.[1]

Lack of interest in reading has been demonstrated again and again in studies of children, young people and adults. And numerous speculations concerning the causes have been advanced.

It has been indicated, too, that there are unjustifiably large numbers of poor readers in our schools. Some studies do show large amounts of reading retardation. For example, in the South Side High School, Newark, New Jersey, of the 247 entering freshmen who were tested in September, 1952, more than 50 per cent tested

Paul A. Witty is Professor of Education at Northwestern University, Evanston, Illinois.

* Reprinted from *Elementary English* 39:562–569, 1962, with permission of the National Council of Teachers of English and Paul A. Witty.

[1] *Reader's Digest*, March, 1956, p. 23.

at or below the sixth grade level.[2] This study reveals a higher frequency of poor reading than is generally reported in such investigations. Yet, other studies show that 15 to 20 per cent of entering high school pupils in some schools read less well, according to test results, than the typical seventh grade pupil. It has been found that most of these pupils can be helped to read more effectively.

However, it should be noted that in most studies of entering high school pupils, *many* superior readers are reported. Such data should make us aware that in our zeal for helping students with reading problems we should not overlook the special needs of superior and gifted students. These pupils are frequently neglected or inadequately challenged. Such pupils are often potential leaders, much needed in the area of human relations. As Harry Passow states: "The daily press and professional journals alike are clamoring about shortages of scientists and engineers. . . . Perhaps our most frightening shortages are not in the general supply of scientists but in those rare persons with imagination, creativity, motivation, competence, and education who can contribute something fresh and basic to our understanding of man's relation with man." [3] To the development of such understanding, the role of reading in the social sciences is essential and unmistakably evident.

Dull Material Discourages Child

Some critics are convinced that certain teaching materials, especially primers and first grade readers, are unnatural and repetitious, and contribute vitally to the inefficient instruction, and lack of interest in reading.

Writers assert, too, that a concern for the interest factor should be shown not only in the primary grades but also at every level of instruction.[4] The desirability of this approach is emphasized by George Norvell who, after analyzing the selections taught in New York high schools, concluded that "To increase reading skill, promote the reading habit, and produce a generation of book lovers, there is no other factor so powerful as interest." [5]

---

[2] Vivian Zinkin, "A Staggering Reading Problem." *The Clearing House, 28,* November, 1953.

[3] Harry Passow, quoted in *Education Digest,* March, 1957.

[4] Paul Witty, "The Role of Interest," Chapter 8 in *Development In and Through Reading,* Nelson B. Henry, ed. 60th Yearbook of the National Society for the Study of Education, Part I. Chicago: University of Chicago Press, 1961.

[5] George W. Norvell, "Some Results of a Twelve-Year Study of Children's Reading Interests." *English Journal 35*:531, 1946. See also George W. Norvell, *What Boys and Girls Like to Read.* Chicago: Silver Burdett, 1959.

The primary objective of a developmental reading program should be recognized clearly at all times: we should seek to help children to become skillful, self-reliant, and independent in using the library and other resources for satisfying interests and needs. This objective will be achieved only if students are enabled to enjoy the act of reading and the results.[6] The first part of this aim will be achieved through an efficient, systematic program of reading instruction. The second part will be realized by the association of reading with interests and needs. Accordingly, children and youth will become skillful readers and will probably continue to enrich their understandings and satisfactions all their lives.

Formal Instruction Necessary

Many school administrators and teachers will doubtless agree that a developmental reading program should be initiated throughout our schools. Instruction in reading today should not cease at the sixth grade level. Help and guidance should be given to all students in studying and reading efficiently the materials of each subject field.[7] Remedial instruction should be offered as a temporary expedient only.

There is a great need to extend opportunities in reading so that children's interests will be satisfied and their needs met judiciously through reading. Accordingly, a balanced reading program includes not only a variety of textbooks and practice books, but also an assortment of narratives, biographies, magazine articles, and factual presentations on many topics.[8] Such needs as the ability to understand oneself and to appreciate one's social environment can be met to varying degrees through the use of printed materials. This approach recognizes the significance of using interesting, varied and individually suitable materials of instruction at every level. And it recognizes too the need for a definite program of instruction designed to apply and extend reading skills in the content fields.

To offer the most helpful guidance and instruction, the teacher requires considerably more information about each pupil's reading than that obtained from tests. For example, the teacher of

---

[6] See Paul Witty, "Reading Instruction—A Forward Look." *Elementary English*, March, 1961.

[7] Elizabeth Simpson, *Helping High School Students Read Better*. Chicago: Science Research Associates, 1954.

[8] Paul Witty, Chapter 2 in *Reading in the High School and College*, W. S. Gray, chrmn. 47th Yearbook of the National Society for the Study of Education. Chicago: University of Chicago Press, 1948. See also the discussions in Henry P. Smith and E. V. Dechant, *Psychology in Teaching Reading*. Englewood Cliffs, N. J.: Prentice-Hall, 1961.

social studies needs to know the nature and extent of the pupil's specialized vocabulary in this area. This appraisal is not always included in a standard test of reading. Nor do standard tests usually contain measures of the pupil's familiarity with, and ability to use, source materials. Moreover, most tests do not examine the ability to read critically.

To be an effective guide, the teacher needs also to know the pupil's rate of reading different kinds of materials. In addition, he should ascertain the nature and extent of each pupil's reading experience. It is clear, then, that to understand a pupil's status in reading, the teacher will employ data from standardized tests and will assemble additional information revealing the pupil's vocabulary, his ability to read and use various types of materials, and the amount and nature of his reading experience.

In offering reading instruction, the teacher requires not only facts about each pupil's reading, but also information pertaining to his interests and to his personal life and social adjustment. Some procedures such as the use of interest inventories, anecdotal records and various forms of observation are helpful in obtaining data of this type. Interest inventories (which include inquiries concerning play activities, hobbies, vocational preferences, wishes, etc.) may yield clues of value in understanding pupils' attitudes, problems, and adjustment.[9] An interest inventory may be used advantageously in studying groups as well as individuals. These data may be employed in association with others to afford a sound basis for planning appropriate and profitable reading experiences for a class or for an individual. Such data will reveal each pupil's readiness for reading at different levels of growth.

Reading in the Content Fields

In considering the role of reading in the content areas, W. S. Gray pointed out that various attitudes range from complete acceptance to total rejection of the idea that "every teacher is a teacher of reading." He also noted that this slogan, which appeared in the 36th Yearbook of the National Society for the Study of Education, *The Teaching of Reading: A Second Report*, was unfortunate in that it designated responsibility without indicating

---

[9] See Witty-Kopel-Coomer Interest Inventories, Northwestern University. See also questionnaires used in Paul A. Witty, Ann Coomer, Robert Sizemore, and Paul Kinsella, *A Study of the Interests of Children and Youths*, a cooperative research based on a contract between Northwestern University and the Office of Education, U.S. Department of Health, Education and Welfare, 1959.

reasons, goals, or methods to achieve objectives. What are the functions of the subject teacher insofar as reading is concerned? W. S. Gray states:

> The basic view presented in this paper is that teachers of different curriculum fields become concerned about reading problems as reading assumes importance in attaining the aims of teaching in those fields. The three major duties of such teachers with respect to reading are to provide optimum conditions under which acquired reading ability may be used in attaining worthwhile goals, to promote growth in many aspects of reading which are unique to given fields, and to provide specific training in reading when for any reason they assign reading materials that are above the reading level of the pupils in their classes. The final level of reading competence attained by pupils in elementary and secondary schools is the product of the effort of all teachers. Whereas the reading teacher lays the foundation of good reading habits, the content teachers play a highly significant role in extending and refining the reading efficiency of pupils in specific areas.[10]

And we might add that special emphasis should be placed on flexibility and ready adaptation of reading skills in order to attain success in the subject fields. A. Sterl Artley states:

> It is not enough to develop proficiency in specific abilities—to teach the child how to locate materials, to select material and evaluate it in the light of the problem at hand, to read at various rates. We might say the job is half done when these abilities have been developed. The second half of the instructional job is that of teaching the child to recognize his particular reading needs and to adapt to those needs the necessary skills—developing the attitude that reading is not a static, inflexible activity, but a dynamic, modifiable activity that changes as conditions change.[11]

We have stressed the importance in a developmental program of the ability to read in the subject fields through effective application and extension of reading skills. Such applications result from emphasis on the ability to adapt reading skills readily to varied needs and purposes.

As a pupil proceeds in school, he encounters a wider and wider range of materials. In modern schools, reading of science and of social studies materials is often introduced in the primary grades. The pupil must learn how to read and to study such materials

---

[10] W. S. Gray, "Theme of the Conference," Chapter I in *Improving Reading in Content Fields*, Supplementary Educational Monograph, No. 62, compiled and edited by W. S. Gray. Chicago: University of Chicago Press, 1947, pp. 4–5.

[11] A. Sterl Artley, "Influence of the Field Studied on the Reading Attitudes and Skills Needed," Chapter V in *Improving Reading in Content Fields, op. cit.*, p. 42.

effectively. Soon he will have elementary books on these subjects to employ for varied purposes. He will increasingly utilize library resources in association with experience units and investigations of various kinds. In the intermediate grades, the program in the subject fields becomes intensified and greater demands are made on the pupil for the selection and application of varied reading skills. He must therefore develop flexibility in applying reading skills. It is clear that a good foundation in basic reading skills is one of the safeguards for successful reading in the content fields. However, beyond these basic skills, there are applications and extensions necessary in each field.[12]

It is worth nothing that Guy Bond and Miles Tinker conclude: "The correlations between general reading tests and reading tests in the content fields range from about .30 to .50." Furthermore they state that "there are many reading abilities (that operate) somewhat independent of each other."[13] A student may be competent in reading materials in one area and not in another. In the elementary school, there are four areas in which reading presents problems because of new vocabulary and concepts, readability obstacles traceable to style of writing, differences in typography, and so forth. The areas include social science, science, mathematics and literature.

One of the most valuable aids in the "teaching of essential study skills and the improvement of reading in the content areas" is the *EDL Study Skills Library* which is "planned as a sequential twelve-year program." The materials stress the skills of interpretation, evaluation, organization, and reference in the areas of science and social studies.[14] The use of these materials is especially valuable in providing the needed application and extension of reading skills in the content areas.

Bond and Tinker point out that within the social studies, difficulties are occasioned by factors such as the temporal sequence of events portrayed, unfamiliar content unassociated with present-day happenings and experience, and necessity for reading and interpreting maps, graphs, charts, etc. Similarly in geography, they

---

[12] See David H. Russell, *Children Learn To Read*, 2nd edition. Boston: Ginn, 1961.

[13] Guy Bond and Miles Tinker, *Reading Difficulties: Their Diagnosis and Correction*. New York: Appleton-Century-Crofts, 1957, p. 352. See also L. C. Fay, "What Research Has to Say About Reading in the Content Areas," *The Reading Teacher* 8:68–72, 1954.

[14] H. Alan Robinson, Stanford E. Taylor, and Helen Frackenpohl, *Teacher's Guide, Levels 4-5-6, The EDL Study Skills Library*. Huntington, N. Y.: Educational Developmental Laboratories, 1961.

indicate that understanding of reading material may depend on the possession of a special vocabulary based on conditions related to housing, food, or occupations; to physical features of the land; and to climate or agriculture in various, often unfamiliar places throughout the world. The interpretation of maps and "interrupted" reading involving reference to materials on various pages also require types of adjustment not previously emphasized. Mathematics presents other unique reading problems with its strong use of a technical vocabulary, symbols, diagrams, complex concepts, and verbally stated problems.[15]

Responsibility for Developmental Reading Program

A developmental program requires the co-operation of administrators, supervisors, and teachers. A primary responsibility of the administrator in a secondary school is to encourage all-school participation in the work. The formation of a committee to study the total reading situation and to make plans for the development and maintenance of the program is a good initial step. This committee should include representatives from every subject field.

In the planning of extension of reading instruction in every area, certain conditions must be met. The reading demands or objectives of each subject should be set forth. We have chosen the social studies field for illustration. In this paper we shall limit our discussion to the following acquisitions: (1) vocabulary and concepts, (2) ability to see relationships between facts, (3) capacity to organize information, (4) tendency to read critically, and (5) ability to use source materials effectively.

Some Reading Proficiencies Essential in All Social Studies

The above list includes some of the skills essential for reading successfully in the social-studies area. In every subject, similar, more detailed lists may be assembled. This is perhaps the first step in embarking on a developmental program that stresses successful reading in the content fields. And it is a step which a teacher or a group representing each subject might follow. Lillian Gray and Dora Reese have discussed effectively and in detail such acquisitions for geography and history, the two social studies subjects commonly studied in elementary and secondary schools. For example, they have attempted to identify the varied skills needed for

---

[15] Bond and Tinker, *op. cit.*

effective reading of geography content. They suggest that pupils be taught directly to:

1. Sense space relations. A thousand miles is a distance difficult for children to understand even though they can easily read the words. . . . To teach directions, children must be taught the location and significance of *north,* and not conceive of it, for example, as the 'top of the map.'
2. Understand how geography influences people and events.
3. Prepare detailed, well-organized reports for class discussion from materials read in different books.
4. Get the facts straight.
5. Sense cause and effect relationships.
6. Recognize generalities, such as the fact that increased altitude indicates a cooler climate.
7. Find the main ideas in an involved paragraph containing cross references and extraneous details.
8. Recognize supporting details.
9. Understand terminology. . . .
10. Classify geographical concepts according to basic human needs: food, shelter, clothing, occupations, recreation, communication, transportation, aesthetic appreciation, government, education, and religion.
11. Compare statements and draw accurate conclusions.
12. Read graphs, maps. . . .[16]

Although we recognize the need for detailed analyses and emphases such as that just given for geography, we shall in this paper limit our discussion to the five items previously cited.

1. VOCABULARY AND CONCEPTS

One of the most important needs of pupils in successful endeavor in social studies is an understanding of the specialized vocabulary employed. The teacher should provide the background of experience and the related activities which help children to understand these words thoroughly and to have clear concepts of them.

This development should be planned with care. The teacher should be alert from the first to detect and correct misconceptions. Significant terms in each unit of instruction should be assembled, studied and discussed. The use of direct experience, photographs,

---

[16] Lillian Gray and Dora Reese, *Teaching Children to Read,* 2nd ed. New York: Ronald Press, 1957, pp. 379–380. Cited by Henry P. Smith and Emerald V. Dechant in *Psychology in Teaching Reading.* Englewood Cliffs, N. J.: Prentice-Hall, 1961, pp. 360–361.

filmstrips, and motion pictures will aid in building backgrounds essential for understanding many new words and phrases.

Discussion techniques may be used to advantage. By encouraging extensive reading, the teacher can help pupils obtain facts or illustrations upon which clear understanding of many terms depends. The use of films and film readers is another way of providing a common background of experience for children. The phenomenal success of children employing film readers suggests their value in improving the efficiency of reading instruction, especially in clarifying the vocabulary employed and in fostering clear interpretation. Some teachers have reported considerable gains in fluency in silent reading and unprecedented gains in reading skill attending the use of the combined approach.[17] These results and indorsements will require validation by careful research. However, there already is clear evidence that the teacher will find the use of the film and the film reader an effective way to foster gains in reading skills.

2. ABILITY TO SEE RELATIONSHIPS BETWEEN FACTS

Pupils also need help in seeing the relationships between facts encountered in different contexts as well as in varied sources. Simple exercises such as the following may help somewhat in the acquisition of this skill. Dates and significant events in an historical presentation may be arranged in two columns in mixed order. The pupils are asked to connect the associated items with lines. However, more important and subtle relationships should also be stressed. For example, the teacher may encourage the students to find the chief products of certain countries and to determine the amount and rate of production. Discussion and objective tests may be used to determine the accuracy of their conclusions. More complex relationships between such factors as resources and productivity or form of government and attitudes of different peoples may also be stressed.[18]

3. CAPACITY TO ORGANIZE MATERIALS

Some pupils appear to have little expectation that they will be required to do more than reproduce a few facts from the accounts they read. They give scant attention to the sequence of ideas and do not differentiate significant items from unimportant details. It is necessary, therefore, to encourage pupils to react more intensely

---

[17] Paul Witty and James Fitzwater, "An Experiment with Film, Film Readers, and the Magnetic Sound Tract Projector." *Elementary English*, April, 1953.

[18] See also Guy Bond and E. B. Wagner, *Teaching the Child to Read.* New York: Macmillan, 1960.

to the content in social-studies presentations. Some pupils may be helped by practice in making outlines in which they differentiate main topics from subordinate themes. Practice in summarizing will also assist pupils to react to ideas as they read and to organize the information they acquire from reading. Since sources of information are so numerous and varied in worth, it is necessary for pupils to learn to evaluate presentations and to submit their findings in well-organized compact form.

4. TENDENCY TO READ CRITICALLY

Charles B. Huelsman has summarized the critical reading skills that were mentioned in one or more of fifteen articles on the topic:

1. To define and delimit a problem
2. To formulate hypotheses
3. To locate information bearing on specific problems
4. To determine that a statement is important for a given purpose
5. To distinguish the difference between facts and opinions
6. To evaluate the dependability of data
7. To recognize the limitations of given data even when the items are assured to be dependable
8. To see elements common to several items of data
9. To make comparisons
10. To organize evidence that suggests relationships
11. To recognize prevailing tendencies or trends in the data
12. To judge the competency of a given author to make a valid statement on a given topic
13. To criticize data on the basis of its completeness and accuracy
14. To criticize a presentation on the basis of the completeness and logic of its reasoning
15. To suspend judgment until all evidence is assembled and evaluated.[19]

Several studies show that many elementary and secondary school pupils lack the ability to read critically. Pupils should be encouraged to study and to contrast the attitudes and points of view of various authors, as well as their sources of information. Attention should also be given to the extent to which authors are impartial and objective in drawing conclusions and in interpreting data.

---

[19] Charles B. Huelsman, Jr., "Promoting Growth in Ability to Interpret when Reading Critically: In Grades Seven to Ten," in *Promoting Growth Toward Maturity in Interpreting What Is Read,* Supplementary Educational Monographs, No. 74. Chicago: University of Chicago Press, 1951, pp. 149–153, cited by Smith and Dechant, *op. cit.,* p. 358.

In the development of "critical reading," specialized approaches have been devised by some teachers. For example, Spencer Brown employed "documentary techniques" to encourage pupils to seek accurate information on which to base their statements.[20] Pupils of varied nationalities and backgrounds visited the homes and neighborhoods of various "racial" groups found within a school district. After discussing their findings and observations, the facts which had been "documented" were utilized in writing a play entitled "America Is Only You and Me." Many elementary school teachers have found that this approach adds authenticity to information obtained from books and leads to a critical attitude toward the printed page. There are many other efforts to help pupils gain skill in critical reading as shown in booklets designed to aid junior and senior high school pupils improve their reading as well as in books designed to foster effective reading of the newspaper.[21]

5. ABILITY TO USE SOURCE MATERIALS EFFECTIVELY

Prevailing practice often neglects the wide range of reading abilities within classes. If a single textbook is prescribed for all pupils, little can be accomplished since a typical class contains pupils of widely differing abilities. In the upper grades of the elementary school the differences in ability between the poorest and the best pupil will probably equal a range of from four to five grades, according to test scores.

The following approach is being used by some teachers in recognition of the range of ability within classes. First, the teacher selects the topics or units to be treated in the social-studies program. For each topic, varied source materials are assembled to meet the abilities within the class. The variety of materials includes factual accounts, biographies, story materials, magazine and newspaper articles, as well as reference sources such as encyclopedias, atlases, and almanacs. Fortunately, there is a substantial and growing amount of literature on every topic of significance in this field.[22]

---

[20] Spencer Brown, *They See for Themselves*, Bureau of Intercultural Education Publication Series, Problems of Race and Culture in American Education, Vol. III. New York: Harper, 1945.

[21] (a) Paul Witty, *Streamline Your Reading*, Life Adjustment Booklet, Chicago: Science Research Associates, 1949. (b) Paul Witty and Harry Bricker, *You Can Read Better*, Junior Life Adjustment Booklet, Chicago: Science Research Associates, 1951. (c) Paul Witty and Edith Grotberg, *Improving Your Vocabulary*, Chicago: Science Research Associates, 1959. (d) Edgar Dale, *How to Read a Newspaper*, Chicago: Scott, Foresman and Co., 1941.

[22] The use of the *EDL Study Skills Library* previously described seems particularly appropriate to provide differentiated instruction within classes.

Co-ordinating the Reading Program—A Concluding Statement

The foregoing concept of reading instruction differs, in some respects, from views previously held. We have seen that modern approaches to reading instruction include emphasis on the reading skills needed in the subject fields. The teacher of every subject has a responsibility for helping the child to read effectively the varied materials employed in instruction, for developing special vocabularies and for building concepts, for providing diversified materials so as to encourage growth for every pupil, for cultivating critical reading, and for fostering reading from varied sources.

When such practices are widely followed in our schools, co-ordination of the reading program will occur. Co-ordination will be facilitated further by the consideration on the part of all teachers of the interests and "developmental needs" of boys and girls and the selection of appropriate, related subject matter and experience.

These procedures are being followed with success in some schools. Not only are they leading to greater skill in reading, but they are helping students appreciate and enjoy the subject matter of the special fields. It is to be hoped that increased numbers of superintendents and supervisors will be led to initiate developmental reading programs in their schools. Certainly there appears to be a great need for stressing reading in the content fields in most schools. Moreover, efforts of this kind have proved abundantly rewarding.[23] This is an approach which when widely followed promises to increase greatly the efficiency of instruction in the modern school.

---

[23] K. B. Rudolph, *Effect of Reading Instruction on Achievement in Eighth Grade Social Studies*, Teachers College Contribution to Education, No. 945, New York, 1949. See also Bond and Wagner, *Teaching the Child to Read, op. cit.*

TEACHERS, COMPUTERS, AND GAMES: INNOVATIONS IN THE SOCIAL STUDIES *

Leonard W. Ingraham

It has been said that the most important function of the schools from kindergarten through college is to join together the students and the teacher in the acquisition of knowledge and the search for truth. With today's higher, wider, and broader horizons, it behooves social studies teachers to employ "jet age" techniques to reach their instructional goals with a speed that beggars the imagination to comprehend—much less to achieve. Just when it began to look as though the "impossible" were literally just that, the teaching machine gave promise of being the vehicle which would rush social studies teachers to a three-point landing in this educational Utopia. The "sonic boom" was loud and clear. They were on their way. As it turned out, however, the programed instruction materials which were produced for the social studies failed to provide the road maps to this promised land.[1] The plane for the social studies teachers never got off the ground.

The teacher, the motion picture, the textbook, the filmstrip, the overhead projector, recordings—all are there, readily available, and waiting for the student.

Now comes the computer. Now comes the teaching game. How do these fit into the social studies scene?

According to Dr. Jerome B. Weisner, Dean of Science at Massachusetts Institute of Technology:

> The computer, with its promise of a million-fold increase in man's capacity to handle information, will undoubtedly have the most far-reaching social consequences of any contemporary technical development. The potential for good in the computer, and the danger inherent in its misuse exceed our ability to imagine. . . . We have actually

Leonard W. Ingraham is Acting Director of the Bureau of History and Social Sciences, New York City Board of Education, New York.

* Reprinted from *Social Education* 31:51–53, 1967, with permission of the National Council for the Social Studies and Leonard W. Ingraham.

[1] The availability of programed instruction in the social studies is considerably less than the number of programs for many other subject areas. For a list of programed instructional materials available, see articles by the author in *Social Education* 27:19–20; January 1963; 28:15–17; January 1964; and 29:28–29; January 1965; also *Programed Instruction Materials 1964–65*, compiled and published by the Center for Programed Instruction, Teachers College, Columbia University.

entered a new era of evolutionary history, one in which rapid change is a dominant consequence. Our only hope is to understand the forces at work and to take advantage of the knowledge we find to guide the evolutionary process.

Computers, harnessed to teaching machines and television hold high promise for educators. The computer could make classroom teaching more, rather than less, an individual activity. Learning with the computer might provide the speed and depth of understanding that programed instruction in printed format was unable to achieve. But they are not yet available to the schools. Computer-based teaching systems are not to be confused with teaching machines and programed learning. The latter dispense instructional material in a fixed sequence of small steps. They are usually followed by a question. All students use the same program. By contrast, using computer-based teaching, the student will study a sequence tailored to his own individual needs.

What should every social studies teacher know about a computer? The computer functions strictly according to detailed instructions, *input,* written by a human programer. The information needed by the computer to perform its task and the procedures to be followed are called "the program." The input is frequently placed into the machine from a typewriter keyboard. It is then translated into electrical impulses and stored on magnetic tape. The heart of the learning machine is the electronic high speed information processor or computer. The control unit of the computer does the work specified by the program. The resulting information is transferred to a device which may print the message, punch holes on a card, or exhibit a visual image on a television-like screen. This is the *output* of the computer.

The student is at the console or *station,* which is connected to the computer by telephone wire or coaxial cable. He will have before him a television screen, a light pen (a device resembling a pocket flashlight), a typewriter keyboard, and possibly earphones and a microphone. He may ask questions or respond to them, by using the typewriter keyboard. Or he may use the light pen to point out an answer to a multiple-choice question which appears on the television screen. The computer's memory will be activated by the light beam. The *incorrect* information may be erased or a revised display may appear on the screen. Due to the immense capacity and speed of the computer, many students may work independently and simultaneously from different locations on the same computer.

Two areas of computer application for the social studies are possible. One is learning history and the social sciences by discovery. A dialogue system would permit the student to conduct a genuine dialogue with the computer. Some relatively difficult technical problems at present prevent the successful development to any depth of subtlety. They are being worked out. We can envisage a program in American history geared to the inquiry and discovery approach. A student might type the following question to the computer: "Why did Booth kill Lincoln?" or "What was the role of the railroad in the economic development of the Mississippi in the nineteenth century?" At the present time, it is very difficult to write programs that will deal with freely constructed questions of such complexity.

In certain curriculum areas in the social studies which have been taught for a considerable time, it is possible to provide a fairly thorough analysis of the types of questions that will be asked. In these subject areas, we can hope for considerable progress toward question-recognition by the computer. The computer can store enough information to give answers. It is important from the standpoint of the program for the computer to recognize precisely what question has been asked.

The second area is simulation and gaming. Simulation refers to the artificial representation of situations occurring in the real world. In computer simulation the student is presented with information about problem situations. It is generally used for the purpose of analysis and learning. The term "game," according to Bushnell, co-editor of *The Computer in American Education,* is often used to denote a form of simulation involving a situation of competition or conflict.

Computer-based games for sixth-grade social studies have been developed by the Board of Cooperative Educational Services in Westchester County, New York, in cooperation with International Business Machines, Inc. The primary aim of this project is to provide and demonstrate computer-based instruction. One of the three games developed is the Sumerian Game, designed to teach sixth graders some basic principles of economics at the time of the neolithic revolution in Mesopotamia.

During an introductory programed tape and slide presentation the child playing the game sees himself as a ruler's son in the city-state of Lagash in the year 3500 B.C. Brief instructions and the initial economic conditions are typed out for the child by the computer. The student assumes the role of Luduga I, priest-ruler of Lagash, and is presented with his first problematic situation: "We have harvested 5,000 bushels of grain to take care of 500 people. How much of this grain shall be set aside for next season's planting, and how much will be stored in the warehouse? The remainder will be given to the people to eat."

The child makes decisions and enters his answers at the computer terminal. The computer immediately returns a progress report, including the harvest reaped from the seed grain set aside for planting, a word index as to the standard of living, and a report on his inventory. A complicating figure affects the second planting. The ruler must take into account the increasing population. At intervals the ruler is presented with technological innovations and disasters which will alter his decisions.

The rule of the first Luduga is devoted to the solution of problems pertaining to an agricultural economy. In the second phase of the game, the child as Luduga II is given the opportunity to apply his surplus grain to the development of crafts. In the third and final stage he is introduced to trade and the more complex problems which confront a changing economy. The rate and trend of development are dependent upon the wisdom of the decisions made by the child.

The essential idea behind the second game, the "Sierra Leone Development Project," is to simulate the economic problems of a newly-emerging nation, placing a secondary emphasis on a study of the country's culture. The simulated economic and social situations used in this game are drawn from actual problems discussed in the Ten-Year Social and Economic Development Plan now in effect.

In the third game, called "The Free Enterprise Game," the player initially assumes the role of the owner of a small toy store. During the first phase of the game, in which the player will be engaged in a retail sales operation, he is expected to be able to increase the net worth and monthly sales of his store, learn certain general concepts and understandings such as:

—The difference between goods and services; public and private services, wants and needs, etc.

—The nature of sales, overhead, profits, assets and liabilities.

—The necessity of capital investment to promulgate growth.

—Sales promotion methods and the concept of small expenditures bringing large returns.

—Basic information about taxes, property and liability insurance, savings and checking accounts, loans, and interest.

—The use and importance of savings.

—The relationship between risk and return.

In the second phase of the game the player is engaged in production rather than sales. This transformation occurs at a point when the player's net worth reaches $100,000 (having grown from the initial figure of $5,000). During this segment the player should learn:

—The laws of supply and demand and the determination of pricing policies.

—The advantages of division of labor (specialization) and mechanization.

—Policies used in hiring, firing, and setting wages.

—The law of diminishing returns as applied to production.

—Transportation and its relationship to production and consumption.

Games without a computer, which have been developed at various institutions throughout the country, run the gamut from those dealing with various democratic processes—from a court of law and the state legislature to family games and those which impart specific vocational or scientific subject matter. The Social Studies Curriculum Program of Educational Services Incorporated is in the process of preparing non-computerized games for: Elementary school level, Seal Hunting, Bush Hunting; Junior high school level, Empire, Adventuring, Revolution; Senior high school level, Steam, Manchester, Galapagos.

Proponents of simulation and games in social studies education claim that intuitive thinking is developed, learning is made entertaining and relevant to student life experiences. Emphasis is placed on developing analytical approaches and organizing concepts transferable to other problems. Learning is achieved by exploratory problem-solving simulations which utilize adult materials. Both bright and slow can share social interactions in the game, while learning from it at different levels. Culturally deprived students seem to respond better to game teaching than to expository methods.

We are just at the dawn of computer-based teaching. Simulation and games will reach the social studies teacher first. The task ahead will be to assign to the machine those things it can do best, and to reserve for the teacher those things which he must provide and control.

Unique among the schools in the United States today are the Nova High School in Fort Lauderdale, Florida, where we find a "coordinator of games," and the West Hartford, Connecticut, schools, where a pilot "Dial Access Information Retrieval System" is in operation.

Yet, educators must be heartened by the sentiments of W. B.

Yeats, who wrote, many years ago, ". . . The visible world is no longer a reality and the unseen world is no longer a dream."

Today in education, the visible is deferring to the unseen—in fact, to the unforeseen. Perhaps now the social studies teacher will not only catch that plane, but will even see it get off the ground, propelled by the combined force of the teaching machine and the computer.

SELECTED BIBLIOGRAPHY

Clark C. Abt, "Games for Learning." Occasional Paper No. 7. *The Social Studies Curriculum Program.* Cambridge, Mass.: Educational Services Inc., 1966.

Layman E. Allen, "Games and Programed Instruction." *Programed Instruction,* March, 1966.

O. Benson, "Simulation of International Relations and Diplomacy," in *Computer Applications in Behavioral Sciences,* H. Borko, ed. Englewood Cliffs, N.J.: Prentice-Hall, 1962.

Sarane S. Boocock, "The Career Game." Baltimore, Md.: The Johns Hopkins University, Department of Social Relations, June, 1964.

Sarane S. Boocock, "Effects of Election Campaign in Four High School Classes." Report No. 1. Baltimore, Md.: The Johns Hopkins University, Department of Social Relations, October, 1963.

Sarane S. Boocock, *The Automation of School Information Systems.* Monograph No. 1. Washington: Department of Audiovisual Instruction, 1964.

Sarane S. Boocock, *The Computer as an Instructional Tool: A Summary SP-1554.* Santa Monica, Cal.: System Development Corporation, 1964.

Sarane S. Boocock, "Computer-Based Simulation: A New Technology for Education." *Audio-Visual Communications Review 11*:March–April, 1963. Entire issue.

Don Bushnell. "For Each Student a Teacher." *Saturday Review,* July 23, 1966.

Cleo Cherryholmes, "Developments in Simulation of International Relations in High School Teaching." *Phi Delta Kappan,* January, 1965.

Editors of *Business Week,* "Can Computers Teach?" June 11, 1966.

Editors of *Fortune Magazine,* "Technology Is Knocking at the School House Door." August, 1966.

Harold Guetzkow *et al., Simulation in International Relations: Developments for Research and Teaching.* Englewood Cliffs, N.J.: Prentice-Hall, 1963.

Marshall McLuhan, *Understanding Media.* New York: McGraw-Hill, 1964.

Bruse Moncreiff, "The Sumerian Game: Teaching Economics with A Computerized P.I." *Programed Instruction 4*:1965.

Richard Wing, "Computer-Based Economics Games." *Audiovisual Instruction,* December, 1964.

Peter Wolff, "The Game of Empire." Occasional Paper No. 9. *Social Studies Curriculum Program*. Cambridge, Mass.: Educational Testing Service, Inc., 1966.

ADDITIONAL SOURCES OF INFORMATION

Center for the Demonstration of Computer Assisted Instruction. 845 Fox Meadow Road, Yorktown Heights, New York 10598.

Institute of Educational Technology. Teachers College, Columbia University, New York 10027.

Project SIMILE. Simulation in Instruction Project. Western Behavioral Sciences Institute, La Jolla, California 92037.

Role Playing Simulation in Instruction. A tape recording of conference held by Department of Audiovisual Instruction at its annual convention in 1966. Available from Tape Duplicating Service, National Tape Repository, University of Colorado, Boulder 80304.

The Contributions of the Social Science Disciplines

*T*HE SOCIAL SCIENCES are generally recognized as the parent disciplines of the social studies. Thus, the elementary social studies program is closely related to history, geography, political science, anthropology, sociology, social psychology, economics, and other social science disciplines. It is assumed that programs based on social science knowledge prepare one to understand human ways and to cope with the complexities of human behavior. Some educators believe that increased contact with social science information of appropriate complexity in the elementary school will promote development of responsible citizenship. Nearly all agree that early contact with social science ideas facilitates the later learning that comes in high school and college.

Traditionally, the content of social studies programs was drawn mainly from history and geography. The other disciplines were often not included at all or were treated in an incidental way. With society's growing awareness of man's need to more fully understand social realities, programs that incorporate only two of the disciplines are not considered adequate. Each of the social sciences deals with fundamental concerns of man, and each has the potential of contributing importantly to the understanding of human behavior and human institutions.

Despite common acceptance of the social science foundation of elementary social studies, there is no agreement concerning the particular *kind* of social science knowledge that should be incorporated in the curriculum. Some suggest that major generalizations drawn from the various social sciences should provide the focus for the content to be taught. They argue that since we cannot teach everything, we must select that which is most basic and most essential. In their view, widely applicable generalizations from the social sciences meet these specifications. Thus, they suggest that teaching generalizations be made the main thrust of the program, and that learning activities be planned and resources used to achieve this end. Implicit in this focus is the assumption that the

318

pupil can apply such generalized knowledge to new and different situations.

A somewhat different position is taken by those who regard generalizations as ephemeral in nature and as having limited educational value, especially when they are presented as immutable truths. They favor an approach that requires children to discover their *own* generalizations, and that in the process the pupils use some of the same investigative procedures used by social scientists. Each social science has developed a set of investigative techniques that constitute its method of inquiry. Advocates of this second approach stress that the most valuable social science learnings are those dealing with the *process* of inquiry. Social science *content* is not regarded as unimportant, but it plays a secondary role to the inquiry process.

Ultimately, of course, the curriculum organization and structure will determine the manner in which social science content is incorporated in the program. In any case, teacher judgment plays an important role in determining what is taught, what is emphasized, and what is omitted. In order to make such decisions in an intelligent way, the teacher will need to understand the rationale underlying the local program and have some knowledge of appropriate guidelines useful in selecting content. The articles that follow provide the teacher with background information concerning the social sciences-social studies relationship and should prove useful in assisting him to select and organize social studies content in a meaningful way.

CHANGING ASPECTS OF GEOGRAPHY AND THE ELEMENTARY CURRICULUM *

Phillip Bacon

In my mind's eye I see them yet, sweeping like a moving mirage over the silent emptiness of the Sahara. These were the nomads, the only true dwellers of this greatest of the world's deserts.

In time I came to know *les hommes bleus au Maroc* well. I recall the father, irascible leader, his stern face bronzed and creased by the searing sun, continually moving his family and his herds like a lost seaman over the interminable ocean of sand. But most of all I remember young Ismail, faithful guardian of his father's flocks.

What a marvelous lad! It was Ismail who could find pasture when starvation seemed imminent. It was Ismail who swiftly warned of danger when the sky took on a yellowish cast, certain sign of the coming of the *chergui*—that devastating wind from the southwest that stirs up sand, withering and smothering everything in its path. And it was Ismail who knew that our only salvation at the time of the chergui was to throw the center post of the tent to the ground, where, crouched together beneath the heavy camel hair fabric of the flattened tent, we waited out the storm.

So it was that I came to understand how man has learned to respond to the challenges of the desert. I became confident that man in the desert, so well illuminated by Ismail, my friend, need not defend his liberty, for in the desert one is always free, nor need he defend visible treasures, for the desert is an empty place, but he defends a secret realm.

In the course of several years of travel, other landscapes and other people came into view. I know now that they should have helped me to differentiate the variety of patterns—physical-biotic-cultural—that one finds distributed over the surface of the earth.

There was, for example, a tiny farm overlooking a fiord that cut deeply into the Norwegian coast. It was summer when I was there, and the father was away from home with the fishing fleet from the nearby coastal village. It was young Olaf, I believe, who told me of

Phillip Bacon is Professor of Geography at the University of Washington, Seattle.

* Reprinted from *Social Education* 31:609–611 ff., 1967, with permission of the National Council for the Social Studies and Phillip Bacon.

the long winter nights, bitterly cold, when he took hay to the barn to bed down the cows. I remember still other cows, and a lovely flaxen-haired girl who followed the melting snow up into the alpine meadows of Switzerland. And there was that wonderful sampan family somewhere in Southeast Asia—I can no longer recall just where, but it was long ago and there were so many places and so many families. Next to Ismail, however, one I will never forget was the boy, Omak, who was learning to hunt the walrus and the seal. His fur clothing, his snow house, his stone lamp with its flickering wick floating in oil seemed, at the time, such perfect examples of man's adaptation to the difficult habitat of the Arctic coast.

From Dreams to Reality

Nostalgic memories of an extended world tour? Certainly—but a vicarious one, made as a child, traveling aboard a series of blue covered geography textbooks, guided by some wonderfully dedicated elementary school teachers. Indeed, most of us who received our elementary school education during and since the 1920's trotted through similar adventures that are now recalled, depending on a whole variety of circumstances, with pleasure, indifference, or abject loathing. Rather anachronistically, too, a great many children attending elementary school today are still herding goats on the Sahara and building igloos along the shores of the Arctic Ocean. Might it not be appropriate, in this event, to paraphrase a popular television show and ask the real Ismail and the real Omak to stand up?

Unhappily, such characters drawn today would likely be no more true to life than the originals. It does seem fairly certain, however, that the real Ismail was never a nomad, unless one counts his fairly recent move from Algiers to Paris; and it may well be that good old Omak is actually a graduate of the University of Alaska who is now teaching his fourth graders in suburban Anchorage about a mysterious little nomad boy named Ismail!

Alas, then, that marvelous kaleidoscope of places and people that seemed so real as a child didn't belong to the real world at all. Or, at best, it was scarcely the representative portrait of the world that one ought to come to know after traveling about it for several years of social studies time. With this thought in mind, one certainly could, for example, ask why spend a month roaming with the nomads, when their numbers represent a terribly small percentage (less than five) of the world's people who occupy desert areas. Furthermore, even if the nomads could be made significant, why wade over the sand dunes when sandy deserts total less than ten per cent of desert surfaces? Why make those fur clothes and the oil lamp seem like such a burst of genius when they were developed by people living in other regions thousands of years before the Eskimos reached the Arctic? Indeed, no Eskimo had the time to sit around in a loin cloth in a sub-zero winter waiting to discover how helpful it would be to have a fur coat! And why, of all things, build igloos when today's Eskimo is more typically busy erecting the geodesic dome of a Distant Early Warning station for the Air Defense Command?

Reflections of Traditional Geography

Certainly Omak and Ismail were not, and are not, descriptive reflections of the sum total of elementary school geography. On the other hand, they are clearly linked to it; indeed, they are rather representative of geography as it has long been viewed by both common school and lay geographers. That this linkage has so long persisted is not difficult to understand. Geography as a field of study has, for centuries, been identified with exploration, and exploration has always focused on places and people located outside the realm of common experience. Further, there is little question but that a certain fascination with "strange lands and exotic people" continues to loom large in the popular mind. That nearly five million people are members of the National Geographic Society, whose magazine rather consistently includes descriptions and photographs of little known areas, is monumental testimony to the appeal of faraway places in geographical literature.

Several years ago, Professor William D. Pattison, in a most useful paper,[1] pointed up several traditions that have been, and continue to be, central to the field of geography. Exploration, both in a real sense and in the sense of the vicarious adventuring of children in elementary school classrooms, is centered in two of these traditions—the "man-land tradition" and the "area studies tradition."

Both of these traditions are clearly acknowledged even by those who have had little or no contact with geography as a scholarly discipline. "Man-land" refers to a search for interaction between man and his physical-biotic environment; "area studies" refers to the characterization of places, ranging in scale from the neighborhood in the primary grades to continents at the intermediate. Both

---

[1] William D. Pattison, "The Four Traditions of Geography." *Journal of Geography 63*:211–216, 1964. Reprinted as Professional Paper No. 25, National Council for Geographic Education.

traditions, unfortunately, have lent themselves to abuse in the elementary curriculum.

Out of the man-land tradition came a special bias, abandoned long ago by academic geography, but one that to this day continues to haunt school geography. This bias, known as environmentalism, is frequently confused with the entire man-land tradition in school geography. We can see its role in reflecting on our stories of Ismail and Omak. Hot and dry—nomadism; severe and prolonged cold— igloos! Of course this is wildly overstating the case. Yet a careful examination of the type study (area study) illustrations developed in so many curricula and texts prepared for the elementary level poignantly illustrates the impact of environmentalism.

Explaining man's behavior as a response to physical controls ignores the essential factor that people in similar physical-biotic environments simply do not make the same choices as to ways of life. What appears to one people as an ideal area for herding goats, appears to another as a marvelous setting for an intensively irrigated market garden, and to still another people as the perfect site for a desert resort replete with swimming pools, golf courses, and casinos. Academic geographers do not assume that man is the product of his physical environment. Neither do such theories have a place in modern school geography. Children, as young geographers, must be granted many opportunities to view the behavior of people in a given physical-biotic environment as a reflection of the attitudes, objectives, and technologies of the people themselves. In doing so they would be committing themselves to the study of environmental perception, a frontier area in modern academic geography.[2]

The man-land tradition, then, can and should continue to play an important role in school geography. It is most important to note, however, that it becomes truly meaningful only as it concerns itself with the real world, a dynamically changing setting as opposed to the static worlds of Ismail and Omak. This implies among a variety of other factors, intensified geographic analysis of urban areas as opposed to romanticized views of rural settings, and strong emphasis on where the people are as opposed to where they aren't.

If environmentalism is the curse of the man-land tradition, what has come to plague the house of geography from the area studies tradition? Out of this tradition sprang the inventory approach to

---

[2] David Lowenthal, ed., *Environmental Perception and Behavior* (Department of Geography Research Paper No. 109). Chicago: The University of Chicago, 1967.

school geography so unhappily recalled by generations of survivors of traditional geography programs. The inventory approach to area study simply refers to the all too prevalent lists of places and products that have so long dogged elementary school geography. While lip service to an avoidance of such drudgery has been given through the years by curriculum developers and textbook authors, the truth is too evident to be denied if one takes the trouble to examine their efforts. A preoccupation with factual detail—as opposed to a search for concepts, models, and principles—has traditionally been the lot of the young victims of an out-moded geography. A review of what Dean Lorrin Kennamer has called the "conceptual elements" of geography [3] is clear indication of a sharp move away from Gargantuan-like collections of miscellanea about places.

The View Ahead

By combing current geographical literature, and by examining the contemporary curricula of leading departments of geography in this country, one could readily find satisfying documentation of the continued existence of each of Pattison's traditions.[4] Geography, regardless of the stance from which one views it, continues to find "its substance from man's sense of place and from his curiosity about the spatial attributes of the surface and atmospheric envelope of this planet." [5] The vast array of facts that might be used to fill out these spatial attributes are virtually limitless and as such lack a constant. Many of the geographical facts that one might learn in grade four, for example, may well be untrue or irrelevant by the time one reaches high school. Certainly, then, the goal for geography as a school subject, as with all fields of study, is to help the learner understand the conceptual structure of the discipline. Without this, as Professor Robert B. McNee has put it, geography would be "too abstract, too dry, too heaped with mountainous detail, too conceptually infertile, or too remote from the world as perceived

[3] Lorrin Kennamer, Jr., "Geography in the Middle Grades." *Social Education* *31*:616, 1967.

[4] Pattison, *op. cit.* Two traditions, area studies and man-land, are discussed above. A third, the "earth science tradition," refers to a study "of the earth, the waters of the earth, the atmosphere surrounding the earth and the association between earth and sun. . . ." Brief discussion of the fourth, the "spatial tradition," follows.

[5] National Academy of Sciences-National Research Council. *The Science of Geography.* (Report of the *Ad Hoc* Committee on Geography, Earth Sciences Division, Publication 1277.) Washington, D.C.: National Academy of Sciences-National Research Council, 1965, p. 7.

by students to be attractive to them as an intellectual challenge." [6]

In counter-action to such unpleasant possibilities, much of the drive in contemporary American geography stems from the "spatial tradition." It is here that one finds concern for a whole gamut of generalizations related to spatial distributions, spatial associations, and spatial interactions. It is an understanding of these spatial relations and processes, along with an understanding of their significance to human activities, that encourages the student to analyze why things are where they are. Much of the work being done on the frontier of the discipline today falls into this tradition. Much of it is highly theoretical and much requires the utilization of sophisticated quantitative techniques. Needless to say, such studies lie well outside the reach of the elementary curriculum. Nonetheless, elementary school geographers can find a sustaining bond of fellowship with the research geographer in even the most rudimentary work that they might undertake in problems concerned with direction, distance, and location. These are spatial problems and, as such, are tied directly to the spatial tradition in the discipline of geography.

Geography is an exciting, dynamic, and wonderfully rewarding field of study. The elementary teacher and curriculum designer who will work toward establishing ties with this discipline cannot help but discover a wealth of ways in which he might link the frontiers of geographic research with geography as a school subject. Chorley and Haggett said it well in stating, "If we move with that frontier new horizons emerge into our view, and we find new territories to be explored as exciting and demanding as the dark continents that beckoned an earlier generation of geographers." [7] If it is time to say *adieu* to our old friends Ismail and Omak, we at least can take comfort in knowledge that we will gain lasting strength through our new grasp of the conceptual structure of the field.

---

[6] Robert B. McNee, "Toward Stressing Structure in Geographic Introduction, or Goodby to *Heavea Brazilliensis* and All That." Paper 4, in Commission on College Geography. *Introductory Geography, Viewpoints and Themes.* Washington, D.C.: Association of American Geographers, 1967, p. 31.

[7] Richard J. Chorley and Peter Haggett, *Frontiers in Geographical Teaching: The Madingley Lectures for 1963.* London: Methuen, 1965, p. 377.

ANTHROPOLOGY IN THE SCHOOLS *

Robert G. Hanvey

In a Chicago high school a student slips an 8mm film cartridge into a projector, sits back to take notes on primate behavior. In Suffern, New York, a seventh grade class listens intently to a tape of the Iroquois creation myth, told by a leading scholar. In a Philadelphia suburb a teacher hands out reprints of matrimonial advertisements from the *Bombay Times;* class begins on a note of ribald hilarity but ends with a serious discussion of caste as it affects biological diversity.

A small group of Minneapolis students ponder a facsimile of an ancient statuette on the table before them, speculating as to the kind of society that might have produced it. In Concord, California, high school juniors read a scholarly article comparing the European conception of authority—as outside the individual and "above"— with the very different conceptions that underlay the fierce individualism of certain American Indian groups. In Massachusetts, fifth grade pupils work through sets of picture cards, sorting scenes of urban and rural life, the beginning steps of a substantial inquiry into the origins and nature of cities.

These separate classroom events have a connection—all occur in the context of experimental units designed to test the contribution of anthropology to the social studies. Such experimentation breaks new ground, for anthropology has been the social science most underrepresented in the traditional social studies program.

Evidence from several quarters suggests that the period of neglect is nearly over. The mere existence of national curriculum projects concerned with anthropology has uncovered a surprising degree of interest among teachers and curriculum workers. Also the experimental materials produced by the projects are beginning to reach a larger audience of educators, to communicate concretely the relevance of the several fields of anthropology to social studies programs.

Physical anthropology, with its focus on the problems of human origins and human diversity; *archeology,* study of early cultures;

Robert G. Hanvey is with the Santa Barbara Public Schools, California.

* Reprinted from *Educational Leadership* 22:313–316, 1965, with permission of the Association for Supervision and Curriculum Development and Robert G. Hanvey. Copyright © 1965, by the Association for Supervision and Curriculum Development.

ethnology, systematic study and comparison of cultures; *linguistics,* study of language, the sine qua non of culture; *social anthropology,* with its attention to the structure and dynamics of societies—all clearly have something to say. Experimental units on biocultural evolution, the emergence of civilization, how to study society, origins of urban life, language and cultures, area studies of Africa, the Middle East, Latin America, films on Eskimo and Bushmen, on archeological digs and domestication of corn, give practical voice to these fields.

The new materials are being produced by several groups.[1] Educational Services Incorporated in Cambridge, active across much of the curriculum spectrum, has specialists at work on units for the elementary school. Also directing its efforts to elementary school applications is the recently activated Anthropology Curriculum Project at the University of Georgia. In Chicago, the Anthropology Curriculum Study Project, sponsored by the American Anthropological Association, is developing and testing high school materials.

Certain other curriculum groups, whose focus is not primarily anthropological, are producing units in anthropology. The School Science Curriculum Project at the University of Illinois, for example, is preparing materials on race, social organization, and archeological method. Some state departments of education—notably Pennsylvania, New York, and Wisconsin—are actively involved in the creation of programs and materials that provide for anthropological contributions, as are curriculum leaders in Minnesota and Indiana.

Experiments in Schools

Neither national projects nor state departments hold any title to experimental work with anthropology in the social studies. Individual teachers and schools have anticipated the current flush of enthusiasm by many years. Programs at the Edsel Ford High School in Dearborn, Michigan, the Francis Parker School in Chicago, the Verde Valley School in Arizona are of long standing.

The number of such schools is small, of course, as is the number of schools engaged in testing the new units. Many of the units planned by the projects are still in production and most of those now in use are in first-draft form and will need revision and larger

---

[1] Project addresses: (a) Educational Services Incorporated, 12 Garden Street, Cambridge 38, Massachusetts; (b) Anthropology Curriculum Project, University of Georgia, Athens, Georgia; (c) Anthropology Curriculum Study Project, 5632 S. Kimbark Avenue, Chicago 37, Illinois.

scale testing. It will be several years at least before the response of the schools to anthropology can be properly measured.

While it is clear that teachers and curriculum people will judge the contribution of anthropology on the basis of the experimental units, specific reactions to these may be less important ultimately than general developments in the social studies and in the society as a whole. Those who study educational change are well aware that there is an ecology of education. They know that the brightest plans pursued with the most capable energies tend often to be submerged, transmuted or accelerated by circumstances, by quiet trends and movements.

So whether anthropology finds a welcome in the elementary and secondary schools will depend only partly on the specific results of classroom experimentation; it will also depend on whether the social sciences in general find a place.

There is some reason to believe that a "readiness" for the social sciences exists in American schools. Certainly, many of those who concern themselves professionally with social education express the belief that there is little continued reason to keep these disciplines in the peripheral position to which they have long been relegated.

A New Warmth

If a new warmth toward the social sciences is evident, it should by no means be taken to represent a simple flirtation with pedagogical novelty. As much as anything it relates to a growing intellectual sophistication among American educators. This is a sophistication that is as impatient with folk ideas about social phenomena as it would be with folk ideas about physiology or the solar system. Teaching a supracultural natural science while promulgating folk explanations of human history and behavior seems less and less tenable. Realization is growing that the social sciences have developed useful ways of studying society, a reservoir of information, and empirical generalizations worth knowing. More important, educators are beginning to recognize that limiting access to such knowledge to a college-educated elite represents a serious inconsistency in a democratic society.

If high school education marks, for the moment, the minimal education we expect of all citizens, then it must be said that the capacity to think systematically about man's nature, his many societies, the whole career of his species—has not been included in our definition of the educated citizen. Knowledge of man produced by the disciplined researches of social scientists has not been generally available to public school students. The high school graduate who has been taught to expect regularities in the affairs of the physical universe will never have heard of the search for regularities in the affairs of men. But the schools seem to be on the threshold of offering access to such understandings, ready in effect *to democratize a social scientific comprehension of man.* It will be in the context of such a development that anthropology may find a role in the schools.

Yet other matters will play a part, too. Our increasing sophistication as a national society makes it tolerable to look at other societies non-invidiously. Non-invidious comparison of societies and their cultures is fundamental to anthropology as a science. But it has not, historically, been a comfortable exercise for the lay citizen and would probably be impossible were we not outgrowing the national narcissism of earlier years.

Trends *within* the social studies may also be preparing the ground for the social sciences. Interest in an inductive pedagogy has generated instructional materials long on data. There will be, inevitably, a corollary demand for frameworks that give such data meaning above and beyond common-sense inference. The social science disciplines offer tool kits of concept, method and theory that enable such frameworks to be built. Many of the units planned by the projects marry data with models of analysis so that students experience, in microcosm, the modes of inquiry of the working scientist.

Certain developments in the social studies promise an increasing need for the special competencies of anthropologists. Among these is the interest in area studies, in "non-Western" cultures. These studies frequently depend on survey materials, aggregates of information. Anthropologists, whose methods call for intensive work in the field and whose training develops a special regard for the *wholeness* of cultures, will be able to offer a complementary approach. This will be characterized by case materials that make depth study possible—and by an emphasis on the interrelatedness of economy, belief systems, social organization, etc.

In Large Perspective

In such contexts, it may be that the *reasons* for the anthropologists' research into other cultures will be found worthy of emulation. The researcher's motives go beyond "knowing about" the particular group studied. He works always toward *general* understandings, toward the discovery of laws that apply to the functioning of all human groups, that make some sense of the minutiae of history.

He studies the economy of a modern African group because, compared with earlier researches, the analysis may throw light on the dynamics of social change. Or he charts an intricate kinship system because beneath its uniqueness lie some truths about human social organization. Or he traces over time and space the movements of a particular tool or technology because he is interested in the general problem of culture diffusion.

This search for an understanding of fundamental social processes and structures marks the work of the anthropologist—and it is not impossible that this will come to be seen as a legitimate goal of the social studies.

One need not discard the conventional content to implement such a goal. The particulars of our own history, for example, grow in meaning when viewed against the backdrop of other human experience. The Westward Movement can be compared to and illuminated by other human migrations. The story of the American immigrant takes on new significance when viewed in the light of systematic studies of acculturation. The Bill of Rights is seen afresh when compared to other societies' institutional devices for safeguarding the autonomy of the individual.

In each instance, *comparison* yields insights into the particulars of our own tradition and produces generalizations about the history of the species and the functioning of its diverse groups.

Those who wish anthropology to play a part in the social studies do not imagine that the discipline can play *more* than a part. (It is noteworthy that the national projects in anthropology are preparing units rather than courses.) Yet the role of anthropology can be an important one, adding significantly to the impact of the social studies.

The explicit curriculum of the schools probably has less influence than any teacher would wish to know. Nevertheless, the influence of those programs we categorize as the social studies can be increased —if such programs demonstrably provide students with the opportunity to see human affairs in large perspective, with the skills of disciplined observation and with new power to explain social phenomena. Anthropology will have a measurable contribution to make to a social studies so conceived.

RECENT DEVELOPMENTS IN POLITICAL SCIENCE *

Peter Woll

To what extent is the study of political science appropriate for elementary and secondary school curriculum? This is an extraordinarily difficult question to answer. It leads to an examination of the importance of transmitting democratic values to students. The discipline of political science at one level tends to exclude value judgments and concentrates upon finding the factors that shape and define political systems. But political science cannot, as it moves to different levels of analysis and purpose, reject values.

Throughout the history of political science in this country numerous prominent scholars have concentrated upon proving the usefulness of democracy, and indicating the places where improvement can be made in our system. Political scientists writing under the guise of objectivity usually put forth a number of value-laden statements, for it is virtually impossible to be entirely objective when dealing with political matters. After examining "facts," scholars often state goals. Woodrow Wilson, for example, in his famous book, *Congressional Government* (1885), after objectively discussing the organization and operation of Congress, went on to point out that the legislature needed far more leadership, organization, and information than it possessed at that time in order to perform its "proper" role in a democratic government by discussion. It was not sufficient, Wilson stated, for the legislature to be involved only in drafting legislation. It must also act as a continual critic of administration and of the affairs of government. He hoped that his study would be helpful in solving the problems in Congress.

More recently, Harold Lasswell, in *The Future of Political Science* (New York: Atherton Press, 1963), suggested that political scientists should use their knowledge to help solve public problems. Lasswell is implying that it is not enough for political science merely to deal with facts, for it must also evaluate the ends of government. This, interestingly, differs somewhat from his earlier statement in the famous book *Politics: Who Gets What, When, How* (New York: McGraw-Hill, 1936): "The study of politics is the study of influence

Peter Woll is Associate Professor in the Department of Politics at Brandeis University, Waltham, Massachusetts.

* Reprinted from *Social Education* *30*:168–172, 1966, with permission of the National Council for the Social Studies and Peter Woll.

and the influential. The science of politics states conditions; the philosophy of politics justifies preferences." His book, he went on to state, deals with political science and not philosophy. The implication was that the study of philosophy should properly be left to philosophers, not political scientists.

The Place of Political Science in Secondary and Elementary Curriculums

There is undoubtedly widespread agreement that when politics is taught to secondary and elementary students some inculcation of values is necessary. Often courses dealing with political science are described as courses in citizenship, implying that it is necessary to teach youngsters the importance of democracy and their responsibilities as democratic citizens. This attitude is well reflected in a recent statement made by two professors of education:

> The word *idiot* is derived from the Greek *idiotes*, which meant "those citizens who do not take part in public voting." Although in ancient Greece the *idiotes* failed to vote because they were not *permitted* to and although the word has taken on a different meaning today, when one considers the large number of Americans who *choose* not to participate in local, state, and national elections, the word (with its 20th-century connotation) may not after all be an entirely inappropriate political adjective. . . .
>
> It is important that American youth emerge from their schooling with solid understandings of and attachments to democratic tenets, processes, and procedures as a way of adult political life. Education for young people in a democracy *is* different from education for children and youth in a totalitarian state.[1]

Here we see clearly reflected the idea that one of the purposes of political education at the lower levels is to "indoctrinate" in the tenets of democracy.

The idea that political science courses must give attention to "citizenship education" poses a dilemma, and also illustrates the difference in approach often taken at the university level on the one hand, and at the secondary and elementary levels on the other. At the university level, citizenship education is generally not considered to be the central core of most political science courses, but rather a more objective approach is taken. True, in many universities, by state law, it is necessary to teach American government

---

[1] Francis J. Sorauf, *Political Science: An Informal Overview*. Columbus, Ohio: Merrill, 1965, p. 75–76. The statement is taken from a concluding chapter by Raymond H. Muessig and Vincent R. Rogers.

and citizenship, as well as state and local government. Nevertheless, the university approach tends to let the validity of democracy as a system of government emerge from an examination of the facts, rather than from any specific indoctrination. Many disturbing conclusions about the viability of the democratic process can be and are presented to college students.

Below the college level, citizenship education is vital, but it is undertaken differently. It is not appropriate to present elementary and even secondary school children with all of the "facts" of political science as they have been recently developed. Students at these levels cannot be expected to analyze the complex facets of the subject. We might not want to suggest to certain groups of students, for example, that non-voters may perform a very important function in a democracy, a conclusion that is tenable but difficult to understand. At lower educational levels we have to explain the democratic process, and recognize the importance of teaching patriotism and loyalty, stemming from a need for what has been called "political socialization" (transmitting the values of the political system to citizens).

Philosophers from Plato and Aristole to the present have been concerned with the role of education in a political system, and have supported the idea that it is necessary for any political system to inculcate its values in young people if it is to survive. This is an entirely proper and necessary undertaking with which there would be little disagreement. *How* this is to take place may be a matter of debate, but all would support the notion that young people must be taught or somehow given respect for the institutions of our constitutional democracy. At the university and college level, once such an inculcation of values has succeeded, we must then move on to analyze more candidly some of the deficiencies and problems of democracy with a view to improving it. At this higher level, it is entirely appropriate to study communism, totalitarian systems, and many other forms of government with a far more objective eye than at the secondary and elementary levels.

All of these considerations are important in any attempt to analyze the relevance of recent developments in political science to elementary and secondary education. We can treat political science in two ways in this regard. First, we can note what information has been gained from recent research, and this may be used as an aid to teachers. On the other hand, there may be developments of use to students. How to use information, of course, will have to be left to the discretion of those who are actually engaged in teaching.

It should always be kept in mind that political science is a fairly sophisticated discipline and deals realistically with matters that might better be treated less candidly at lower levels. This will depend upon the caliber of students with which one is dealing, whether or not they are going on to university and graduate levels of education, and a variety of other factors. Political science has not conclusively been able to explain the nature and success or lack of it of our political system or of other systems, and it is important that both teachers and students recognize that studies in political science suggest only tentative conclusions for the most part. This is particularly difficult, of course, for the indiscriminate student to realize.

Recent Developments and Research

Political science today roams very widely. Scholars study all aspects of American government—the workings of the legislative, executive, and judicial branches; the role of political parties, elections, and the nature of voting behavior; state and local government, problems of federalism, and so forth. Apart from this, attention is focused upon the international arena with international relations, defense policies, international organization and law being at the center of attention. Comparative government deals with such problems as the factors determining stability or instability in emerging states, as well as with problems of supranational authority such as the European Coal and Steel Community and other aspects of foreign governments. Political theory includes large doses of sociology, psychology, and related disciplines. Because of space limitations, the best way to cover some of the more important recent developments in political science is to discuss generally a few key books that present significant research findings or contain new ideas.

The nature of "political socialization"—that is, the way in which attitudes towards the political system are developed and transferred —is the subject of several recent and important studies. How do people learn political attitudes? What effect does the learning process have upon their support of a democratic or other political system? In other words, how is "political socialization" connected with the political system? In the well known book by Gabriel A. Almond and Sidney Verba, *The Civic Culture* (Princeton: Princeton University Press, 1963; Boston: Little, Brown and Company, 1965, paperback edition), it is suggested that there is a direct connection between the way in which attitudes are learned and the support of democracy.

The Civic Culture contains an analysis of the attitudes of a cross section of the people of five countries—the United States, Great

Britain, Germany, Italy, and Mexico. The purpose of this study was to find out the connection between political and social attitudes on the one hand, and the effectiveness and stability of the democratic process on the other. Questions were designed to determine exactly how citizens felt about their government, and the political system generally. Did they think that they could influence local and national government? Did they actually attempt to exert influence upon government officials and governmental policies? Did they view partisan activities favorably? Did they feel a sense of participation in national affairs? Did they feel that they would be treated fairly by the governmental bureaucracy? These and many other questions were designed to determine whether or not there was a "civic culture"—that is, a culture which supports the democratic process by fostering favorable attitudes towards political participation, trust in the government, in political elites, and in people generally.

In this cross-cultural review of attitudes it was found, for example, that individuals in the United States consistently feel they have had more influence in family decisions, more freedom to participate in school discussions and debate, and that they have been consulted about job decisions more frequently, than people in countries such as Italy, Germany, and Mexico. Somewhat surprisingly, respondents in the United States felt a greater sense of identification with school, job, and family than did those interviewed in Great Britain. This comparative study comes to a tentative conclusion that those who are socialized toward greater participation in the nonpolitical areas of life are more likely to feel that they are able to participate in politics and influence governmental decision-making.

The final conclusions of this important study, although they cannot be stated fully here, bear very directly upon secondary and elementary school political science courses. The authors point out that:

> The civic culture is not the political culture that one finds described in civics textbooks, which prescribe the way in which citizens ought to act in a democracy. The norms of citizen behavior found in these texts stress the participant aspect of political culture. The democratic citizen is expected to be active in politics and to be involved. Furthermore, he is supposed to be rational in his approach to politics, guided by reason, not by emotion. He is supposed to be well informed and to make decisions—for instance, his decision on how to vote—on the basis of careful calculation as to the interests and the principles he would like to see furthered. This culture, with its stress on rational participation within the input structures of politics, we can label the "rationality-activist" model of political culture. The civic culture shares much with this

rationality-activist model; it is in fact such a culture *plus something else.* It does stress the participation of individuals in the political input process.[2]

What must be added to political participation in order to enable a civic culture—that is, one which supports the democratic process —to exist? There are many things, but one of the most important is a division of labor, a recognition that government must in many important respects be left to a circulating elite, but at the same time there must also exist a feeling that influence can be exerted, and that those in the government can ultimately be held to account for their actions. Another important ingredient of the civic culture, according to Almond and Verba, is trust of the elite. There must be a feeling that the government will deal fairly with citizens, and generally handle political matters well in terms of the interests of the community. It is important that the myth of participation be maintained and that people feel they can influence political events, even though this may not in fact be entirely the case. The information contained in *The Civic Culture* should provide a very good basis for class discussion at a very advanced level among discriminating students. It is, however, of primary value for teachers to gain a perspective on the subject of political science and new approaches of systematic comparative analysis.

A book of particular interest to teachers will be *Children and Politics,* by Fred I. Greenstein (New Haven: Yale University Press, 1965). This book attempts to analyze the way in which children learn about politics, and the way in which early "political socialization" occurs. The study is based upon an analysis of New Haven school children in grades 4–8, representing different socio-economic backgrounds and reflecting a cross section of the population. Among the conclusions reached, teachers and school principals will be interested to find that when asked what role is "most important," 80 per cent of the fourth-grade children interviewed picked the President of the United States, whereas "school teacher" was listed by 35 per cent of the sample, and 22 per cent selected the role of school principal. This reflects the very benign attitude that, not only fourth-grade, but other grades of children held toward the great institution of the American Presidency.

In many respects the conclusions of the study are not surprising, pointing out that children of these ages have a very limited knowledge of the political system. Their awareness extends to the

---

[2] *The Civic Culture,* paperback edition, pp. 29–30.

Presidency, the mayor of their city, and local more than state government. Knowledge of partisan politics tends to be totally absent. What feelings are expressed more often than not reflect the family attitude, and depend upon the extent to which there is political discussion at home. The differences in political participation that show up later in life between those of higher and lower socio-economic status are not apparent by the eighth grade, for roughly the same number of children from these two groups reflected a desire to participate in politics. This book will certainly provide interesting insights into the political attitudes of fourth-through eighth-grade students, and may give teachers some new ideas on how to enliven the subject of political science in the classroom at these levels. The questionnaire that was used is included in an appendix of the book.

One of the most interesting developments of the last decade in political science has been the expansion of the Survey Research Center of the University of Michigan, which has conducted a series of systematic surveys of electoral behavior from which new conclusions have been reached regarding the role of voters and the significance of elections within the democratic political process. The results of many of these surveys are analyzed in V. O. Key's book, *Public Opinion and American Democracy* (New York: Alfred A. Knopf, 1961).[3] This is a book that should be read by all who are concerned with American government and the relationship between public opinion and policy formation. Key goes into the question of the extent to which pressure groups, political parties, and other organs of public opinion actually influence the decision-making process. He also discusses the way in which public opinion is formed dealing with the mass media and the educational system, as well as the impact upon the public of pressure groups and political parties.

Key's conclusions generally support Almond's thesis that democratic process cannot rely completely upon active voters. Excessive activism is an unnatural situation which tends often to produce or reflect tension rather than a healthy political environment. Public opinion in relation to public policy is more often than not very vague, and the interaction of pressure groups and parties with the governmental process often revolves around the elites of interest groups along with the elites of the bureaucracy and other decision-entities of "the people" on the one hand, and "the government" on

---

[3] See also Angus Campbell, Philip E. Converse, Warren E. Miller, and Donald E. Stokes, *The American Voter*. New York: Wiley, Sons, 1960.

the other. The power of elites does not mean that the democratic process is not healthy, but only reflects the nature of electoral and political behavior about which very little can be done.

Unlike Almond, who was concerned with a broad "civic culture," Key deals more with the governmental process and agencies that directly or indirectly influence it. He demonstrates that the relationship between public opinion and government is very nebulous indeed, and results in a tremendous amount of discretion being left in the hands of political decision makers. Governmental perception of public opinion may actually be more important than public opinion itself, although it is often difficult for Congressmen or bureaucrats to perceive a general public opinion, regardless of their frequent statements to the contrary. General popular mandates simply do not exist in most areas of public policy, and, as Key points out, "Even if mass opinion assumes forms incompatible with a national interest, the articulation between government and mass opinion is so loose that politicians enjoy a considerable range of discretion within which to exercise prudence and good sense." The opposite proposition is also true: If governmental decision-makers assume attitudes incompatible with the national interest (whatever this may be), they will, within boundaries, be able to act regardless of a public expression of opinion to the contrary. This means that we must place great trust in our government, which in fact we do (according to Almond), and that the future of the democratic process depends upon *responsible leadership* which must exist without the guidance of a clearly articulated public opinion.

Discussions of leadership lead to another interesting book, which reflects an important school of thought in American political science. This group holds that the separation-of-powers and checks-and-balances system has produced a "deadlock of democracy," which prevents effective democratic leadership. This thesis is well articulated in James M. Burns, *The Deadlock of Democracy* (Englewood Cliffs, N.J.: Prentice Hall, 1963). The separation of powers gives to the President and Congress separate constituencies, so that the dependency of each upon the other is reduced to a minimum. The President is not always able to act as the focal point of leadership for his party in Congress. Voters who have selected a liberal Democratic President, for example, may find him frustrated by a conservative congressional majority, just as more conservative Republicans voting for the President may find, if he is elected, a Democratic and more liberal majority in the Congress. This entire system, it is held, essentially nullifies the choice of the people.

Burns, and others of this school of thought, feel that something has to be done to strengthen the nature of our party system and make it more disciplined and able to transmit public opinion into policy through the leadership of the Presidency. Where public opinion does not exist and provide a mandate, it is necessary for the President to act as leader if our democracy is to survive. How can changes be brought about in the system? Essentially, the proposals relate to bringing the constituencies of Congress and the President closer together, and breaking the conservative grip of the machinery of Congress. Various constitutional devices can be employed for this purpose, such as electing Congress and the President every four years rather than on the basis of staggered terms as it is now done.

One of the central problems of Burns' thesis is that the very factors that give to the President an independent position in relation to Congress have actually strengthened his leadership rather than diminished it, because of the conflicting interests in the community. In other words, in the absence of the separation of powers, we would more likely have a multi-party system which would increase the present diversity of our national government. We cannot have unity at a national level unless it exists within society, and with a diversified and geographically dispersed country such as ours an independent Presidency can provide leadership in times of crisis that otherwise would be absent. General de Gaulle recognized this in France when he sought to imitate at least parts of the presidential system in the Fifth Republic to create an independent institution that could provide leadership in a very dispersed political community.

Recent political science, in addition to these general and important studies, has also provided insights into other aspects of American government. It would be impossible here to list all of the recent literature, but perhaps a few key books will serve to provide a basis for further reading. Beginning with the Presidency, there is very little that has been said that adds to the material of Clinton Rossiter, *The American Presidency* (New York: Harcourt, Brace, 1960) and Richard Neustadt, *Presidential Power* (New York: John Wiley, 1960), but a different dimension is discussed in Aaron Wildavsky, *The Politics of the Budgetary Process* (Boston: Little, Brown, 1964), which deals with the Presidency and the Bureau of the Budget along with other elements in the budgetary process, including congressional committees. Because of the highly personal nature of the Presidency, much of the scholarship in the area has been historical, for the institution does not lend itself to the kind of survey research analysis done on voters and other groups.

Turning to Congress, one of the most important recent works is that of Charles L. Clapp, *The Congressman: His Work as He Sees*

It (Washington, D.C.: The Brookings Institution, 1963). Clapp presents an insider's view of the workings of Congress, and covers the attitudes of Congressmen concerning their role in government, and the way in which they formulate legislation and deal with constituent grievances. Much direct quotation from the Congressmen themselves is included, and there is even a section on the wives of Congressmen and the difficulties and problems that they face. Another work on Congress is that of Lewis Froman, *Congressmen and Their Constituencies* (Chicago: Rand McNally, 1963). This is a book that deals, as the title implies, with constituency influence upon Congress and the nature of congressional constituencies generally. It presents the results of a variety of behavioral surveys. A more general work on Congress that contains the views of many is that of Robert L. Peabody and Nelson W. Polsby, *New Perspectives on the House of Representatives* (Chicago: Rand McNally, 1963). This book consists of articles and selections dealing with Congress, and is particularly useful for an understanding of the literature of the field.

With respect to the judicial process, readers might take particular note of John P. Roche, *Courts and Rights* (New York: Random House, 1961; second edition, 1966), which is both a general analysis of the nature of the judicial process and an examination of the important areas of civil liberties and civil rights. The current controversy over the activism of the Supreme Court stems from its opinions in many fields, including legislative apportionment. These are summarized in Howard E. Hamilton, *Legislative Apportionment* (New York: Harper and Row, 1964), which also contains a general analysis of the area of apportionment.

Finally, the effects of the emergence of the federal bureaucracy upon our constitutional democracy are analyzed in my own book entitled, *American Bureaucracy* (New York: W. W. Norton, 1963), and a variety of selections from important current research relating to all fields of American government are included in my *American Government: Readings and Cases* (second edition, Little, Brown, 1965). Much of the current research has been published in article form in scholarly journals, and these are included in the latter work.

Hopefully, the preceding remarks and suggestions for reading will be helpful to teachers in their attempts to relate the discipline of political science to the classroom. Nothing is more important than that the future citizen understand and appreciate our political system, even though he may not wholly participate in it. Of course, participation should always be encouraged, and citizens should always feel that they can potentially influence the course of government. This is a necessity for a healthy democratic process.

THE DILEMMA OF HISTORY IN THE ELEMENTARY SCHOOL: PRODUCT OR PROCESS? *

Ambrose A. Clegg Jr., and
Carl E. Schomburg

What is history? Why study it in the elementary school? This is the dilemma that faces anyone who examines the role of social studies in the elementary school curriculum.

History has been defined as an inquiry into the past with a view toward a better understanding of the present. While a historian may pursue his inquiry and investigation of the past solely for the development of scholarly knowledge, the role of history in the elementary school curriculum has often been quite different. Typically history has been looked on as an essential element in training for citizenship. A well-informed citizen, it has been argued, needs to know the background of his own cultural heritage, its myths and heroes, in order to make effective decisions about the present and future.

Traditionally, history has been the mainstay of the social studies curriculum in the elementary school. Such early books as Peter Parley's *History of the United States* (1828), helped to transmit the national heritage during the early years of our independence.[1] The McGuffey *Eclectic Readers* helped to build a background of legends, myths, and heroes of both the ancient and modern world as well as to give training in the 3 R's. As years passed during the middle of the nineteenth century, history began to share its place in the elementary school curriculum with geography, civics, and more recently with economics, sociology, and anthropology.

Lawmakers apparently believed that a knowledge of our history was necessary for elementary school children for effective citizenship. State legislatures, past and present, have mandated the

Ambrose A. Clegg, Jr., is Visiting Associate Professor of Education at the University of Washington, Seattle; Carl E. Schomburg is Coordinator of Elementary Education at the University of Houston, Texas.

* Reprinted from *Social Education* 32:454–456 ff., 1968, with permission of the National Council for the Social Studies and Ambrose A. Clegg, Jr., and Carl E. Schomburg.

[1] Edgar Knight has noted that one history of the United States and three of New England had appeared by 1821, and that during the next decade eleven histories of the United States and three state histories had been published. *Education in the United States*, 2nd ed. Boston: Ginn, 1941.

teaching of state and national history and the celebration of a number of national holidays such as Washington's and Lincoln's birthdays, Memorial Day, Labor Day, Veterans' Day, as well as local holidays such as Independence Day in Texas, Patriot's Day in Massachusetts, Admission Day in California, and Huey P. Long's birthday in Louisiana. As early as 1827, Massachusetts required the teaching of American history in all towns of more than five hundred families,[2] and today every state requires that it be taught in the elementary and secondary schools.[3] While this legislative requirement has probably preserved the identity of immigrant groups and promoted sectional and class interests in some parts of the country, it has also helped to develop an awareness and pride in the national consciousness.

Today the history of one's state or region is often taught in the fourth grade, usually with strong emphasis on the state's early origins, first settlers, and the development of local institutions. American history is usually taught in the fifth grade as a chronological survey from the early explorers to the present. In some cases, this may be combined with geography of the various regions of the nation. The sixth grade usually combines a broadly based study of the ancient world as a background for Western civilization. These practices find their rationale and place in the curriculum as part of the familiar K-6 expanding environment approach to the study of man and his society.

It is interesting to note, however, that while the expanding environment approach proceeds on a sound logical and psychological basis from the familiar to the unknown, from the simple to the complex, there appears to be little justification, apart from tradition or legislative mandate, for the largely chronological organization or grade placement of the historical narrative of American history.

Indeed, there is considerable evidence to suggest that from the point of view of psychology of learning and child growth and development patterns, that the persistent emphasis on chronological order is misplaced. In that sense, history does not belong in the elementary school. But there are ways that history can focus on the "now and then" in the elementary school that are both psychologically and academically sound. We shall return to these later.

---

[2] Richard E. Gross and W. V. Badger, "Social Studies," in *Encyclopedia of Educational Research*, 3rd ed., 1960, p. 1297.

[3] William H. Cartwright, "Selection, Organization, Presentation, and Placement of Subject Matter in American History." *Social Education* 29:435–444, 1965.

Some Basic Issues and Problems

The current ferment in the entire social studies field, K-12, has helped crystallize a number of major issues and problems regarding the role of history in the elementary school curriculum. These concern: (a) the relation between history and the social sciences, (b) curriculum goals, (c) methodology, (d) lack of a theoretical basis in learning theory, and (e) history as an inquiry process. Let us now turn to each of these and discuss them in some detail.

There has been much concern in recent years about the relation between history and the social sciences. Curriculum revision has focused on the identification of important concepts and generalizations from the various disciplines, and the nature of a fundamental structure presumed to underlie each. Yet historians are inclined to claim that history has no universal concepts, no underlying structure as do the social sciences; rather, there may be many competing structures. More often, historians tend to refer to history as one of the humanities and also a social science. Mark Krug,[4] for example, refers to it as a social science because it uses a carefully disciplined method of inquiry. But he also claimed it was a humanity because its final conclusions were intuitive and highly individual; they belong to the world of art.

> When history is written in the grand tradition of a literary narrative, it becomes important not only as a scientific record of a segment of the past, but also as an artistic and aesthetic experience. Thus, history is also a branch of literature and belongs not only to the social sciences, but to the humanities.[5]

If this is true, it raises serious questions about history in a conceptually oriented curriculum modeled after the mode of inquiry of the social sciences.

A second basic issue is the relationship of history to major curriculum goals. Is the nature and intrinsic value of history and its subject matter of such importance that it should be studied primarily for itself in the sense of a separate scholarly discipline? Or is it in some way more directly related to the developmental needs of youth, to persistent social problems, to concepts of social change,

---

[4] Mark Krug, "History and the Social Sciences: The Narrowing Gap." *Social Education* *29*:515–520, 1965. See also Krug's address, "New Concepts and Approaches to Social Studies—Implications for Teacher Education," presented at the National Council for the Social Studies Convention, Seattle, Washington, November 22, 1967, in which he discussed this issue at some length.
[5] *Ibid.*

or to the modern demands of citizenship? All of these have been posed at various times as appropriate philosophic criteria for the selection and organization of the curriculum. As we noted at the beginning of this article, the often professed purpose of history is its assumed relationship to the task of training for citizenship. Yet the teaching of it continues to be, for the most part, the recitation of the narrative of the American past with little or no connection with the current or the future tasks expected of the citizen. This is the essence of Professor Anthony's [6] objections to many of the new social studies programs. And similarly it is the lack of relevance that Shaver refers to when he calls for a redefinition of social studies.[7]

A third issue involves the methodology of teaching. Currently there is considerable interest in the use of inductive or inquiry teaching, the use of original source materials, and "the tools and methods of the historian." In contrast, the deductive method often depends on the synthesis of previous work of scholars, Professor Fenton's [8] recently developed material in the use of the inquiry method appears to give promise as a useful technique for the study of history. So also does the current work by Kounslar and Frizzle [9] at the junior high school level. What is critically needed in addition are well-designed research programs that carefully test out the assumptions implied in those teaching methods that involve inductive or deductive modes of thinking.

Another major issue concerns the failure to relate learning theory more closely to the methods presently advocated in the teaching of social studies. The terms "problem solving" and "reflective thinking" have been too cosmic. They need to be defined much more precisely in behavioral terms and at the bits and pieces level of day-to-day operation so that clearly defined teaching strategies can be developed and managed by the classroom teacher. In this respect, Taba's [10] identification of three cognitive tasks gives much clearer

[6] Albert S. Anthony, "The Role of Objectives in the 'New History'." *Social Education 31*:574–580, 1967.

[7] James P. Shaver, "Social Studies: The Need for Redefinition." *Social Education 31*:588–592, 596, 1967.

[8] Edwin Fenton, general ed., *Holt Social Studies Curriculum.* New York: Holt, Rinehart & Winston, 1966. See also programs as *Comparative Political Systems, Comparative Economic Systems, Shaping Western Society, History of the United States,* all of which are based on an inductive approach.

[9] Allan O. Kounslar and Donald B. Frizzle, *Discovering American History.* New York: Holt, Rinehart & Winston, 1967.

[10] Hilda Taba, *Teaching Strategies and Cognitive Functioning in Elementary School Children.* U.S. Office of Education, Cooperative Research Project No. 2404. San Francisco State College, February, 1966.

direction to the classroom teacher than do many of the more classic statements on problem solving.

Neither Inquiry nor a Disciplined Study

The irony of all this is that what passes for history as taught in the elementary school is neither inquiry nor a disciplined study. What we may call "school-book history" tends to focus on the *product* of the historian, not the *process* of an inquiry into the past, disciplined by a rigorous method of investigation. What we also overlook is that the product of the historian's efforts is *an* interpretation of the material. We conveniently ignore the fact, too, that there may be varying and conflicting interpretations of the same data. Unfortunately, the historian's original scholarship and interpretive comment are often three or four times removed from the distillations that appear in the elementary school social studies texts. Somehow in the translation process we have lost sight of the assumptions, the biases, the perspective, and the tentativeness of the original in an effort to emphasize the narrative of the agreed upon facts. Thus we have clothed history with far more certitude than the historian ever intended. As a result, school-book history tends to be the approved recorded narrative of the past. In the terms of the anthropologist, history in the elementary school consists largely of passing down the myths and legends of our national heritage as part of the initiation of youth into the culture of the society.

The Process of "Historying"

As we have suggested above, history is not only a product, it is also a *process*. It implies the act of "inquiry" in the same way that "inquiry" is so much a part of modern curriculum developments in the natural sciences.[11] To express this in the sense of the verb, we have to resort to such awkward phrases as *doing* history, or *historying*. It is an activity, a process, not a passive absorption of someone else's account. Pupils are expected to work actively with the materials of history.

The relics or residue of the past constitute the materials of history. These may be such primary or original sources as artifacts,

---

[11] J. Richard Suchman, *The Elementary School Training Program in Scientific Inquiry*. U.S. Office of Education Title VII, Project No. 216. University of Illinois, January, 1964.

records, documents, diaries, newspapers, or pictures of past events. Other useful sources are the many available secondhand accounts of those who have talked to eyewitnesses, and the records of the remembered stories of others. Also included are the narratives of those who wrote the "history" of a contemporary period, for example Herodotus's account of Greece in his day, or a current figure such as Arthur Schlesinger, Jr., who has recently provided both an eyewitness account and an interpretation of the Kennedy administration.

"History Is What the Historians Do" [12]

The process of doing history or historying [13] involves both the activity of inquiring and the use of a carefully disciplined approach to the selection, analysis, and interpretation of evidence. Clements [14] has outlined a basic strategy or model [15] that is applicable to history as well as to any social inquiry. It includes such tasks as (1) identifying a heuristic or leading question, (2) selecting ideas or concepts that will be useful for analyzing the leading questions, (3) using the concepts to formulate propositions or hypotheses about the leading questions, (4) locating and collecting various sources of evidence, (5) cross-examining the evidence, and (6) preparing a report that presents the conclusions or interpretations of the study.

The tasks identified in Clements's model are not beyond the competency of elementary school children. Traditionally we have just not become involved in doing history as a process of inquiry in the elementary school. This is not to suggest, as some would advocate, that the schools train junior historians in the technical aspects of the craft. Rather, it is to argue as Henry Johnson [16] urged more than a quarter century ago, that children become critical students of how the historian produces his product, so that they can read and interpret history with an equally critical eye.

---

[12] Isaiah Berlin, "History and Theory, the Concept of Scientific History." *History and Theory* I, No. 1, 1960.

[13] We deliberately continue to use these concocted words to emphasize the sense of active engagement with materials of the past.

[14] Millard Clements, "The Disciplines and Social Study." *Effective Thinking in the Social Studies.* Thirty-seventh Yearbook of the National Council for the Social Studies. Washington, D.C., 1967, pp. 72–75.

[15] In an earlier work Clements referred to this as the "mystery model," comparing the process to that used by the detective in the fictional novel to solve the murder mystery. See M. Clements, W. Fielder, and R. Tabachnick, *Social Study: Inquiry in Elementary Classrooms.* Indianapolis: Bobbs-Merrill, 1966.

[16] See especially "School History and the Historical Method." *The Teaching of History*, Rev. ed. New York: Macmillan, 1940, Ch. XV.

With some relatively minor changes in our procedures teachers could easily shift the focus from learning the product to engaging in the process of historying. For example, third or fourth graders traditionally study their local community. Because ready-made texts are seldom available, teachers (1) plan field trips to important sites, (2) help children find old records in the town hall or in early newspapers, (3) arrange for the visit and interview of a long-time resident, (4) collect and organize their findings on large charts, and (5) help the children prepare a book of stories, a series of oral reports, a mural, or perhaps present a play about some dramatic episode from the town's past. If these activities are not too heavily dominated by the teacher, then it can be said that the pupils are actively engaged in doing history at a relatively simple level.

Many suggestions have been made elsewhere for actively engaging pupils in the process of inquiring about times past. Vincent Rogers [17] has suggested some interesting uses of original documents in connection with the colonization of Jamestown, the stereotype of slavery, and the rush to settle new lands in the West. Clements *et al.*[18] have presented many examples of historical inquiry in a variety of settings: ancient and modern, local and national. And in a more specialized area, Clifford Lord [19] has edited an entire series of monographs on "localized history" with individual books on every state as well as major cities, important watersheds, and the principal ethnic groups that have immigrated to this country.

The Balance Between Product and Process

As noted above, the bulk of what passes as history in the elementary school consists largely of learning the accumulated traditions of the national heritage. While recognizing the value of this knowledge as a necessary part of the socialization process, the focus of this article has been to suggest that the balance be redressed to give the process of *doing history* its appropriate place in the curriculum. The issue is not an "either-or" proposition. Rather, an appropriate balance of history as both a product *and* a process needs to be established in the elementary social studies curriculum.

---

[17] Vincent Rogers, "Using Source Material with Children." *Social Education* 24:307–309, 1960.

[18] Clements, *op. cit.*

[19] Clifford Lord, ed., *Localized History Series*. New York: Teachers College Press, Columbia University, 1964.

Summary

This article has examined the role of history in the elementary school in terms of the dilemma of product or process. The product of the historian's work was seen to be of value in that it served to acquaint the pupils with the past traditions of the nation, its legends, and its heroes. On the other hand, the pupil develops a false and misleading sense of certainty and truth in the highly distilled and antiseptically neutral account of the agreed upon facts that he reads in some school textbooks. To redress the balance between product and process and to nourish the spirit of intellectual inquiry, Clements's model was suggested as a useful strategy for actively engaging pupils in the process of doing history, using the materials and the methods of the historian at an elementary level.

ANTHROPOLOGY FOR PUBLIC SCHOOLS: PROFITS AND PITFALLS *

Joseph A. Francello

Within the social sciences, probably no one discipline has received the attention of late as has the field of anthropology. This attention has come from educators, students, and the public in general. The latest pronouncements of Margaret Mead on American teen-age problems, anthropological field work in New Guinea, East Africa, and the Near East, are reported speedily and voluminously in the mass media. On college campuses throughout the entire United States, courses in anthropology attract greater and greater numbers.

It is not surprising, therefore, that among educators the question of how anthropology could be incorporated into the public school curriculum receives more and more attention. Does the anthropological approach promise a new and better understanding of man's long and difficult path through the ages? Can the public schools profit by the addition into the curriculum of courses utilizing the insights and techniques of the anthropologist?

Joseph A. Francello is on the faculty at Edinboro State College, Edinboro, Pennsylvania.

* Reprinted from *The Social Studies* 55:272–275, 1965, with permission of the McKinley Publishing Co. and Joseph A. Francello.

Before attempting to answer these questions, it would be advisable to arrive at some understanding as to what anthropology is about.

By simple definition, anthropology is the study of man in accordance with the recognized principles and techniques of the scientific method. It is *both* a natural and social science in that the anthropologist is interested in man as a physical being as well as man as a social being. Man, the physical specimen, is the primary interest of the physical anthropologist while man, the social animal, is of primary interest to the cultural anthropologist.

The main concern of the cultural anthropologist is the behavior of man as he responds to those values and attitudes which his culture makes known to him. With the exception of those basic drives which originate out of man's needs as an organism, all of man's behavior is learned. Behavior traits taken as an integrated whole and identified with a specific group of people form what the anthropologist refers to as culture.

In what way can the public schools profit by the work of the anthropologist? I believe there are both profits and pitfalls in attempting to relate this to the social studies curriculum of the public schools.

Among the profits, I see seven worthwhile contributions which anthropology can make:

1. Clearing up the concept of race—one has only to pick up a newspaper to see the timeliness of such a contribution. Race is something about which Americans can well stand clarification.

Anthropology offers scientific evidence that race is a valid *biological concept* but is invalid as a *socio-cultural concept*. Heredity bestows certain physical characteristics such as skin pigmentation, body type, hair covering, facial features, and stature which are used as criteria for classification into racial categories. The racial concept is not a valid one when applied to cultural considerations, however, because all races have the potential to develop any set of behavior patterns. All races are equal in their capacity to learn and to profit from this learning—if they so choose. There is no scientific proof that any race is superior to another.

2. Repudiation of "instinctive behavior" and "human nature" as explanations for human behavior.

The anthropologist rejects the concept of instincts, believes instead that man has three basic biological drives to satisfy his need for food, protection, and reproduction. How man goes about satisfying these drives comes as a result of learned behavior. It is through learned behavior that we know what to eat, what clothing we should wear, the kind of shelter we wish to live in, what kind of marriage our society considers desirable, proper behavior toward other mortals and correct behavior toward the gods or god. Man's behavior is not a result of "human nature" which is the same the world over and which we must passively accept as inevitable. Rather, man's behavior is the result of what his particular culture defines as "human."

3. The rejection of the concept of superior and inferior cultures.

In the eyes of the anthropologist, all cultures are equal. They are different due to the fact that man has learned to meet his problems in different ways. He may have chosen to emphasize certain aspects of cultural development and others not so much. For this reason some cultures, such as ours, may be advanced in the area of technology but may be experiencing a culture lag in other areas such as law, property concepts, and spiritual matters. Leaders of so-called underdeveloped areas of the world, of which Nehru would be a good example, have made it clear they want our technology but do not want our materialism, alcoholism, juvenile delinquency, high crime, and divorce rate.

4. The concept of cultural variability—this says that values, ethics, and morality are defined by the culture one lives in.

There is no absolute set of values which applies equally to all peoples in all cultures at any given time. What is considered proper behavior toward your fellow man in one culture may be highly improper in another. That which is considered immoral in one culture may scarcely raise interest in another. The actions of man must be weighed in terms of the culture within which the individual involved has been molded and which provides the basis for his behavior. The Comanche brave, who was raised in a society that looked upon horse stealing as a means of proving one's manhood, was most bewildered by the white man's determination to "hang the hoss thief" when the horse was located tied behind his tipi. There definitely was a lack of understanding of the other fellow's values in this case.

5. Greater tolerance toward other people and other ways of life —this means more than tolerance as verbalized in the American slogan.

When we say "regardless of race, creed, or color," we are usually referring to fellow Americans who have slightly different backgrounds but who nevertheless are a part of our total culture. Anthropology goes beyond this because it advances the cause of tolerance toward all peoples of the world—even those who do not want to change their way of life. That is a more profound test of tolerance than the usual American experience of dealing with various ethnic groups within our own country.

6. Better understanding of ourselves—we see that man has basically the same problems and needs and that he tries to solve them as best he can.

This can give us a better insight into why we do certain things and why we refrain from other modes of action. Our great confidence in overcoming obstacles to the production of goods causes us to leap into urban renewal projects—undertakings designed to improve the physical environment of the city. When it comes to improving the social aspect of life in the city, say in breaking the ghetto restrictions on Negro housing, we don't quite have the confidence and verve. Our culture does a much better job in providing good housing than in providing good neighbors. This has been our conditioning regarding peoples who appear "different" whether they be Negro, Oriental, Jew, or just plain foreigner.

7. Increased consistency with our role as a world leader—where we hope to inspire confidence among peoples of many different cultures.

When the United States was developing the West, it could afford to concentrate on history and especially the greatness of American history. Now that we have reached our present position of development and power, we must make a departure from our traditional approach toward other cultures. It must no longer be only a matter of pride in how we developed our greatness, but also a recognition that other peoples and cultures have equally worthy accomplishments, even though some aspects of their cultures might be primitive by our standards.

The benefits to be derived from the use of anthropological insights and techniques in the public school curriculum should not lull us into thinking, however, that we have discovered a panacea which will take care of all the ills which afflict the social studies program. I feel there are a number of serious hazards and pitfalls which raise questions that must be thought out carefully before attempted implementation of such a program.

Five major pitfalls which could bring about disastrous consequences if not anticipated properly and if steps are not taken to ameliorate their effect are:

1. Others are strange; too bad that they are missing so much not being more like us—an easy attitude to acquire and one which is evident in social studies classrooms in too many instances already.

The introduction of anthropological subject matter could make this condition worse unless competent and skillful guidance on the part of the teacher kept this within bounds.

2. We are more complex, hence we must be superior—an understandable conclusion for an American to arrive at in view of the emphasis we place on things being "bigger and better."

The concept of proceeding from a simple stage to a complex one may be interpreted by the student as going from the inferior to the superior. The values of our culture place greater worth on the complex in comparison to the simple. The industrial revolution has conditioned us to regard items which include many operations in their manufacture as having greater value than those which have only one or a few operations connected with their production.

3. They are technologically backward; therefore they are backward in everything.

This was an error made by the early anthropologists of 19th century Europe who considered non-Europeans as basically inferior due to their lack of industrialization. This is also an error made by American tourists today who judge the worth of a country by how close it comes to our own standards. The teacher who attempts to reverse this trend will have his work cut out for him as the students will reflect the emphasis which American culture places on technology and material goods.

4. This is a "snap" course—students think anyone can pass it and administrators think anyone can teach it.

Only teachers with a good background in the social sciences and course work in sociology and anthropology should teach courses utilizing the anthropological approach. This will help safeguard against the abuses of the easy-to-pass course taught by whatever teacher had that hour open on the schedule.

5. Community taboos regarding certain areas of human behavior —sensitivity toward certain topics which could inflame public opinion and bring down the wrath of the good citizenry upon the teacher. From a realistic standpoint, will it be possible then to cover certain aspects of human relationships which are an integral part of anthropological study? One had better know his community!

The community in which you teach may be reacting to some specific social problem which has spread alarm and anxiety among the citizenry. For example, there may be great concern about contemporary morality and, as is always the case, it is supposed to be degenerating. How will you handle such topics as Samoan premarital sexual relations or Eskimo wife-borrowing? If the community is extra-sensitive to the dangers and challenges of the cold war, how will you handle collective ownership of property as it exists among many primitive peoples? In the face of problems connected with juvenile delinquency, how will you handle the acceptance of private law with its emphasis on individual revenge which is the concept of law in many primitive societies?

As is true in so many problems in education, there is no simple solution. Anthropology all by itself cannot save the world or even social studies. Anyone grasping at it as an all-purpose cure-all is due for disappointment. Its advantages must be carefully appraised, caution observed regarding potential dangers and limitations, and highly qualified and motivated people given a chance to test its potentialities in the classroom. All by itself, no,—but as one important facet contributing to a better understanding and tolerance of other people and other cultures, anthropology can be a mother lode of opportunity.

GUIDELINES FOR INCORPORATING ECONOMICS IN THE INTERMEDIATE GRADES *

Lorraine H. Scheer and Vincent Patrick

Economics offers a way of deciding the relative merits of alternative action. In short, it equips a child for orderly thinking about ways to satisfy his wants by the use of scarce resources which have many uses. The world is governed by economic laws and the sooner a child is taught the simple grasp of certain helpful funda-

Lorraine H. Scheer is on the faculty at the University of Tulsa, Oklahoma; Vincent Patrick is Coordinator of the Economic Education for Tulsa Public Schools.

* Reprinted from *Social Education* 30:256–258, 1966, with permission of the National Council for the Social Studies and Lorraine H. Scheer and Vincent Patrick.

mentals about these laws, the sooner he is prepared to conduct his own life wisely.

The purpose of this article is to set forth guidelines which will enable a teacher to include economic concepts in the intermediate grades. The authors do not propose that economics at this level should be taught as a new subject, but rather as a new dimension of the social studies. Economics fits naturally into the already established curriculum, and intermediate-grade pupils readily learn economic concepts.

The ideal situation would be to have full administrative support; to have each intermediate-grade teacher well-versed in economics; and to have social studies textbooks stressing economic concepts. Unfortunately, this ideal is presently unattainable. In too many of the schools, the administration prefers to have its teachers avoid this subject as it is "too controversial." Too many of the intermediate-grade teachers have had little, if any, formal training in economics, and social studies textbooks too often stress history, physical and political geography, and citizenship. Economics is not even mentioned in passing.

Within this setting, how can intermediate-grade teachers include economics in their curriculum?

The reason the study of economics is considered to be controversial is that economic "viewpoints" are often confused with economic principles or relationships. For example, in developing economic understandings related to income, a teacher in a working-class district may seem to overstress management's viewpoint in a current wage dispute; or a teacher in an upper socio-economic area may seem to overstress labor's point of view. In either situation she risks trouble, for she has expressed a "viewpoint" rather than an economic principle, and a viewpoint to which the immediate community is unsympathetic.

Economics does not consist of a set of pat answers to a problem. It is a body of concepts and working relationships. For example, the heavier the tax burden imposed on society for government services, the less income there is available for private spending; the greater the degree of specialization, the higher the level of production will tend to be; as the price of a good or service goes up, sales tend to go down. Rather than teaching viewpoints, the teacher of economic concepts should stress rational, objective thinking—an understanding of cause-and-effect relationships. When economics is taught in this framework, the school administration need have little fear of the subject being "too controversial."

To overcome the lack of economic materials developed for the intermediate grades, the following suggestions are offered.

Integrate economics with other materials. Although it is acknowledged that economics may be more effectively taugh as a separate subject, the authors also realize the time limitations which may make this impossible for both the student and the teacher. Today the introduction of another new subject is almost impossible in an already crowded curriculum. However, much of the social studies materials currently studied is rich in economic content. The economic concepts need only to be crystallized. For example, as students study the migration of people westward—a popular social studies unit—the concepts of scarcity, specialization, factors of production, enterprise, profit, and opportunity costs can be introduced.

In planning an economics program, teachers may want to use materials which are familiar to them, but, at the same time, add emphasis to the new dimension—economics.

Define economic concepts. Before attempting to include economics in classroom material, determine the economic concepts which are to be emphasized and the understandings the child should associate with each concept.

A concept is an abstract idea which is understood within the experience of the child. As the child's level of learning deepens, the understandings associated with the concept also expand. For example, using the concept of *money*, a fourth-grade level of understanding is:

> In an exchange society, money is necessary. Barter just will not work.
> Anything can be used for money if it is acceptable as a medium of exchange and has a high degree of scarcity.

At the fifth grade, the concept of money can be reintroduced, but the understandings associated with the concept are broadened.

> By the use of a fractional reserve system, banks create money.
> When banks issue a loan, money is created. When the loan is completely paid, money is destroyed.

As the child's knowledge of the history of the United States increases, the concept of money can be further expanded.

> There is a relationship between the money supply and prices. As the money supply increases, prices may go up. As the money supply decreases, prices may go down.

Methods of defining concepts. One way of clarifying economic concepts and understandings currently used in intermediate-grade material is to have the material reviewed by economists.[1] As stated earlier, many social studies units are rich in economic content. However, since most teachers are not aware of the economic content, it is rarely stressed or even mentioned. Economists can crystallize the economic concepts and understandings in the materials presented.

Once the concepts and understandings are clarified, then an educator—either a teacher, supervisor, or a committee—should determine the appropriate grade level at which the concepts can be introduced. Here, then, economists and educators work together as a team, complementing one another. Economists, skilled in economic knowledge, determine the concepts which appear in the present curriculum content. Educators, skilled in the knowledge of how children learn, determine the child's depth of understanding and suggest appropriate learning activities.

But what if an economist is not available for such services? In this situation, make use of the many materials which have already been developed by various organizations and individuals.[2] These materials set forth economic concepts and understandings with suggestions for the appropriate grade level.

Limit scope of study. Economics is a broad discipline. In integrating economics into the intermediate grades, do not attempt to each all there is to learn about the entire field. This would be a herculean feat. However, the basic structure of the economy, in its entirety, can be presented with increasing complexity and depth

---

[1] For economic concepts used in intermediate grade materials, see *Adventure in Learning, A Tentative Course of Study for Grade Five*, Tulsa, Okla.: Tulsa Public Schools, 1965. Also see Vincent Patrick and Lorraine Scheer, "Review of Elementary Textbooks, in the Primary Grades," Tulsa, Okla.: Tulsa Public Schools, 1965. (Mimeographed)

[2] See James D. Calderwood, *Developmental Economic Education Program: Part I, Economic Ideas and Concepts* and *Developmental Economic Education Program;* and *Part II, Suggestions for Grade Placement and Development of Economic Ideas and Concepts*, New York: Joint Council on Economic Education, 1964. Also Rudolph Trenton, "Handbooks of Economic Information Related to the Tiegs-Adams Social Studies Series, Grades Four to Six," Stillwater, Okla.: Oklahoma Council on Economic Education; "A Few Economic Understandings," Tulsa, Okla.: Tulsa Public Schools, Social Studies Office, 1965 (mimeographed); "Economic Education Supplement to Teaching Guide for Social Studies, Health and Safety Education, and Tentative Guide for Science, Grades Four to Six," Austin, Texas: Austin Independent School District, 1960; "Preliminary Scope and Sequence Materials," Seattle, Wash.: Seattle Public Schools; "Economic Education, A Project in Pinellas County Schools," Pinellas Park, Fla.: Pinellas County Schools; J. F. Barron and Marilyn L. Hoff, *Some Concepts Essential to a Basic Understanding of Economics*, Monograph 110, Chicago: Southwestern Publishing Company, 1964; *Suggested Procedures and Resources for a Minimum Course in Economics*, Curriculum Development Series No. 4, Harrisburg, Pa.: Department of Public Instruction, 1962.

as the child moves toward maturity. After defining the economic concepts and understandings to be introduced at each grade level, it is best to develop learning activities within the learning abilities of the student.

For example, an intermediate-grade child can understand the concept of international trade as the exchange of money, goods, and services between countries. He can also grasp the idea that the value of the American dollar is not necessarily the same as the value of the Canadian dollar.[3] However, at this level of learning, the child should not be introduced to theoretical intricacies of international trade beyond his scope of comprehension. Teachers should present ideas which the child can grasp at his level of understanding. Economics should not be made dismal and dull by an attempt to teach the entire complexities of the discipline in one year.

Teach concepts. In teaching economics, too often institutions are described without clarifying the abstract idea underlying them. It is important to teach the *why* as well as the *what*. The fifth-grader, learning the complexities of the American banking system, should also understand why banks exist as well as how they operate as financial institutions. The student should be led to understand the importance of money in an economy and the role of banks in fostering economic activity.

Simplify terminology. Economics is often described as a study of the obvious stated in incomprehensible terms. Like all other social sciences, economics has its own terminology which must be translated into the vocabulary of the intermediate-grade child. Until economic materials have been developed especially for the intermediate grades, one of the tasks of the teacher is to rephrase the technical language into simple words which the child can understand readily. For example, a ten-year-old can understand what the word *technology* means when it is rephrased as special *knowledge* or *know-how; capital goods*, as *tools*.

The more thorough the background of a teacher in any subject, the greater her confidence in her own ability and command over the intricacies of the subject; this, in turn, facilitates the task of teaching. Unfortunately, few intermediate-grade teachers have had as thorough a grounding in economics as one might desire. Teacher training, therefore, is an important element in the development of an economic program. An in-service course, conducted by economists, is one way of overcoming the lack of economic background among intermediate-grade teachers. Many such courses are now

---

[3] *Adventure in Learning, op. cit.,* pp. 83–84.

being offered by various school systems throughout the nation.[4]

Another method of developing economic background for the teachers is by the use of the "Our American Economy" films.[5] Each film might be followed by group discussions in which not only the economic content of the film is extended but the teachers might also exchange ideas as how best to implement the economic content of the film in the classroom. Here, then, is a two-pronged approach: building economic background, and developing materials simultaneously.

Until such time that economics is included in the pre-service teacher-training programs, in-service courses, workshops, and short courses must be conducted to strengthen the economic background of teachers.

All teachers at all grade levels should be prepared to impart economic knowledge to their students, who, as future adult citizens, will be able to cope with the difficult economic problems which face them. Students who have been grounded in basic economic laws and have developed an objective, rational way of thinking as well as a knowledge of fundamental economic principles will be far better prepared to arrive at solutions than their parents have been.

---

[4] During the 1964-65 school year, in-service training courses in economics were conducted by the following schools: Tulsa (Oklahoma) Public Schools; Wichita (Kansas) Public Schools; Contra Costa County Schools, Pleasanthill, California; Downey (California) Unified School District; San Diego (California) County Schools; New Haven (Connecticut) Public Schools; Atlanta (Georgia) Public Schools; Minneapolis (Minnesota) Public Schools; Omaha (Nebraska) Public Schools; Pittsburgh (Pennsylvania) Public Schools; and Seattle (Washington) Public Schools. Also, in the summer of 1965, 51 economic workshops were held at various universities throughout the nation. Inquiries regarding future workshops should be directed to the Joint Council on Economic Education, 1212 Avenue of the Americas, New York 10036.

[5] For a summary of The American Economy film series, see Harlan Smith, *Study Guide for Selected Sixty-Session of the American Economy TV Films*, New York: Joint Council on Economic Education, 1965.

THE ROLE OF HISTORICAL GEOGRAPHY
IN THE AMERICAN SCHOOL *

Daniel Jacobson

The Nature of Historical Geography

Historical geography, like other branches of the mother discipline, is concerned primarily with *place*. It attempts on the one hand to reconstruct the past geographies of particular sites or areas, on the other to trace the changes that occur on the landscape at particular places through time.[1]

Geographers in the United States have emphasized particular aspects of historical geography. They have been concerned with discerning the "stages of human occupance" of regions—that is what the late Professor Whittlesey called *sequent occupance*.[2] They have emphasized the changing scene in both rural and urban settlements and have worked on changing settlement patterns, on transportation media, on the evolution of industries. They have investigated "the historical record of man's use, alteration and rearrangement of his only potentially permanent resources: water, soil, vegetation and animal life." [3]

While these gropings seem impressive geographers have really only begun to scratch the surface. Much of the work has been fragmentary and unstructured. Much remains to be done—on the physical side of historical geography, on the growth of population and resulting changes in land utilization, on the evolution of regional landscapes. The Eastern Seaboard, for example, with a long record of research in history, shows no comparable record of research in historical geography, albeit the picture is improving.[4]

The fact of the matter is that American geographers in general

Daniel Jacobson is Director, Social Science Teaching Institute, Michigan State University, East Lansing.

* Reprinted from the *Journal of Geography* 64:99–105, 1965, with permission of the National Council for Geographic Education and Daniel Jacobson.

[1] Preston E. James and Clarence·F. Jones, eds., *American Geography Inventory and Prospect*. Syracuse, N. Y.: Syracuse University Press, 1954, p. 71.

[2] Derwent Whittlesey, "Sequent Occupance," *Annals of the Association of American Geographers 19*:162–165, 1929.

[3] James and Jones, *op. cit.*, p. 89.

[4] See Erich Isaac, "Jamestown and the Mid-Atlantic Coast: A Geographic Reconsideration." *The Journal of Geography 57*:17, 1958.

For a fine recent example, see Harry Roy Merrens, *Colonial North Carolina in the Eighteenth Century*, Chapel Hill: University of North Carolina Press, 1964.

have shown little interest in historical processes and sequences and that historical geography as such definitely lies on the fringes of the mother discipline.[5] During the past decade (1954–1964), for example, only ten percent of the articles in the *Annals of the Association of American Geographers* have been devoted to historical geography;[6] the *Geographical Review*'s percentage was even smaller—less than four percent.[7] *The Journal of Geography*, reflecting in part the lack of concern of professional geographers, devoted less than two percent of its feature articles to historical geography during the same period.[8]

Data and Methodology

Of course, the ardor of individual historical geographers has not diminished. Geographers continue to delve into old land records, newspapers, census reports and business and industrial directories. They continue to read local histories, letters, diaries, geological and geographical descriptions and travellers' accounts of particular places. They continue to consult old maps, gazetteers and almanacs and spend precious hours poring over old photographs and engravings. They go into the field to examine particular sites and areas and to see what history has left for them to see. The data, by and large, are historical; the methodology, however, is geographical.[9] Geographers use historical evidence to reconstruct the geography of the past—to trace the changes that occur on the landscape through time.

The Teaching of Historical Geography

The nature of the field, its peculiar emphases, the lack of interest shown in it by professional geographers and its methodology all have implications for the teaching of historical geography in the

---

[5] Carl O. Sauer, "Forward to Historical Geography," *Annals of the Association of American Geographers 31*:2, 1941.

The same is reproduced in John Leighly, ed., *Land and Life*, Berkeley and Los Angeles: University of California Press, 1963, p. 352.

[6] Between September, 1954, and September, 1964, 246 articles appeared in the *Annals of the Association of American Geographers;* 25 were devoted to historical geography.

[7] Between July, 1954, and July, 1964, 279 articles appeared in the *Geographical Review;* 11 were devoted to historical geography.

[8] 561 articles appeared in *The Journal of Geography* between September, 1954, and May, 1964; 11 were devoted to historical geography.

[9] H. C. Darby, "The Relations of Geography and History," in *Geography in the Twentieth Century*, Griffith Taylor, ed. New York: Philosophical Library, 1957, p. 643.

modern American school program. Equally significant, of course, are the ramifications of the learning process—particularly the readiness of school children to learn the subtle nuances of place, space and time.

But let one pause for a moment to consider the role of historical geography in the programs of schools to date. There is no real history of the teaching of historical geography in American elementary and secondary schools. History, *per se*, has long dominated the so-called social studies programs. Social studies teachers, inadequately trained in geography, have rarely been able to provide the necessary geographical dimensions in their teachings. They have certainly been unacquainted with the approach through historical geography.[10] Geography teachers, often trained by geographers who themselves cared little about historical processes, have themselves contributed little to the teaching of historical geography.

Where then does one begin? What are the values of historical geography in the school program? How early can historical geography be introduced? What are the logical sequences to be followed? What do children know and understand of place, space and time?

The Teacher

A proper beginning, perhaps, can be made with the teacher. He or she must be well trained in *both* history and geography. A full year of college work in historical geography should be mandatory. Additional work in allied fields, particularly archeology and cultural anthropology, could well be included. Teachers in the elementary grades in particular should be familiar with the psychology of the young child and the learning process. They should know much about the history and geography of their local area, and be familiar with local historical source materials. They should have a general acquaintance with the history and geography of the United States. High school teachers need an even broader training. They should know much about adolescent psychology and the learning process. They, too, should know much about the history and geography of their local area, but this should be fortified with a broad general knowledge of the entire continent. They should know enough about source materials and methods of historical and geographical research to enable them to direct small research

---

10 Phillip Bacon, "An Approach to Social Studies Through Historical Geography," in *New Viewpoints in Geography* (Twenty-Ninth Yearbook of the National Council for the Social Studies), Preston E. James, ed. Washington, D.C., 1959, pp. 144–161.

projects in the local area. The order, of course, is a tall one; but it is not one that is impossible to fill.

Why Historical Geography?

Why historical geography? Because, as Professor Bacon points out, historical geography is an "effective means of capitalizing on the child's interest in the past in combination with an opportunity to strengthen his natural ability to deal with basic spatial concepts." [11]

Today's children, unlike yesterday's, are bombarded with many stimuli from both near and far. The most immediate are not always the most stimulating. Teachers and psychologists claim that children are intensely interested and highly motivated to explore not only the "far away" but the "long ago." [12] The implications for school curricula are clear. Historical geography offers at least one opportunity to dip into the past, to test the appeal and glamour of the near and far and to teach the deep significance of what Professor Warman calls "perpetual transformation." [13]

The Tender Years

The basic themes implicit in historical geography can be handled very early in the school program—even as early as the first three grades.

> To assume that we should wait to encourage and help children to gain concepts of time and change until they can handle true chronology is to deprive children of one of the important learnings of early childhood. To defer help and encouragement in this area is to frustrate a basic intellectual need of today's young children. Adults must shuttle back and forth with children from the present to the past as they react to the ever-present urge to understand what has gone before. This dipping into the past without concern for a logical development of chronology from the past to the present does not violate basic patterns of learning.[14]

---

[11] *Ibid.*, p. 150.

[12] Kenneth D. Wann, Miriam S. Dorn, and Elizabeth A. Liddle, *Fostering Intellectual Development in Young Children*, New York: Bureau of Publications, Teachers College, Columbia University, 1962, p. 39.

[13] Henry J. Warman, "Major Concepts in Geography," in *Curriculum Guide for Geographic Education*, Wilhelmina Hill, ed. Normal, Ill.: National Council for Geographic Education, 1964, pp. 21–22.

[14] Wann, *et al., op. cit.*, p. 53.

Rather, the idea of a changing landscape might—even in these tender years—provide a framework for the further development of concepts relating to place, space and time.

A point of departure for such studies might well be the American Indians and their use of the local landscape. Teachers might seek answers to the following questions: What was the local area like prior to its discovery by Europeans? Who were the Indians? How many were there? How did they earn their livelihood? What kind of houses did they build? What type of settlement pattern did they establish? How did they use their land?

The Lenni-Lenape may be taken as a case in point.[15] They were Indians of Algonkian stock who occupied eastern Pennsylvania, southern New York and all of New Jersey. Their villages were placed on high ground near rivers, lakes or bays. Several were located in the valleys of the Passaic and Raritan rivers.

A typical village was dominated by the *Big House* where the Lenni-Lenape held their social and religious ceremonies. The family wigwams were scattered with no real plan around the "Big House." Not far from the wigwams stood the village sweat lodge, the maize cribs and the bark-covered storage pits.

The Lenni-Lenape hunted in the nearby forests; they gathered berries, fruits, herbs, nuts, bulbs and roots; they fished in the streams and went to the sea over well-defined paths to gather shellfish; they farmed the land.

The men cleared the trees; the women prepared the fields. Stone hoes were used to remove rocks and pebbles. Earth was heaped into small mounds two to three feet apart and a half dozen maize seeds were planted in each. Beans and squash were also planted—often in the same field.

But Lenni-Lenape population was small. Best estimates for pre-Columbian times indicate only between 2,000 and 10,000 Indians for the entire state of New Jersey. Few then occupied the Passaic and Raritan river valleys. The Lenni-Lenape impact on the landscape, therefore, although important, was in the light of later history relatively slight.

Familiarity with the local scene—like the example from pre-Columbian New Jersey—will lead pupils to raise similar questions about peoples and places in more remote areas. The teacher, knowl-

---

[15] The Lenni-Lenape reconstruction is based largely upon Dorothy Cross, "The Indians of New Jersey," *Proceedings of the New Jersey Historical Society* 70:1–16, 1952, and William W. Newcomb, Jr., *The Culture and Acculturation of the Delaware Indians*, Anthropological Papers, No. 10, Museum of Anthropology, University of Michigan, Ann Arbor, 1956.

edgeable on the Lenni-Lenape, or the Creek, Sioux or Blackfoot must also know her way in the realms of the Haida, Hopi and Nez Perce. She must know much about the American Indians in general; she must know much about the geography of the United States. Fortunately a fine device is readily available to assist the teacher in classifying the Indian tribes and cultures—a map of the culture areas.[16] It can be used to delimit various aspects of Indian culture in both place and time. Because it is based upon the ramifications of a single attribute the economy or food area is especially useful for young children.[17]

Having established the Indians in place and time it would be well to bring on the Europeans. Their coming, of course, marks a turning point in the history of the landscape. What peculiar notions did these intruders have on building homes, settlements, on land utilization in general? What culture patterns did they eventually establish upon the landscape? How did *they* use the land?

The English, for example, displaced the Lenni-Lenape on the Raritan and Passaic rivers. They made a new impact on the New Jersey landscape. One English group—fresh from Connecticut—under Robert Treat brought the idea of the compact agricultural settlement to the lower Passaic.[18] They hoped their new town would have its village green, its town lots dispersed about the green and the common fields beyond. But the founders were compelled to consider the local environment—the position of the neighboring marshlands, the ponds and brooks, the Lenni-Lenape trails, the small hillocks just beyond the marsh and, perhaps most important of all, the Passaic River itself.

A line was drawn from the bend in the river in the north to the encroaching marshland in the far south. Near the northern end of the line a small area, triangular in shape, was set aside for a market place; immediately to the southeast a larger triangle was planned for a training ground; less than a mile south of the training ground, along the same line, a large common was planned. A broad road—eight rods wide—was to link the common and training ground. Roads less wide were planned to parallel the main road on either side. A fourth road—six rods wide—was to cut the other

---

16 An excellent discussion of the Indian culture areas appears in Harold Driver, *Indians of North America*, Chicago: University of Chicago Press, 1961, pp. 12–20.

See also Map 2. *Culture Areas.*

17 See the map Food Areas of the New World, in Clark Wissler, *The American Indian*, New York: Peter Smith, 1950, p. 2.

18 The discussion is based upon Daniel Jacobson, "Origins of the Town of Newark," *Proceedings of the New Jersey Historical Society* 75:158–169, 1957.

three at right angles. It was along these four roads that the earliest settlers of Newark were to establish their town lots. Before long the plans were put into operation. Homes of oak and cedar went up along the broad road. Fences were built to keep cattle and pigs from the marsh. A meeting house was constructed; a cattle pound was built. The town of Newark had begun to make its impact on the New Jersey landscape.

Imagine the possibilities, at the elementary level, for the teacher of historical geography in the city of Newark. She takes her class on a stroll through the central business district. She continually asks, "What do you see that is old?" "What is new?" The stroll begins near the city's public library. Nearby is Washington Park, the old market place and across the street the gleaming new Mutual Benefit Life Building. The stroll continues down the broad street—actually called Broad Street today—past the new YMCA building. The teacher notes a soft layer of green grass under which a parking lot has recently been erected. She points out that the class is standing in the old training ground reaching back to the days of Robert Treat. In Military Park, as the training ground is called today, she points to the Robert Treat Hotel. The walk continues to the corner of Broad and Market streets—as of old the heart of the city—and then past the old church, the city hall and the areas now marked for slum clearance. The class rests on benches in Lincoln Park—the old town common. All the children are asked to look up Clinton Avenue toward Elizabeth Avenue. Was this modern artery once a Lenni-Lenape trail? Is it a relatively new road? Just how old is it?

And in every city, town and hamlet in America the opportunities are similar. Persistence and change are basic ingredients in the historical geography of every place. There is much to learn; there is much to be learned. The writer avers that young children will enjoy the learning, and that the groundwork will thus be laid for future studies in place, space and time.

The Upper Elementary and Junior High School Years

It is well known that "the child begins to think geographically before he learns to think historically." [19] The idea of place or space is more easily mastered than that of time. Fifth graders, for example, are already well oriented in concepts of space and area. They have a feeling for distance and elevation. They are aware,

---

[19] Bacon, *op. cit.*, 150.

too, of local community time, life-cycle time and personal time; they continue to fall short, however, on chronological time.[20] Pupils entering even the seventh and eighth grades have an understanding of chronological time that is far from mature.[21]

The challenge presented by the inability of upper elementary and junior high school students to grasp chronology can be met successfully through the skillful use of historical geography.

Two dates, not remotely separated in time, can be used in a problem-solving orientation in which the data for one of the dates is known. Teachers in New Jersey, for example, are especially fortunate in that *Gordon's Gazetteer* is available for the early 1830's.[22] It can well be used as a starting point. 1880 or 1890 could serve as the second date.

Newark was already a bustling manufacturing community in the early 1830's.

> Between 1830 and 1833 the population leaped from 10,953 to nearly 15,000—an increase in excess of the growth experienced during the entire previous decade. One hundred nine new dwellings rose in the town in 1832—the year of the cholera—and as many in 1833. Eighteen shoe factories, ten carriage plants, nine hat factories, thirteen tanneries, as well as soap and candle plants, iron and brass foundries, sawmills, breweries and dyeing establishments dominated the landscape. Three hundred fifty tailors were preparing garments for the local and southern markets. Watches, locks, guns, whips, plows and pumps were being manufactured and twenty-five boats were in operation on the recently completed Morris Canal. Pumps were maintained, cisterns built, the first reservoir completed, and cast iron pipe substituted for wooden conduit—but the problem of procuring for the town an adequate water supply had not been solved.[23]

If available, other sources can be used to complete the picture of the town in the early 1830's. But what of the unknown quantity? What of the city of 1880 or 1890? What was it like? What had happened to its population, its streets, its dwellings, its manufacturing enterprises? Was the Morris Canal still in operation? Had the city solved its water supply problem? How much of the town of 1830 was still in place? What in the city was new?

With the teacher acting as guide and information source the students attempt to answer the questions. They dip into the past.

---

20 *Ibid.*

21 Kopple C. Friedman, "Time Concepts of Junior and Senior High School Pupils and Adults." *School Review 52*:233, 1944.

22 Thomas F. Gordon, *Gazetteer of the State of New Jersey*, Trenton (1834).

23 Daniel Jacobson, "The Pollution Problem of the Passaic River." *Proceedings of the New Jersey Historical Society 76*:189, 1958.

They use every available resource to get a picture of the Newark of 1880 or 1890. They are encouraged to use primary sources—real historical documents—perhaps, for the first time. They learn to "taste" their history and to apply it to place.

Opportunities in the High School Program

Opportunities for an approach through historical geography can be made equally rich in the high school program. For the first time—beginning in grade 10—students are able to deal with problems relating to place, space and time with adult maturity. At this vital juncture (one might delay it until grade 11 or 12) it would be appropriate to introduce a course in the "Historical Geography of the United States"—an elective course, *a la* Ralph Brown, open to select students.[24]

Regional studies could be made on numerous themes: population and land utilization in the urban northeast, the rise and demise of cotton culture in the changing south, cultural succession in the Great Plains, water use in the southwest and the like. The local area would again be used for research purposes. Students could work in the field and in the archives. The problem-solving orientation could now be used upon three or even four dates. Individual students might wish to delve into problems relating in space and time, to land occupance, settlement patterns, house types, water supply or even of man as an anthrogeomorphic agent.[25] The research possibilities are limitless. They can be planned in accordance with students' interests and abilities.

Conclusions

Although it is true that "Geographers have always recognized a field of historical geography,"[26] they have not flocked in great numbers to worship at its shrine. Much, therefore, remains to be done. The field is an open one. The same can be said for historical geography as a school discipline, for the teaching of historical geography has no real history in American elementary and secondary schools. Its values, however, are quite obvious. Its study can center students' attention on place during the tender years and

---

[24] Ralph H. Brown, *Historical Geography of the United States*. New York: Harcourt, Brace, 1948.

[25] The term *anthrogeomorphic* is adapted from Berl Golomb and Herbert M. Eder, "Landforms Made by Man," *Landscape 14*:7, 1964.

[26] Richard Hartshorne, *Perspective on the Nature of Geography*. Chicago: Rand McNally, 1959, p. 101.

furnish them with their first real notions of time. In later years its study can sharpen these notions, permit students to do research both indoors and outdoors and give them a better understanding of their local community or area. In high school the concepts and content of historical geography can be used to broaden the students' basic knowledge of the entire continent. Its study can serve to sharpen students' powers of observation and their ability to criticize, interpert and analyze historical data in terms of place.

Nearly 20 years ago Erling M. Hunt pointed out that ". . . there seems to be no likelihood whatever that a course in or including the human geography of the United States will be introduced into the high school program." [27] Perhaps the times were not ripe. But in the middle '60's geographers are about ready to make much progress. In that progress, historical geography is prepared to play an important role.

THE PROBLEM OF CHILDREN'S HISTORICAL MINDEDNESS *

Leo J. Alilunas

One of the pioneer psychologists who became interested in the study of children's historical interests and abilities was John Dewey. In his new psychology he attacked faculty psychology, which fallaciously assumed that the mind was made of parts called faculties and that certain subjects were especially intended to develop certain mental powers. Thinking, said Dewey, was not simply knowledge stored up by virtue of taking "intellectual" subjects. Various subjects might serve the purpose of arousing inquiry and reflection. He protested vigorously against the presentation of isolated knowledge, historical and geographical, in the name of teach-

---

[27] Erling M. Hunt, "The Relation of American History to the Other Social Studies," in *The Study and Teaching of American History*, Richard E. Thursfield, ed. (Seventeenth Yearbook of the National Council for the Social Studies), 1946, 185.

Leo J. Alilunas is on the faculty of the State University of New York, Fredonia.

* Reprinted from *The Social Studies* 56:251–254, 1965, with permission of the McKinley Publishing Co. and Leo J. Alilunas.

ing. For Dewey it was not the question of how to teach the child history but first of all what history is for the child.[1]

Dewey held that the best discipline for the child came out of the conditions of his own experience and not of the manufacture of isolated intellectual problems. He did not believe that history should be taught for its own sake but for its functional value in helping the child to understand the world in which he lives. On this point he said: "A knowledge of the past and its heritage is of great significance when it enters into the present, but not otherwise. And the mistake of making the records and the remains of the past the main material of education is that it cuts the vital connection of present and past, and tends to make the past a rival of the present and the present a more or less futile imitation of the past." [2]

Dewey did not conceive of method as just a logical presentation of history. The purpose of pedagogy was not to impose facts upon the child in a process of storing knowledge but to have the child use facts in the development of his social growth. He respected children's interests as signs of their intellectual development. Dewey sought to apply his pragmatic ideas about the teaching of history in the elementary school of the University of Chicago, a school he established in 1896. Attacking history and geography as "informative studies par excellence," Dewey directed instruction in the elementary grades so that children studied transportation, inventions, and industries, using history and geography in functional learning situations. Children made implements. They engaged in clay-modeling, painting, and dramatization. They visited museums and other community institutions. Dewey sought to direct instruction in history and geography so as to serve the needs and interests of children, and not to make them learn terms, places, and events in meaningless recitations.[3]

Except for Dewey's writings, there were very few systematic studies of children's concepts of history before 1920. Harold Rugg, Professor of Education at Teachers College, Columbia University, pointed out this fact in a challenging manner in 1921 when he reminded Henry Johnson, Chairman of the Committee on History and Education for Citizenship of the American Historical Association, that for thirty years the professional historians had domi-

---

[1] John Dewey, "The Psychological Aspect of the School Curriculum." *Educational Review*, April, 1897, p. 36.

[2] John Dewey, *Democracy and Education*. New York: Macmillan, 1916, p. 88.

[3] Leo J. Alilunas, "John Dewey's Pragmatic Ideas About School History and Their Early Application." *The Social Studies*, March, 1950, pp. 111–114.

nated the organization of history instruction in the elementary and secondary schools with their armchair methods rather than scientific procedures.[4] In 1936 the Department of Superintendence of the National Education Association listed three methods of determining history content for children—present practice, opinion of individuals or groups, and studies of child interest and ability. The report emphasized that the third approach had influenced the school history program very little.[5]

While a graduate student in educational psychology, this writer reviewed, as a seminar project, the research on historical concepts of American children. Findings have indicated that children show a gradual development grade by grade in their ability to make proper historical concepts. Differences between grade groups are less significant than differences among children within a grade group. Children have special difficulty with abstract terms dealing with financial and political aspects of history. They have more knowledge about things in the present such as in matters affecting their home, food, clothing, and shelter. The more intelligent children are more consistent in forming their concepts. Most children are especially weak in their ability to do inferential thinking, perhaps because their school instruction has not provided adequate opportunity for developing such ability. All children do not derive the same meaning from the same material which they read. Various factors—their background of experiences, their mental ability, and their mind set—account for differences in historical conceptualization. Children learn and retain definite quantitative terms in history better than they do indefinite terms of quantity. Mere ability to identify a historical term is no indication that a child understands that term. Children learn casually about many things in their experiences away from school. The school should aid the children in organizing these experiences for the purpose of making proper concepts.[6]

In his review of children's concepts, David H. Russell has stated that any group of children of the same chronological age shows a wide range in understandings of different types of concepts, and the range usually increases as children grow older. Knowledge of

---

[4] Harold Rugg, "How Shall We Reconstruct the Social Studies Curriculum? An Open Letter to Professor Henry Johnson." *The Historical Outlook*, May, 1921, p. 188.

[5] National Education Association. Department of Superintendence. Fourteenth Yearbook, *The Social Studies Curriculum*, p. 168, p. 176. Washington, D. C.: National Education Association of the United States, 1936.

[6] Leo J. Alilunas, "A Review of the Research on the Historical Concepts of American Children." *Educational Administration and Supervision*, September, 1945, p. 344.

concepts is related to the experiential background, the chronological age, the mental age, the socio-economic background, and, in some cases, the sex of children. Children may know a concept thoroughly, partially, inaccurately, or not at all. Children may have some concept of past versus present at about eight years. In general, they understand time lines at about thirteen years, and approach some maturity of understanding time words and dates at about sixteen years of age. Children need considerable first hand, multisensory vicarious experiences in order to develop breadth and depth in their historical concepts. With increasing age children become more able to handle verbal materials and to do abstract thinking about problems of the "far away and the long ago." [7]

Jerome S. Bruner believes there has been an underestimation of the ability of children to learn. His hypothesis is that any subject can be taught effectively in some intellectually honest form to any child at any stage of development. He points to the lack of research concerning devising learning episodes for children at different ages and in different subject matters. He states research is needed concerning what kinds of materials should be used and at what age with what effect. Bruner admits that organizing instruction in history is more elusive than the teaching of mathematics and the sciences.[8] Sand's research has indicated the difficulty of establishing continuity and sequence in the social studies curriculum.[9]

Vincent R. Rogers has urged the application of Bruner's ideas about the structure of a discipline and the presentation of basic ideas to young children in a form they can understand to the teaching of history in the elementary school. He is especially intrigued by the idea of teaching the methodology of history to children, and suggests that much of this can be taught to and understood by young children. At the end of his article [10] he raises the perennial types of questions that have been brought up in the years of research. How important is the mental ability? What deductive and evaluative thinking can children do? In asking such questions he is really asking about the form of history which children are capable of understanding.

---

[7] David H. Russell, *Children's Thinking.* See Chapter 5, "Children's Concepts." Boston: Ginn, 1956.

[8] Jerome S. Bruner, *The Process of Education.* See Chapter 3, "Readiness for Learning." Cambridge, Mass.: Harvard University Press, 1960.

[9] Philip Ole Sand, "Continuity and Sequence in the Social Studies Curriculum." *Journal of Educational Research,* April, 1951, pp. 561–573.

[10] Vincent R. Rogers, "History for the Elementary School Child." *Phi Delta Kappan,* December, 1962, pp. 132–135.

Rogers seems genuinely interested in seeking ways of "building the foundation for a mature understanding of history." But a *mature* understanding comes with *maturity*. Willard C. Olson has concluded from years of research on child development (using the longitudinal approach) that achievement in learning comes from *maturation*. He urges respect for learning readiness, be it the teaching of reading or history.[11] The history of historians needs, as John Dewey long ago reminded us, to be "psychologized" for the child.[12]

Some children, the bright ones, seem to have more capacity for historical mindedness in studying topics in a chronological sense and in doing inferential thinking about the past. They especially need to be weaned away from the standardized, textbook methods of history teaching and provided with better opportunities to pursue their intellectual interests more creatively. There are many unexplored areas of research pertaining to the development of a program of elementary school history suited to the needs and interests of gifted children. Educational psychologists, historians, social studies specialists, teachers of elementary school history and the other social studies, and directors of educational foundations need to undertake a vigorous program of cooperative research in studying and applying learning theories as they pertain to children's historical mindedness. For years far too many children have been subjected to a "forced feeding" brand of history teaching and the result has been a confusion of "verbalization with true understanding." [13]

There is some danger that educational reactionaries may impede much needed research concerning children's interests and abilities as they relate to the study of society, both present and past. In the new era, and as one of the many effects of the "cold war" between the United States and the Soviet Union, the exponents of the "essentialist philosophy of education" have become militant in their attacks on schools. The exponents of "hard peda-

---

[11] Willard C. Olson, *Child Development*. Boston: Health, 1949, pp. 118–162, 325–350. Also see Leo J. Alilunas, "History for Children—Too Much Too Soon," *The Elementary School Journal*, December, 1951, pp. 215–220.

[12] One of the positive outcomes of the Ford Foundation project to improve teacher education is the encouragement of liberal-arts professors to find exposure to educational psychology in improving their own classroom work and in gaining more insight into the problems of teaching their discipline in the schools. *The New Teacher: A Report on Ford Foundation Assistance for New Patterns in the Education of Teachers*. New York: Ford Foundation, Office of Reports, 1962, p. 31.

[13] Charles A. Harper, "Why Do Children Dislike History?" *Social Education*, October, 1937, pp. 492–494.

gogy" are urging citizens to emphasize the "training of the mind" (so did Dewey) rather than "life adjustment." (Dewey did not believe the training of the mind and life adjustment to be antithetical aims of education.) They want the teaching of the "basic" subjects (history rather than the "social studies"). They stress the society-centered approach to learning and are intent on keeping the child-centered learning theorists who have expounded "gestalt psychology" on the defensive. They want history taught not only formally but separately. (There is even a sign of schism between historians and geographers in vying for a place in the curriculum.) [14] The traditionalists seek to drive the "child-centered educationists" out of the temples of learning, while flinging epithets about functionalism and integration.[15]

In these days of focus on the structure of the discipline it is well to heed what John Dewey said concerning the nature of and the emergence of children's societal interests. This writer believes that the manifested interests of children have to be reckoned with.[16] Herbart's principle of apperception still is a challenge to teachers concerned with the problem of children's historical mindedness. History for children is not the same psychological phenomonon as history for historians. For children, history is initially a process of relating the past to their direct experiences. With maturity, they gradually develop a capacity for indirect intellectual experiences and thus become ready to study the past for its own sake. As children grow older and gain a sense of chronology, their history becomes more closely identified with the history of historians.

---

[14] Robert N. Saveland, "Whatever Happened to Geography?" *Saturday Review,* November 17, 1962, pp. 56–57, 77.

[15] In its propaganda the Council for Basic Education asserts the following "seven deadly dogmas" have taken hold of American elementary schools: The dogma of readiness, the dogma of interest, the dogma of the whole child, the dogma of freedom, the dogma of integrated subjects, the dogma of scientific knowledge, and the dogma of professionalism. Washington, D. C.: The Council for Basic Education. *Reprint Series Bulletin,* No. 1, June, 1958, pp. 7–14.

[16] See the story of the nine-year-old who had observed all the landmarks of the nation's capital from the top of Washington Monument but was most impressed by his birdseye view of four baseball diamonds on one park! Dorothy Barclay, "Making our History Come Alive," *The New York Times Magazine,* April 8, 1956, p. 48. Drew Pearson has told the story of Jim Wright, a Congressman from Texas, who took his ten-year-old son to Washington's home at Mt. Vernon. The boy wandered about the grounds and came back enthusiastic about the "swell woods." "Yes," said Mr. Wright, "but how did you like George Washington's house?" "Oh," replied the boy. "You mean that big old house over there?" Drew Pearson, "Washington Merry-Go-Round" column, *Buffalo Courier-Express,* May 12, 1955.

THE ROLE OF LAW IN THE SCHOOL CURRICULUM *

Tom C. Clark

To meet with you, the members of the distinguished National Council for the Social Studies, is a high privilege. I shall always cherish it. It is a rare treat! After all, I spent a third of my life listening to teachers and now at long last they must listen to me for one night.

Your National Council is one of the most important organizations in our country. You deal with youth, and during the greater part of their day they are your special charges. In your classes they are not only learning the social studies but, more importantly, they are learning how to deal with their fellow man and developing virtues and vices that will shape their future lives. In your hands, therefore, lies not only their destiny, but through them you determine the fate of our nation.

My casual study of the social studies curriculum indicates it has become compartmentalized into history, government, economics, geography, and sociology. Of late, however, there has been a growing uneasiness that the curriculum has not kept pace with that of the physical sciences. In an endeavor to appraise the problem, many research and development programs have been organized, each seeking the answer to the question, "How can we improve the knowledge of young people in the social studies?" Some 50 nationally oriented projects are now under way under various auspices, both public and private. I am sure that each of these projects has merit, although it appears there may be some duplication.

It is well that the Council itself be disturbed over the inadequate coverage that the present social studies curriculum gives to the role of fundamental legal principles in our society. A year ago yesterday *The New York Times* reported that the CBS National Citizenship Test indicated that 34 per cent of our citizens had a "poor knowledge" of their rights and duties as citizens, while 47 per cent had only a "fair" one. An earlier test by the Purdue Opinion Poll, among students, indicated that 37 per cent did not object to the use of third degree tactics in crime detection; 43 per cent

---

The Honorable Tom C. Clark is former Associate Justice of the Supreme Court of the United States.

* Reprinted from *Social Education* 31:185–187ff., 1967, with permission of the National Council for the Social Studies and The Honorable Tom C. Clark.

were undecided as to the value of freedom of speech; 34 per cent would prohibit the circulation of petitions, and a like number opposed integration in the public schools. Moreover, a recent Crime Commission survey shows that 7 per cent of all the persons charged with murder, 24 per cent of those charged with rape, 34 per cent of those charged with robbery, 52 per cent of those charged with burglary, and 61 per cent of those charged with auto theft were released to the juvenile court—all in their early teens or younger.

It is also true that millions of our citizens know little or nothing about the Constitution, the Bill of Rights, the nature of our government and the distinguished heritage that is ours. You read about the citizen who, a few years ago, tore the Bill of Rights from a bulletin board in a public building and denounced it as subversive material; you heard of civil rights leaders denouncing court orders and refusing to obey those that did not suit their mood; you know, I am sure, that we have 15 million functional illiterates in our population, and that some 65 million citizens over the age of 18 years do not have a high school education. Our problem is our failure to teach our people democracy as written in our fundamental law—individual rights rather than individual riot—respect for law and obedience to constituted authority. These principles must be brought home to youngsters and adults alike. This is your challenge tonight!

It appears to me that an understanding of the social studies, save perhaps geography, requires study of our fundamental principles. Indeed, the validity of the governmental action that you teach, when challenged, must be tested by the yardstick of constitutional law. To understand the operation of government one must, therefore, be acquainted in general with the manner in which the courts have performed the juristic function of elucidating constitutional doctrine. During its 176 years of organization, the Supreme Court of the United States has decided over 4,000 cases involving some question of constitutional interpretation. These cases probably cover over 50,000 pages in our reports. I do not say that you or the students should study all of these pages. What I do say is that every social studies course should stress governmental structure less and give more attention to its processes. The student would then get a better picture of his government, of its history, of its economics and its sociology.

We would all like to report that in fact the rights of the individual had become as secure and recognized as their universal verbal acclaim. But we all know this is not true. And, unfortunately, of late individual duty and obligation has not only lost its validity in fact but is rarely acclaimed by our orators. If you want to read of the dynamism of the first 175 years of United States history, the best place to get it is in Charles Warren's *Supreme Court in American History*. It places a new dimension on American life; namely, that the Judiciary is the branch of government that has transferred theory and doctrine into actuality—American dreams into American practice! It teaches that if we are to have good citizens we must have, as the Virginia Declaration of Rights declared, "frequent recurrence to fundamental principles." We must teach people not only to obey the law but also to understand it. We have too many today that do neither! What is the cause of this? I must confess that I do not know but I do believe that you, the social studies teachers of America can remedy it.

Your Yearbook for 1966 is entitled *Political Science in the Social Studies*. It is not yet circulated, but I had the good fortune of a preview via galley proofs. A reading of the papers in it indicates that my view as to the role of law in social studies is a dissent. However, I do not feel ill at ease in that position. The reason for its rejection, it is said, is that the law is "a very poor predictor"; that the amount of legal information is so monstrous that teachers could never master it; indeed most lawyers, it is said, specialize in only one branch of law themselves; that knowing the number of amendments to the Constitution, the number of Cabinet departments, etc., is in a few years an exercise in obsoletes.

I say, if prediction is one of the functions of the social studies teacher, the judicial process is, I believe, one of the most accurate predictors available. History shows that *Marbury v. Madison* was the forerunner of one of the most effective tools of liberty in America, *i.e.*, the technique of judicial review; the *Civil Rights* cases were a barometer of what was to come in business; the *Northern Securities* of what to expect in antitrust; the *West Coast Hotel* case of what was coming in minimum wages and hours of labor; the *segregation* case in integration; and *Griffin v. Illinois* in the field of individual rights. If a teacher wishes to be a seer, the fundamental law of our country is the best indicator yet devised. Other criticism of the law's role reflects "a straw man" technique, often used by lawyers. No one has advocated that statute law, administrative decision, and law reviews be introduced into social studies. My thesis is that "recurrence to fundamental principles" be woven into the social studies curriculum. Indeed, your National Council is doing this very thing in your bulletin *Judgment* which is being inserted in *Social Education* four times a year. To decry this approach by saying that the monstrous amount of legal information is more than the teacher can handle is likewise without validity. No one says that the teacher should undertake to become a lawyer. It is the basic principles of law—the "recurrence to fundamental principles"—about which I speak. And let me say it is my view that the study of the structure of government, *i.e.*, the number of amendments to the Constitution, etc., has been overworked. What we need is an understanding of the fundamental legal principles on which our government rests—not statistics, statutes, structure, and superfluity.

I am also disappointed that more emphasis has not been placed on the role of these fundamental principles in your convention program. I believe only one or two items in your extensive agenda have to do with legal fundamentals.

And, if you will pardon me, your program *Judgment* is great; but it only includes celebrated cases on individual rights. It fails to cover the responsibilities and duties of the citizen. We need more frequent recurrence to that fundamental principle. The recurring obligations of the citizen could be brightly illuminated through the use of landmark cases spanning the whole life of our judiciary.

In short, my view is that the judiciary is one—if not the most—powerful instrument in our governmental machinery. I ask you, reflect tonight, what force in American government has triggered a more tremendous exercise of governmental power in every field of public activity, including health, welfare, education, juvenile problems, and industrial and economic relations? What power has equally and as surely curbed the excesses of legislative action? Nor has the Executive escaped judicial edict when he overstepped the powers granted in Article II. And finally, tell me what force has given more life and reality to the rights of the individual through the Bill of Rights and the Fourteenth Amendment; to freedom of speech, of press, of religion; of equal opportunity in education; to public facilities; and to the right of counsel?

You know and recognize what force! In the development of improved curriculum you have referred to it. Your project, *Judgment*, is an example. Moreover, several of the various surveys depend upon it. They have enormous potential. I am particularly impressed with the program at Columbia. It appears to be close to my views and has drawn together a most distinguished group of educators, public officials, corporate officers, lawyers, judges, clergymen, and publishers under the directorship of Alan F. Westin. Its brochure warns us: "Today, in most schools, instruction in constitutional liberty and the rule of law is largely formal, bland and irrelevant to the life of the student. Neither the root values of our free society nor the central concept of due process of law are taught in ways that create understanding and interest in the average student, let alone the disadvantaged or gifted child."

I am hopeful that the Columbia project will develop materials and instructional techniques among teachers—through "frequent recurrence to fundamental principles"—that will weave the role of law into conventional courses and give more life to social studies curriculums.

Students must be attracted to such courses just as they have been to the sciences. This we have neglected. The place to begin is in the K-12 curriculum. I do not suggest a new course covering the role of law. I do not ask that you teach law *per se*—not at all. Rather than giving the role of law equal time, I merely suggest that it be used as an integrating force in the conventional social studies. In your research for more effective tools in social studies learning, it might well be the common denominator. If you could develop the social studies into more of a scintillating drama with a storybook finish, it would soon catch the eye of the student. Often a law case can be used as the base from which historical, legal, political, and sociological forces can be radiated with telling effect. In this way the law itself will not be studied as law *per se* but only to interlace the patterns of family living, economic enterprise, political and governmental activity, and sociological development.

Your *Judgment* program is, as I have said, excellent, but it is not enough. There must be more "frequent recurrence to fundamental principles." Curriculum, as I see it, should be designed so as to include day-by-day correlated study of democratic living and effective citizenship, through and under law. This would meet the prime objective of social studies; namely, responsible citizenship; the day-by-day living study of human relations under constitutional government. By utilizing events familiar in the lives of children—for example, beginning with the law behind the traffic light and extending to that behind Telstar—the living law will become a part and parcel of the child's very being. This would not violate your conventional classroom procedures or interfere with the rigidity of school organization, but it would serve as an assist to teachers in developing students who would examine and analyze, through discussion and argument, the conflicts of life.

While each of the projects now in progress will contribute much to improvement, it is hoped that in some way they might all be coordinated in a mammoth crusade for the efficient modernization of the social studies. No single group can effect this save your National Council itself. In it are the teachers who can get the job done.

We in the judiciary had to create in the field of judicial administration a joint coordinating committee that brought together all of the projects in that area. Perhaps you might take a leaf from it. In this way duplication would be eliminated, money saved, and the over-all work expedited. Perhaps you could develop state and regional teacher seminars devoted solely to a study of the practical problems—not the theories—the exchange of ideas and the development of teaching techniques in a dynamic social studies program. Indeed, the American Bar Association might be enlisted as a co-sponsor. It has had experience in the publishing of legal books for laymen, such as *Law Books, USA;* the Federal Bar has its *Equal Justice Under Law;* and the National College for State Trial Judges now carries on three monthly sessions each year for trial judges. It is the most effective instrument for the improvement of the administration of justice in America. The social studies should have a similar program. The College has found that law is more than rules and books.

And so you might conclude that the teaching of responsible citizenship requires more than history and governmental structure—more than a knowledge of civil liberties—more than geography, economics, and sociology. It means knowing how the democratic process works and why it works in the way it works; it includes a familiarity with how government is conducted and how political decisions are made; and, most important of all, how the citizen can affect and be affected by this process. Through that "Frequent recurrence to fundamental principles," each of us will know of one's responsibility not to abuse the privilege of citizenship but by becoming informed of the whole process of government to live within and under the law. As you develop among students an awareness of the value of the democratic processes and a desire to participate in their operation you will, I believe, have solved one of the most disturbing problems of our time—disrespect for constituted authority—disobedience to law and its processes.

As you meet here in Cleveland you have a great opportunity. If the nation could speak to you tonight I believe it would say:

"I am the nation. I was born on July 4, 1776; the Declaration of Independence is my birth certificate; the Constitution and its Bill of Rights my charter of freedom. The bloodlines of the world run in my veins because I have always offered freedom to the oppressed. I am many things and many people. Indeed, I am 195 million souls—and the ghost of millions of others who have lived and died for me.

"I remember the Alamo, the Maine and Pearl Harbor. When freedom called I answered—and I stayed until it was over. I left my heroic dead in Flanders fields, on the rock of Corregidor, on the bleak slopes of Korea, and in the steaming jungle of Vietnam.

"I am big. I sprawl from the Atlantic to the Pacific—my arms reach out to embrace Alaska and Hawaii—three million square miles throbbing with industry. I am more than five million farms.

I am forest, field, mountain and desert. I am quiet villages—and cities that never sleep.

"I am 130,000 schools and colleges, and 320,000 churches where my people worship God as they think best. I am a ballot dropped in a box, the roar of a crowd in a stadium and the voice of a choir in a cathedral. I am an editorial in a newspaper and a letter to a congressman.

"Yes, I am the nation, and these are the things that I am. I was conceived in freedom and in freedom I wish to spend the rest of my days. This my charter guarantees. But tonight I am troubled. There is disorder, disbelief, disrespect, distrust in my land. This we cannot let be. Education has always been my guardian genius and so to you, the educators, I turn. Yours is a growing responsibility to prepare my people—especially my youth—for a life, devoted to the great principles laid down in my charter: I have faith that you will well and faithfully devote yourselves to this task; that all my people may have instilled in their bosoms the loyalty, the integrity, the courage and the know-how to keep my institutions and their lights of liberty ever burning bright not only for themselves but as well for those who are oppressed wherever they be. Yes, I am the nation. I have been and am great. But remember this well: in my youth lies my strength. You must not let them fail. In you lies my salvation; in your hands my destiny. Shoulder to shoulder—side by side—may you plan for my continued glory under God—together forever and forever together."

A CONCEPTUAL STRUCTURE
FOR GEOGRAPHY *

Preston E. James

The current ferment of curriculum revision in America provides geographers with both a challenge and an opportunity to formulate appropriate conceptual structures that can be made clear to the fraternity of education. There is no need here to give additional support to the point that facts slip quickly away unless they are relevant to a framework of theory.

Preston E. James is Chairman of the Department of Geography at Syracuse University, New York.

* Reprinted from the *Journal of Geography* *64*:292–298, 1965, with permission of the National Council for Geographic Education and Preston E. James.

The words "concept" and "conceptual structure" have been used in such different contexts and with such varied meanings that they are now dangerously close to becoming meaningless. But if they do become meaningless we shall have to invent new words to refer to the general body of theory that distinguishes our field, and that justifies the place it takes in the curriculum. This paper provides no new theory, but only restates in simple language ideas that have been current in the geographic profession for many decades.

First of all it is important to understand that there are just three fundamentally different ways of organizing units of study in a curriculum. One is to build units around concepts that have to do with specific processes or with groups of similar processes. Thus a unit of study in science is built around a physical process or a biotic process, without reference to when the process takes place or where. A unit of study in social sciences is based on concepts of human behavior. This is the *substantive* principle of curriculum organization, and the one on which most curricula are structured. Another way of organizing units of study is around concepts of time sequence. This is the *chronological* principle, most commonly (but not exclusively) associated with history. And the third way of organizing units of study is to make use of concepts of areal association and interconnection among things and events of unlike origin, where different kinds of processes interact in particular places. This is the *chorological* principle, most commonly (but not exclusively) associated with geography.[1] A well-balanced curriculum for elementary and secondary grades will make use of each of the three principles of organization at different times.

Geography is that field of learning which undertakes to develop concepts based on the chorological principle. In this field, therefore, attention is focused on the areal associations of things and events that result from unlike processes, and on the interconnections among the facts thus associated. Geography is also responsible for developing and teaching the arts of communication and analysis through the use of maps.

There are three purposes to be served by the teaching of geography. One is to provide a general understanding of the arrangement of things and events over the whole surface of the earth, so that by the end of the 9th or 10th grades, at least, students should be able to look at a globe without finding any large areas about which they are completely uninformed or are unable to predict what kinds of associated features they would be likely to find if

---

[1] Richard Hartshorne, *Perspective on the Nature of Geography.* Chicago: Rand McNally & Co., 1959, pp. 173–182.

they paid the area a visit. The second purpose to be served is to teach the pupils to ask geographic questions, and to devise ways of finding and testing the answers to such questions. The third purpose is to teach the language of the map. This paper deals only with the concepts useful for achieving the first of these purposes: namely, world coverage.

What Is a Geographic Concept?

A concept we may agree, is a mental image of a thing or event. In this meaning it is opposed to a percept which is the direct observation of a thing or event. Out-of-doors one can look at a specific hill—this is the percept of a thing—and if the hill is covered with plants and used in some way by man, it becomes an area, or segment of earth space, within which things of unlike origin are associated and interconnected. But in the classroom one develops a mental image of "hill" in general. This is a concept. Out-of-doors one can observe the formation of a gully during a rain. This is the percept of an event. In the classroom we develop a mental image of gullies in general. This is the concept of the event, or sequences of events that result in the formation of gullies. A long list of such concepts can be matched against percepts: valley, river, lake, farm, factory, airfield, or such events as the harvesting of a field of wheat, or even the impact of government on an individual when a census is taken. There are many glossaries of geographic terms, but there is still need for research to identify those concepts that should be taught, and the grade level at which they should be taught.

But geography, because of the nature of the field, must inevitably deal with concepts that can never be matched with percepts. The curved surface of the earth limits the range of vision, even when observations can be made from the moon. The basic instrument of perception is man himself. The things he perceives and the mental images he develops are related to the fact that his eyes are some five feet above the ground and some three inches apart. If the observers were ant-size creatures, the mental images of things and events on the face of the earth would be quite different. The ant would not think of a hill as a unit, nor would the process of gully formation come within the field of direct observation. Similarly there are many features of the face of the earth that lie beyond the perception of man. No one has ever directly observed a hilly upland. The mental image of such a general category of surface is based on the observation of many specific hills and valleys. No one has ever perceived the formation of a river system. Geographers must deal with many concepts that lie beyond the range of direct observation: climatic regions, soil associations, types of farming regions, or even the politically organized territory we call a state, etc.

The distinction between concepts that can be matched with percepts and those that cannot is of sufficient importance to merit special terms. The writer describes those features that can be directly observed from a single place as topographic features, and the mental images of such features are topographic concepts.[2] Concepts that refer to things and events too widely spread to be observable from one place are described as chorographic concepts. Concepts that refer to those highly generalized features that occupy the major part of the earth's surface are global concepts.

It is clear that the only geographic unit is the whole surface of the earth.[3] Like all fields of learning, geography must make a selection of segments of human knowledge sufficiently restricted to be comprehended. Geographers must set off pieces of the whole, or segments of earth-space. Since no two pin points on the face of the earth are identical, any segment of earth-space, however small, represents a generalization from which irrelevant details have been eliminated. The segments of earth-space that geographers define as homogeneous are identified by the existence of some kind of areal association of things or events of unlike origin. These are called *regions*.[4]

The region, so defined, is one of the core concepts of geography. The word is not to be confused with the popular meaning of region as a large, vaguely-defined area containing some kind of homogeneity; nor is the regional method to be confused with the compilation of groups of unrelated facts that are summarized within some kind of arbitrary area.

A distinction must be made between generic regions and genetic regions.[5] Generic regions are defined as homogeneous in terms of stated criteria—a hilly upland with an associated pattern of land use and settlement, for example. The definition of a genetic region requires not only the identification of areal associations, but also of the processes, or sequences of events, that have produced the areal associations.[6] This involves the reconstruction of past geographies (that is, of past areal associations of things or events of

---

[2] Derwent Whittlesey, "The Regional Concept and the Regional Method," in *American Geography Inventory and Prospect*, P. E. James and C. F. Jones, eds. Syracuse, N. Y.: Association of American Geographers, Syracuse University Press, 1954, p. 61.

[3] Hartshorne, *op. cit.*, pp. 108–145.

[4] Whittlesey, *op. cit.*, pp. 21–22.

[5] Edward A. Ackerman, *Geography as a Fundamental Research Discipline*, research paper 53, Chicago, 1958.

[6] Preston E. James, "Toward a Further Understanding of the Regional Concept." *Annals of the Association of American Geographers 42*:195–222, 1952.

unlike origin), and the tracing of geographic change through time. This is called historical geography. The recognition of segments of earth-space within which unlike things and events are interconnected to form systems of related parts is the operative definition of the regional method. Such segments of earth-space may be based on a wide variety of phenomena and processes, and may be defined at very different scales or degrees of generalization, ranging from topographic to global. A conceptual structure is a series of related concepts, forming a system.

An Approach to Global Geography

We seek, then, a structure of related concepts to provide an understanding of the causes and consequences of the arrangement and interconnections of the major physical, biotic, and cultural features of the earth. So infinite is the variety of things and events that are interconnected on the earth that many different kinds of conceptual structures could be formulated. The problem is to identify a minimum number of such structures which are useful in providing the framework of a global understanding for Americans. Surely, we may agree that the conceptual structures we want must be relevant to the great contemporary problems: the adequacy of the earth to support the world's rapidly increasing population; the causes and results of the world arrangement of wealth and poverty; the meaning of the conflict between autocracy and democracy. Any conceptual structure that fails to throw new light on these questions may be judged as being poor.

Applying the regional concept on a global scale, we suggest a series of related concept-systems. First, we suggest regions based on *ecosystems* in which the areal associations of things and events resulting from physical and biotic processes, without the intervention of man, are identified. Second, we proceed to regions based on *habitats,* wherein man modifies his natural surroundings through interference with physical and biotic processes. And third, we suggest regions based on the interconnections between habitat features and *culture* features, in which changes in the *significance* of habitats are correlated with the processes of economic, social, and political change in the modern world.

ECOSYSTEMS

Ecosystems are produced by areal associations of interconnected physical and biotic processes, without the interference of man. There are at least five major groups of physical and biotic things and events that are involved in forming these areal associations: surface features, climates, water, biota (wild plants and animals), and soils. Each of these elements forms a sub-system of related parts, and each could be made the subject of a course of systematic study by itself. But it is the interconnected areal associations of all these things and events that form the earth's major ecosystems.

There are two principles involved in the global arrangement of such ecosystems. First, all those things and events that are related to the pattern of surface features and rocks are irregularly distributed with reference to the poles and latitudes. And second, all those things and events that are related to the pattern of climates are regularly distributed over the earth. This basic regularity of climate, and of climatically related phenomena, is the result of the distribution of energy over the earth, and of the mechanisms that tend to equalize energy. The circulation of the atmosphere produces a regular pattern of rainfall and temperature. The distribution of water on the land is related to climate. So also are the patterns of plants and animals. The great soil groups are clearly associated with climate, water, and biota. The circulation of water in the ocean basins is another mechanism for redistributing energy, and this process develops a basic regularity in the movement of water, the temperature, salinity, and other properties of the oceans.

The actual pattern of ecosystems, however, is a compromise between the principle of regularity and the principle of irregularity. For the relatively simple patterns of climatically-related features that would exist if the earth were all level land or all water are, in fact, distorted by the irregular disposition of the continents and ocean basins, and by the unique surface configuration of each continent. Yet the underlying climatic pattern is never wholly obscured; rather the irregularity of surface only distorts the regularity of climate.

As a result it is possible to predict the nature of the ecosystem that would be found in any part of the globe. If one knows the latitude of a place, and whether it is on the eastern, interior, or western part of a continent, or on the eastern or western part of an ocean, and if one recalls the unique surface patterns of seven continents, the basic world patterns fit nicely into place. A pupil who develops this mental image of the world can be expected to pass the so-called thumb test. With eyes closed he places the thumb on a globe. When he sees where his thumb is resting he can predict the physical and biotic character of that part of the world, whether his thumb is on land or water. He fails the test if he cannot make the necessary prediction.

HABITAT

A habitat is an ecosystem that has been modified by human action. For the nearly two million years that the earth has been occupied by the *genus homo,* the ecosystems have been subject to changes introduced by man. The distinguishing characteristic of man-made changes, as opposed to changes resulting from natural processes, is that they are carried out in accordance with a plan of action that extends beyond the immediate. But many changes started by man have spread beyond the range of human plan. Changes introduced at some point in the balance of the ecosystem have repercussions of an unexpected nature throughout the system. Even where primitive man was present in small numbers, his fires, set for the purpose of aiding in the hunt or of clearing the land for crops or pasture, have had a profound and unplanned impact on the original vegetation. In fact, wholly new habitats have been created in certain parts of the pattern of ecosystems—as when grasslands were created where once there was an intermingling of brush and woodland. But these changes of the vegetation took place so long ago that related soils have developed under the new plant cover, and animals adjusted to the new environment have become established. The "natural" surroundings of man are, therefore, partly man-made.

Nevertheless the global pattern of habitats closely reflects the previous pattern of ecosystems. Furthermore, the principles of regularity and irregularity can also be applied to the prediction of habitat patterns.[7]

THE CONCEPT OF SIGNIFICANCE

Habitats are significant, not only because they have in part been created by human action, but also because they provide the "natural" surroundings of man's occupancy of the earth. Any human society, if it is to survive for long, must form a workable connection with the earth resources. The habitat is the resource base of man's societies. Answers to many questions regarding wealth and poverty, and the capacity of the earth to support the human population must be provided by reference to the habitats with which man is associated. It is of the utmost importance, therefore, to develop a valid concept regarding the significance to man of the features of the habitat.

---

[7] Preston E. James, *A Geography of Man,* 2nd ed. Boston: Ginn & Co., 1959, pp. 25–37.

The dominant concept in American geography until the 1920's was known as "environmental determinism." Many persons not in contact with modern geographical thinking still accept the concept that the nature of man's physical and biotic surroundings either determines, or at least sets limits to man's ways of making a living. Adherents to this concept point out such habitats as the dry lands, or the polar lands, or the mountain lands are always difficult for human settlement. Oranges, they insist, cannot be grown in the polar lands. No nation can be strong, they say, without coal.

The study of the relations of man to his habitat by the methods of historical geography, however, reveals the inadequacy of the concept of environmental determinism. No land can be properly described as rich or poor, friendly or unfriendly, except in relation to a particular group of people, for the land which may be considered to be richly endowed for people who live by hunting may be considered as poorly endowed for a people who wish to live by farming. Slopes that can be cultivated with the hoe are too steep to cultivate with plows. Soils that are productive for one kind of crop raised with certain farming methods may be quite unproductive for other crops raised by other methods. Even such a resource as coal clearly has a different meaning for people who have the technical skill to make use of it from what it means to people who lack such skill. Climates which the Greeks thought would prohibit the development of civilized living are now occupied by people with high standards of material comfort. The people flocking into Southern California do not think of dry lands as difficult for human settlement.

The cornerstone of the conceptual structure of geography, and the connecting link between habitat and human inhabitants is the concept of significance. It may be stated as follows: the significance to man of the physical and biotic features of his habitat is a function of the attitudes, objectives, and technical skills of man himself. This is cultural determinism. This concept in no sense eliminates the need for studying man's natural surroundings; nor does it accept the often-repeated idea that as man's technology becomes more advanced, his dependence on the natural resources of the earth decreases. It is not that the habitat ceases to be significant to the people of the industrial society. It is, rather, that its significance changes and becomes more complex. With every change in man's attitudes and objectives, and with every advance in his technical skills, the habitat must be reappraised. This kind of reappraisal is known as *sequent occupance*. The concept of *sequence occupance* is an operational definition of the changing significance of habitat.

CULTURE REGIONS

Attitudes, objectives, and technical skills are included in the idea of a culture. Since the geographic study of habitats has no meaning for man without tracing the interconnections with the culture of the inhabitants, one more step is required to complete the conceptual structure of geography. This is the formulation of some kind of theoretical framework for the definition of culture regions. How can homogeneities of culture be defined so that they are useful in demonstrating the changing significance of habitat, and so that the major divisions of the world in terms of man's ways of living can be identified?

The writer has presented his ideas regarding a framework of theory for the definition of culture regions at a previous meeting of the NCGE.[8] Cultures, or distinctive ways of living, originate in particular places which can be described as culture hearths. From these areas of origin the new way of living spreads, producing conflict and destruction along the advancing front where the new way of living is in contact with the older. In the whole history of *homo sapiens* (who appeared some 50,000 years ago as the only surviving species of the *genus homo*) there have been only three periods of major culture change, when man's ways of living were fundamentally changed. First was the agricultural revolution, when crops were first planted and animals domesticated. The second great revolution took place when the "Early Civilizations" appeared in six different locations on the earth. And now we are in the midst of the third great period of revolutionary culture change.

The Industrial Revolution and the Democratic Revolution first appeared about the middle of the 18th century around the shores of the North Sea in Europe. The content of these revolutions, and the reasons for the location of these fundamental changes are presented elsewhere.[9] Spreading in somewhat different patterns from the area of origin, each of these revolutions makes contact with pre-industrial and pre-democratic societies. The first result of this contact is conflict and confusion, as the old ways of living collapse and as reactions against the new are set up by those who resist change. The Industrial Revolution brings economic development, produces the population explosion, changes the relation of human society to the resource base, changes predominantly rural popula-

---

[8] Preston E. James, "Geography in an Age of Revolution." *Journal of Geography 62*:97–103, 1963.

[9] Preston E. James and Nelda Davis, *The Wide World*, New York: The Macmillan Co., 1960, and Preston E. James, *One World Divided*, New York: Blaisdell Pub. Co., 1964.

tions into predominantly urban ones, produces the technical skill greatly to increase the food, clothing, and shelter available for man, but requires a fundamental shift of the system of values if the new skills are to be applied effectively. All the world is struggling with the problems posed by the substitution of machines and controlled inanimate power for human and animal muscles.

The Democratic Revolution is no less profound. The stage is set for the uncompromising struggle between autocracy and democracy, between the idea that the individual has no right but to serve the state and the idea that the state should be erected on the principle of individual dignity and of equality before the law. The reaction against the Democratic Revolution has been violent, especially where Facism or Communism are adopted.

The world is now sharply divided as a result of the impact of these two revolutions with pre-existing ways of living. The first result of this impact is to increase the contrast between wealth and poverty, between autocracy and democracy. It is possible to define some eleven major regions in each of which the impact of these revolutions with pre-industrial and pre-democratic societies has produced a distinctive process of culture change. Within each of these eleven regions the present conditions and conflicts are similar, and in each the processes of change follow similar courses.

A Global View

The thumb test must include not only an understanding of the ecosystems and habitats based on the principles of regularity and irregularity, but also must include an understanding of the changing significance of habitat. With each change in the culture the meaning of the resource base must be reappraised—and this is a period of profound and revolutionary culture change. The processes of change associated with each of the culture regions bring about changes in the capacity of the earth to support its population, and changes in the meaning of wealth and poverty. The thumb test calls for some understanding of the interconnections among these diverse things and events, and how such interconnections are arranged on the face of the earth.

The student who gains this kind of organized concept of the earth can no longer regard the contemporary conflicts as meaningless. A global picture of change emerges, in which each individual is challenged to play a constructive part. In playing such a role the first step is to understand and appreciate the differences that distinguish one part of the earth from other parts. This is one of the three purposes of teaching geography.

CONTENT FOR ELEMENTARY SOCIAL STUDIES *

Bruce R. Joyce

Scholarly knowledge has reached the point where complete factual knowledge of any field has become an impossibility even for the advanced scholar. More than ever before in the history of education, we need to devise a method of analysis which will enable us to sort out the truly important and organize it in such a way that the relatively few things we are able to teach will have maximum educational effect.

The Notation of Structure

For a good many years educators have worked for an arrangement whereby the central ideas used in the various scholarly fields be identified by practicing scholars and translated into a form which would assure that even the younger pupil be taught up-to-date ideas and ways of thinking. Chapter XIV of Dewey's *Democracy and Education* deals with the "Nature of Subject Matter" and suggests that the logical arrangements of a discipline consist in an organization of the major ideas of that field.[1] It would be ineffective, he suggests, to present these ideas via lectures to each child, but, he argued, if the scholar and educator would work together, a means might be devised so that the learner could be led to construct advanced ideas out of his own experience.

Charles Hubbard Judd similarly proposed: "Let a specialist in a given field indicate those lines of thought which his special study has shown him to be significant and worthy of attention on the part of pupils in schools. Then let some teacher who understands the way in which ideas should be presented to immature minds organize a teaching unit based on the material furnished by the specialist."[2]

Alfred North Whitehead, speaking to the problem of selection

Bruce R. Joyce is Associate Professor of Education at Teachers College, Columbia University, New York.

* Reprinted from *Social Education* *82*:84–87, 1964, with permission of the National Council for the Social Studies and Bruce R. Joyce.

[1] John Dewey, *Democracy and Education*. New York: Macmillan, 1916, especially Chapters 13 and 14.

[2] Charles Hubbard Judd, *Education and Social Progress*. New York: Harcourt, Brace, 1934, p. 263.

from available content, made the suggestion in a little different form when he suggested that few especially illuminating ideas be identified and that these be introduced early and reiterated until the learner can use their power. "Let the main ideas which are introduced into a child's education be few and important, and let them be thrown into every combination possible. The child should make them his own, and should understand their application here and now in the circumstances of his actual life. From the very beginning of his education, the child should experience the joy of discovery. The discovery which he has to make, is that general ideas give an understanding of that stream of events which pours through his life, which is his life." [3]

Recently, Jerome Bruner has restated and popularized this approach to the analysis of subject matter.[4] Bruner's formulation rests on the contention that the product of scholarly endeavor is a series of major ideas or relationships which explain the findings of the field. The scholar collects facts and thinks about them. The relationships he sees or thinks he sees among them are the heart of his knowledge, for it is in the light of these relationships that the facts are explained. These relationships Bruner refers to as elements of the *structure* of the discipline.

For an example of the development of a major structural idea, we might turn to anthropology. That each human society has developed distinctive modes of behavior, or norms, was established early in anthropological research, and as an idea was recognized from the time of the ancient Greeks. However, the idea that culture conditions the psychological makeup of individuals awaited the 1930's. Ruth Benedict found that the culture of the Southwest Pueblos was strikingly different from the surrounding cultures and sought for an explanation. She concluded that the difference was produced by the "psychological set" of the cultures. Thus, she concluded that culture affects the very personality of its members. Benedict thereby created a new relationship among anthropological data, one that has resulted in numerous studies of personalities in differing cultures.[5] By seeing a new relationship among facts, she made the facts more understandable and gave rise to a search for more information to see if this new idea would stand up. We shall

---

[3] Alfred North Whitehead, *The Aims of Education and Other Essays*. New York: Macmillan, 1929, p. 3.

[4] Jerome Bruner, *The Process of Education*. Cambridge, Mass.: Harvard University Press, 1960.

[5] Milton Singer, "A Survey of Culture and Personality Theory and Research," in *Studying Personality Cross-Culturally*, Bert Kaplan, ed. Evanston, Ill.: Row and Peterson, 1961, p. 23ff.

return later to this function of structural ideas—guiding future searches for information.

The potential utility of structural ideas in education is very great. Since they are the part of a discipline which has the greatest "explaining power" the learner who masters them will be able to understand information much more coherently. Also, since they are relatively few in number, they are more manageable than the masses of data from which they are drawn—they are a kind of map of the fields of raw data—and the child who is introduced to them will have at his command the most powerful scholarly ideas which we possess.

Bruner has provided us with a series of hypotheses concerning the application of structure to education.

1. The major structural ideas of scholarly disciplines are essentially very simple.
2. These ideas can be developed in a form that even young children can discover (in childish terms, at first, and progressively in more sophisticated forms).
3. Structural ideas can be utilized as organizing themes in curriculums, being reiterated and rediscovered in more complex and adequate terms.
4. The child who is taught in such a way that he discovers the structural ideas in discipline will be advantaged in that:
   a. Structure facilitates memory. Learning how things are related makes it easier to remember facts.
   b. Structure provides intellectual power by ensuring greater comprehension of the area concerned.
   c. Structure facilitates transfer of learning to new situations and problems.
   d. Structure is the language of the scholar. By learning structure the learner is brought closer to the leading edge of the discipline. He learns to think with the most advanced minds in the field.[6]

These hypotheses are so tantalizing that one might ask why we don't immediately proceed to select those structures which appear to help us best accomplish our objective of social education and proceed to the experiments we will need to test these hypotheses.

However, an attempt to find the major ideas which lie in the social sciences will not be an easy task.

When one concentrates on the mathematics curriculum, he can call together mathematicians and educators, and they can concentrate their attention on the structure of a single discipline. Furthermore, it is clear that a portion of the curriculum will be focused on mathematical content alone. The political scientist, asked to

---

[6] Bruner, *op. cit.*

contribute to a discussion of the social studies, knows that the content from his discipline will be mixed with that of several others. His ideas have to be placed in context with those of the economist, historian, and so on. What may be a more serious problem in the examination of the social sciences is that the older ones have not had a tradition of quantitative methods. Their structures have, therefore, not been expressed in the terms of mathematical logic which so helps us sort out the content of the natural sciences. The new social sciences, while they have been built on a tradition of quantitative approaches, have the problem of newness. Their content is emerging and developing at such a rate that their taxonomies, terms, and methods are less discrete and definite than are those of the older disciplines. A third problem is that the social world itself is so elusive, so much in flux, and holds still for study so less readily than does the physical world. For example, social psychology defines attitudes in several ways, and attitudes manifest themselves in many ways and vary enormously according to numerous conditions. This uncertainty in the social sciences is reflected in the relatively different statistical levels of confidence which are utilized in the social and the natural sciences. The psychologist will accept a proposition at the 5 per cent level. Imagine a physicist who reported that we could accept his observation that day is brighter than night, with the probability that he could be correct 19 out of 20 times! But that is the relative uncertainty with which we live in the social sciences.

Eventually, any approach to the determination of the social sciences to find their structures will have to take the form of a long-term effort by scholars representing the several social sciences and educators who combine both acquaintance with behavioral sciences and sophistication in translating ideas into operational constructs which can be approached by children. Let us look further into the nature of structures and see if we can find some clues about the possible shape of such an inquiry.

Structures and Strategies

We should begin by looking briefly at some notions concerning the nature of knowledge that should be taught. The contemporary struggle to determine what content will be useful dates at least from Comenius' attempt to focus attention on content that will be socially useful.[7] Comenius saw education as the process by which the child approaches and solves problems, acquiring ideas about the

---

[7] John Ames Comenius. *Selections*. Lausanne, Switzerland: UNESCO, 1957.

nature of the world in the process. His contemporary, John Locke, no foe of independent thought, nonetheless saw childhood as a time for learning the essential knowledge which will prepare the youngster later to be a rational thinker. He believed that the products of past thinkers should be presented to the child who should master these products against the time when he, too, would be able to be an independent thinker. This view of Locke's was typical of many of the views of subject matter through to the end of the nineteenth century. Once something had been "found out" it took its place as a fact and might be learned by someone. The child would not necessarily be let in on the hypothetical nature of "facts."

The pragmatists struck hard at the notion that knowledge was fixed. They emphasized the distinction between physical reality and our conceptions of physical reality. As our conceptions of reality are imperfect and changing, subject matter becomes transient and imperfect—the product of the mind rather than a necessary accurate representation of external reality. Thus, Dewey was able to say, "All knowledge, as issuing from reflection, is experimental in the literal physical sense of experimental. . . . It involves the explorations by which relevant data are procured and the physical analyses by which they are refined and made precise; it comprises the readings by which information is got hold of, the words which are experimented with, and the calculations by which the significance of entertained conceptions or hypotheses is elaborated." [8] Prior to the work of the pragmatists many laymen and school teachers thought knowledge consisted of rather formal and unchanging concepts. The pragmatists turned the concept into the hypothesis. One experiments, and one concludes. The conclusion is a hypothesis which merits further experimentation, not a concept which will last forever. The hypothesis is expressed in words whose meaning varies with the experience and feelings of the perceptor.

While this view of knowledge is in accord with what is happening in every scholarly discipline, the textbooks and methods of schools have largely concentrated on the identification of verbal conclusions which are presumably to be taught to children. To read an elementary-school history text, for example, is to find statements of conclusions to be learned—most of these books, in fact, cover ground too quickly to permit the presentation of data from which the conclusions were deduced. Knowledge, then, at least the conception of it which we frequently teach children, becomes a system of pronouncements. In other words, when we ask children to learn state-

---

[8] John Dewey, *Essays in Experimental Logic*. Chicago: University of Chicago Press, 1916.

ments as if they represent fixed and unchanging ideas, we are teaching them a conception of the nature of knowledge which is out of line with current scholarly thought.

Structure and Certainty

Let us turn again to the question "What is structure?" Bruner explains that it is "the way things are related." What he means, really, is that structure is the way we think things are related. He gives the example of an inchworm crawling up graph paper held at various inclinations. The inchworm varies his angle of progression across the graph paper so that his angle of climb does not exceed a certain proportion. We have discovered a *relation* between slope and climb. Now, one may ask how the identification of that relationship helps us select content for the child to learn. It doesn't, very much, but before we make a hasty conclusion, let us examine some other living organisms to see if they control their movements in patterns analogous to those of the inchworm. We can look, for example, at movements of the sunflower plant. Lo and behold, we find that the sunflower reacts to direction and intensity of illumination, turning it blossom to face the light source. We could examine further examples, but the point is clear. We have discovered what we presently call tropism, an innate tendency to react to a stimulus in a definite way. Now, the tropistic relationship between organisms and stimuli becomes a structural idea in those sciences which study the behavior of living things. A person who discovers the idea of tropism is prepared to investigate many behaviors in living things.

Bruner suggests that if we can identify major ideas like these we will have identified the organization of the discipline concerned. By teaching these structural ideas, or by introducing them to the child, we will help him to identify an organization for the things he learns, an organization which will be in accord with the way the scholar organizes the information from his discipline. If we follow these structural ideas, says Bruner, we will avoid teaching fragmented bits of knowledge from a field, because the structural ideas are themselves of relationships which have been at least tentatively established. The child will thus have better comprehension of the field and an easier time remembering what he has learned, and his learning will be much closer to the front-line thinking in the field. Further, since learning which stresses structural relationships within a field emphasizes the identification of relationships, a program of instruction which is centered around structures will emphasize the discovery of relationships by the child and hence prepare him to be an independent thinker. Bruner rather carefully stresses that the structural idea which the child forms need not be the same form as the idea possessed by the scholar. The child should discover the structures in a form which he can handle, and then rediscover more and more complex and adequate forms of the structure as he proceeds through the curriculum. This practice in revising ideas will teach him to hold them tentatively and prevent him from developing the erroneous notion that present knowledge will last for all time.

Joseph Schwab has approached the idea of structure in a manner similar to Bruner. Schwab emphasizes the changing ideas of subject matter which recent scientific discoveries have forced upon us. "Forty years ago, it was possible for many scientists and most educators to nurse the illusion that science was a matter of patiently seeking the facts of nature and accurately reporting them. The conclusions of science were supposed to be nothing more than the summaries of these facts. . . . By the mid-twenties, the revolution in physics had gone so far that we were faced with the fact that some of the oldest and least questioned of our ideas could no longer be treated as literally true—or literally false. . . . Our old assertions about these matters were changed because physicists agreed to treat them in a new way—neither as self-evident truths nor as matters for immediate empirical verification. They were to be treated, instead, as *principles of inquiry*, conceptual structures which could be revised when necessary in directions dictated by large complexes of theory, diverse bodies of data, and numerous criteria of progress in science." [9] In other words, the scholar looks for new information in terms of ideas which spring from the old. "A fresh line of scientific research has its origin, not in objective facts alone, but in a conception, a construction of the mind. And on this conception, all else depends. It tells us what facts to look for in the research. It tells us what meaning to assign to these facts." [10]

Put another way, scholarly inquiry results in a series of tentative ideas about the relationships between the facts. These relationships give rise to further inquiry which frequently requires that the ideas be modified or discarded completely. Previous conceptions of scholarship gave us the "impression that the goal of all the sciences was a congeries of well-tested hypotheses," [11] or a series of statements

---

[9] Joseph P. Schwab, "The Concept of Structure in the Subject Fields." An address presented to the Twentieth Annual Meeting of the Council on Cooperation in Teacher Education of the American Council on Education, Washington, D.C., 1961.

[10] *Ibid.*

[11] *Ibid.*

on which we would be able to bank. However, the view that science is the discovery of relationships on the basis of which further research is carried out in order to add to and modify these relationships, "renders scientific knowledge fragile and subject to change." [12]

We are now in a position to make a tentative statement of the function of structural ideas.

First of all, they are expressions of generalizations concerning the data of a field. They are the ideas which show how things are related in any given sphere of inquiry.

Second, they are the basis for organizing knowledge in a field. Facts are classified according to the way they relate to other facts. In the example of tropism, for example, the behavior of certain animals and plants would be classified together because of their similarity.

Third, structure guides the search for future knowledge. It does this in two ways. Sometimes knowledge is looked for because a relationship has been discovered in another place. For instance, when Benedict hypothesized that certain cultural differences were the product of a psychological set produced by that culture in the American Southwest, it behooved other anthropologists to see if psychological sets could be detected among the aborigines of Northern Australia, for example. At other times, the awareness that a structural idea is inadequate gives rise to research. Sociology had to invent the idea "anomie" to explain certain normless behaviors which have been observed in mass societies where norms have usually been thought to be particularly strong. As the guide for research, structure serves as a kind of "strategy" for a discipline, a tactical guide to use when venturing into previously unexplored territory.

I have presented evidence that structures should be thought of as tentative and changing, and that they should be discovered by the learner rather than laid out for him. Bruner has given us several hypotheses to test, among which are the propositions that we will be able to identify simple forms of structural ideas which even young children can discover and apply to their own problems.

Let us assume that we will be able to identify structures in the social sciences. What will be some of our tasks before they will be useful in education?

First, we will have to be satisfied that they can be discovered in a form which will be useful in citizenship education. The learner has to have potential use for the ideas or they will wither and be

---

[12] *Ibid.*

of little good to him. Insofar as is possible, we want the ideas we present to become part of his permanent intellectual equipment, available as he needs it to attack new problems. The ideas should be ones which will serve one or more of the following functions:

1. Illuminate his study of some topic, such as American history, which he will meet many times in school and life. If the idea can illuminate an area which will recur, then it will have much opportunity for exercise.
2. Be applicable to the study of social and personal problems which will make up part of the curriculum. It should help the child as he studies contemporary affairs, or local government structures and functions, or problems of democratic organization in his classroom. The study of economic relations in his own community should, if properly conducted, result in the development of some structural ideas which the child can apply to the study of economic relations in other nations, or in colonial times, for example.

In other words, even as the structure of a discipline provides the scholar with a strategy which he can use to approach the acquisition of knowledge, so the learning of structural ideas should provide the child with a systematic method of attack on areas where he seeks new knowledge. If he learns how rainfall and land use are related in the United States, he should use that relationship as he looks at either land use or climate in Austria. If he learns that political beliefs were related to economic interests in Revolutionary times, he should seek to find if the same relationship holds true today. In other words, if structural ideas are to be useful educationally, it will be because we have found a method for helping children learn to use them as they pursue research on their own.

In this writer's opinion, structural strategies will be useful in all aspects of the social studies curriculum, especially in terms of our view of social education as preparing the child with the modes of thought necessary to effective citizenship. Topics for study in social studies curriculum might be thought of as coming from four sources. These are: topics dealing with past times, topics from contemporary cultures, topics centered around contemporary affairs as they happen, and topics centered around the conduct of the classroom. Let us examine very briefly the possible application of structural ideas to topics drawn from these four sources.

All the social sciences bear on the study of the community, one of the topics dealing with contemporary society. The very young child can find economic functions in his community that he can apply to the study of other communities. A six-year-old I know classified several communities which she knows according to available consumer goods. "This one you can buy gas and some groceries. That one has more, you can buy shoes and some clothes, and they have a movie. The next one has almost everything, just like Newark does, but they're not like the city, which has even more."

All the social sciences apply to the study of history. Sociology, for instance, can supply the idea of values to the study of the ancient Greek society, to American Colonial and Revolutionary times, and to the Civil War. Contemporary affairs in the community can illustrate how land use has become important to city government, as in the case of the second graders who studied the need for a park in their town, or a third grade which found that there were laws which prevented building a factory in the center of town. The classroom provides a perfect laboratory with which to experiment with ideas about the political behavior of men.

Identification of teachable forms of social science structures will not solve all the problems of social studies content. It should, however, aid in the identification of themes which can focus and strengthen elementary social studies instruction and provide the basis for content continuity with secondary education. It also will enable the testing of Bruner's exciting hypotheses concerning the benefits of teaching structures and strategies for children's thinking.

Further, although most social studies curriculums do not reflect it, there exists much basic scholarship in the area. I refer specifically to Hanna's work at Stanford, which certainly can and should be extended in terms of structures and strategies.[13]

---

[13] Paul R. Hanna and John R. Lee, "Generalizations from the Social Sciences," Section one of Chapter III, "Content in the Social Studies" of the Thirty-Second *Yearbook* of the National Council for the Social Studies, John U. Michaelis, ed. *Social Studies in Elementary Schools*. Washington, D.C.: National Education Association, 1962.

The Social Studies and the Humanities

*T*HERE HAS ALWAYS BEEN A CLOSE KINSHIP between the social studies and the humanities. Whether history belongs to the social sciences or to the humanities has never been resolved. Many historians allow that it can be either, depending on the approach and the style of inquiry applied. In a real sense the humanities represent some of the aesthetic products of human societies and their cultures—their art, music, literature, poetry, drama. With increasing emphasis on culture studies in the elementary school, it follows that the humanities take on added importance.

The humanities contribute to the enrichment of the social studies in a number of ways. Much of their value is inherent in their providing an additional dimension of meaning to social studies concepts. Much of social studies education has dealt with the study of people meeting their basic needs. Basic needs are often interpreted as food, clothing, and shelter. This formula of basic need satisfaction is applied to studies of the local community area as well as to the study of foreign groups. These are the simplest and most apparent needs that human beings have. But human beings have other needs as well, and it is through the satisfaction of these other needs that they acquire much of their "human-ness." These needs have to do with the expression of feelings and aesthetic impulses in a way that will endure throughout an individual's life span. Man creates poetry and stories that are passed on from one generation to the next. He paints or carves drawings on the walls of caves. Later in his development he composes music and invents sophisticated instruments through which he can express himself musically. He writes literary pieces that are printed. These, too, are important needs that in one way or another all human beings share. If social studies programs are designed to help pupils understand human societies, the aesthetic and cultural products of a society can provide important insights into the core values that guide the behavior of people. Perhaps this is the most important contribution of the humanities to social studies education.

The humanities are important because they provide children with experiences that are in themselves satisfying. Like virtue, they provide their own reward. They could be experienced quite apart from social studies and hold value for pupils. Placing them within the context of social studies gives them added meaning. A Japanese painting, an Eskimo carving, or a recording of a melody of frontier music can be appreciated and enjoyed simply as works of art. Experiencing them while related units are being studied in social studies can make these art objects even more significant to the learner than they otherwise might be.

When properly taught the humanities often carry delicate affective overtones that are long remembered by pupils. They sensitize pupils to man's efforts to create the beautiful and to his attempt to express his feelings through the arts and literature. In the humanities man reaches beyond himself, yet he himself is the creator. In the humanities we find man at his best.

Much of what the child learns in social studies will erode over a period of time. Battles and political campaigns won and lost will fade from memory. Dates and places will be lost to the retrieval system. Men who achieved great goals, with a few obvious exceptions, may or may not be remembered. But those experiences that precipitate deeply moving responses to art, beauty, drama, and literature become a permanent part of the individual's response to life itself. Decades later the individual will still recall that "I had a teacher once who loved . . ."

CHILDREN'S BOOKS:
MIRRORS OF SOCIAL DEVELOPMENT *

Richard L. Mandel

How does our society inculcate its basic values?

To throw some light on this problem, we examined two sets of American children's books. Such books are a highly valuable source of information about the methods a society uses to instill its basic value system, because those methods are most clearly observable while a society is rearing its children.

The growing child has not yet learned how he should judge and act. He is in the process of acquiring his society's most fundamental system of values and motivations, which will make up his basic attitude and behavior orientation for the rest of his life. Thus, the society, unconsciously more than consciously, makes demands on the child for the fundamental kind of character its every socialized member must possess.

What is important for us is that these demands are being made in clear and simple terms so that the child can easily understand and fulfil them.

For our study, we have selected two sets of children's beginning readers from two periods of United States history: the mid-nineteenth century and the mid-twentieth century. We will analyze, compare, and contrast the books to discover differences in ways used to inculcate social character in the young reader.

Our essential assumption, then, is that widely read books written for and about children reveal the methods used to form the normative social character sought by the child's society. We can establish several concrete indications that the fictive world of the books does indeed reflect the world of their readers.

For each period we will rely on a series of books that have a fairly consistent set of characters. Such a series will give us a well-developed picture of the child's life during the period under consideration. Since we are dealing with social character as developed by the society in the upbringing of its children, we have selected two series that depict the activities of children. In the two

Richard L. Mandel is Administrative Assistant to the President of the School Board, Baltimore, Maryland.

* Reprinted from *The Elementary School Journal* 64:190–199, 1964, with permission of The University of Chicago Press and Richard L. Mandel. Copyright © 1964.

series the storybook characters are the age of the intended reader, who was undoubtedly supposed to identify with them. By analyzing the characters, we can hope to understand what was expected of the child.

For the contemporary series, I have chosen the well-known Dick and Jane books for beginning readers up through the second grade (1). For the mid-nineteenth century series, I have chosen the Rollo series by Jacob Abbott (2–12). The tremendously popular Rollo books were published from about 1844 to 1860. Like the Dick and Jane books, the Rollo books under consideration are intended for beginning readers about six to eight years old.

Rollo and Dick

Rollo lives on a farm owned and run by his father. Mother spends her day doing housework. She is assisted by a servant girl who figures very little in the stories and by Rollo's older sister Mary. Father has an orphaned, teen-age boy Jonas to help manage the farm.

Mary and the kind, hard-working Jonas are depicted as "good" children who are respected by everyone. They, with their clear-cut characters, serve as foils for Rollo, whose character is not quite so simple.

Rollo's father is fairly well off, and he can afford to give his son a substantial number of toys, books, and treats of various kinds, including excursions and even the privilege of accompanying him on extended journeys.

Rollo's family is very religious by current standards. God as an authority and overseer constantly figures in conversations; and prayers are said every night.

Although life on the farm is fairly autonomous, visits by relatives who live nearby, occasional trips to a nearby town for supplies and farm business, and going to school all keep Rollo in contact with the world outside his father's farm.

Each of the Rollo books centers on some aspect of Rollo's life. Note the titles: *Rollo Learning To Talk, Rollo Learning To Read, Rollo at Play, Rollo at Work, Rollo at School.* These books try to follow the normal pattern of a child's development. Thus, Rollo and the young reader grow up together.

Dick, Rollo's contemporary counterpart, lives on Pleasant Street in the suburbs. Almost all his activities take place right in his neighborhood. Mother stays at home doing the housework, but occasionally she has time to go on a trip to the zoo or to join Father in games with Dick and his sisters, Jane, who is about Dick's age, and Baby Sally. Father works in the city and comes home every evening. Unlike Rollo's parents, Dick's mother and father have a good deal of time for their children.

Dick and Jane have a great many toys and pets. They go to the country regularly to visit their grandparents, who own a farm.

Whereas Rollo walked some distance to school and met a whole new group of people there, Dick goes to school with the same neighbors he plays with every day.

Like Rollo, Dick and Jane and their friends grow up with the reader. The individual books, however, do not center on a single topic. Rather they concern themselves with the over-all life of the children and have such titles as *We Look and See*, *We Work and Play*, *Fun with Dick and Jane*, and *Friends and Neighbors*.

Natural Evil Versus Natural Good

Rollo's life on the farm is full of hard work and is not easy. Beneath all that is said and done in the Rollo books, there is an undercurrent that the world is indeed a serious place, fraught with sources of trouble. Learning to live properly in society is a job that requires constant attention and concentrated effort.

This idea is implied in the purpose of the Rollo series, as expressed by the author in his "Notice to Parents" in *Rollo at Work* and reaffirmed in all subsequent volumes. The purpose of the books is to help in "cultivating *the thinking powers* . . . promoting the progress of children *in reading* . . . cultivating the *amiable and gentle qualities of the heart*" (5: 5).

Rollo must be trained to develop inner powers and qualities to protect himself against the evil prevalent in the world around him. This basic mistrust of the world is expressed in many ways. There are always "bad boys" Rollo must avoid playing with; he must never become familiar with strangers.

Even more important, however, is a feeling that while Rollo is potentially a good boy, he is filled with bad impulses and tendencies that he must be constantly on the watch for and that he must learn to suppress.

The Rollo series consists of experiences, most of them unpleasant, in which Rollo does something naughty or careless that has bad consequences. He interrupts his mother at her work, causing her to make a mistake; he leaves something that had been intrusted to him on a rock while he plays, and he loses it; he loses interest in a tedious job his father gave him, and he does not get it done on time. More often than not, if the evil in the world does not punish Rollo for letting down his guard, the evil within him, momentarily given rein, somehow gets him into a tight spot.

Often we see the two evils combining. When Rollo forgetfully goes into a field he has been told not to enter, a farmer leaving the field accidentally locks Rollo inside. When Rollo carelessly plays with a strange little boy, the boy accidentally breaks his knife.

But for Dick the world is certainly not dangcrous and full of forebodings of evil. We get the impression that his world is waiting eagerly for any child who will walk in and introduce himself. Strangers excite interest; the children on the block eagerly await and welcome new neighbors.

Bobby, a new boy, is watching Jim and John dig for potatoes in their garden. He would like to join them, but he is shy and afraid to ask. When he finally summons up the courage and asks, the two boys unhesitatingly accept him, and some unknown force rewards him by enabling him to find the biggest potato.

Nature never conspires against the careless child; there are no "bad boys" to avoid. Everyone—from Big Bill the friendly policeman to Zeke the handyman—is ready to help a child out of a scrape, whether he has lost five pennies or has lost his way in a game.

Similarly, there is no indication that there is anything within the child that he must learn to control. Dick and his friends merely follow their impulses toward play and fun. They have a good time, approved and fostered by the adults around them.

This contrast between Rollo and Dick will be clarified and enlarged upon as we discuss other problems, but we may make our first generalization now:

I. In the first group of books, the world is full of dangers and evil temptations, and the child himself is full of evil impulses that he must learn to control. In the second group, the world is full of good possibilities, and the child himself has only good impulses which should be given rein and encouragement.

Precept Versus Experience

With all the potential for badness outside and inside Rollo, it is natural that he should be given some sort of mechanism to protect himself from danger. From the first, Rollo is being taught a code of Christian virtues, which he is to adopt in order to resist the evil around and within him.

The first step in inculcating such a set of rules for behavior is to impress the child with the wisdom and the sanctity of authority.

Rollo, by negative example of what happens if he ignores authority, must be taught to obey his parents unquestioningly.

The following is typical of a story in the first Rollo book:

> Here is a picture about powder. Don't you see it flashing—blazing up? There are some boys; they have been playing with powder. They are bad boys; their mother told them they must not play with powder, for they would get hurt; but they did not obey her. They went away out into the woods;—do you see the trees there? Well, they went out into the woods, where their mother could not see them, and played with the powder. They were bad boys; they disobeyed their mother. The powder exploded; it flashed in their faces, and burnt their eyes. Do you see the smoke? and see! one of the boys has put his hands up to his face, because it has burnt him; and there is another boy lying upon the ground. Poor boy, I am afraid he is very much hurt; perhaps it has put his eyes out, so that he will never see again. Poor boys, if they had done as their mother told them, they would not have been burnt so. But they were bad boys, they disobeyed their mother, and now you see how they are punished [2: 23].

Unquestioning obedience having been established, it remains for society to give the individual inner strengths and virtues so that he can confront new situations with his own established mechanisms. Rollo is constantly doing wrong things. His father must constantly point out the mistakes he has made so that he will not make them again.

Rollo has been eagerly looking forward to an excursion and has insisted all day, in spite of threatening clouds, that it will not rain. He persists in this conviction even after drops begin falling. His father reasons with him:

> "You are *self-conceited*—vainly imagining that you, a little boy of seven years old, can judge better than your father and mother, and obstinately persisting in your opinion that it is not going to rain, when the rain has actually commenced and is falling faster and faster. You are *ungrateful* to speak reproachfully of me, and give me pain, by your ill-will, when I have been planning this excursion, in a great degree, for your enjoyment, and only give it up because I am absolutely compelled to do it by a storm; *undutiful* in showing such a repining, unsubmissive spirit towards your father; *unjust* in making Lucy and all of us suffer, because you are unwilling to submit to these circumstances that we cannot control; *selfish* in being unwilling that it should rain and interfere with your ride, when you know that rain is so much wanted in all the fields, all over the country; and *impious*, in openly rebelling against God, and censuring the arrangements of his providence, and pretending to think that they are made just to trouble you" [4: 80].

The excerpt is taken from the fourth book of the series, *Rollo at Play*, the subtitle of which is *Safe Amusements*. Notice that even playing means playing properly, at the right time, in the right way, with the right people and toys. Every situation and action has for Rollo a potentiality for wrong behavior.

From the world of simple obedience to outer authority, through the world of inner virtue, Rollo is led to the man's world of law. In a later volume, Rollo becomes involved in a situation in which a friend loses a knife that was lent to him by another boy. Rollo's father discusses the law of bailment with his son. This is the conclusion of their conversation:

> "I want you to remember what I have said, and practice according to it. Boys bail things to one another very often, and a great many disputes arise among them, because they don't understand the law of bailment. It applies to boys as well as men. It is founded on principles of justice and common sense, and, of course, what is just and equitable among men, is just and equitable among boys.
>
> "You must remember that whenever anything belonging to one boy is intrusted to another in any way, if it is for the benefit of the bailee, if any accident happens to it, he must make it good; unless it was some *inevitable* accident, which could not have been prevented by the utmost care. If it is for the benefit of the bailor, that is, the boy who intrusts it, then he can't require the other to pay for it, unless he was grossly negligent. And if it was for the common benefit of both, then if the bailee takes what may be called good care of it, he is not liable to pay; if he does not take good care, he is" [9: 74].

This is how the important moral and social values are presented to Rollo and inculcated into his thought and behavior.

Since Dick's world is seen in a different way, and since Dick himself does not have Rollo's tendencies, no such code needs to be impressed upon him.

Situations that would call for long talks by Rollo's parents turn out well for Dick and his friends. There is no need to be constantly on guard, no need to master a set of abstract moral principles.

Tom goes to the store and buys some cookies; on the way home he gives all of them away to the friends and neighbors he meets. No lecture ensues on being carelessly spendthrifty or too free with people. By coincidence, Mom has just finished baking a batch of cookies, and Tom can eat them.

Again, Bobby takes the biggest apple from a pile and puts it in his back pocket. The apple gets stuck there, and he cannot sit down in class, but no moral about greediness is forthcoming. The teacher merely cuts a slice out of the apple to remove it. It is no longer the biggest apple, and everyone has a good laugh.

Jane takes her sister Sally's toys and opens up a store; Dick takes his mother's food and opens up another store. Rollo's parents would have a field day in a situation like this, when toys and supper are found missing. Here is what happens in *Our New Friends:*

> "I see," said Mother with a laugh. "You took many things, but you did not ask for them. Now Sally wants her toys, and I must take all the food."
>
> So Dick and Jane helped take everything into the house again. Soon they did not have anything in the two stores. Not an apple or an egg or a cookie. Not a car or boat or ball or doll. Not anything for anyone to buy. But soon Dick and Jane were glad. Soon they had a very good dinner [1: 137].

Where does Dick find his source of moral and social value? The problem involves the very complex consideration of identity, which we will discuss later. But from what has already been said we may present our second generalization:

II. In the first group of books, social behavior is handed down with unshakable authority to the child in a complete set of established rules and virtues which he must live up to. In the contemporary books, no such abstract rules are instilled in the child, but he seems to get his ideas about right and wrong from everyday social experience.

Father Versus Peer Group

We have discussed the inculcation of Rollo's abstract code of moral behavior. What motivates Rollo to accept and follow this code? How does this motivation come about?

Besides the character of Rollo himself, Rollo's father is unquestionably the most important fact in the book and in Rollo's life. After Rollo's mother has taught him to talk, Father figures in every stage of Rollo's development and activity.

In every situation Father presents the problem to be solved or the goal to be achieved and explains in the detail we have observed why an action is right and should be done or why an attitude is good and should be held. Father doles out punishments and rewards; he corrects and encourages.

It is Father who introduces Rollo to society, giving him work to prepare him for the bigger and bigger jobs ahead, teaching him the correct forms of social behavior, taking him on trips to encounter the larger world around the farm.

Yet there is very little of what we would call sympathetic kindness on Father's part. He is willing to lead only if Rollo is willing to try and follow. His love is not given freely, but must be earned.

Two stories from *Rollo Learning To Read* will serve to illustrate. In the first, Father discusses with Rollo the boy's plans for the day and points out that what Rollo calls *mine* really does not belong to him at all, since Rollo neither produces nor earns any of the things he uses. They really belong to his father, who lends them to Rollo as long as his son deserves them:

> "Well," said his father, "I shall let you wear these clothes of mine then. I am very glad I have got a house, and some breakfast, and some clothes for my little Rollo boy, since you have not got any of your own. But I think if I get a house for you to live in, and breakfast for you to eat, and clothes for you to wear, you ought to be a very careful, faithful, obedient, little boy" [3: 108].

Even more striking is the story called "Selling a Boy," in which a poor father tries to sell his own son to get bread to eat. He is offered first one, then ten, then a hundred dollars for his boy. Each time he rejects the money because it is not enough to compensate for his good companion who will be unable to share the bread and may be treated harshly. The father finally determines not to sell his son, but to find work to support them both. The conclusion:

> This is a fictitious story. It is written to teach children that if they are good, and kind, and obedient, their fathers will love them, and work hard, if necessary, to get them bread, and will not sell them, even if any body should offer them a thousand dollars [3: 180].

Father then is the giver of gifts: reading, social code, material well-being. These gifts, however, are given only to the child he loves, and Rollo must earn Father's love and respect by becoming like Father. Only as Rollo masters the rules and achieves the goals established by Father, can he be sure of his love and the security derived from it; and it is Rollo's father himself who continually embodies all the moral, social, and material virtues toward which Rollo must strive. By identifying with Father, Rollo becomes like Father, is rewarded by Father, knows he has done right, and is secure and happy.

While Rollo had a definite system of rules to work with and a specific authority to hand them down and motivate him to accept them, Dick has no such obvious rules. It is thus more difficult to find his source of authority. By setting down general observations about the Dick and Jane books, however, some particularly striking and relevant aspects of Dick's life will become apparent.

The books consist almost exclusively of conversation among the children; there is very little narrative. The children seldom interact with their parents or other figures of adult authority. When this interaction does occur, it is the adults who react to a situation established by the children.

The children spend their time having fun while playing with one another, while going to school, or while participating in humorous little incidents described as *funny* or *silly*. An unbelievable amount of time is spent at parties they host for one another and in planning and attending social events, usually birthday parties, at which gifts are given. The children frequently visit relatives and neighbors and go in groups to places like zoos and construction sites.

Perhaps we should also note that while Dick has a sister his own age and a baby sister he plays with, Rollo, for all practical purposes, appears to be an only child. Mary is always inside the house helping Mother, and Jonas is in the field working with Father.

We arrive at the conclusion that Dick's behavior is distinctly gregarious and what we would call social in nature; he is continually and intensely involved with his peer group.

Bobby is rewarded for trying to make friends as recorded in the potato story. Tom is rewarded for generously sharing his cookies. Even Dick and Jane seem to be rewarded for playing store, although their game involved taking what did not belong to them.

As we have suggested, while Rollo is adopting precepts, Dick is adapting to social experience. These stories obviously demonstrate the value of experience that involves interaction with friends. We are dealing with a friendly world. The character of the good people who populate this world is molded by daily interaction with their peers, who become their authority for correct social behavior.

As would be expected from our first generalization, there is a noteworthy lack of negative examples in these stories. One can assume, however, that Bobby would have been "missing something" if he had not forced himself to make friends. His uneasiness about his hesitancy indicates this, and he is suitably rewarded for his friendly behavior by finding the biggest potato. We feel that all the children would feel uncomfortable at being removed from their group.

In *Friends and Neighbors* there is, in fact, the story of John Hill who visits Grandma Hill on Pleasant Street and is uneasy because he fears there will be no boys and girls to play with: "Oh Grandmother! I don't think I'll like the city. I don't see any children to play with me" (1: 57). Of course his fears disappear as soon as he is happily welcomed by all the children of the neighborhood

Here is our third generalization:

III. In the first group of books, the child finds his source of identity and motivation in his father. In the second group of books, the child's identity is confirmed and his social behavior is molded by his peer group.

We should recall that the explicit purpose of the Rollo primers included the cultivation of *"thinking powers"* and of *"amiable and gentle qualities of the heart"*—inner strengths to be instilled in the child. The only explicit purpose of the Dick and Jane books is to teach the child reading—a basic element of much contemporary social experience.

Thus our essential assumption, that the content of the books accurately reflects their societies' methods of inculcating basic social character, seems to be borne out in this case. The internal content of the books correlates closely with their external purpose in their respective societies.

One World Versus Two Worlds

We have of course been oversimplifying at every turn, but we must keep in mind that our materials themselves are purposely oversimplified for the benefit of their readers. Indeed, that is why we choose them. One more comparison can be made which will serve as our conclusion by incorporating the other three.

The dangerous nature of the world in which Rollo lives requires that a definite authority be established, the imitation of which will protect the child. There is only one world, one authority, one source of identification and motivation. Rollo must grow up to be like his father to satisfy the demands made upon him. The law of bailment "applies to boys as well as men . . . and, of course, what is just and equitable among men, is just and equitable among boys" (9: 74). "The men's way is best," says Rollo (9: 91). There is one ideal of social character, and Rollo's training serves to bring him ever closer to achieving that ideal as embodied in his ever present father.

Dick's world requires no constant watchfulness with confirmed inner virtues always on hand to protect him. His identity and motivation are found in the free and easy interaction readily available to him. His world is distinct from the world of adults. Indeed, adults foster the autonomy of Dick and his group. Each individual finds self-confirmation and a source of meaning in social interaction with his peers.

IV. In the first group of books, the child's social character is developed by his being brought into the world of adults. In the second group of books, the child finds acceptance and meaning from being a member of his peer group, and his social character seems to have its source there.

Our children's books mirror broad trends in methods of inculcating American social character. How these changing methods relate to different kinds of social character and what the social and historical reasons are for such changes are problems for further study. In these investigations, children's books undoubtedly will continue to provide a valuable and lively source of information.

REFERENCES

1. William S. Gray, Marion Monroe, A. Sterl Artley, May Hill Arbuthnot, *We Look and See, We Work and Play, We Come and Go, Fun with Dick and Jane, Our New Friends, Friends and Neighbors, More Friends and Neighbors.* Chicago: Scott, Foresman, 1956.
2. Jacob Abbott, *Rollo Learning To Talk.* Boston: Phillips, Sampson, 1855.
3. Jacob Abbott, *Rollo Learning to Read.* Boston: Phillips, Sampson, 1855.
4. Jacob Abbott, *Rollo at Play.* Philadelphia: Hogan & Thompson, 1850.
5. Jacob Abbott, *Rollo at Work.* Boston: Phillips, Sampson, 1855.
6. Jacob Abbott, *Rollo at School.* Boston: Phillips, Sampson, 1855.
7. Jacob Abbott, *Rollo's Vacation.* Boston: Phillips, Sampson, 1855.
8. Jacob Abbott, *Rollo's Experiments.* Boston: Phillips, Sampson, 1855.
9. Jacob Abbott, *Rollo's Museum.* Philadelphia: Hogan & Thompson, 1850.
10. Jacob Abbott, *Rollo's Travels.* Boston: Phillips, Sampson, 1855.
11. Jacob Abbott, *Rollo's Correspondence.* Boston: Phillips, Sampson, 1855.
12. Jacob Abbott, *Rollo's Philosophy. Part I: Water.* Philadelphia: Hogan & Thompson [undated].

MINORITY AMERICANS IN CHILDREN'S LITERATURE *

David K. Gast

Introduction

The social and economic integration of minority peoples in America has been a slow process ever since the first colonists took land from the native Americans. But it has been especially slow for American citizens of American Indian, Chinese, Japanese, African, and Spanish descent, who, by virtue of their racial, religious, and other ethnic characteristics, have been largely excluded from the mainstream of dominant culture in the United States.

Social scientists of the present day generally agree that there are no inherent cultural predispositions or traits among people of different races or geographical areas, but that man is a product of his cultural environment. The shaping of this product begins at birth. Children literally "learn what they live." They learn prejudice against, and intolerance of, people who are racially, religiously, and culturally different from themselves. In turn, the objects of prejudice internalize the self-debasing concepts that are held of them in the mirror of the majority. The source of these learnings can be traced to parents and other adults, peers, mass and minor media, and teaching materials. The American public school, functioning as a social sorting and screening device with Protestant, white, middle-class bias, has not always facilitated integration of the minority American into the mainstream of dominant culture, nor has it effectuated, through its academic portrayal of minority Americans, a social conscience on the part of the majority American. Studies of past and present teaching materials have shown that the American of minority race, creed, or color, has not been given fair representation in school textbooks.[1] The role of the minority American in the development of our country

David K. Gast is Associate Professor of Education, San Diego State College, Imperial Valley Campus, Calexico, California.

* Reprinted from *Elementary English* 44:12–23, 1967, with permission of the National Council of Teachers of English and David K. Gast.

[1] American Council on Education, Committee on the Study of Teaching Materials in Intergroup Relations, *Intergroup Relations in Teaching Materials*. Washington, D.C.: American Council on Education, 1949; Lloyd A. Marcus, *The Treatment of Minorities in Secondary School Textbooks*. New York: Anti-Defamation League of B'nai B'rith, 1961; Abraham Tannenbaum, "Family Living in Textbook Town," *Progressive Education* 31:133–140, 166–167, 1954.

has largely been neglected. When he does appear in textbooks, the minority American is stereotyped.

But textbooks are not the only teaching materials that convey concepts of inter-group relations to school-age children. One source of such learning has been children's literature. Yet very few studies have been designed to analyze the images of minority groups as presented to children in fictional literature. The limited research which has been done has shown that minority peoples have been stereotyped and that stereotypes are perpetuated in the face of the changing reality of social fact. The need for a current investigation into the nature of characterizations of minority Americans in contemporary children's literature has been clearly indicated in previous studies.[2] The purpose of the present study[3] has been to fill this need.

The Problem

The problem of this investigation consisted of an analysis of characterizations of minority group Americans as presented in contemporary children's literature. Answers were sought for the following questions: (1) What are the characteristics of and concepts about present-day American Indians, Chinese, Japanese, Negroes, and Spanish-Americans in contemporary children's fiction? (2) What are the identifiable stereotypes imputed to minority Americans in the literature? (3) How does treatment of minority Americans in contemporary children's fictional literature compare with that in related studies of adult magazine fiction and school instructional materials?

Three hypotheses were established for the study: (1) Stereotypes of American Indians, Chinese, Japanese, Negroes, and Spanish-Americans are not found in children's literature. (2) Treatment of minority Americans in recent literature dignifies the differences in race, creed, and custom of minority peoples. (3) Treatment of minority Americans in recent literature emphasizes similarities

[2] American Council on Education, Committee on Intergroup Education in Cooperating Schools, Hilda Taba, director, *Literature for Human Understanding*. Washington, D.C.: American Council on Education, 1948, p. vi; Marie L. Ram, "Analysis of the Lois Lenski Literature from a Sociological Point of View (Parts One and Two)," unpublished doctoral dissertation, University of Buffalo, Buffalo, New York, 1958, as reported in *Dissertation Abstracts 19*:3308, 1959.

[3] This paper is based on the writer's doctoral dissertation: David Karl Gast, "Characteristics and Concepts of Minority Americans in Contemporary Children's Fictional Literature," unpublished doctoral dissertation, Arizona State University, Tempe, Arizona, June, 1965.

rather than differences among minority and majority Americans with regard to behavior patterns, attitudes, and values.

The Population

The population of the study was defined as all children's fiction in book form about present-day (1945–1962) American Indians, Chinese, Japanese, Negroes, and Spanish-Americans, first published between 1945 and 1962 for kindergarten through eighth-grade reading levels and noted in one or more of the following guides: H. W. Wilson Company's *Children's Catalog*, tenth edition, 1961, and the 1962 and 1963 supplements to the tenth edition; The American Library Association's *A Basic Book Collection for Elementary Grades* and *A Basic Book Collection for Junior High Schools*, both published in 1960; the American Library Association's *Subject Index to Books for Primary Grades*, second edition, 1961, and *Subject Index to Books for Intermediate Grades*, second and third editions, 1950 and 1963 respectively.

Books included in the study were identified by one or more of the following factors in the listings: (1) book title and bibliographical data; (2) Sears Subject Index heading; (3) grade reading level; and (4) résumé or review of the book. This technique insured inclusion of books exhibiting most of the necessary characteristics. Four required definitions of the population that could not always be identified in the listings were: (1) contemporaneousness of the story; (2) a continental United States setting; (3) minority characters of U.S. citizenship; and (4) minority Americans in significant roles in the story.

After an initial selection, forty-two books met the criteria established for the population and were analyzed as a total sample.

The Method

To obtain the characterizations, concepts, and stereotypes in children's literature dealing with contemporary American minorities, the investigator devised two analytic instruments based on the Berelson and Salter technique.[4] The Katz and Braly List of Verbal Stereotypes [5] was also employed as a measure of stereotyping.

---

[4] Bernard Berelson and Patricia Salter, "Majority and Minority Americans: An Analysis of Magazine Fiction," in *Mass Culture*, Bernard Rosenberg and David Manning White, eds. Glencoe, Ill.: Free Press, 1957, pp. 235–251.

[5] Daniel Katz and Kenneth Braly, "Racial Stereotypes of One Hundred College Students." *Journal of Abnormal and Social Psychology 28*:280–290, 1933.

These instruments were applied to the literature by three coders and the investigator.[6]

The analytic operations took two forms, based on two units of analysis defined by Berelson as the "character" and the "item." [7] The first unit of analysis, an example of "character" analysis, dealt with the major and minor characters in the story. This unit was in two parts; first, the coding of seven characteristics for each of the characters; and second, the application of the Katz and Braly list to each of the characters to discover stereotypes. The character instrument, Form C, was used for this unit of analysis. The second unit, an example of "item" analysis, dealt with each book as a whole to ascertain the concepts, explicit and implicit, in the story. The book instrument, Form B, was used for this unit of analysis. The coding of the seven characteristics constituted "What Is Said" categories,[8] while the application of the Katz and Braly List of Verbal Stereotypes and item analysis of explicit and implicit concepts in the stories constituted "How It Is Said" categories.[9]

There was an *a priori* definition and delimitation of terms with respect to descriptions in the various categories of characteristics given to the coders. A brief analysis preceded the study to discover the need for further definitions and refinements of terms and agreement among the coders in regard to the categories of analysis.

The characterizations in each book were limited to one major character and a maximum of five minor characters. Characters were selected by the first coder to read the book. In the case of disagreement among the coders, the judgment was based on majority opinion of the coders and the investigator.

In the first unit of analysis, the seven characteristics for which data were secured were: role in the story (major or minor) ; physical traits (age, sex, general physical description) ; status position (occupation, economic status, educational level, social class) ; social origin (racial or ethnic group, religion) ; personality traits; goals and values; and plus-minus position (general approval-disapproval of a character by others in the story). Documentation in the form of a phrase or full sentence quotes was supplied by the coders for

---

[6] The coders who participated in the study were a San Diego State College professor of elementary English and children's literature holding an Ed.D. degree, a San Diego State College librarian with an M.S. in Library Science degree in public school librarianship, and an elementary school teacher with an M.A. in Education degree.

[7] Bernard Berelson, "Content Analysis," in *Handbook of Social Psychology*, Vol. I, Gardner Lindzey, ed. Cambridge, Mass.: Addison-Wesley, 1954, p. 509.

[8] *Ibid.*, p. 510.

[9] *Ibid.*, p. 511.

each decision as to the characteristics chosen. Since pictorial representations are significant in children's literature, especially at the lower-grade reading levels, coders also used documented pictorial clues as a basis for judgment on characteristics. The data for each characteristic were tabulated and charted separately for each minority. Further analysis was facilitated on each chart by separate enumerations for (1) male-female, (2) major character-minor character, and (3) age: children (1–12 years of age), teenagers (13–19 years of age), adults (20–59 years of age, or parents in story presentations), and old-timers (60 years of age and older or grandparents in story presentations).

The second part of the first unit of analysis required the coders to choose five adjectives from the Katz and Braly list which best described each of the characters analyzed. These words were compiled for each minority group analyzed and listed in rank order of mention to determine stereotypes of the various minority Americans. Charting procedure of this data was identical to that of the characteristics above.

The second unit of analysis concerned itself with the concepts or "lessons" in the story and involved the use of Form B. This form was filled out only after each character in the book had been analyzed. Consideration of the characteristics of each character in the story, plus the plot of the story determined the coders' choice of concepts. Coders noted whether the concept was implicit or explicit in the story in the respective sections of Form B.

On both forms, only characteristics and explicit concepts which were documented by both page number and quote were accepted. Documentation was not required in the identification of implicit concepts or in the choice of Katz and Braly adjectives as they were not based on references to discrete parts of book content.

The findings of the present study were compared with those of previous related research, namely, "Majority and Minority Americans: An Analysis of Magazine Fiction" by Berelson and Salter;[10] *Intergroup Relations in Teaching Materials* by the American Council on Education, Committee on the Study of Teaching Materials in Intergroup Relations;[11] *The Treatment of Minorities in Secondary School Textbooks* by Marcus;[12] and "Family Living in Textbook Town" by Tannenbaum.[13]

---

[10] Berelson and Salter, *loc. cit.*

[11] American Council on Education, Committee on the Study of Teaching Materials in Intergroup Relations, *loc. cit.*

[12] Lloyd A. Marcus, *loc. cit.*

[13] Tannenbaum, *loc. cit.*

Findings

The population. Based on the criteria of selection detailed above, forty-two children's books constituted the population of this study. Of the forty-two books analyzed, thirteen were about American Indians, two were about Chinese, five were about Japanese, sixteen were about Negroes, and six were about Spanish-Americans. One hundred fourteen minority American characters were identified for analysis.

Social origin. In the analysis, thirty-one Indian, seven Chinese, eight Japanese, fifty Negro, and eighteen Spanish-American characters were identified. The total group represented forty-three children, fifteen teenagers, forty-three adults, and thirteen old-timers. The major roles in all of the stories were held by children or teenagers. Books about the Negro, while greater in number, tended to treat teenage characters. Books about Indians, Chinese, and Japanese had no significant teenage characters. Books on Indians and Spanish-Americans emphasized male characters far more than female, while books on Chinese, Japanese, and Negroes generally gave numerically equal representation of male and female characterizations. Indian and Spanish-American stories also contained larger use of male major characters than did the books about the other minorities.

None of the Indians, Chinese, Japanese or Negroes was identified as Roman Catholic while virtually all of the Spanish-American characters were. Of the minorities surveyed, the Indians, Chinese, and Spanish-Americans appeared to have held to traditional ethnic religious beliefs while the Japanese when identifiable as to religious belief, embraced the basic Protestant tradition of the dominant culture. Protestant Christianity was shown to be the religious belief of approximately one-half of the Negroes in the literature. The other half were unidentifiable as to religious belief.

Ethnic subgroups within the Indian and Spanish-American minorities were represented in the children's fiction. Of the thirty-one books concerning Indians, twenty-seven described Navahos, two described Cherokees, one described Havasupi and one described Seminoles. Books about the Spanish-American minority were equally divided into three ethnic subgroups: Spanish (shepherds and farmers of New Mexico), Mexican (persons of Mexican descent living in the Southwest), and Early-California Spanish (persons tracing their heritage back into the early history of California).

Physical descriptions. The physical descriptions of minority American characters portrayed: (1) American Indians as having brown skin and black hair and as wearing traditional costumes;

(2) Chinese as having black hair and the epicanthic eye fold and favoring traditional garb; (3) Japanese as having black hair and the epicanthic eye fold and favoring the clothing of the dominant culture; (4) Negroes as generally having brown skin and black kinky hair, but often (in nearly half of the characterizations, especially female) Caucasoid facial features and straight hair; and (5) Spanish-Americans as having brown skin and black hair and favoring traditional costumes only in the case of the Mexican subgroup.

Status position. The status position analysis of minority Americans included analysis of occupation, educational level, economic status, and social class and can be summarized as follows: (1) American Indians in the literature did traditional on-reservation work of shepherding and handicraft, were poor and of the lower-class, and did not aspire to go to college. (2) Chinese were portrayed as semi-skilled workers of the lower socio-economic class with adequate incomes. They valued the schools of the dominant culture and Chinese language school, but were not shown as college oriented. (3) Japanese evinced middle-class standards of living with apparently comfortable incomes. Gardening and floriculture made up the identifiable occupations of the Japanese, and college orientation was inferred in only one book. (4) Negroes were portrayed as having a wide range of vocations and they were shown to value college attendance as a goal. They were evenly distributed as to lower—and middle-class status rating. (5) Spanish-Americans were shown as poor people of the lower-class having no college aspirations and holding a variety of non-professional occupations.

Personality traits. The personality traits imputed to minority Americans did not vary to a great extent. "Dependable" and "unselfish" were the first-ranking traits coded for every group. "Authoritarian" was third-ranking for Indians, Chinese, and Spanish-Americans and fifth-ranking for Negroes. Negroes and Chinese were generally portrayed as extroverts while Japanese and American Indians were shown as introverts. Optimism was a high-ranking trait of the Japanese, Negroes, and Spanish-Americans. Generally, minority Americans were portrayed as being individuals and stereotyped personality traits were not found.

Goals and values. "Self-realization" was found to be a major goal for all of the minority American characters analyzed in this study. It ranked first for the Japanese, Negro, and Spanish-American minorities, and second for the American-Indian and Chinese minorities. "Future orientation" was a first-ranking value set for the Chinese and a second-ranking value set for Japanese and Negroes, indicating that these groups looked to the future for self and group improvement. "Past orientation" was a first-ranking value set for the American Indians and Chinese-Americans while it was only eighth-ranking for the Negroes, third-ranking for the Spanish-Americans, and not found for the Japanese. As can be seen, the Chinese were ambivalent with regard to past-future orientation. The Negro group was the only minority for whom the goal of "social acceptance in the dominant culture" ranked first. In comparison, this goal ranked third for the Chinese, sixth for the Spanish-Americans, and seventh for the American Indians and Japanese. Generally, American Indians, Chinese, and Spanish-Americans were shown to have ethnocentric goals and values, while the basic values of the Japanese and Negroes were not ethnocentric.

Plus-minus position. The analysis of the plus-minus positions of minority Americans demonstrated that negative attitudes towards the minority characters by their peers or members of the dominant culture were very rarely emphasized by the authors of the literature. One exception to this was the stories about Negroes, where themes of prejudice and intolerance illustrated the Negro's struggle for equality.

Stereotypes. The stereotypes imputed to the 114 characters analyzed were measured by the application of the Katz and Braly List of Verbal Stereotypes to the characterizations. The Japanese and Negro minorities were stereotyped as being the most "conventional" of the minority Americans while the American Indians, Chinese, and Spanish-Americans were shown as being "tradition-loving" and "loyal-to-family ties." The dominant American middle-class virtues related to kindness, industriousness, love of tradition, conventionality, intelligence, neatness, and ambition were high-ranking stereotypes for the groups as a whole. The first hypothesis of the study, that stereotypes of the respective minority groups would not be identified in the literature analyzed, had to be rejected. Stereotypes were identified. However, the large majority of the stereotypes were positive and complimentary. One-fourth of the adjectives on the Katz and Braly list were never chosen as stereotypical of characters in this study, and all but two of the terms that were not chosen were negative and non-complimentary.[14] The implications of these findings must be tempered by the fact that the Katz and Braly List of Verbal Stereotypes was developed in 1933 and the climate of public opinion of which stereotypes are a part may have changed since that time.

Concepts. Two hundred twenty-six concepts were identified in the unit analysis and were categorized for each minority under the

[14] See Table I, page 429.

following headings: (1) Concepts Showing Ethnic Uniqueness, (2) Concepts Showing Minority Group Pride, (3) Concepts Showing Conventionality, (4) Concepts Showing Social Roles (of the given minority) in the Dominant Culture, (5) Concepts Dealing with Prejudice, and (6) Concepts Showing Brotherhood.

The findings of the unit analysis were in basic agreement with those of the individual character analysis of the members of the respective groups. The Japanese and Negro groups were found to be more similar to the majority Americans in cultural values, socio-economic aspirations, and way of life than were the American Indians, Chinese, and Spanish-Americans.

Comparisons. The comparison of the present study with the four selected studies indicated that: (1) The treatment of minority Americans in children's literature evidenced virtually no negative stereotypes, while magazine fiction and school textbooks contained non-complimentary stereotypes. (2) The children's fiction presented a more up-to-date treatment of minority American life than did school textbooks published during the same period. (3) The children's fiction portrayed far more intergroup and interracial cooperation and equality than did the magazine fiction, school textbooks, and elementary readers. (4) The minority Americans were not shown as problem-makers for the dominant culture in the children's fiction as they were in the textbook studies. (5) The children's fiction often portrayed the minorities as aspiring to middle-class values and standards of living while the textbook studies indicated that minority groups had lower socio-economic standards and goals.

On the basis of the findings of the present study and a comparison of those findings with previous, related research, the second and third hypotheses of this study can be supported. The treatment of minority Americans in the literature of the present study dignified the differences in race, creed, and custom of minority citizens and, for the most part, emphasized similarities rather than differences between minority and majority Americans with regard to behaviors, attitudes, and values.

Conclusions

The results obtained from the analysis of the data derived from the population of the present investigation warrant the following conclusions:

1. Recent children's fiction generally portrays American Indians, Japanese, Negroes, and Spanish-Americans as having adopted

the dominant middle-class American values related to cleanliness, kindness, intelligence, ambition, hard work, and success.

2. Recent children's literature generally contains complimentary stereotypes of present-day American Indians, Chinese, Japanese, Negroes, and Spanish-Americans. Middle-class Anglo-American virtues make up the new stereotypes imputed to these minorties by the authors of the literature. Traditional, non-complimentary stereotypes have largely disappeared from the literature. The image of the Negro in children's fiction represents an almost exact reversal of traditional Negro stereotypes with one exception—"Negroes are musical."

3. Recent children's literature generally portrays American Indians, Chinese, and Spanish-Americans as having lower-class socio-economic status. Negroes are portrayed as being evenly distributed as to lower- and middle-class status rating. Japanese are shown to be of the middle-class in socio-economic status.

4. Recent children's literature contains occupational stereotypes of all minority groups except the Negro. The Negro is represented in a wide range of occupations, including white-collar jobs and the professions, which are not recorded for the other minorities. The common stereotypes of the Indian craftsman, the Chinese cook, the Mexican shopkeeper, the Japanese gardener, and the Spanish shepherd are perpetuated in the recent literature.

5. Recent children's literature, with one exception, portrays the Negro minority as the only minority whose members seek higher education and attend college. The exception is found in the American Indian minority where one college educated character is portrayed. The findings leading to this conclusion may be in part due to the large number of upper-grade books about teenage Negroes, and the lack of such books for the other minorities in the population of this study. But it also relates to findings of the present investigation showing the Negro adult in white-collar and professional positions.

6. Recent children's literature portrays Japanese and Negro minorities as being more thoroughly assimilated into the dominant culture and as having more social interaction with Anglo-Americans than the American Indians, Chinese, and Spanish-Americans. The Japanese and Negro minorities are shown to have less ethnic or racial identification than the other minorities and are portrayed as living among Anglo-Americans in integrated neighborhoods. In contrast, Chinese are shown to live in "Chinatown," American Indians are portrayed as liv-

ing only on reservations, and Spanish-Americans are depicted in rural settings.

7. Recent children's literature portrays American Indians and Spanish-Americans as living a simple and virile life, close to nature. These minorities are generally pictured as living serenely, with few material comforts, in remote and sparsely populated areas of southwestern United States. They are said to have an innate understanding of, and reverence for nature and a particular fondness for animal life.

8. Recent children's fiction about American Indians and Spanish-Americans emphasizes male characters and perpetuates the male-superiority tradition, while children's fiction about Chinese, Japanese, and Negroes presents no disparity between the number or importance of male and female characters, and does not perpetuate male-superiority in the characterizations.

9. Recent children's fiction about American Indians, Chinese, and Spanish-Americans contains no portrayals of individuals who have lost or abandoned their ethnic culture and are assimilated into the dominant culture. The authors of the literature portray these minorities as taking pride in their ethnic cultures and clinging to traditional patterns of life while accepting some of the material goods and economic motivations of the dominant culture.

10. Recent children's fiction stereotypes the American Indians and the Mexican-American subgroup of the Spanish-American minority as wearing their ethnic garb. This is especially evident in the primary-grade books, which utilize a greater number of pictures than the intermediate- and upper-grade level books. Though not always identified by name of tribe, Indians are illustrated in the literature wearing moccasins, headbands, turquoise and silver jewelry, and other traditional garb of Indian tribes, especially the Navaho and Hopi, who inhabit the southwestern area of the United States. Mexican-Americans are depicted in the fiction as sombrero- and sandal-wearing innocents who revel in traditional holidays and customs. This stereotype of dress perpetuates the image of the Mexican-American as a friendly foreigner and a tourist attraction in the Southwest.

11. Recent children's literature generally portrays Negroes as being brown-skinned people who often have Caucasoid facial features and straight hair. Negro females are pictured in the literature as generally lighter in color and more Caucasian in appearance than Negro males. This new image of the Negro differs from that found in earlier literature which caricatured

the Negro by over-emphasizing Negroid facial features, kinky hair, and black skin. It appears that the authors and publishers of the recent literature, while emphasizing themes of social equality in the books about Negroes, have deemphasized physical differences between Negroes and Anglo-Americans by portraying light-skinned Negroes as representative of the Negro minority.

12. In recent children's literature, social acceptance in the dominant Anglo-American culture is the predominant theme in books about the Negro minority, while it is only a minor theme in books about American Indians, Chinese, Japanese, and Spanish-Americans. Negroes are portrayed in the literature as having to overcome prejudice and social restrictions in their struggle for equal social and economic opportunity in the United States. American Indians, Chinese, and Spanish-Americans are portrayed as having little contact with Anglo-Americans because of their geographical isolation or "segregated" living conditions and apparent ethnocentrism. The Japanese minority is portrayed in the literature as encountering no prejudice and as being completely accepted by the Anglo-Americans.

13. Recent children's fiction is more complimentary to minority Americans when compared with literature analyzed in previous studies. Non-complimentary stereotypes and the "minority as a social problem" concept that were found in previous studies are not to be found in the children's literature of the present study. The children's literature contained themes of brotherhood and racial equality, while in school textbooks such themes were slighted and often were not to be found.

14. Recent children's literature dignifies the differences in race, creed, and custom of the minority Americans, and emphasizes the similarities rather than the differences between minority and majority Americans with regard to behavior, attitudes, and values.

15. Recent children's literature contains a dearth of books about Negroes in the picture book and primary-grade reading levels, while upper-grade books about Negroes are not uncommon. There are more stories about Negro teenagers than there are about young Negro children of early elementary school age. It can be concluded that intermediate- and upper-grade books about Negro teenagers allow for more sophisticated treatment of the problem of social acceptance faced by Negroes which is the major theme in the literature about Negroes.

16. Recent children's literature contains a dearth of books concerning American Indian, Chinese, Japanese, and Spanish-American teenagers and their problems and aspirations, while stories of Negro teenagers are numerous. The books concerning minorities other than the Negro primarily portray child-family relationships and do not emphasize themes of social acceptance. The readers of the literature concerning minority Americans will have Negro teenage characters with which to identify, but they will find almost no other minority American teenage characters portrayed in the literature.

Recommendations

The results obtained from the analysis of the data derived from the population of the present investigation warrant recommendations for action programs and for further research which are presented below.

ACTION PROGRAMS

On the basis of the results of this study, the following recommendations for action programs are suggested:

1. The use of contemporary children's literature about minority Americans should be increased in supplementing reading and social studies textbooks in the public schools. This recommendation is imperative if a balanced and "culturally fair" presentation of American life is to be afforded to school children.
2. Textbooks should be made available which contain stories about or portrayals of minority Americans living in the dominant culture as citizens having equal rights and sharing in the American way of life.
3. Authors and publishers of children's literature should increase: (a) the number of books concerning Negroes in the picture book and primary-grade reading levels, and (b) the number of books concerning American Indian, Chinese, Japanese, and Spanish-American teenagers in upper-grade reading levels.
4. Authors and publishers of children's literature should increase the number of books showing American Indians, Chinese, and Spanish-Americans who live among and associate with Anglo-Americans.
5. Authors and publishers of children's literature should consciously avoid occupational stereotypes and misleading overgeneralizations concerning the ethnic background, culture, and

traditions of minority Americans. This recommendation particularly relates to portrayals of American Indians, Chinese, and Spanish-Americans.

FURTHER RESEARCH

The results of this investigation emphasized the need for the following types of research:

1. Content analysis studies should be made of the characterizations of individual American minority groups in children's fictional literature. The findings of the present study warrant further investigation.

2. Content analysis studies should be made of the characterizations, concepts, and stereotypes of minority Americans in children's fictional literature published before 1945. Such studies would provide a stronger basis for evaluation of, and comparison with the present study and future studies of contemporary literature. Previous research along these lines has been very informal and valuational.

3. A qualitative and quantitative comparison should be made of recently published books having historical settings and recently published books having contemporary settings. This kind of research might indicate first, a change in the historical portrayal of the minority Americans and second, the proportions of the literature which deal with the past, present, and future realities.

4. A qualitative and quantitative comparison should be made of children's fiction appearing in the Wilson and the American Library Association guides to children's literature and children's fiction not listed therein to determine (a) differences between such literature, and (b) possible biases of the guides.

5. Experimental studies should be made to test the assumption that attitudes favorable to minority Americans are developed by readers of contemporary children's fiction concerning minority Americans. Such literature is reputed to effect an understanding of minority Americans and a reduction of prejudice, but this assumption needs more than judgmental support.

6. Investigations should be made of current stereotypes of racial, ethnic, and religious groups in America. Experimental and descriptive studies are needed to check the present validity of past enumerations of stereotypes as they pertain to various minority groups in the United States.

TABLE I

Rank Order Enumeration of the Stereotypes of 114 Minority American Characters on the Katz and Braly List of Verbal Stereotypes

Kind (46)	Conservative (4)	Sophisticated (1)
Industrious (36)	Happy-go-lucky (4)	Suave (1)
Tradition-loving (32)	Pleasure-loving (4)	Suspicious (1)
Conventional (30)	Straightforward (4)	Witty (1)
Loyal to family	Talkative (4)	Cowardly *
ties (29)	Efficient (3)	Extremely
Intelligent (23)	Progressive (3)	nationalistic *
Neat (23)	Quick-tempered (3)	Frivolous *
Ambitious (20)	Revengeful (3)	Gluttonous *
Artistic (18)	Arrogant (2)	Grasping *
Generous (18)	Imitative (2)	Humorless *
Musical (16)	Impulsive (2)	Individualistic *
Reserved (16)	Lazy (2)	Materialistic *
Practical (15)	Loud (2)	Mercenary *
Alert (12)	Ostentatious (2)	Methodical *
Faithful (12)	Stolid (2)	Passionate *
Gregarious (11)	Aggressive (1)	Physically dirty *
Superstitious (11)	Argumentative (1)	Ponderous *
Courteous (10)	Brilliant (1)	Pugnacious *
Honest (9)	Conceited (1)	Quarrelsome *
Quiet (9)	Cruel (1)	Radical *
Very religious (9)	Deceitful (1)	Rude *
Meditative (8)	Evasive (1)	Sensual *
Boastful (6)	Ignorant (1)	Shrewd *
Imaginative (6)	Jovial (1)	Slovenly *
Persistent (6)	Naive (1)	Stupid *
Sensitive (6)	Scientifically-	Suggestible *
Sportsmanlike (6)	minded (1)	Treacherous *
Stubborn (5)	Sly (1)	Unreliable *

* Not chosen as stereotypical of minority Americans in the present study.

LITERATURE ENLIVENS
THE SOCIAL STUDIES *

Mildred A. Dawson

In discussing how literature enlivens the social studies, our immediate concern is with its contribution to the goals implicit in the social studies curriculum. We want the children to become familiar with the story of our country—the Westward Movement, the development and meaning of the Bill of Rights, the contributions of pioneers, inventors, industrialists, and labor to the greatness of the United States. Our pupils, too, should learn the course of world history, not only its contribution to our nation but also the background that makes each foreign land what it is in its ideals, religious status, current economic and social conditions, and its relations to the rest of the world.

Knowing the sweep of history, the children should normally and naturally gain some understanding and permanent interest in such current affairs of the "Atlantic Community," the rapid emergence of African nations into independent members of a world-wide organization, the turmoil of Southeast Asia.

Along with history comes geography with its interplay between man and his environment, as well as sociology and economics as factors influencing the direction which citizens in every clime and at every time take. It is not only in relation to 1964–1965 that children should be concerned with the problems of the culturally deprived, but at every stage of history.

Currently our civilization is being transformed through space-age science; but the inventions such as the wheel, the printing press, the steam engine, the varied harnesses for electrical energy, and the modern agents of instantaneous communications have had their earth-shaking consequences. Children should learn about the progress of the human race.

Thus far we have been largely concerned with the social studies' goals of transmitting information in the form of history, anthropology, geography, and the like. But ultimately the goals are di-

Mildred A. Dawson is Professor of Education at Sacramento State College, California.

* Reprinted from *Education* 85:294–297, 1965, with permission of The Bobbs-Merrill Company, Inc., Indianapolis, and Mildred A Dawson. Copyright © 1965.

rected toward making good citizens, of developing in children the values that will develop interested, constructive citizenship locally, nationally, and world-wide. It is to such goals that literature can make a significant contribution.

The Role of Literature

We teachers of the social studies rely heavily on textbooks, reference books, and parallel readings of an informational nature as a foundation and organizer of the materials in our courses. True it is that the authors of these printed materials are generally persons of wide knowledge, good judgment, and vision in the area of the social studies. Yet, from the tremendous mass of available information, they must select rigorously and present a severely restricted set of facts presented in the most economical style.

These basic materials of the social studies tend to be skeletal, cold-bloodedly factual, pedestrian in style. They are unlikely to stir the reader's blood, to build strong pride in the character and acts of great men, to give insight, to develop ideals. If we are interested in developing patriotism, world citizenship, feelings of responsibility for making a contribution to humanity, we will have to look beyond textbooks, parallel readings, and encyclopedias.

It is in our best of juvenile literature that the men of history come alive with their problems, motivations, achievements, even failures and inherent weaknesses. It is a trade book, carefully authentic, that can reveal great men as persons and clearly indicate to its reader the ideals, goals, behavior that he himself may well emulate. The deeper goals of the social studies can be fully realized only as the life and conditions of the past or far-away become explicit through the pages of true-to-life fiction, biography, and books of travel.

Literature activates the past and the distant as it deals with living men, on-going events, localized current conditions—geographic, economic, sociological. Through perusing the pages of a well-written book, a pupil can gain insight, feel sympathy and empathy, sense the values of patriotism, formulate rules of conduct. In other words, literature causes the basic teachings of the social studies to be *absorbed* or *assimilated*.

In what may seem to be a lighter vein but actually is not, we might consider a major goal in the social studies to be encouraging children to read *just for fun*. With the shortened and shortening work-week, there is increased leisure, more time for recreation— and what better way to spend a few hours per week than to read significant articles in periodicals or a book of biography, travel, or insightful fiction? Let us help the teacher of reading to make lifetime readers of our girls and boys!

Some Examples

Let us consider a few of the books among many thousands to which we may turn in enlivening our lessons in the social studies. An understanding of early peoples will result as children read authentically historical fiction such as Haugaard's *Hakon of Rogen's Saga* (early Vikings) or books about early Americans like Mc-Neer's *The American Indian Story* and Haig-Brown's *The Whale People*.

Colonial and pioneer times come to life as children admire the bravery of early colonists in Smith's *Pilgrim Courage*, see superstitions of witchcraft in Speare's *The Witch of Blackbird Pond*, fight Indians with Edmonds' *The Matchlock Gun*, go traveling in Coatsworth's *Away Goes Sally*, roam the fields with Mason's *Susannah, the Pioneer Cow*, live the pioneer life in Steele's *Westward Adventure* and Laura Ingalls Wilder's *Little House* books, colonize California in Politi's *The Mission Bell*, or see the sweep of history in Caudill's *Tree of Freedom*.

The stress and strain, the horrors of battle will become real as child-readers identify with the Civil-War teen-ager in Keith's *Rifles for Watie*. Or, civics of today become intriguing through books such as Johnson's *The Congress*.

Or let's turn to biography. Primary children will thoroughly enjoy the colorful and carefully authentic d'Aulaire biographies of great Americans of the past or Dalgliesh's *The Thanksgiving Story*. With older children, the past fairly glows as they read Daugherty's *Daniel Boone*, Sandburg's *Abe Lincoln Grows Up*, or the scholarly volumes by May McNeer, Genevieve Foster, and Clara Judson. There are remarkably fine series available, too, as for instance the *Landmark Books* or the *Childhood of Famous Americans*.

The early days of Poland and medieval England are vividly relived in Kelly's *Trumpeter of Krakow*, De Angeli's *The Door in the Wall*, and Gray's *Adam of the Road* (all beautifully literary in style). Or let the children turn to the old favorite, Pyle's *Otto of the Silver Hand* and to the recent book on Biblical times, Speare's *The Bronze Bow*.

The children may gain insight of modern times as they read Lattimore's *Little Pear*, Flack's *The Story of Ping*, or Bemelmans' *Madeline*. Older children may sympathetically "visit" Latin America through such books as Clark's *The Secret of the Andes* and *Magic Maize* or, instead, "see" Europe in such books as Dodge's *Hans Brinker* and Spyri's *Heidi*.

One of America's problems is the development of understanding among our own people for fellow citizens who manifest regional and cultural differences. Sympathetic understanding, even empathy, come as children read such books as Credle's *Down, Down the Mountain,* Justus' *Here Comes Mary Ellen,* Clark's *In My Mother's House,* Krumgold's *And Now Miguel,* De Angeli's *Thee, Hannah!* and Lois Lenski's regional series.

Insight, not only into the problems of others but into deep-down personal disturbances, may result from living with the characters in Estes' *One Hundred Dresses,* Beim's *The Smallest Boy in the Class* and *Two Is a Team,* De Angeli's *Bright April,* Enright's *Kintu,* Sperry's *Call It Courage,* Speare's *The Witch of Blackbird Pond* or De Angeli's *The Door in the Wall.* Here we have such problems as intolerance, economic, religious, or social; differences in size or dress; overpowering fear to be overcome; physical deficiency.

The books mentioned above are examples of the diverse, high-quality literature to which teachers of social studies in the elementary school can turn as they seek to achieve personalized learnings about the people, events and conditions of present and past, close at hand and far away. Children's books can indeed enliven the social studies for boys and girls who are growing toward responsible citizenship.

BIBLIOGRAPHY

Jerrold Beim, *The Smallest Boy in the Class*. Morrow, 1949.

Jerrold Beim, *Two Is a Team*. Harcourt, 1945.

Ludwig Bemelmans, *Madeline*. Viking, 1939.

Rebecca Caudill, *Tree of Freedom*. Viking, 1949.

Ann Nolan Clark, *In My Mother's House,* Viking, 1951; *Secret of the Andes,* Viking, 1952.

Elizabeth Coatsworth, *Away Goes Sally*. Macmillan, 1934.

Ellis Credle, *Down, Down the Mountain*. Nelson, 1934.

Alice Dalgliesh, *The Thanksgiving Story*. Scribner, 1954.

James Daugherty, *Daniel Boone*. Viking, 1939.

Marguerite De Angeli, *Bright April,* Doubleday, 1946; *The Door in the Wall,* Doubleday, 1949; *Thee, Hannah!* Doubleday, 1940.

Mary Mapes Dodge, *Hans Brinker* (many editions).

Walter Edmonds, *The Matchlock Gun*. Dodd, 1941.

Elizabeth Enright, *Kintu*. Rinehart, 1935.

Eleanor Estes, *The Hundred Dresses*. Harcourt, 1944.

Marjorie Flack, *The Story of Ping.* Viking, 1933.
Elizabeth Gray, *Adam of the Road.* Viking, 1942.
Roderick Haig-Brown, *The Whale People.* Morrow, 1963.
Erik Haugaard, *Hakon of Rogen's Saga.* Houghton, 1963.
Gerald Johnson, *The Congress.* Morrow, 1963.
May Justus, *Here Comes Mary Ellen.* Lippincott, 1940.
Harold Keith, *Rifles for Watie.* Crowell, 1957.
Joseph Krumgold, *And Now Miguel.* Crowell, 1953.
Eleanor Lattimore, *Little Pear.* Harcourt, 1931.
Lois Lenski, *Cotton in My Sack,* Lippincott, 1949; *Corn-Farm Boy,* Lippincott, 1954.
May McNeer, *The American Indian Story.* Farrar, 1963.
Miriam Mason, *Susannah, the Pioneer Cow.* Macmillan, 1941.
Leo Politi, *The Mission Bell.* Scribner, 1953.
Howard Pyle, *Otto of the Silver Hand.* Scribner, 1957.
Carl Sandburg, *Abe Lincoln Grows Up.* Harcourt, 1928.
E. Brooks Smith, *et al., Pilgrim Courage.* Little, 1962.
Elizabeth Speare, *The Bronze Bow,* Houghton, 1961; *The Witch of Blackbird Pond,* Houghton, 1958.
William O. Steele, *Westward Adventure.* Harcourt, 1962.
Laura Wilder, *Little House* series. Harper, 1953.

"THE CURIOUS WHETHER AND HOW" *

Ruth Kearney Carlson

Three of our American poets offer guidelines for an individualized approach to teaching the social studies. Emily Dickinson thought that "wonder is not precisely knowing"; Whitman spoke of "the curious whether and how"; and Frost saw it as "a pursuit of a pursuit forever," a course which brings about "an interminable chain of longing." This wondering, doubting, and longing about life should be fostered in young readers, who use many thinking processes in the creative and critical reading of literature related to the social studies.

Individualized or personalized reading usually means that the child selects his own materials; proceeds at his individual pace, not in competition with his peers; records his progress with his teacher; works on skills as needed; and relates his reading with

---

Ruth Kearney Carlson is Professor of Education at California State College, Hayward.

* Reprinted from the *School Library Journal* 11:27–29, 1965, with permission of the R. R. Bowker Company and Ruth Kearney Carlson.

other curricular areas. In planning such an approach to material in the social studies, one should consider at least eight possible organizational patterns. These are:

exploratory reading—"the curious whether and how";
specialized investigations, or depth reading, focused on one particular subject area;
historiography and research study;
critical reading by genre;
reading for social sensitivity and the understanding of human relationships;
a concentration on thematic units of social studies content;
the "basic concepts" approach; and
the aesthetic and artistic form of reading and interpretation.

Exploratory Reading

To be successful exploratory reading requires: mastery of word attack and comprehension skills, a vast variety of novels, biographies, and informational volumes, a creative teacher or librarian who is able to provide the right book for the right child, a questioning learning climate, and time for the child to engage in his pursuit of knowledge.

In providing for an exploratory reading program, the teacher may develop a modified Dalton contract unit with the child, offering information on possible avenues to explore, determining an approximate time schedule with a deadline for investigation, and a way of sharing the learner's study with others. Such a "contract" should not focus the reading upon one particular subject area, but should rather give the child an opportunity to sample many tidbits of the available literature. Some idea of the gamut of new books in the social studies area can be seen from this brief list.

BEHN, Harry. *The Faraway Lurs.* World, 1963. 190 pp. $3 Gr. 7-10
A story set in Denmark during the Bronze Age, telling of the love between Heather, daughter of the chieftain of the Forest People, and Wolf Stone of the Sun People.
————. *Omen of the Birds;* illus. by author. World, 1964. 157 pp. $3.50 Gr. 7-10
A book with the unusual setting of the Etruscan city of Tarquinia. The novel recreates life of the Etruscans, Greeks, and Romans of long ago.
BLEEKER, Sonia. *The Masai; Herders of East Africa;* illus. by Kisa N. Sasaki. Morrow, 1963. 155 pp. $2.75 Gr. 5-7
An informative book about the Masai which discusses the his-

tory, cultural patterns, taboos, social customs and rites. The concluding chapter discusses the contemporary scene. Index included.

FEIS, Ruth Stanley-Brown. *Mollie Garfield in the White House;* illus. with photographs. Rand McNally, 1963. 128 pp. $2.95 Gr. 5-8

Author is grandchild of President James A. Garfield; old prints and photography are included as well as an index.

KROEBER, Theodora. *Ishi; Last of His Tribe;* dr. by Ruth Robbins. Parnassus, 1964. 206 pp. tr. ed. $3.95; libr. ed. $3.87 net. Gr. 7-10

A story about the last surviving member of the Yahi tribe. He was finally helped by an anthropologist who understood the Yahi customs and language.

PIKE, Edgar Royston. *Mohammed; Founder of the Religion of Islam.* Roy, 1964. 127 pp. illus. $3.50 Gr. 8-12.

Part of this biography is autobiographical. The other part considers such topics as the Koran, Islam, and beliefs and practices of Moslems today.

REYNOLDS, Quentin James. *Winston Churchill.* illus. with photographs. Random House, 1963. 183 pp. $1.95 Gr. 7-9

A biography written in an interesting style, which includes early photographs, index, and bibliography.

ROBINSON, Charles Alexander. *Alexander the Great; Conqueror and Creator of a New World.* Watts, 1963. 158 pp. $2.95 Gr. 7-9

Offers an analysis of Alexander's world with an excellent account of campaigns and battles.

SAVAGE, Katharine. *The Story of the United Nations.* Maps by Richard Natkiel. Walck, 1962. 224 pp. illus. $4.00 Gr. 8-12

A history of the United Nations until 1961. Includes maps, bibliography, index.

TREECE, Henry. *Horned Helmet.* illus. by Charles Keeping. Criterion, 1963. 118 pp. $3.00 Gr. 7-10

Story of Beorn, an orphaned Icelandic boy, who shipped with a Viking crew at the beginning of the 11th century.

WILLIAMS, Ursula Moray. *The Earl's Falconer.* illus. by Charles Geer. Morrow, 1961. 189 pp. $2.95 Gr. 5-8

An unusual story of medieval days concerning feudal life and falconry.

After pupils have explored their individual interests, they may place the author and title of the books which they have read on cards, which might be organized under such categories as medieval or ancient history. Their studies are followed up with creative reports: imaginary round table talks, a television program, tape recordings with mood background music, and reports using an opaque projector.

Focused Ideas and Specialty Reports

The "specialty report" focuses on one topic or area of study, such as World Wars I and II or Russia. Requirements for such a report include: a variety of books in the library; a contractual form or outline which offers a core list of books; a helpful librarian or teacher who can suggest additional sources; and some provision for sharing ideas.

Sources for specialized lists of topics include such journals as *Elementary English, Horn Book,* and the SCHOOL LIBRARY JOURNAL. One list is "The Civil War in Children's Books; selected titles published 1958–1961" (SCHOOL LIBRARY JOURNAL, October 1961). Elvajean Hall offers "What to Read About Russia" (*Junior Libraries,* November 1959).

Pupils may also become interested in pursuing some series of books which focus upon particular areas. For instance, Leonard Wibberley has written several books for pupils in grades 7 to 11 published by Farrar, Straus. These include *John Treegate's Musket* (1959), *Peter Treegate's War* (1960), *Sea Captain from Salem* (1961), and *Treegate's Raiders* (1962). Genevieve Foster has written several Scribner simplified biographies for grades 3 to 6, including *Abraham Lincoln* (1950), *Andrew Jackson* (1951), *George Washington* (1949), and *Theodore Roosevelt* (1954), as well as more complex biographies for grades 6 to 9, including *Abraham Lincoln's World* (1944), *Augustus Caesar's World* (1949), *George Washington's World* (1941), and the *World of Captain John Smith* (1959). Gerald White Johnson has written a trilogy of books for Morrow which include *America Is Born* (1959), *America Grows Up* (1960), and *America Moves Forward* (1960). SCHOOL LIBRARY JOURNAL for October 1964 offers an extensive list of series books concerned with social studies and science.

Walter J. McHugh has developed a *Pupil Specialty Guide Book for Curriculum-Related Pupil Activities* (Castro Valley School District, Castro, California, 1964). It offers a list of specialized reference sources which a child might use to obtain information, steps in organizing a research report, and many creative ways to present such a report.

Historiography and Research

The scientific procedures used by historians in writing history may be learned by pupils who read books written by authors who illustrate the use of basic sources. Three books of this type are one edited by Rhoda Hoff, *Russia: Adventures in Eyewitness History* (Walck, 1964), which includes 57 excerpts about Russian history, written by persons ranging from Ovid to Dumas and Gorky; a diary by Laura Ingalls Wilder, *On the Way Home; The Diary of a Trip from South Dakota to Mansfield, Missouri, in 1894*, with a setting by Rose Wilder Lane (Harper, 1962) and a history of *The Crusades* by Régine Pernoud (Putnam, 1963) which uses such original sources as letters and chronicles.

After studying such books as these, pupils can examine other factual books more critically to determine authenticity of sources, biases, significance of publication date, competence of the author, and other details necessary in the judgmental aspects of critical reading.

Critical Reading by Genre

Pupils may conduct individual investigations of the biography, novel, or essay. As historical novels are read, students can consider such questions as (1) *story style:* is the plot contrived, pedestrian, fast moving, or involved and confusing? (2) *characterization:* are characters real persons or do they appear as wooden automatons? Am I able to empathize with them? (3) *dialogue:* is the dialogue appropriate, natural, or artificial? Is it related to a region or period of time? (4) *authenticity:* do the historical and geographical facts appear to be authentic? What sources did the author use for his information?

Reading for Social Sensitivity

The growing child needs many experiences with types of literature which make him empathize with the problems of mankind. For instance, he may read *Across Five Aprils* by Irene Hunt (Follett, 1964) and glean historical data about family life in Illinois during the Civil War; or he may gain a sense of compassion for young Jethro Creighton, who grew many more years than five between his ninth and his fourteenth birthday. Here is a book that offers a balance of bloodshed, hate, and tears with love, loyalty, and compassion.

In *Blue in the Seed* (Little, 1964) Kim Yong Ik depicts the little Korean boy who learned to accept the fact that difference is only a superficial thing. In *It's Like This, Cat* by Emily Neville (Harper, 1963), a young adolescent faces growing up problems in the Gramercy Park neighborhood of New York. Ester Wier's story *The Loner* (McKay, 1963) offers the story of an orphaned nameless boy, an itinerant crop-picker, who learned to be accepted and loved by others.

Three helpful bulletins in the area of using literature for human understanding are: *Literature and Social Sensitivity* by Walter Loban (National Council of Teachers of English, 1954) ; *Diagnosing Human Relations Needs* by Hilda Taba and others (American Council on Education, 1958) ; *Reading Ladders for Human Relations*, revised and edited by Muriel Crosby (American Council on Education, 1963).

The thematic unit and basic concepts approaches to individualized study are kinds of units which are often developed by county and city curricular staffs working with teachers, librarians, and consultants. The thematic unit may be topical, such as a unit based on the chronology of a particular historical period such as the Civil War, World War II; or a unit on the "Launching of a New Nation" might be thematic, with such a theme as "Man's Search for Recognition" or "The Quest of the Unknown." In developing the concepts or generalizations of a unit of study, students work cooperatively and inductively on experiences designed to foster an understanding of such concepts as interdependence or freedom.

Reading to Develop Aesthetic Appreciations

Children can be assisted in appreciating the qualities of good literature if they experience such a book as *Island of the Blue Dolphins* by Scott O'Dell (Houghton Mifflin, 1960). This is a novel which is artistically created, informative, and one which offers a feeling of man's dependence upon his environment. The true loneliness of the female Robinson Crusoe, Karana, penetrates the 184 pages of this volume as O'Dell beautifully interprets a lonely island, where the sea was a pale "blue stone." Childhood must experience such writing as a distillation of the blue crystal moments of experience.

CHILDREN'S LITERATURE FOR INTEGRATED CLASSES *

Ruth Anne Korey

At present, without doubt, teachers have a mandate to discover and develop materials for improving instruction of Negro children and, at the same time, to build a better curriculum for white children. Whether we happen to be teaching in an integrated or a segregated school, this is now a prime responsibility.

An excellent bibliography, entitled *Books about Negro Life for Children,* has been compiled by Augusta Baker.[1] It can be procured by mail for fifty cents. This list is especially useful in selecting books to purchase for the school library.

Another approach is to visit the children's department of a public library, particularly one in a neighborhood which has a Negro population. Consultation with the children's librarian, reference to the card catalog, and browsing along the shelves will guide the teacher to many worthwhile titles. This method was used by the present reviewer. Following are some of the books which can be recommended to other teachers who are just beginning to learn about appropriate literature for an integrated classroom.

Picture Books

The Caldecott Award for 1963 went to *The Snowy Day,* written and illustrated by Ezra Jack Keats.[2] This is an example of what might be called the "casual" Negro book. It relates the experiences of a small boy on a snowy day in the city. The incidents recall the usual activities of any child playing in the snow. It just happens that the pictures show the small hero as a Negro, even as it just happens that each of us is born white or Negro or whatever we may chance to be.

A similar and equally delightful book in the "casual" manner is Marie Hall Ets' *Gilberto and the Wind.*[3] Both stories are suitable for kindergarten or first-grade units on weather and should be

Ruth Anne Korey is Associate Professor of Education at Fordham University, New York City.

* Reprinted from *Elementary English* 43:39–42, 1966, with permission of the National Council of Teachers of English and Ruth Anne Korey.

[1] New York Public Library, 1963.

[2] Viking Press, 1962.

[3] Viking Press, 1963.

included along with the usual excellent books which are available on this topic for young white children.

The "planned" approach is apparent in other picture books which carry a more explicit message. *New Boy in School* by May Justus, for example, tells of a Negro boy's adjustment in an all-white class.[4]

In the picture-book category, there is a factual book which is suitable for almost any grade. This is *Red Man, White Man, African Chief* by Marguerite Rush Lerner, winner of a special award from the National Conference of Christians and Jews.[5] It explains how different amounts of melanin in the skin determine whether people are white, yellow, red, brown, or black. The account is simple enough to be read to children in the primary classes, and scientific enough to interest sixth graders. An appendix provides additional and advanced data for parents and teachers.

Juvenile Fiction

Beyond the primary grades, we find a sharp distinction between boys' books and girls' books. As we all know, girls read or listen to boys' stories, but boys will have nothing to do with books written for girls. Hence the teacher will supply titles for both but must confine oral reading to fiction for boys.

A Summer Adventure by Richard W. Lewis is a good choice for reading aloud.[6] Without any reference to his race, the story describes the experiences of a ten-year-old Negro who visits the zoo with his class and decides to spend the summer collecting animals for his own backyard.

Books dealing with sports can be depended on to attract slow readers whose main interest is athletics. Both white and Negro characters appear in *Little League Heroes* by Curtis Bishop [7] and in *All-American* by John R. Tunis.[8]

A number of stories with Negro protagonists may be classified as historical fiction. *A Lantern in the Window* by Aileen Fisher [9] and *Escape to Freedom* by Ruth Fosdick Jones [10] are exciting stories of the Underground Railroad. Such books help to enliven social studies, a subject which is difficult for underprivileged children and often disliked by them.

Still another group of stories with Negroes as important partici-

---

[4] Hastings House, 1963.
[5] Medical Books for Children, 1960.
[6] Harper, 1962.
[7] Lippincott, 1960.
[8] Harcourt, 1942.
[9] Nelson, 1957.
[10] Random House, 1958.

pants are those which are concerned with adjustment between black and white children. Alice Cobb's *The Swimming Pool* [11] and Jesse Jackson's *Call Me Charley* [12] are books of this type.

Many stories for girls seem dull and sentimental by contrast with those for boys. However, girls in their pre-teens are less critical than adult readers and seem to enjoy stories about home life or scouting, such as *Bright April* by Marguerite De Angeli,[13] *Sal Fisher at Girl Scout Camp* by Lillian S. Gardner,[14] and *Melindy's Happy Summer* by Georgene Faulkner.[15]

Biography

Life stories of successful Negroes are important in building the Negro child's self-esteem and in gaining appropriate respect from his fellow pupils. Courses of study which deal fully with the contributions of various European national groups have often neglected to include important Americans of the Negro race.

There are certain names that most teachers know, such as George Washington Carver, Booker T. Washington, Ralph Bunche, Joe Louis, and Jackie Robinson. A little study will enable us to add to this list. Such knowledge makes literature lessons more effective and also enriches the teaching of social studies, science, music, and art.

For example, it is good for a teacher to know that the pilot of one of Columbus' ships was a skillful navigator named Pedro Alonzo Nino. Similarily, when a class is studying the exploration of the Southwest, it is worth noting that Esteban, a Negro, was a leader of the group which discovered Arizona and New Mexico.

There is one book to be found in most public libraries which will give the teacher a start on her collection of outstanding Negroes. This is the beautifully written and illustrated *North Star Shining* by Hildegard Hoyt Swift.[16] In free verse she recounts the accomplishments of the Negro race, of illustrious Negro individuals, and of Negro heroes in World War II. The book as a whole gives an inspiring overview of the subject, and parts of it may be used for choral speaking.

The First Book of Negroes by Langston Hughes,[17] published in

---

[11] Friendship Press, 1957.
[12] Harper, 1945.
[13] Doubleday, 1946.
[14] Watts, 1959.
[15] Messner, 1949.
[16] Morrow, 1947.
[17] Watts, 1952.

1952, contains information about the Negro in history and also discusses frankly the social discrimination faced by Negro children both in the North and in the South. Apart from the lists of famous names it provides, the book is useful as an introduction to that phase of critical reading related to date of publication. "Which parts would have been different if the author had been writing today?"

Details of the achievements of outstanding Negroes can be obtained from individual biographies in the children's department, from books in the adults' section of the library, and from juvenile and general encyclopedias.

If, as Johnston has suggested,[18] there are books which should be recommended to every child, the biography of *Amos Fortune, Free Man* by Elizabeth Yates [19] is deserving of a special place. It tells the story of one Negro in colonial New England but epitomizes the whole experience of the American Negro—his life in Africa, his forced transfer to the American continent, his life as a slave and as a free man. Despite its theme, the book is filled with sheer goodness—the admirable character of Amos, the kindness and integrity of the many whites and Negroes he meets. The teacher will enjoy this book. It is truly a classic and, for the pupils, provides a splendid introduction to the biography shelves in the library.

Books about Africa

The topic of Africa appears in several places in the elementary school course of study. Teachers are therefore familiar with textbook and supplementary materials related to that continent. Recent sweeping changes in the map of Africa have caused us to read widely in newspapers and other periodicals so that what we teach will be true as of the present moment. The revised article on Africa in the 1962 edition of the *World Book Encyclopedia* [20] is helpful. Separate reprints, which can be obtained from the publisher, may be used in language arts lessons on the encyclopedia.

Many new children's books have appeared dealing with the entire African continent and its history, with specific areas, and with its people, its flora, and its fauna.

Negro organizations have asked that more attention be given to Africa in our curriculum. Among the children's books for the

---

[18] A. Montgomery Johnston, "The Classics of Children's Literature." *Elementary English 39*:412–414, 1962.

[19] Dutton, 1950.

[20] G. H. T. Kimball, "Africa," in *The World Book Encyclopedia*, I. Chicago: Field Educational Corporation, 1962, pp. 86–107.

teacher to consider are: Langston Hughes' *The First Book of Africa* [21] and Efua Sutherland's *Playtime in Africa*.[22] The latter presents photographs of children in the new Africa, looking much like our own pupils, and avoids the pictures of primitive tribes which some sensitive Negro children find embarrassing and distressing in an integrated classroom. There are directions for many games as well, some similar to American playground activities and others interestingly different.

Conclusion

The books which have been mentioned are listed only as suggestions. These and similar books will furnish materials and impetus for modifying the present curriculum to meet new needs.

Why are such changes necessary? As a recent song tells us, "The answer, my friend, is blowing in the wind." We can formulate these reasons as follows:

1. Negro children, handicapped in academic work by all-white textbooks and children's literature, may be helped to learn to read more easily if they can readily identify with the characters in a book.

2. Negro children, long underprivileged in social and economic background, may be inspired toward meaningful careers by the example of many Negroes who have made important contributions to our national life.

3. Negro children, suffering emotional problems resulting from inferior social, economic, and political status, may gain greater confidence in their own worth and ability, and thus may be freed from psychological impediments to learning.

4. White children, facing a new era in race relations, will be helped toward understanding and appreciation of Negro classmates as human beings like themselves, with a history and a potential for contributing to the welfare of the nation.

5. The teacher, whether white or Negro, will add to his own education and interests by learning as much as possible about new areas of social studies and literature.

6. The teacher will be more effective in class work and therefore will be a happier individual through becoming conversant with facts and materials related to the vital interests of the pupils.

---

[21] Watts, 1960.
[22] Atheneum, 1962.

HELPING ELEMENTARY SCHOOL CHILDREN UNDERSTAND MASS PERSUASION TECHNIQUES *

William W. Crowder

Today's young people are bombarded with propaganda and mass persuasion techniques on every hand. They are told what to eat. They are told what to wear. And they are even told what to say and think. One source reports they are subjected to 1,518 sales messages a day.[1] Because of this endless flow of appeals, young citizens must be taught to think critically, to make up their own minds intelligently, and to avoid being misled or fooled into precipitant reactions, later to be regretted.

Clearly then, elementary school teachers must help their pupils understand these efforts to engineer consent, and must assist them to gain perspective in a mad world of ballyhoo and sucker psychology.

What, one might ask, is propaganda? It is "an association or scheme for propagating a doctrine or practice, and comes from the Latin word *propagare* which describes the gardener's practice of pinning the fresh roots of a plant which will later take on a life of their own."[2] In a more general sense, it is an attempt to persuade others in favor of a set of beliefs, policies, or attitudes desired by the propagandist, or against those he deems unworthy.

As is suggested by this definition, some attempts to manipulate opinion are "good," others are "bad," and much lies between the two extremes and is neutral. Propaganda against crime, disease, and highway accidents is considered beneficent. But attempts to sell bogus stock or to encourage racial prejudice would be looked upon unfavorably by most of us. In some instances the alternatives are as much alike as tweedledum and tweedledee and offer no real choice.

William W. Crowder is Associate Professor of Education at Purdue University, Lafayette, Indiana.

* Reprinted from *Social Education 31*:119–121, 1967, with permission of the National Council for the Social Studies and William W. Crowder.

[1] Vance Packard, *The Status Seekers*. New York: Pocket Books, 1964, pp. 271–272.

[2] J. A. C. Brown, *Techniques of Persuasion: From Propaganda to Brainwashing*. Baltimore: Penguin Books, 1963, p. 10.

How can the school help its young people understand propaganda? Four avenues will be suggested in this paper.

1. Young people should be taught to recognize and understand the major propaganda devices. These have been identified by C. R. Miller [3] and Leonard W. Doob.[4] Seven of the most common are:

Name calling. This procedure involves attaching a label or tag to a person in an attempt to besmirch him. He may be called a "pink," a "Communist," or a "free-thinker."

Glittering generality. This is a gimmick used to describe a person or product in a favorable light and is usually the opposite of name calling. Such nebulous terms as "pure," "modern," "honest," and "democratic" are examples.

Transfer. This involves joining a symbol or idea toward which the reader has favorable attitudes with another symbol whose acceptance is less sure or less certain. The attractive girl on the billboard probably has nothing to do with the performance of the automobile she is seated in, but the linkage provides a means of influencing the reader in a positive way.

Testimonial. In this device, the name of a famous movie star is often used to endorse brand "X" toothpaste, thus giving the impression that popularity and success can be traced to the use of the product.

Card stacking. This involves rigging the facts by concealing certain information or by emphasizing other information. A chart of a company's earnings may be constructed in such a way as to suppress losses over a long period, while the dividends of the last few years are highlighted.

Plain folks device. Here the propagandist tries to become "one of us," or the politician rolls up his sleeves, loosens his tie, and decides to just "talk."

Band wagon procedure. This entails an appeal to the group instinct and urges one to "do it" because everyone else is doing it.

These seven are the major devices, but there are others. Harter and Sullivan [5] list 77 such techniques. But in reality, awareness of them is not enough, for mere recognition does not imply a true perception of their intent. Another step is necessary.

2. Elementary school children must be encouraged to study the

---

[3] C. R. Miller, *How to Detect and Analyze Propaganda.* New York: New Town Hall, 1939, p. 14.

[4] Leonard W. Doob, *Propaganda and Its Psychology and Technique.* New York: Holt, 1935, pp. 99–107.

[5] D. Lincoln Harter and John Sullivan, *Propaganda Handbook.* Philadelphia: Twentieth Century, 1953, p. viii.

meanings of words and their specific relation to other words as they analyze indoctrination. The first two devices, name calling and glittering generalities, lean heavily upon the misuse or abuse of words to disguise the issues. For example, what does "conservative" mean? Are there not degrees of conservatism? Is this characteristic exhibited in every act of the person?

All this means that young people must be helped to realize that one word may have a variety of meanings. For example, in the sentence, "Fresh troops were rushed into the battle," the meaning is unclear until the definition of the word "fresh" is clarified. Does it mean rested, young, healthy, or does it carry the idea of more? To understand the true intent of the writer or speaker, one must first come to grips with the word he employs.[6]

Here again, certain words implanted in propaganda may be used to distort a particular point of view or to color it for a specific reason. As an example, what is meant by "Great Society Democrats" or "Northern Republicans"? There can be little doubt but that such words are not used to depict the exact attributes of a person as often as they are employed to suggest an *opinion* about him.

Among other things, elementary school children must be taught to examine the motives of a writer as revealed by his choice of words. Does his position appear to be coldly scientific, analytical, and logical? An exhaustive discussion by a daily newspaper columnist on social security or on the cold war, when probed thoughtfully, may turn out to be an emotionally laden appeal to stir up mass protests. A writer or speaker with axes to grind is likely to practice the art wherever he finds an audience.

As might be expected, a study of semantics will further demonstrate to children that certain proverbs are motivational contrivances. It has been pointed out by other writers that most wise sayings contain strategies for action and over the years assume a kind of authority. If one wishes to pursue individualism, he might justify it by "Paddle your own canoe." But on the other hand, if he desires the company of others, he might call forth "A friend in need is a friend indeed." Many advertisers use old maxims, or make up their own slogans. After all, there is nothing wrong with using such techniques, but teachers must be sure their students understand this drumbeat of the hucksters. A study of old sayings will prove useful to an elementary class as it pursues the place of mass persuasion in modern communication media.

3. Today's young citizens must be made aware of the emotional

---

[6] Albert L. Walker, Keith G. Huntress, Robert B. Orlovich, and Barriss Mills, *Essentials of Good Writing.* Boston: Heath, 1959, p. 319.

motivations upon which propagandists play.[7] A study of advertisements in newspapers and magazines and of concerted efforts to mold opinion will reveal several basic psychological needs to which they appeal. They include the desire for financial success, social acceptance, security, sex, good health, comfort, and social status. Some of these overlap, but each is fundamental to one's well-being and happiness.

Take, for example, the desire for financial success. Advertisements or announcements of stock for sale in a newly-formed company with a name like Electronics, or Computer Processing, are accompanied with evidence of growth of other companies, the implication being that, if one wants $5,000 to become $350,000 within a few years, he should place his money with this fledgling. Elementary school pupils, especially those in the middle grades, can study the folderol of such ads, examine closely the word meanings, and under most circumstances, conclude the absurdity of their claims.

The desire for social acceptance can be equally as strong as the wish for wealth. Although a study of class structure and social prestige may not be appropriate for all elementary school children, many youngsters can profit from it. Celia Stendler has shown that "awareness of social class symbols develops gradually over a period of years" and concludes that pupils in "The two upper grades, especially the eighth, are very much like adults in their ratings [of social class symbols]."[8] To this end it might be interesting for a seventh- or eighth-grade class to study advertisements to determine which ones arouse a response for improving one's social status.

These and other desires, hopes, dreams, and fears, eternal in the human breast, are the target of every bamboozler. They engender within him a preposterous fandango of efforts to manage the intellect through the use of logic, suggestions, statistics, and psychology, and appeal to the senses of smell, touch, taste, and hearing.

That being so, surely none can remain neutral in this battle of words; nor indeed, would such posture be desirable. For even the uncommitted, like huge boulders unmoved by a torrential mountain stream, influence the water's course by the very fact of their immobility.

4. In the last analysis, teachers must lead their pupils to self-awareness and self-understanding so that they will be able to make

---

[7] See, for example, Vance Packard, "The Molding of Tender Minds," in *The Status Seekers*. New York: Pocket Books, 1961, pp. 195–215.

[8] Celia B. Stendler, *Children of Brasstown*. Urbana: University of Illinois Press, 1949, pp. 88–92.

relatively rational choices for themselves. These decisions must have as their foundation a wide acquaintance with the humanities, social sciences, ethics, and social psychology. For only through a knowledge of these and other subjects can individuals come to know themselves, their problems, and the solutions to their problems. True it is that almost all English which endeavors to persuade will use techniques similar to the celebrated seven, as Bresler [9] comments. Plainly, too, children must be taught that distinguishing sense from nonsense, value from vice, demagoguery from pedagogy, and the socially good from the socially evil is no small task. It is, in fact, the job of a lifetime.

Aided by a knowledge of propaganda devices, an awareness of semantics and the basic appeals it makes, as well as an understanding of themselves, today's youth will possess the skills necessary to become model, not muddled, thinkers.

DEVELOPING LIFE VALUES THROUGH READING *

May Hill Arbuthnot

When Longfellow uttered his portentous warning, "Life is real! Life is earnest!" he neglected to add that life can also be a lot of fun and more full of intriguing people and interesting things to do and see than one lifetime can possibly encompass. The problem is to make the most of life and, as adults, we do have to admit that growing up is also a chancey process. What forces, for instance, made you what you are? And when and where did you begin to grow into the You that is sitting here today? As a group of teachers we may not be in the higher echelon of world shakers, but on the whole we are a fairly competent lot of people. What image of ourselves grown to maturity made us so and prevented us from going in the direction of the unhappy law-breakers of one kind or another?

[9] Marvin Bresler, "Mass Persuasion and the Analysis of Language: A Critical Evaluation." *Journal of Educational Sociology 33*:17–27, 1959.

May Hill Arbuthnot is Associate Professor Emeritus, Case-Western Reserve University, Cleveland, Ohio.

* Reprinted from *Elementary English 43*:10–16, 1966, with permission of the National Council of Teachers of English and May Hill Arbuthnot.

As teachers we would be the first to admit that the child's home and the people he is associated with are of paramount importance in forming his ideals of what he himself wants to be. But for the most part these influences are beyond our control. Today we are also concerned about the influence of mass media on the child's developing image of himself. And again his use of these media, outside of school, we can do little about except to know their scope and character. Certainly all forms of mass media—newspapers, pictorial magazines, moving pictures, radio and television—are very much with today's child. Along with their fine documentaries and other substantial offerings, today's child is bombarded daily with closeups of brutality, banality, scandal, and violence. Over the din of the Beatles with their screaming hordes, Western heroes forever fighting and movie Queens forever misbehaving, what chance to make a deep impression, for instance, has the image of Herbert Hoover's quiet dedicated life? The hopeful element in this mass presentation of savage and silly examples of maturity is their evanescence. Pictures and words come and go with great rapidity and are immediately replaced by something equally brief and easily forgotten. But are they forgotten? We know so little about the image of himself that is gradually forming in that secret, inner world of the child's mind and spirit. But one thing we do know. If we can induct children into a genuine enjoyment of books, we can guide them to stories in which they will discover pictures of noble maturity and of children growing and changing into more competent and more lovable human beings at every stage of development.

Reading an absorbing story is a continual process of identification. The child sees himself as the smart, third Little Pig or as Tom Sawyer or Caddie Woodlawn or whoever his current hero may be. Then, because even fluent, rapid reading is a slower, steadier process than the interrupted, piecemeal presentation of television with its station identifications and endless commercials, the hero image in a book has a chance to make a deeper, more lasting impression. Books are a bright hope if we can find the right book for a child at the right time.

For the Youngest—Reassurance and Achievement

The youngest children in our schools, the prereaders and beginners in reading, just because they are small and inexperienced, are uncertain, insecure and generally find themselves in the wrong. Someone is always saying, "Don't do that," or "No, you aren't old enough for that." So, of course, these young pilgrims need lots of reassurance about their place in the world, that they are loved, needed and capable of doing things on their own. Notice how their first picture stories stress both loving reassurance, and also achievement. For example, these qualities account, in part, for the popularity of *The Happy Lion* series by Louise Fatio with pictures by Roger Duvoism. The Lion, like small children, is cribbed, confined, and misunderstood. But he has ideas of his own, whether it is going for a walk in the town or getting himself a beautiful lioness, he carries out his plans gently but firmly. And children, after feeling sorry for him, chuckle over his achievements and say, "read it again." Then they pore over those inimitable pictures which are completely one with the text and they triumph again with the Happy Lion.

This autumn has brought one of the most beautiful and satisfying picture stories for the prereaders that we have had. It is called, *Whistle for Willie*, written and illustrated by Ezra Jack Keats, who did the Caldecott Medal book *Snowy Day*. This new one is even more beautiful, in luscious pinks against the whole spectrum of colors, and with the same little colored boy in a pink and white shirt trying desperately to whistle for his dog, Willie. Failing, he crawls into a big carton to practice. Then, feeling more grown-up by the addition of his father's hat, he plays father, and all sorts of other things, but always working for a whistle. Suddenly, there is Willie his dog, and suddenly Peter whistles! Willie stops dead in his tracks and then comes flying. Here is a climax and from that point on, sheer triumph! But there is more to this slight story than this briefing indicates. There is the enviable pattern of big boys whose dogs come when they whistle and a little boy struggling to be equally competent. There is an understanding mother, a proud father, love and achievement happily combined to make a small masterpiece.

If you look back over the picture stories that have enjoyed lasting popularity with children, you discover how these two notes—reassuring love and independent achievement—recur over and over again from *Peter Rabbit, Little Black Sambo*, and *Millions of Cats*, through the *Little Tim* and *Madeline* series to last year's splendid and more mature story of *Hans and Peter* by Heidrum Petrides. All of Robert McCloskey's beautiful picture stories stress reassurance. When children identify their own helplessness with the Ducklings or with Sal picking blueberries or losing a tooth or with the family in *Time of Wonder*, they come away from these books feeling that they too, when their time of trial comes, can weather the storm. They are stronger, more confident children for such books. And at an older level, the importance of Alice Dalgliesh's *The Bears of*

Hemlock Mountain lies in the fact that Jonathan was genuinely afraid. Nevertheless, he went ahead with his scary undertaking and discovered in himself unexpected resources. A fine achievement tale for the primary.

Certainly, the carefully selected folk tales we use with young children—the fours and fives, sevens and eights—present a lively gallery of up-and-doing heroes and heroines, as, for example, the dauntless Bremen Town Musicians, the Three Pigs, Three Billy Goats, Boots, Beauty, Snow White and their like. These and the more complex tales for the older children are saying to the child, "If you show kindness as well as courage, if you beware of silly credulity and use your head as well as your heart, you too can accomplish wonders." These old stories are worthwhile if only to build in children the firm conviction that evil need not be endured; that giants, ogres and all the other big bullies in the world can be laid low, and meanness, greed and cruelty exterminated. Our generation may not have finished the job but some progress has been made and maybe the next generation will do better. Anyway, these old tales are good medicine for children to grow on, so don't miss the beautiful new editions of single tales illustrated by such artists as Marcia Brown, Adrienne Adams, Eric Blegvad, and many others. These entrancing editions are bound to revive the popularity of these old tales, and it is about time.

Middle Years—7-10, Curiosity and Zest for Living

Love and achievement continue to motivate stories for all ages, but by the middle school years children seven, eight, and nine should be developing a lively curiosity about an ever expanding world and should have such a gay, coltish zest for living that they seek fun, adventure, and sometimes pure nonsense. Apathy and boredom in these transition years are unthinkable, and yet teachers say there are plenty of both, especially among deprived children in our big cities. Perhaps the bite of frustration and failure has set in. In these years, 7 to 10, the child has taken a giant step. He has learned to read for himself, but alas, not fluently! There's the rub. Learning to read is all very exciting to begin with, but when difficulties pile up, discouragement mounts. These are the years when teachers must try consciously to fill the gap between what the slow learning child can read for himself and what he would like to read. There is often a lag of from one to three years between reading skill and the ability to understand and enjoy. Teachers must fill that gap with plenty of practice in easy-to-read books and by reading aloud to their children books that delight them but are well beyond their reading ability.

There are many lists of easy-to-read books but frequently the content is too immature for the children who need them. Take Else Minarek's *Little Bear* books. They are charming for the fives and sixes, but babyish at seven and eight. Here the books of Clyde Bulla help mightily. He has an easy but never commonplace style and a stepped-up content which the sevens and even the elevens respect and enjoy. He always tells a lively adventure story and his books fit into many subject matter areas as the titles indicate— *Squanto, Friend of the White Men, Down the Mississippi, The Sword in the Tree,* and others. Alice Dalgliesh's *The Courage of Sarah Noble* will balance these boys' stories and give even the mildest little girls a sense of achievement. While we are on historical fiction, these may be good years to read aloud one of William Steele's stories of pioneer boys to introduce children to these books —*Tomahawks and Trouble, Winter Danger,* or any of them. Their importance lies in the fact that besides being exciting adventure stories, these ignorant, wrong-headed boy heroes grow and change in the course of a story, forged into something stronger and better by trials of endurance that call out all their stamina. Such books build up children's self-respect. They are antidotes for discouragement, apathy, and giving up the struggle. It is far too easy for children to accept failure and to downgrade themselves accordingly. Strong stories are energizing. The hero image gives them a clear idea of a competent maturity and the satisfaction of putting up a good fight.

Children also need a sense of fun along the way. The more school or home or personality difficulties increase, the more a child needs the release of laughter or even pure nonsense. Laughter can break tensions and restore balance. Nonsense verse or what children call "funny stories" help. If they can read for themselves those two indestructibles—*Mr. Popper's Penguins* or *Mary Poppins*—they'll chuckle and recover from the doldrums. If they can't, then take time to read one of them aloud. Or if you prefer, choose Oliver Butterworth's *Enormous Egg,* about the hen that hatched out not an Ugly Duckling, but no less than a mammoth dinosaur, amiable but outsize for domesticity. For a group of children to laugh together is to break down hostilities, tensions, and unhappiness. It is well worth the time. And E. B. White's matchless *Charlotte's Web,* which *is* beyond their reading skill but not their enjoyment level, will give them not only the therapy of laughter but the therapy of tears. Children need both. How else can they learn compassion?

These examples of the child's "funny stories" have all been in the field of fantasy, but there is also humorous realism to reassure routine-weary youngsters. If they cannot read Beverly Cleary's

Henry Huggins, read them the first book and they'll tackle the next one as soon as possible. The hilarious Huggins' adventures with Ribsey, the dog, and the neighborhood children lead naturally to Keith Robertson's *Henry Reed, Inc.,* one of the funniest books available. Henry, with his complete lack of humor, decides to go in for research. He puts up a sign, "Henry Reed, Inc. Research," to which his pushy girl neighbor adds, "Pure and Applied." He explains that only girls keep diaries "about their dates and different boy friends. But pirates and explorers keep journals." So, in his journal he records their summer adventures in research and these should leave any child a little better able to laugh at himself when he gets into absurd messes of his own making. The second book, *Henry Reed's Journey,* is as amusing as the first. Both are enhanced by some of Robert McCloskey's funniest drawings.

In these years the child's curiosity is boundless, or should be, and so are the informational books written to answer his questions and promote new ones. In any field of science, from dinosaurs to insects, and from stones to stars, there are excellent books at almost any reading level you desire. The same is true in the field of the social studies. But factual books are not the province of this paper which is concerned with literature for children. Fiction may also meet his curiosities about people, places, and ways of living. So his fiction goes back in time to include historical events of long ago and out in space to embrace the diverse regions and peoples of our United States and of other lands. Stories about Amish, Indians, Negroes, Jewish families, ranchers, farmers, fishermen, migrant workers, city folk, all give a colorful and sympathetic introduction to diverse peoples and customs in this vast country of ours. Young readers get delightful glimpses of life in other countries in such old favorites as Chinese *Little Pear* by Eleanor Lattimore, or Hungarian *The Good Master* by Kate Seredy, or Natalie Carlson's tender and humorous story of Paris *The Family Under the Bridge,* or Harry Behn's Mexican *The Two Uncles of Pablo.* From all these areas of reading—historical, regional, foreign lands—children get the reiterated truth that peoples of every age or place or country have similar difficulties, suffer deprivations and failures, and are more alike than different in their struggles to achieve a place in the sun.

For these middle years you may have noticed a dearth of recent titles, but there is nevertheless rich treasure in the books available if you are not too dedicated to recency. And why should you be? Just remember, it is the children who are forever recent, the books don't have to be, and a strong book twenty years old is worth a dozen bits of mediocrity just off the press.

Preadolescents—10 to 12 or 14, Compassion and Courage

In the last years of elementary school reading there is such a wide variation in reading abilities and social maturity that placing books by age levels is complete nonsense. A thirteen-year-old who thoroughly enjoyed *The Agony and the Ecstasy* and could discuss it eagerly, play by play, is not going to be satisfied with *Caddie Woodlawn*, nor will a twelve-year-old who has a struggle to get through *Henry Huggins*, give more than a passing glance at *Rifles for Watie*. Adults who guide children's reading in the years from ten to twelve or fourteen are pretty much on their own and can let those brashly graded reading lists fall where they may.

Oddly enough there is one area of reading where children and adults frequently meet on common ground and that is the well-written story about animals. By well written we mean authentic, true to the animal species, and neither humanized nor sentimentalized. For instance, *The Incredible Journey* by Sheila Burnford, which meets all these standards, was intended for adults but the children took it over. The same thing happened to Marjorie Rawlings' *The Yearling* and to that poignant little masterpiece by the late James Street, *Good-Bye, My Lady*. And, of course, the values of such books and those by Marguerite Henry, Jim Kjelgaard, Joseph Lippincott, the Georges and others, are manifold. Of first importance, however, is the fact that they stir the readers' compassion for animals. Albert Schweitzer calls this "reverence for life, all life worthy of development." Such reverence is made up of sensitivity to the needs and sufferings of others, compassion and a strong identification that we call empathy. These are all aspects of the same emotion, love. Going out to others selflessly is the most civilizing force in life. Never have we needed it more.

Teachers who have worked in the deprived areas of big cities where children have never been responsible for farm animals or pets, know all too well the horrible acts of sadism practiced by unthinking children against small animals, especially defenseless cats. Only this autumn there have been two such terrible examples of cat-torture that they have made the front pages of the papers. These could not have happened had those children ever cherished a pet cat or a rabbit or a dog of their own. And next to owning or growing up with animals are the vicarious experiences of reading about them. The process of identification that goes on when a child reads about *Smoky* or *Lassie* or *King of the Wind* means that he suffers with and for the animal hero. He also senses the nobility and sacrifice of the great gorilla in Lucy Boston's *Stranger at*

Green Knowe or the patient endurance of mistreated Smoky or the curious loyalty and first aid the cat gave her two dog companions in *The Incredible Journey*. Perhaps compassion and reverence for life are ambitious terms for the child's emotional response to these books, but certainly they evoke tenderness and the desire to cherish and protect. These are the qualities that make the well-written animal story of great importance to young readers of every age and the reason why a story about animal torture in the bull ring, ballet style, seems regrettable.

The last years between childhood and the budding maturity of youth are hard on children. These preadolescents need almost as much encouragement as the youngest. They try their wings and fall flat on their faces. Failure is bitter and it takes courage to get up and try again. They are acutely aware of their own imperfections—too fat or too skinny or not sufficiently sought after. They are even more critical of the frightful imperfections of their parents. In no book has this ever been more accurately reflected than in those opening paragraphs of Emily Neville's *It's Like This, Cat*. Here they are:

> My father is always talking about how a dog can be very educational for a boy. This is one reason I got a cat.
> My father talks a lot anyway. Maybe being a lawyer he gets in the habit. Also, he's a small guy with very little gray curly hair, so maybe he thinks he's got to roar a lot to make up for not being a big hairy tough guy. Mom is thin and quiet, and when anything upsets her, she gets asthma. In the apartment—we live right in the middle of New York City—we don't have any heavy drapes or rugs, and Mom never fries any food because the doctor's figure dust and smoke make her asthma worse. I don't think it's dust; I think it's Pop's roaring.
> The big hassle that led me to getting Cat came when I earned some extra money baby-sitting for a little boy around the corner on Gramercy Park. I spent the money on a Belafonte record about a father telling his son about the birds and the bees. I think it's funny. Pop blows his stack.

By the way, whoever said this book lacked style? It may not have the lyric style of *Wind in the Willows*, but a family conflict is not a lyric. Styles do and should differ, and this is valid for the subject it describes. Incidentally, notice how in these brief paragraphs, the reader gets the theme, problem, and conflict of the entire book, as well as the brash, caustic judgments of youth. The fact that in the course of the story Dave comes to reevaluate his parents and even to see a new image of his own maturity through his father's eyes, makes this a choice book and one of our best big-city stories of a boy growing up.

There are different kinds of courage and it takes a special kind to accept physical handicaps or humiliating failures. That was the special value of the Newbery Medal book by Marguerite De Angeli, *The Door in the Wall.* Young, active, ambitious Robin has to accept the cruel fact of his semi-paralyzed limbs. But thanks to Brother Luke's ministrations and his philosophy—"Always remember . . . thou hast only to follow a wall far enough and there will be a door in it. . . ." Robin learned to use his hands again and to get around agilely on crutches. The conclusion is not a cure, but a heart-warming triumph for Robin that should give courage to all permanently handicapped children. The thing is to find a door in every wall.

To come to grips with failure is part and parcel of growing up. Most children's stories grant the hero success in the end. That happened to David in that remarkable book of 1963—*The Loner* by Ester Weir. This is a great book. But there is a recent book that is memorable because in *Skinny* by Robert Burch, the boy's failure to achieve his heart's desire is unalterable. Skinny is an illiterate, eleven-year-old orphan. Miss Bessie has taken him in temporarily to help her in her small town hotel. The work and Miss Bessie suit Skinny fine, and he dreams of adoption. Everyone likes Skinny but at the end of a happy summer the dreaded orphanage is inevitable. The board has refused Miss Bessie's request to adopt Skinny because she is unmarried. Everyone keeps saying, "The orphanage is only forty miles away." To which Skinny replies sadly, "Forty miles is a far piece." And so it is, a far piece from love and a home. But at least he can return to Miss Bessie for vacations and at long last he is going to learn to read and write. It is a sad ending but somehow the right one, for the reader knows that Skinny will make out wherever he lands. He'll put his grief behind him and do with a flourish whatever there is to do.

In Joseph Ullman's older book *Banner in the Sky,* Rudi also saw his bright hope destroyed. This is a new step for children in their reading and in facing life. Things do not always come out happily in the end. Hopes are blasted, struggles are defeated, but the young reader must catch from his reading the image of the hero who picks himself up after defeat to make a new start. That is what reading in these last years of childhood must reiterate, and that is what all of Rosemary Sutcliff's magnificent historical novels are saying over and over. They were discussed last year in detail, but get your good readers into these books as soon as they can handle them.

Still another kind of courage, often thankless, is the patient's plodding courage to endure. The recent *Across Five Aprils* by Irene Hunt tells such a story. It is another Civil War book, usual in subject but unusual in treatment. Five years of war are seen through the eyes of Jethro, a farm boy, nine years old when war begins and fourteen when it ends. With his brothers gone off to fight, his father paralyzed, even his beloved school master gone too, all the back breaking toil of maintaining the farm falls on young Jethro. The unusual quality of this book lies in the vivid portrayal of every person in the story, even minor characters. It is a beautifully written chronicle of the enduring courage of one unsung hero, a boy, who did what had to be done.

Another 1964 story of courage at a more mature level is Ann Petry's relentless account of the Salem witch-hunting hysteria, *Tituba of Salem Village*. Tituba was a slave, and from her arrival in Salem, her dark skin and unusual skills made her suspect. There is a grim foreboding and suspense about this story of mounting evil that grips the reader from the first page to the last. Yet with others hanged or burned, Tituba, honest, brave, and patient, miraculously survived. Only mature readers can take this bitter record of white civilization gone wrong. But it has a message for today, not underlined in the book, but there nevertheless. This is probably the most powerful book of the season in the juvenile field, not to be missed by good readers.

Conclusion

In suggesting some of the needs of children at different ages that books can help to satisfy, the list began with reassuring love and independent achievement. It ends with much the same—compassionate love and the kind of courage that is another phase of achievement. These qualities, by the way, motivate fiction for all ages and help to tie children's books into the whole stream of literature. But in children's books, the quality of love must grow and change as the child matures, until he can begin to see himself vicariously through his book heroes as loved and bestowing love, as dealing compassionately with others and, above all, as picking himself up after failures or shattered hopes or grievous mistakes to try again. These are some of the things strong books can do for children besides giving them keen enjoyment. Books can show them patterns of compassionate love and courageous achievement of many kinds.

ART IN THE SOCIAL STUDIES *

Thomas A. Hamil

A picture is not *worth* a thousand words. It is different than a thousand words. A picture makes its own message, not a translation of a verbal message. Visual communication is direct, swift, and powerful.

Members of the literate culture are not often aware of the power of nonverbal communication.[1] But when we notice the reactions of the viewers to a show of avant-garde painting, of the trance compelled by the flickering television image, or the shudder when a flashing red light is seen in the rear-view mirror of our car, we may appreciate that all communication is not in words. The strong impact of vision is sensed in such expressions as "eye-sore," or "it delights my eyes."

Although many cognitive elements may be introduced in a picture, it is the emotional effect that is most noticed. Two pictures may show the appearance of a medieval village, for example, but the illustrator's use of color, technique, and the aspects of the scene he stresses may give the feeling of a romantic fictional past or the awareness of the squalor and poverty of the Dark Ages. Both pictures may give the same facts, but the reaction to them will be completely different. The viewer is reached on an affective level as well as through the information presented.

Children are often more comfortable with visual than verbal messages. They are constrained by vocabulary and grammar in their verbal communication, whereas visual communication seems more direct. Visual communication is natural to man. We have a 30,000-year heritage of visual art that seems as understandable now as when painted. Of course, our understanding may be different than the intentions of the painters, but we can appreciate the symbols on our own terms. Children also seem ready to accept art on their terms. Many works that are confusing to adults are accepted by children. I recall watching a little girl and her mother looking at a nonobjective painting. The mother looked perplexed; the little girl squealed delightedly, "Oh, isn't it noisy!"

Thomas A. Hamil is an author and illustrator of children's books and a pre-doctoral associate at the University of Washington, Seattle.

* Prepared especially for this volume by Thomas A. Hamil and printed with his permission, February, 1968.

[1] J. Ruesch, *Nonverbal Communication.* Berkeley: University of California Press, 1956.

This is not to say that understanding through vision is automatic. It takes training to see as a hunter sees, or as a botanist sees, or as a painter sees. Work in visual expression has as one of its goals the development of visual acuity.[2] Children may develop their vision by looking at paintings and by working with the problems of visual expression. Some symbols in art require sophistication for full understanding, but some understanding, on a personal level, seems possible for everyone who is willing to look.

The Use of Art in the Social Studies

We expect to find the pages of type in our textbooks relieved by pictures. They are treated often as decoration to give the reader a pause in his study. But we expect illustrations to give information also. They may be considered supplementary, extending the ideas in the text, or they may contain their own body of facts that would be impossible to put into words. Some information must be shown. Imagine trying to describe the face of Lincoln.

As with all sources of fact, pictures must be carefully considered before the teacher uses them. Editors and illustrators try to be accurate. But illustrations have appeared with freshly attired pioneers, or Mongol warriors astride Western cow ponies! Obviously, teachers cannot go through the research necessary to certify each picture. But awareness of the importance of the information contained in the illustrations may help the teacher keep alert to errors. An accurate picture can be a research tool.

The teacher can ask questions that encourage careful looking by her students. The level of questioning can proceed from basic identification of things in the picture to conjecture of possible uses, outcomes, sources, and so forth.[3] Probing questions may bring out more from a picture than from the pages of type. The picture is open-ended; there are no limits to the suppositions that could be drawn from it.

Pictures not only show facts but they often reveal emotion. Scenes of historical events may show the setting and costumes and people involved and also show how the people felt on the occasion.

Paintings not only give information about an era, but the paintings may be a primary source. Scollon described the change in the attitudes of Americans shown in the sequence of portrait art.

---

[2] G. S. Wright, Jr., "Elementary Art to Develop Visual Sensitivity." *School Arts* 2:19–21, 1963.

[3] B. S. Bloom, ed., *Taxonomy of Educational Objectives: The Classification of Educational Goals, Handbook I: The Cognitive Domain.* New York: McKay, 1956.

Early portraiture was done in imitation of European court paintings; later they became more and more indicative of individualism as men were portrayed in the gear of their trade.[4] A great deal can be learned from the subjects chosen by painters and how they dealt with those subjects. There are many examples: symbolic animals in many hunting cultures, the comparison of the idealized human in Greek art and the portraits of Rome, the absence of figures in Islamic art, and so on.

Art As a Means to Social Study

Art may be used by children as a means of study. In the social studies, we are concerned about the reading abilities of our pupils because so much of our material is verbal. But there is a great source of data that the reader and nonreader can share in the visual arts. Pictures may provide the means to find information and also the means to record information when it is found. The research skills can apply equally to gathering facts from illustrations as well as from texts. Many of the topics we study may be put directly into visual terms. Why write about the appearance of a California mission? Many topics are available in well-illustrated trade books that provide a research tool for all pupils. The illustrations may be used as a perfectly respectable method for learning, even for excellent readers.

Pictures can build a strong background for concept formation.

> . . . for it was not so much by the knowledge of words that I came to the understanding of things, as by experience of things I was enabled to follow the meaning of words.
>
> Plutarch[5]

A picture can come close to experience. The degree of the response to a picture depends on its quality. Pictures can be as dull as last year's memorandum if they present information without style. Or, the symbolism of a picture can be too obscure for the pupil to respond. But a painting that gives the information needed in an appealing form involves the child in a vicarious experience from which he can build his ideas.

There is one aspect of art that is used a great deal in elementary school social studies—that is the use of art as a presentational

---

[4] Kenneth M. Scollon, "The Arts: Overlooked Witnesses of History." *Social Education 31*:29–32, 1967.

[5] Quoted in B. Bettelheim, *The Empty Fortress*. New York: Free Press, 1967, p. 89.

method. In most classrooms, the walls display maps, drawings, and murals that relate to the social studies content. Here is the place to add richness to the pupils' learning. These displays can be made artistically pleasing as well as factually accurate.

The first step toward good art in the social studies is to have the children do their own drawings. Copies of illustrations are generally stilted and add no personal quality to the work. Details, the facts of the drawing, may be taken from paintings of the period or from illustrations, but the drawing should be the child's own expression. Only by taking the material of his study and putting it into his own expression can the child learn. As M. P. Follette commented:

> Concepts can never be presented to me merely, they must be knitted into the structure of my being, and this can only be done through my own activity.[6]

Also by working with the problems of art, children can be made more aware of the artist's approach to those problems. The child then becomes a contributor to knowledge, not a mere recipient.

Develop the appreciation of the children in the works of children by showing the products of their peers from their own school, other schools in the area, and examples from around the world. The commonality of interests may present an important social lesson. Within the school district, schools of different social classes or with ethnic variations may trade pictures to build an appreciation of the views of others and to share their views. Diversity may be more apparent than real when we are made aware of the similarity of our arts. Children's art is an important facet of the world's art. When pupils see their work as a part of this art and not in competition with adult art, they may be more willing to display their work.

An awareness of the expressive quality of color can be encouraged. Descriptive color may contribute little to a drawing, especially if the color is stereotyped. Using colored paper as background for pastel or tempera paintings may bring more exciting effects than the usual manila paper. A huge combine roaring across a field may take on real drama if presented with brilliant colors.

The use of color can also be stimulated by short walks around the schoolyard. Skies are not always blue, nor leaves green. Looking at a plant will show the wide variation of colors in its leaves. A

---

[6] M. P. Follette, *Creative Experience*. New York: Longmans, Green & Co., 1924.

word of caution in this regard, however. Children need to develop their own symbols before they can give them meaning.[7] Respect the child's symbol even while you bring him outside to look.

A variety of media will encourage the visual presentation of your social studies material. Crayons can be used dozens of ways. They can be broken and used for big, flat effects; they can be used with the paper placed on top of a textured surface, like wood or canvas, so the colored areas will have texture; they can be pressed hard against the paper so a deep layer of wax is left, then that wax polished with a paper towel to give a shiny, rich surface. There are many possibilities.[8] Paints, clay, papier maché could all be used for social studies reporting.[9] Murals might be made from torn paper, squares of paper cut from magazines, bits of cloth or other materials, as a change from tempera on butcher paper. There is no limit to the variety that can be introduced. Be willing to give new ideas a try, or better, be willing to let your class give new ideas a try.

Variety can be stimulated by bringing reproductions of art work into the class. They are available free, or for very little cost, through museums of art and other sources. Magazines carry pictures of architecture, sculpture, ceramics, dancers, and paintings that can be collected and used. How much better to have a reproduction of a work of art done *at* the time you are studying than to use an illustration *about* the time studied. Don't shy away from work that doesn't happen to be in your taste; give the children the chance to form their own opinions.

The child should be involved in choice. He should have as many opportunities as possible to decide and follow through on that decision. Art gives a chance for this social learning at a basic level. The child should choose his materials and techniques and see for himself the outcomes of that choice. The work should be an expression of the child, not an example of his ability to follow instructions. In this regard, the duplicated sheets of social studies material for coloring are a flagrant example of the misuse of visual media. The practice of providing those sheets robs both art and the social studies of any meaning.

There are activities used in the social studies that are related to art but that do not have the expressive quality. Those are the

---

[7] R. Arnheim, *Art and Visual Perception*. Berkeley: University of California Press, 1954.

[8] N. Laliberte, *Painting with Crayons*. New York: Reinhold, 1967.

[9] For example, F. Wachowiak, and T. Ramsay, *Emphasis: Art*. Scranton, Pa.: International Textbook, 1965.

constructing activities. The object in construction is to replicate items for study. Maps, models, costumes, stage settings, or artifacts may be reproduced. The purpose in construction is to make the replication as accurate as possible. The details of construction should be checked from many sources. Someone's recollection of a Western movie is not enough research for constructing an Indian village. The children should be taught, for example, that the diverse cultures of the American Indians had many different ways of building homes and villages. Books and magazines, paintings and films can be used to check authenticity. A museum is an ideal place to seek an authority who can check the children's work or give some ideas for reference.

As nearly as possible, the construction should duplicate the materials and methods of building the original. There is no reason for making model pueblos out of cardboard when there is mud and clay available. There are limits to the practicality of using some materials, but the effort should be toward trying to find the closest substitute rather than duplicating the appearance only. The children will learn a great deal more in their attempt to build as the original was built. In the construction of maps, accuracy again becomes important. The children will be limited in their ability to make an accurate map, but they can become aware of the care taken by cartographers in the process.

Work with the evidences of art and the materials of art can add richness to a social studies program. There is no facet of the social studies that could not benefit from the inclusion of art works or from the use of art materials as a reporting medium. The arts give us a strong bond with the qualities of people.

> The life of the arts, far from being an interruption, a distraction, in the life of a nation, is very close to the center of a nation's purpose— and a test of the quality of a nation's civilization.
>
> President John F. Kennedy [10]

Through the social studies, it is important that the life of the arts becomes a part of the life of the children.

---

[10] Quoted on a poster by Art Education Inc., 1967.

Evaluating the Outcomes of Instruction

BASICALLY, SOCIAL STUDIES INSTRUCTION is a communication system with feed-forward and feed-back dimensions. Feed-forward involves establishing instructional objectives for the child—planning and managing learning contacts—and determining how well the individual has learned. Feed-back is communication from the child or from some source related to the instructional setting that provides data and information on the extent to which success has been achieved in attaining instructional objectives, or on problems pupils have encountered in their learning.

What could otherwise be successful instructional communication sometimes breaks down because of failure to base evaluation precisely on instructional objectives. When this occurs, evaluation may be made of relatively unimportant matters rather than of the attainment of major instructional targets. Teachers evaluating classroom learning and school district personnel evaluating entire programs must, therefore, begin the process by clearly delineating how instruction is expected to change learner behavior. In short, what can he do after instruction that he could not do prior to it? What skills should he be able to perform? Which concepts should he be able to describe and to apply? What generalizations should he know and what should he be able to do with them?

If the initial step is that of deciding what the pupil is expected to learn, the second step should be that of determining what will be acceptable to the evaluator as a performance criterion or demonstration that the expected behavior, in fact, has been learned by the individual. In some cases, a pencil-and-paper test may be used to evoke and evaluate the expected performance. In other circumstances, role playing or some other kind of subjective procedure might be appropriately used. Many evaluation episodes combine objective and subjective procedures. In any event, the evaluative procedure used is always one designed to evoke performance that can be judged in accordance with expected or desired outcomes.

In evaluating social studies achievement, teachers are handicapped by the absence of a variety of innovative, creative, and effective instruments that will provide valid and reliable data. The need for such devices and procedures is nowhere more apparent than in the affective domain. Typically, social studies programs claim to develop attitudes and values, yet there is a considerable amount of uncertainty as to the impact of school programs on the values and attitudes of pupils. Precision is lacking in both the teaching and evaluating of affective learnings. Thus, teachers often rely on their own subjective judgments as to whether or not pupils show evidence of growth. The unreliability of such evaluations is well known and raises serious questions relative to the whole matter of the school's role in the affective area. An extreme position on this issue is taken by those who insist that if a given behavior cannot be accurately and reliably identified and evaluated, it must be rejected as an objective of instruction.

Evaluation is perhaps the weakest link in the social studies instructional chain. Certainly there is urgent need for fresh insights and more productive approaches to evaluation than we have at the present time. There is also a need for teachers to familiarize themselves with existing instruments and techniques of proven value. Social studies instruction will be more effective as evaluation improves and as dependable data on how well pupils have learned are fed back into the instructional system. When this happens, the prospect of wise and correct judgments concerning pupil achievement and teaching success is enhanced. The articles that follow provide the reader with some leads to the improvement of evaluation in elementary social studies.

PROBLEMS AND PRACTICES IN SOCIAL STUDIES EVALUATION *

Richard E. Gross and Dwight W. Allen

One of the great stumbling blocks to any satisfactory, large-scale implementation of the emerging "new" social studies will be the evaluational aspects. If the "new" social studies, as promised, are thoroughly updated, highly objective, inquiry-directed, individualized, and process- and skill-oriented, assessment of student progress will be much more difficult and even less effective than present evaluation of the outcomes of traditional content and instruction. The social studies of tomorrow promise much, but proof of efficacy will be sadly lacking unless serious attention is given to helping teachers and school districts strengthen their capabilities in this crucial area. New courses, units, and lessons, as well as new media and approaches, will demand much from us that is new and improved if we are adequately to ascertain pupil understanding, competency, and attitudes. The learner involved in simulation, independent study, source interpretation, an interview in the community, small group role playing, or in case analysis will, indeed, be difficult to rate—especially when we are limited by current evaluative attitudes and practices.

How can we be so pessimistic? Several years ago one of the authors conducted a national study of evaluational ideals and practices of classroom teachers of the social studies. This had not been previously reported in print and was the first such systematic survey made since 1934. The results were disquieting, and in this paper we will summarize some of the findings without delving into the details of the research.[1]

The responding sample included more than 600 members of the National Council for the Social Studies selected at random from its mailing list. The respondents then represented a group of pro-

Richard E. Gross is Professor of Education at Stanford University, Palo Alto, California; Dwight W. Allen is Dean of Education at the University of Massachusetts, Amherst.

* Reprinted from *Social Education 31*:207–208ff., 1967, with permission of the National Council for the Social Studies and Richard E. Gross and Dwight W. Allen.

[1] See Dwight W. Allen, "Evaluation in Social Studies Classrooms: Ideals and Practices." Doctoral dissertation, School of Education, Stanford University, 1959. Available from University Microfilms, Ann Arbor, Michigan.

fessionally oriented individuals whose practices could be assumed to be in advance of the evaluation procedure followed by a general sampling of instructors. Teachers were asked to reply, both in terms of an ideal and of their own practices, to 60 questions related to three elements of assessment: (1) What should be covered in social studies evaluation; (2) The administrative procedures for testing; and (3) Kinds of examinations and test items.

Some of the more general conclusions are summarized here:

1. Teachers frequently fail to relate their assessment practices to the aims they claim for their offerings.
2. Teachers are often inconsistent in their conception of evaluation.
3. Teachers are reticent, even ideally, to use the full range of evaluation techniques now available.
4. The use of many evaluation devices is misunderstood and such devices are often misused.
5. Teachers place a great amount of blind faith in the indirect accomplishment of their objectives.
6. All the purposes of evaluation are not understood by many teachers.
7. Teachers indicated by their answers that in general they have a low level of statistical sophistication.
8. Teachers almost unanimously accept both essay and objective test items.
9. A disproportionate amount of time seems to be spent in the correction of English errors in social studies work.
10. The theory of sampling and test instruction is not understood by teachers.
11. More than half of the teachers ignore the value of student-constructed test items and only about half encourage pupil-grading and self-evaluation.
12. Few teachers employ item analysis or other checks upon their testing and evaluation procedures.
13. Teachers, by their practices, encourage students to regard grading as a coercive weapon to be used against them.
14. Very few teachers perceive the major implications of the evaluation program which carry beyond the grading of students.

The above conditions are not surprising to anyone who has carefully observed classroom practices in evaluation. Such findings tend to confirm some of the previous research results of one of the authors gathered a decade earlier with a smaller and narrower sampling of history teachers.[2] Here it was also revealed that instructors failed to use the wide variety of assessment opportunities available and that paper-and-pencil tests were weighted far too heavily in the total narrow process of evaluation and grading.

The major investigator of the more recent study found four basic reasons why social studies teachers have not been more concerned with examining and improving their evaluation practices. First of all, they have been satisfied with their evaluation, and with its accuracy and adequacy. The statistical neatness of objective tests and numerical averaging lends an aura of exactness to the grading process and disguises the many subjective elements which are anterior components.

A second reason is the fact that so many of the social studies objectives are vague and ambiguous and overlap other curricular areas and do not readily lend themselves to precise measurement. This obscures the fact that there are also many specific objectives which are readily measurable in skill areas, content areas, and methods of problem solving.

Thirdly, there is no doubt that many teachers are either unfamiliar with many methods or do not understand their purpose and use sufficiently well to be comfortable in their utilization. Tests have been regarded as a panacea of evaluation, and teachers have automatically turned to tests (and even then only to certain favorite types) whenever evaluation is considered necessary.

Fourth, teachers regard evaluation as an unfortunate appendage of teaching, rather than as an integral part of it. So long as teachers do not comprehend the integral relationship of the full range of evaluative techniques with teaching objectives and activities, evaluation will never be utilized in its full potential.

Allen also concluded that there was a strong indication in the replies to the questionnaire that teachers often set their goals in terms of pre-determined evaluation techniques. Instead of really considering the most effective teaching situations, it appears that many teachers adapt their teaching procedures to the most easily contained evaluation program. This practice holds many implications for teacher education, both in-service and pre-service, and warrants further investigation.[3]

Several special problems of evaluation in the social studies merit our further consideration. These factors complicate additionally the difficulties that beset assessment in our field.

---

[2] Richard E. Gross, "Evaluative Practices in United States History Classes," *The Social Studies*, January, 1953, pp. 23–26.

[3] Dwight W. Allen, *op. cit.*

1. We are plagued by the broad and imprecise goals that are held for the social studies; add to these the future-oriented socio-civic purposes commonly expected to result from social education, and it becomes immediately apparent that improved measurement devices may become available long before we can agree upon criteria and more immediate aims that are sufficiently specific so that their attainment may be ascertained. In many ways this is perhaps the fundamental problem besetting the social studies today.

2. Unfortunately, even as we become more specific, the problems of validity rise. Experiments with the teaching process which we have conducted at Stanford University in recent years reveal the incredible complexities of any single act of instruction. For example, in a simple teacher explanation to a class about an event, more than one hundred variables in the situation may be easily identified. We need much more careful and rigorous research so that we can know just what causes what. More precise planning may help, but to teach a typically compounded affair, such as a revolution or an election, is difficult enough in itself; to validly evaluate key factors in pupil comprehension remains, as matters now stand, largely a pious hope.

3. A related question now appears. Do the instruments we attempt to apply in evaluation really ascertain what we believe they do? We indicated previously that the "new" social studies will call for a more sophisticated program of assessment than now commonly followed. Yet even as we build the necessary measures of skill, we remain dogged by a doubt that has not been alleviated to date: Are such tests of competency actually measures of the qualities implied or are they largely indexes of ability to apply knowledge previously learned? While the social studies share this problem with judgment procedures in other disciplinary fields, adequate assessment of admittedly fundamental skill competencies in our field must wait on the evolution of largely new instruments.

4. Among the major purposes of the social studies are those reflecting desired socio-civic attitudes. To what extent does our teaching really affect attitudes? How can we best ascertain overt, let alone covert, behavior changes in these vital areas? Indeed, should such highly personal attributes be rated? Are we really trying in the best ways known to help youth build sound and worth-while value systems? Can a purely objective social-science approach ensure progress in this domain? Until we have better answers to these queries, perhaps teachers are to be forgiven their transgressions in regard to attitudinal assessment. But if attitude growth is a desired end, we must find ways to evaluate progress—otherwise the sham of our stated purposes will shame us no end.

5. The heart of the social studies program should rest in controversy. Often in controversy there is *no* answer, or there is the possibility of a variety of hypotheses that either can't all be tested or that will not satisfy many who are involved. A social studies curriculum moving on the frontier of ferment and change calls for evaluation of a non-traditional means; but more than that, to what extent can pupil grasp of value-laden, emotionally tinted issues actually be evaluated? Certainly new conceptions of testing and rating of problems in this area are demanded or we make a mockery of our purposes and our instruction.

6. Unhappily, the great bulk of commercial and standardized tests in the field of the social studies has been found wanting by experts. Observe the reviews in the last three Mental Measurement Yearbooks; they give at best but limited hope for long-time improvement. While achievement-type tests have been scored roundly, reliable measures of skills and attitudes have been found even more lacking. Banks of tested items will eventually provide significant help for concerned teachers, but producers of tests must now become as creative and innovational as they have not been in the past. Until we gain much improved tests of this nature, teachers must use current measures with caution and are well advised to continue to try to evolve devices that best suit their own purposes.

We have not painted a bright picture in this important area. However, unless we are continually concerned, not only over employing evaluation wisely in ascertaining pupil progress, but also in establishing realistic aims, in setting up purposeful curricula and courses, in critically reviewing instructional materials, and in judging the efficacy of our teaching process, we fall short of our responsibilities as professionals. Indeed, until we accept such a comprehensive and evolving concept of evaluation, we dare give no one a grade but ourselves.

THE PROBLEM OF EVALUATION IN THE SOCIAL STUDIES *

Robert L. Ebel

Your approaches to the teaching problem, and to the evaluation problem, are basically sound. Both the maintenance of good educational programs and the improvement of educational procedures require good evaluation. Good evaluation, in turn, can only be made in relation to the goals of instruction. Too often when teachers make tests they forget their goals and remember only the subject matter they used in trying to achieve those goals.

I should warn you, however, that my answers to your question are going to be more complex and less satisfying than either you or I would wish them to be. The plain fact is that we do not have many evaluation instruments which will do the job you want done. What is even worse, our disappointing experience in trying to measure some of these outcomes is beginning to convince us that part of the job simply *cannot* be done. I even suspect that part of of it *should* not be done. On the brighter side, there is much more we can do, and do better, than we are typically doing in evaluating student progress in the social studies.

Three broad categories of educational achievement are reflected in various degrees by the listed objectives:

I. Objectives primarily concerned with knowledge and understanding

    A. Transmit our cultural heritage

    B. Teach important historical facts and generalizations

    C. Teach time and space relationships

    D. Acquaint students with basic historical references

    E. Provide instruction and practice in locating information

II. Objectives primarily concerned with attitudes, values, and feelings

Robert L. Ebel is Professor of Education at Michigan State University, East Lansing.

* Reprinted from *Social Education* 24:6–10, 1960, with permission of the National Council for the Social Studies and Robert L. Ebel.

F. Promote moral and spiritual values

G. Promote the attitude that history is interesting and useful

H. Promote good mental health

I. Promote aesthetic sensitivities

J. Develop democratic citizenship

III. Objectives primarily concerned with instruction and practice in intellectual skills

K. Writing notes from lectures and references

L. Writing essay examinations

M. Judging the validity of evidence

N. Drawing sound conclusions from data

O. Working in a group

P. Facility in oral expression

The overlap among these three categories is substantial. Most of us have attitudes, feelings or values attached to much of the knowledge we possess. Conversely, most of our attitudes, feelings, and values have some basis in knowledge and understanding. Intellectual skills are heavily loaded with knowledge, and also have values attached to them. Thus some of the differences among the three categories are differences in the relative contributions of knowledge, feeling and practice to the attainment of the specific goals.

You may have noticed that my grouping omits entirely the second objective in your list, "Provide intellectual exercise for the discipline of the mind." The notion of mental discipline has been the target of considerable psychological criticism. Its most naive form, which assumes that the mind is analogous to a muscle that can be strengthened by exercise in learning anything, especially something difficult to learn, has been generally discredited. Even the notions of general mental *functions* such as memory, reasoning, and will, which were supposed to be separate faculties independent of mental content, have been generally discarded. Modern studies of human and animal learning, and of brain function, suggest that the mind guides behavior by serving as a semi-automatic ready-reference storehouse of ideas derived from experience and reflection. The effectiveness of a mind seems to depend on how many of these ideas are stored in it, how accurately they represent the world outside the mind, and how easily they can be made available for recall and recombination when the occasion demands.

If by intellectual exercise is meant increasing the store of ideas, and if by discipline of the mind is meant improved accuracy and increased integration of these ideas, then this is indeed an important objective—so important, in fact, that it encompasses most of the others. If this is not what is meant, some further clarification may be required. In any case, I cannot suggest any tests which might be used to make a separate evaluation of it.

Knowledge and Understanding

For the measurement of knowledge and understanding in the social studies a number of excellent tests are available. The Cooperative Test Division of the Educational Testing Service offers social studies tests in its series of Sequential Tests of Educational Progress, and in its end-of-course achievement tests. The World Book Company offer tests in world history and in American history as parts of its Evaluation and Adjustment series. Science Research Associates distributes the test of Understanding of Basic Social Concepts from the Iowa Tests of Educational Development. Oscar Buros' *Fifth Mental Measurements Yearbook* [1] lists 60 tests in the social studies, with critical reviews of 23 of them. Not all of the tests listed are of high quality. The reviewers are rather critical of some. While the reader must occasionally discount the idiosyncrasies of particular reviewers, their comments are usually unbiased and always informative. This is the best available guide to educational tests of all kinds. It should be consulted by anyone who seeks better tests for specific goals.

You may have hoped for a more specific recommendation of a few tests exactly suited to measure achievement of the goals you listed. Unfortunately, this is not possible. In only a few cases have these particular goals been made the focus of specific test construction efforts. Even if tests of each goal were available, it is unlikely that the test author would conceive of these goals precisely as you do. So many facts and ideas are involved in our cultural heritage, and there are so many different value judgments that can be made of them that tests from different sources are almost certain to differ widely. Hence, even in this easiest area of educational measurement, you are not likely to find ready-made tests to meet your needs.

---

[1] Highland Park, N. J.: Gryphon Press, 1959.

What, then, is to be done? One solution is to make tests of your own, based on a very specific definition of each goal in the area of knowledge and understanding. This is a difficult task. In the absence of substantial expert assistance (and liberal finances) it is not likely to be done very successfully.

Another solution is to get along with the published tests that come closest to covering the goals as you have defined them. This will be cheaper, and cost less effort, but may not be any more satisfactory in the end. What is really needed, it seems to me, is some nationwide effort by social studies teachers and other educators to agree on a definition of basic goals in this and other areas of common educational concern. Then the effort to build really good tests of the agreed upon goals would be justified, and we would have a means for making sound evaluations of the achievement of our common goals. Unless a teacher foolishly devoted his whole teaching to the attainment of these common goals, completely suppressing his own special interests and disregarding local conditions and individual pupil needs, this would place no straitjacket on the curriculum. But if we are committed to the defense of the freedom of states, schools, teachers, or even pupils, to define all their own goals in whatever way they think best, then the task of getting meaningful measures of the degree of achievement of these diverse goals becomes almost impossible. The price we pay for what may be an excess of freedom seems rather high.

Attitudes, Values, and Feelings

Adequate measurement of achievement toward goals in the realm of attitudes, values and feelings present other, and still more difficult, problems. There is the problem of getting agreement on a clear definition of just what is meant by "democratic citizenship" or "aesthetic sensitivities." There is the problem of obtaining valid indications of the students' true attitudes, values and feelings. Direct questions in a test situation indicate mainly how the student thinks he *ought* to feel. Indirect, disguised tests are often low in relevance and reliability. The instability of pupil behavior from time to time and from situation to situation makes any single observation quite limited in significance. Finally, it is very difficult to create a test situation which is realistic enough to give valid indication of a student's probable behavior in a natural non-test situation.

For these reasons, good tests in the area of attitudes, values and feelings are quite rare. I know of none in the realm of moral and spiritual values. Remmers' multi-purpose instrument, *A Scale for*

Measuring Attitude Toward Any School Subject, might be used to reflect general attitudes toward history, but probably would not indicate specifically the students' attitudes of interest in history and appreciation of its usefulness, and possibly not the students' genuine attitudes. Good mental health is a complex, poorly-defined concept. Clinical diagnosis is the best basis for estimating mental health, and even that leaves much to be desired. There are tests of specific kinds of aesthetic sensitivity in art, music, and literature. I wonder if these kinds of aesthetic sensitivity are commonly regarded as goals for a course in the social studies? If not, the concept of aesthetic sensitivity may require further definition. Even when so defined, I doubt that we could do more than measure knowledge of aesthetic principles. There are some tests of civic knowledge. There have been some attempts to predict good civic behavior, but there again the problems of trait definition and test validity have been so troublesome that no existing test can be recommended.

This lack of good, ready-made instruments is bad enough. What is even more discouraging is the lack of any promising techniques for the measurement of attitudes, feelings and values. It is gradually becoming apparent that the difficulties of measuring these traits with paper-and-pencil tests are inherent in the nature of the traits, and in the limitations of formal, written tests. Techniques of testing which are reasonably effective in measuring knowledge and understanding may never be even passably effective in measuring an individual person's attitudes, values and feelings simply because these are specific to situations which cannot be realistically reproduced by any test. Further, deficiencies in these traits can easily be hidden from the prying questions of the tester, behind a mask of conventionally correct responses.

Does this mean that teachers should abandon the pursuit of goals in this area? To some extent, yes. Many widely approved goals with respect to attitudes, values and feelings are generally acceptable only when they are left undefined. What consensus could we get in defining the activities of a good citizen, or the nature of ideal spiritual values? People in different localities, and of different political, religious, or philosophical persuasions would define them quite differently. Is tolerance a virtue or a fault? No teacher can avoid influencing pupils to adopt his own particular attitudes and values, but I doubt that these should become formal goals of teaching, or objects for testing, unless they are the predominant view of the culture, or unless they can be supported as rational consequences of valid knowledge about the world and man.

This suggests that some of our attitudes, values and feelings are determined by the knowledge we possess. I am persuaded that this cognitive basis for feelings is very influential, and that it constitutes a proper and productive focus for teaching and for testing. Consider the goal of good mental health. How can a teacher promote good mental health? One way is to understand mental hygiene and the causes of mental illness well enough so that most of his acts in dealing with students tend to improve rather than impair the student's (and the teacher's) mental health. Another is to teach a knowledge and an understanding of mental health to the students themselves. Good tests of this kind of knowledge can be built. But no paper-and-pencil test is likely to do an adequate job of assessing mental health or diagnosing mental illness. That is a task for the specialist who knows how to use complex clinical procedures.

Similarly, one could build good tests of knowledge about good citizenship, about aesthetics, about moral and spiritual values and about the uses of history. Imparting of relevant knowledge does not guarantee development of desired attitudes, values and feelings, but it surely must contribute substantially to their development.

The chief alternative to the development of desirable attitudes, values and feelings via knowledge is to develop them by indoctrination or conditioning. Many of our most cherished feelings were developed in this way. As children we learned acceptable social behavior largely through a complex system of rewards and punishments, and only secondarily on the basis of rational understanding of the *why* of the correct form (if indeed it was rational!). Indoctrination is almost the only way of teaching very young children, but it becomes progressively less necessary and less desirable as their minds develop. It is a more appropriate technique in the home than in the school. I seriously doubt that teachers, especially teachers of the social studies at the high school level and beyond, should intentionally have much to do with indoctrination or conditioning. Their attempts to develop desirable attitudes, values and feelings should have mainly a cognitive, rational base, depending on knowledge and understanding.

This emphasis on knowledge, rather than on attitudes, values and feelings, troubles some teachers greatly. Knowledge alone is not enough, they say. It is what a person does with his knowledge that counts. Arthur Guiterman said it this way:

> Theology, literature, languages, law
>   Are peacock feathers to deck the daw
> If the lads that come from your splendid schools
>   Are well-trained sharpers or flippant fools.[2]

---

[2] Arthur Guiterman, "Education," in *Death and General Putnam*. New York: Dutton, p. 74, 1935.

He is right, of course, and so are the teachers. But they err, I think, if they assume that instances of misbehavior are caused mainly by deficiencies in attitudes, values and feelings which the school could correct if it only would try hard enough. Character traits are important determinants of behavior, but so are environmental circumstances. Teachers err if they assume that character is largely independent of knowledge, or that the same techniques of teaching and testing that have served for knowledge will serve also for attitudes, values and feelings. There is little in the experience of teachers or testers to support such assumptions. To evaluate individual achievement in these non-cognitive areas we may have to settle for measurement of relevant knowledge of how one ought to feel. We do not yet have good tests to do even this job, but we know how to make them.

For the rest of our evaluation of typical behavior, as influenced by attitudes, values and feelings, we may have to rely on systematic but informal observation of pupil behavior in real, non-test situations. This does not relieve us of defining clearly the traits we wish to observe. It does not promise to yield reliable measurements with little effort. But techniques for observing and recording typical behavior seem to offer more promise than any test-like instrument designed to probe a student's attitudes, values and feelings.

Nearly 30 years ago, Truman L. Kelley, writing on "Objective Measurement of the Outcomes of the Social Studies," stressed the importance of attitudes.[3] His emphasis on developing the basic determinants of behavior, rather than its superficial manifestations, seems eminently reasonable, and he said many true and wise things in supporting his thesis. Social studies teachers could profit much from re-reading his words today. He recognized the difficulties of measuring attitudes but was confident that these *could be* overcome, if only because they *had to be* overcome.

Today many of us are less sanguine. The experience of 30 years of generally unproductive efforts is beginning to convince us that we have set ourselves an impossible task, like squaring the circle or building a perpetual motion machine. Kelley himself later reported the unsuccessful outcome of an "Experimental Study of Three Character Traits Needed in a Democratic Social Order."[4] He commented, "This study emphasized the universal difficulty which has been experienced by those who have endeavored to obtain objective character measures of school children." But he did

---

[3] *Historical Outlook 21*:66–72, 1930.
[4] *Harvard Educational Review 12*:294–322, 1942.

not lose faith in eventual success, ". . . for it still seemed practically axiomatic that traits of character and attitudes and interests are essential determiners of human conduct, independent of intellectual, sensory, and motor abilities and attainments."

Since 1942 an enormous amount of work has been done on personality testing. A great many tests have been developed. Some interesting findings have been reported, and some interesting theories proposed. But much of what goes on in the name of personality assessment is not much better than horoscope casting or tea leaf reading. We still have no personality test of demonstrated value that is practically useful in measuring the effectiveness of learning or teaching in the classroom. We may never have. It may be that our search for the "structure" of personality, and our attempts to "measure" its dimensions will be as fruitless as previous attempts to find the fountain of youth, or the philosopher's stone. Perhaps the problem needs to be reformulated. It may be that the really basic, stable determinants of behavior, so far as behavior is internally determined, are not attitudes, values and feelings, but ideas—rational, cognitive, teachable, testable.

Intellectual Skills

The third category of goals was concerned mainly with intellectual skills. Here again there are no good, ready-made tests that can be recommended. To the extent that these skills rest on knowledge—and this is a considerable extent—they can be tested by conventional paper-and-pencil tests. To the extent that they rest on facility gained through practice, performance tests judged with the help of rating scales offer the most promise. The best solution may be a combination of knowledge and performance tests as a basis for evaluating skills in note taking, essay examination writing, effective group participation, and oral expression.

There are two objectives in this area—judging the validity of evidence and drawing conclusions from data—that may be so greatly conditioned by a student's background knowledge that the influence of generalized skill on his behavior may be relatively unimportant. I wonder if there are broadly applicable rules for judging the validity of evidence, principles which do not depend on the particular nature of the evidence under consideration. I wonder if the interpretation of data is an abstract procedure, like the diagraming of a sentence, that can be applied with reasonable uniformity to all kinds of data. If so, knowledge about these rules and procedures can be taught and tested *as abstract principles.* But I am persuaded that attempts to test these skills by asking a student to judge specific evidence or interpret specific data will reveal mainly how much he already knows about the source of the evidence or data, its meaning, and the problem to which it applies. In short, I wonder if these are important enough as abstract skills to deserve the status of goals of instruction.

Recommendations

What, then, would I recommend for the evaluation of student progress toward the goals of teaching in the social studies?

First, that goals be defined specifically enough so that one can judge how satisfactory a given test will be.

Second, that goals which cannot be defined specifically and with general acceptability, or which hypothesize traits of dubious independence from other more obvious and easily measurable traits, be eliminated or de-emphasized.

Third, that goals which have statewide or nationwide, not just local, validity be emphasized.

Fourth, that command over essential knowledge be emphasized as a primary goal of instruction, even in the areas of attitudes, values, feelings and intellectual skills.

Fifth, that social studies teachers continue to search for, or to construct, evaluation instruments of acceptable validity in terms of specifically defined goals.

Sixth, that the *Mental Measurements Yearbook* be consulted for guidance in judging the usefulness of available tests.

Seventh, that social studies teachers recognize and accept the necessity of building some new tests, whose quality will depend on how much effort and money they are prepared to spend on them, and on how much expert help they get and accept in creating them.

That I have completed this discussion without clearly recommending a single specific test for you to use is something I regret very much. It reflects the complexity of some problems of educational measurement. Even more, it reflects our failure to be realistic in setting our goals, and to be objective and precise in defining them. I am persuaded that the main reason why educational measurement sometimes seems inadequate is that we persist in setting impossible tasks for it to do. But I am also persuaded that if we concentrate on the right problems, and work on them energetically and intelligently, we can improve educational measurement substantially.

EVALUATION IN THE SOCIAL STUDIES *

John Jarolimek

In this discussion, the term "evaluation" will be taken to mean all those techniques and procedures that the teacher and pupils, individually or jointly, use to determine the progress being made in achieving the goals and purposes of social studies education. The concept of evaluation assumes that the teacher has certain objectives and aspirations for his pupils, for his class and for himself that he hopes to achieve. Evaluation helps him to know whether or not, or to what degree, he is successful. The purpose of evaluation in the elementary social studies is, therefore, basically an instructional one and must ultimately be defended on its ability to enhance instruction and learning.

If evaluation is to be of value as an instrument of instruction, it must convey to the pupil a knowledge of desired responses, expected ways of behaving and the degree to which his own performances measure up to what is expected or anticipated. Pupils could probably not learn if their performances were not judged as to their correctness. Evaluation must help the pupil know when he is performing in satisfactory ways. This knowledge is ordinarily given by the teacher to the pupil through the use of some system of reward when pupil behavior is in line with what is expected—approval, complimentary comments, high scores on tests, and so on. Similarly, inadequate responses are made known to the pupil through the withholding of such rewards. Punishment, once widely used to discourage incorrect responses, is no longer sanctioned as a follow-up to evaluation. In any case, before any indication of the degree of goodness of performance can be conveyed to the pupil, the teacher must make a value judgment concerning it. The validity of that judgment depends on how effectively the teacher has evaluated the performance. Evaluation, therefore, is an important ingredient in learning because it provides the learner with feedback regarding his success or lack of it.

Obviously, evaluation will be more effective when both teacher and pupil know exactly what is expected of them in the learning task. This means that the teacher and pupils must know what achievement *is* in the social studies. Otherwise, neither of them

---

John Jarolimek is Professor of Education at the University of Washington, Seattle.

* Reprinted from the *Grade Teacher* 80:60ff., 1963, with permission of Teachers Publishing Corporation and John Jarolimek.

would know when progress has been made. Clearly, this calls for understandable, well-defined goals and behaviors. One cannot make a judgment about the adequacy of a performance unless he can differentiate between a good one and a poor one. Teachers who are vague about their goals and purposes in teaching confuse children in the learning process. The learner must, in some cases, wait until the teacher has evaluated his performance before the goals of instruction become clear to him. No matter what the stated goals of instruction are, however, the system of evaluation employed will more correctly identify what the real goals of instruction are.

Social studies education concerns itself with three different types of learnings—the development of understandings (facts, concepts, generalizations, principles), the development of attitudes (feelings toward others, accepting responsibility, love of country and fellowman), and the development of skills (reading a map, thinking critically, solving problems, using references).

It is important for the teacher to know that each of these learnings deals with different intellectual processes and must be taught differently and evaluated differently. Procedures that are appropriate for evaluating growth in skill development are not always appropriate for evaluating growth in understandings or attitudes. For example, a pupil may demonstrate his skill at reading a map by doing well on a teacher-prepared test in which he must use a map. Explaining the skill or telling about it may not be an adequate test of the pupil's actual proficiency in its use. However, if the learning to be evaluated was the pupil's understanding of the concept "retailing," the teacher could very well learn much about the pupil's knowledge of it by listening to how the pupil uses the term or how he explains it. Growth in pupil attitudes presents a different evaluative situation, because, in this case, the teacher must observe behavior that is based on the value system of the pupil. This is not always easy to do because pupils know the type of behavior expected and, when being observed, will perform in the "right" ways rather than in ways that reflect their true feelings.

The diversity of the learning outcomes sought in social studies has many implications for the teacher in the evaluation process. It means that many different types of evaluative procedures and devices will have to be utilized. It means, too, that evaluation of social studies learnings needs to be done not only during the social studies period but informally at many times when the teacher is able to observe samples of pupil behavior.

Evaluation of social studies learnings at the primary grade level must of necessity rely more heavily on informal procedures than on formal ones. This is not to say that informal procedures are less important in the middle and upper grades; rather that they can be augmented by more formal devices as the pupils grow in their ability to handle ideas symbolically through the use of language skills. One might correctly say that no evaluative procedure or device has superiority over all others, but rather that particular procedures are selected and utilized because, under a given set of circumstances, they will yield more information than some others would. All evaluative procedures have both strengths and limitations.

Informal evaluative procedures include discussion, observation, conferences with pupils, checklists, examination of work samples, experience summaries, short teacher-made tests and similar practices. They are important because they often provide the teacher and the pupil with information concerning social studies progress that is difficult to obtain through the use of formal written tests. The major limitations of these procedures are that the observations are often unsystematically obtained, the data may lack objectivity and reliability, pupil behavior may be mistinterpreted, the evaluative devices are often difficult to interpert and defend, and the data so obtained do not lend themselves well to quantitative expression and analysis. The effectiveness of informal evaluative procedures depends upon the teacher's skill in overcoming these limitations.

The teacher who employs informal evaluative procedures must be careful to systematize his observations. Some type of record keeping is essential. Moreover, he will attempt to objectify his observations by indicating fairly specifically what it is that is being evaluated. For example, unless the teacher has been careful to preserve a sample of a pupil's work at one time, his judgment about the goodness of the pupil's work at a later time is mainly conjecture. Having the two samples side by side would provide much more convincing evidence as to which one is better. Teachers need much in the way of objective, documentary evidence when they are attempting to evaluate pupil progress in social studies learnings through the use of informal procedures.

Formal evaluative procedures consist of comprehensive teacher-made tests, commercially prepared tests such as those provided in teacher's manuals, and standardized tests. Of these, the standardized tests are usually the best prepared from the standpoint of test construction; the teacher-made test least good. Comprehensive teacher-made tests that provide a good sampling of learnings to be evaluated, test depth of understanding, are technically sound and are reliable, are difficult to construct. Often teachers base such tests on factual content, the correctness of which can be verified easily by the textbook or encyclopedia. The assumption implicit in this procedure is that if the pupil responds correctly to such items, he also has a knowledge of the concepts and understandings with which they deal. This assumption lacks validity more often than not and the whole procedure not only leads to poor social studies teaching but also to faulty study habits on the part of the pupils. When teachers construct their own written tests, they should do so with the objectives of the unit before them. Test items should be designed that require the pupil to exercise thought, apply his factual knowledge, and demonstrate understanding of basic ideas and concepts rather than stressing simple recall.

Standardized tests have value in providing an objective "yardstick" that can be used to determine the extent to which the achievement of a pupil or class is below, at or above that of the norming population. They also provide an objective record of the pupil's achievement in the social studies from year to year as he progresses in school. Insofar as possible, standardized tests should be used to measure basic understandings and concepts of a generalized nature, or to measure social studies skills. They have less value when they call only for recall of facts or for knowledge that is highly specific to a particular curriculum pattern. The misuse of standardized tests is widespread; some of the more flagrant abuses in social studies being to teach specifically for the content of the test, using the test norm as a standard that all pupils are expected to attain, ignoring curricular validity of the test, and judging teacher competence on the basis of pupil test scores.

It remains to be said that evaluation reflects the values sought in social studies education. How does one know if he is doing a good job if the job itself is vague or unclear? Currently, evaluation in social studies education needs to be more precise, more rigorous, less sentimental. This can be achieved only when the basic purposes of elementary social studies become more precise and more clearly defined in terms of the difference that social studies education is supposed to make in the way pupils in a democratic society live.

RESERVE BOOK

RESERVE

DISCHARGED
NOV 28 1962

DISCHARGED 1978